A passage from a poem by William Wordsworth.

The meaning I take from it today may be a little different
from the original meaning of the poem. And now, as I write
this in the spring of 2011, it may be a little early to read
out loud. Yet I would like to record it here.

Though nothing can bring back the hour
Of splendour in the grass,
of glory in the flower,
We will grieve not, rather find
Strength in what remains behind.

—Hiroyuki Asada, 2011

Hiroyuki Asada made his debut in *Monthly Shonen Jump* in
1986. He's best known for his basketball manga *I'll*.
He's a contributor to artist Range Murata's quarterly manga
anthology *Robot*. *Tegami Bachi: Letter Bee*
is his most recent series.

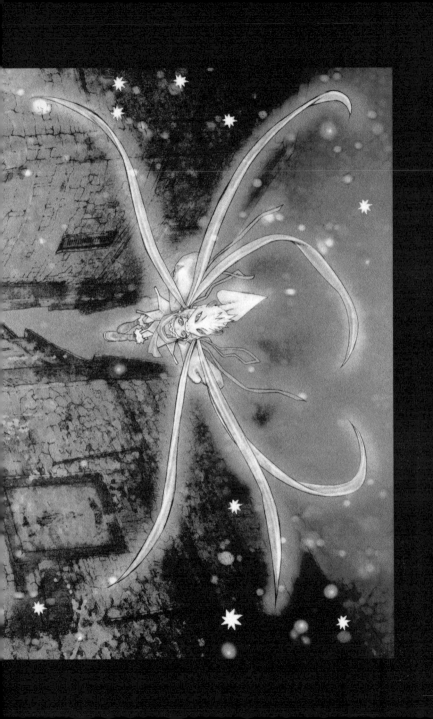

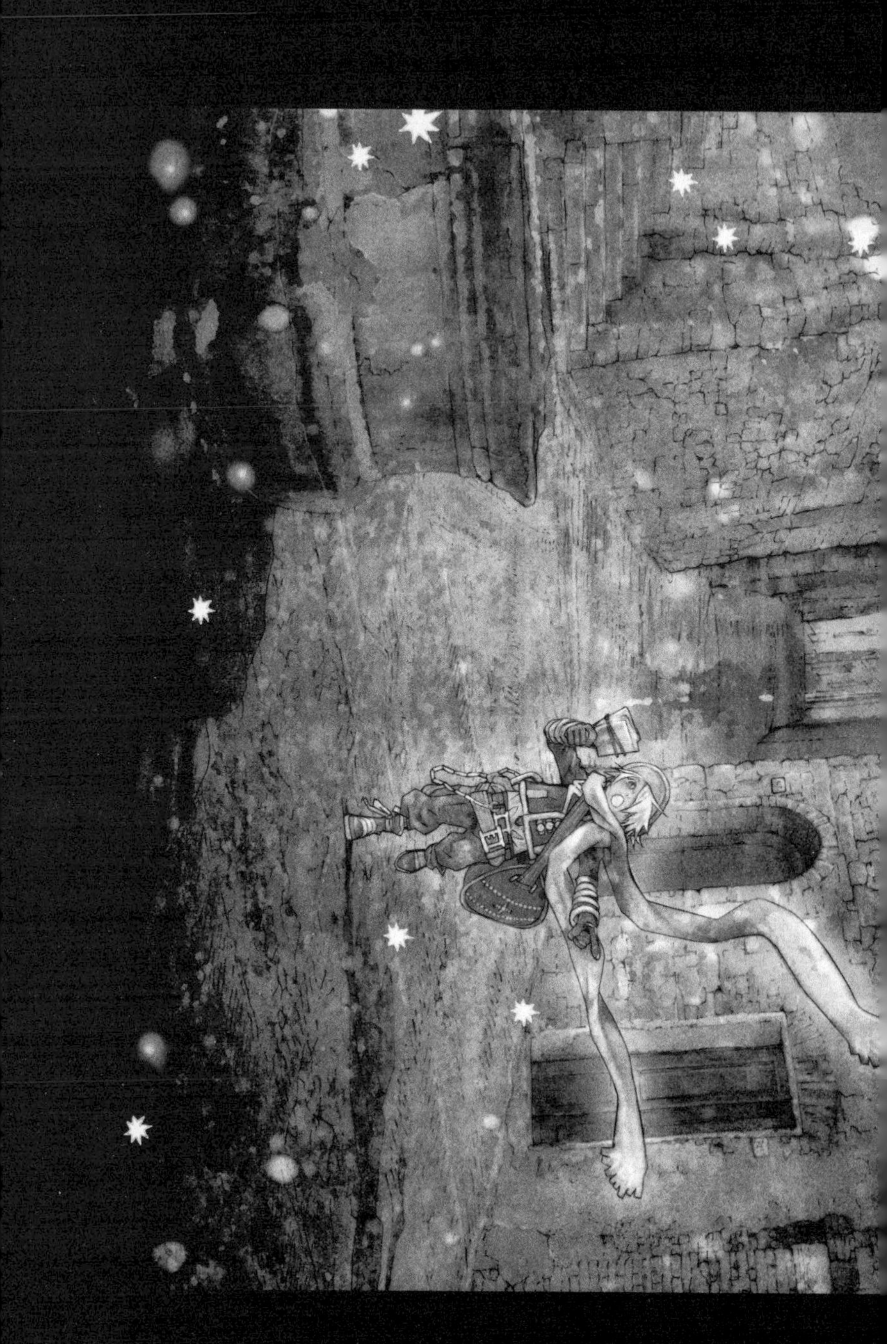

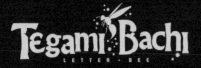

TEGAMI BACHI
LETTER · BEE

Volume 12

SHONEN JUMP Manga Edition

Story and Art by Hiroyuki Asada

English Adaptation/Rich Amtower
Translation/JN Productions
Touch-up & Lettering/Annaliese Christman
Design/Amy Martin
Editor/Shaenon K. Garrity

Printed in the U.S.A.

Published by VIZ Media, LLC
P.O. Box 77010
San Francisco, CA 94107

10 9 8 7 6 5 4 3 2 1
First printing, February 2013

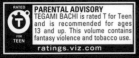

RATED T FOR TEEN

PARENTAL ADVISORY
TEGAMI BACHI is rated T for Teen and is recommended for ages 13 and up. This volume contains fantasy violence and tobacco use.
ratings.viz.com

Tegami Bachi
LETTER · BEE

VOLUME 12
CHILD OF LIGHT

STORY AND ART BY
HIROYUKI ASADA

This is a country known as Amberground, where night never ends.

Its capital, Akatsuki, is illuminated by a man-made sun. The farther one strays from the capital, the weaker the light. The Yuusari region is cast in twilight; the Yodaka region survives only on pale moonlight.

Letter Bee Gauche Suede and young Lag Seeing meet in the Yodaka region— a postal worker and the "letter" he must deliver. In their short time together, they form a fast friendship, but when the journey ends, each departs down his own path. Gauche longs to become Head Bee, while Lag himself wants to be a Letter Bee, like Gauche.

In time, Lag becomes a Letter Bee. He learns that Gauche has lost his *heart* and become a marauder named Noir, working for the rebel organization Reverse. After many adventures, Lag returns with the unconscious Gauche, throwing the Beehive into an uproar.

When Gauche awakens, it seems like cause for celebration, especially for Gauche's beloved sister Sylvette. Sadly, Lag discovers that Gauche has not recovered his *heart* and has no memories of his life before he became Noir.

Meanwhile, the Beehive prepares to battle Cabernet, an enormous, ravenous Gaichuu created by Reverse...

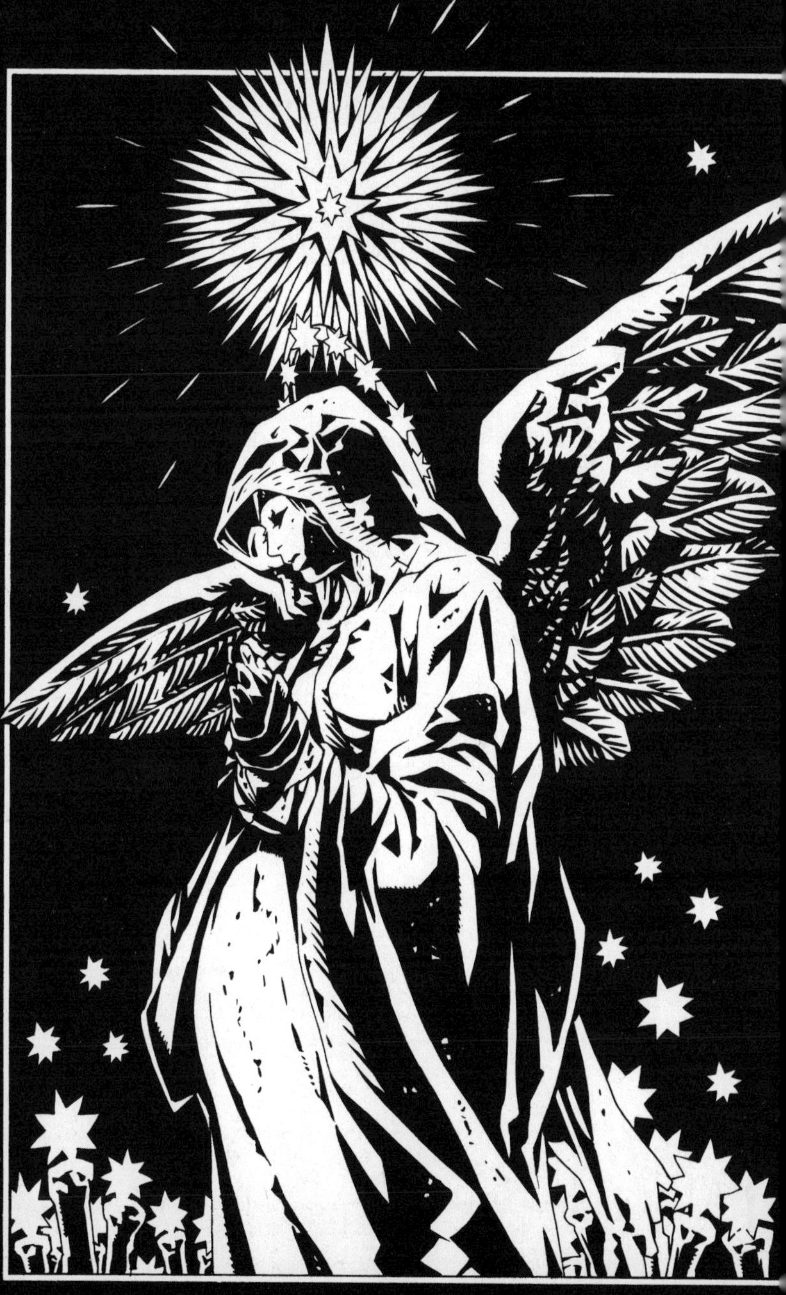

List of Characters

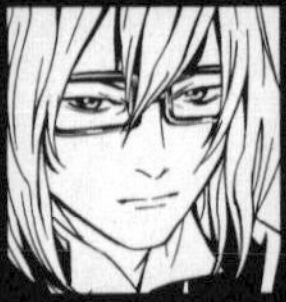

LARGO LLOYD
Ex-Beehive Director

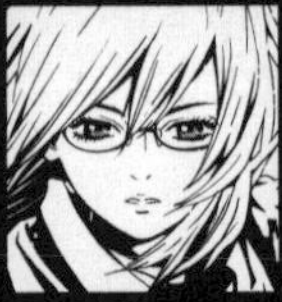

ARIA LINK
Section Chief of the Dead Letter Office

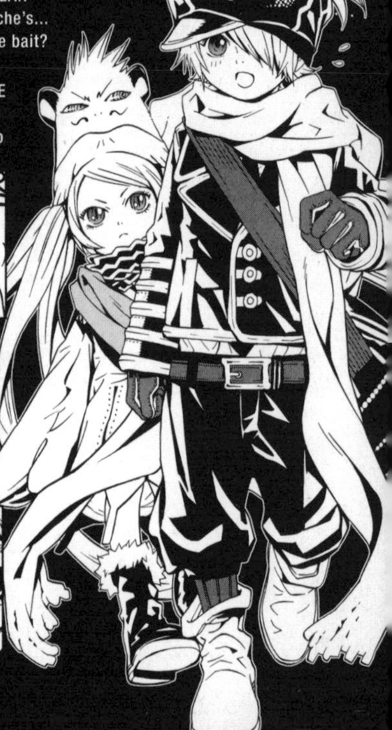

STEAK
Niche's... live bait?

NICHE
Lag's Dingo

LAG SEEING
Letter Bee

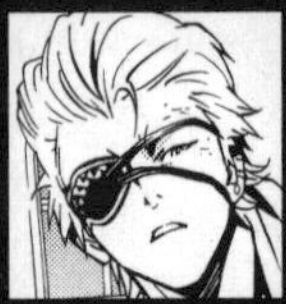

DR. THUNDERLAND, JR.
Member of the AG Biological Science Advisory Board, Third Division and head doctor at the Beehive

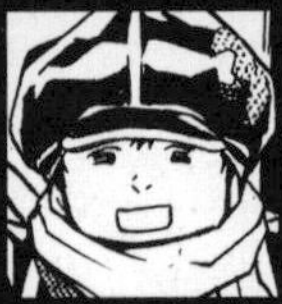

CONNOR KLUFF
Letter Bee

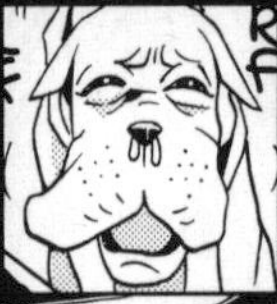

GUS
Connor's Dingo

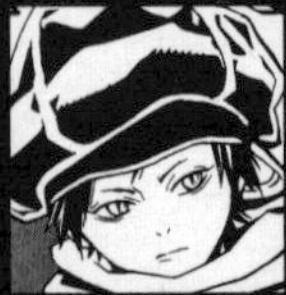

ZAZIE
Letter Bee

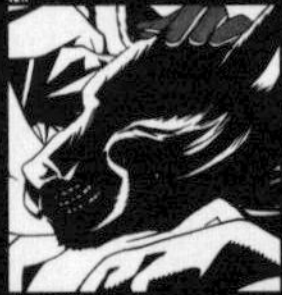

WASIOLKA
Zazie's Dingo

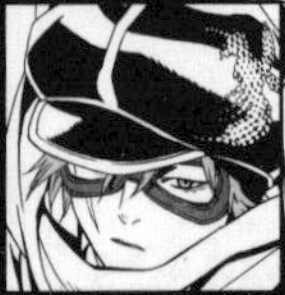

JIGGY PEPPER
Express Delivery Letter Bee

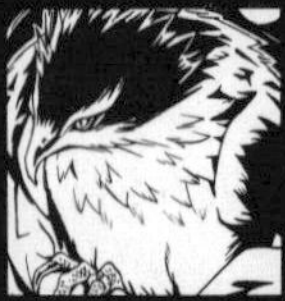

HARRY
Jiggy's Dingo

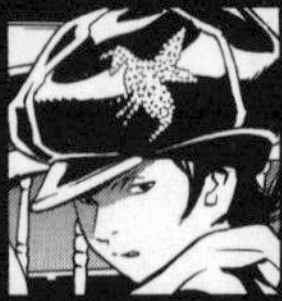

MOC SULLIVAN
Letter Bee

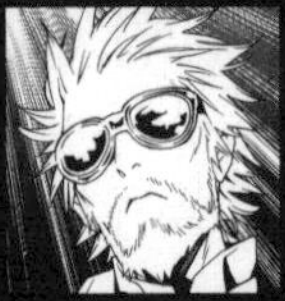

CHALYBS GARRARD
Inspector and ex-Letter Bee

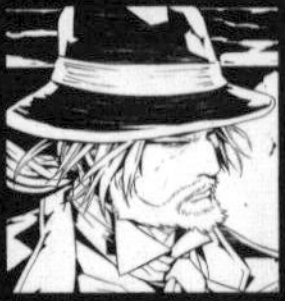

HAZEL VALENTINE
Inspector and ex-Dingo

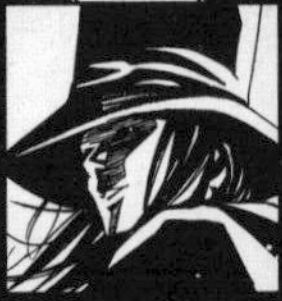

LAWRENCE
The ringleader of Reverse

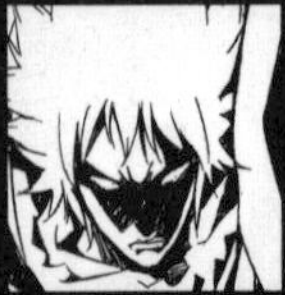

ZEAL
Marauder for Reverse

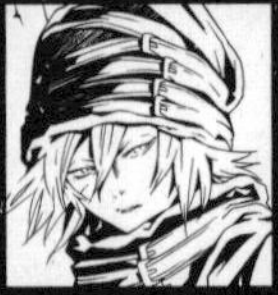

NOIR (FORMERLY GAUCHE SUEDE)
Marauder for Reverse and an ex–Letter Bee

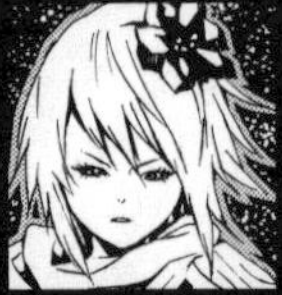

RODA
Noir's Dingo

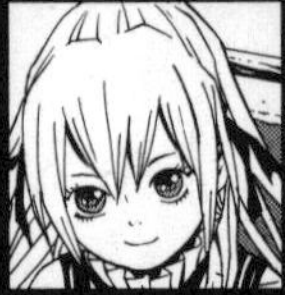

SYLVETTE SUEDE
Gauche's Sister

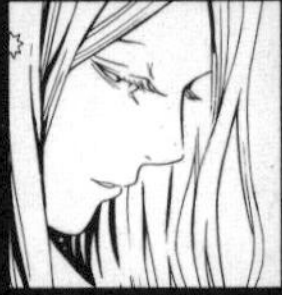

ANNE SEEING
Lag's Mother (Missing)

Tegami Bachi

LETTER • BEE

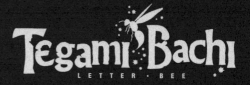

VOLUME 12

Child of Light

In all things... the heart must take prece-dence.

The heart rules over all things...

...and all things come from the heart.

—THE SCRIPTURES OF AMBERGROUND, 1st verse

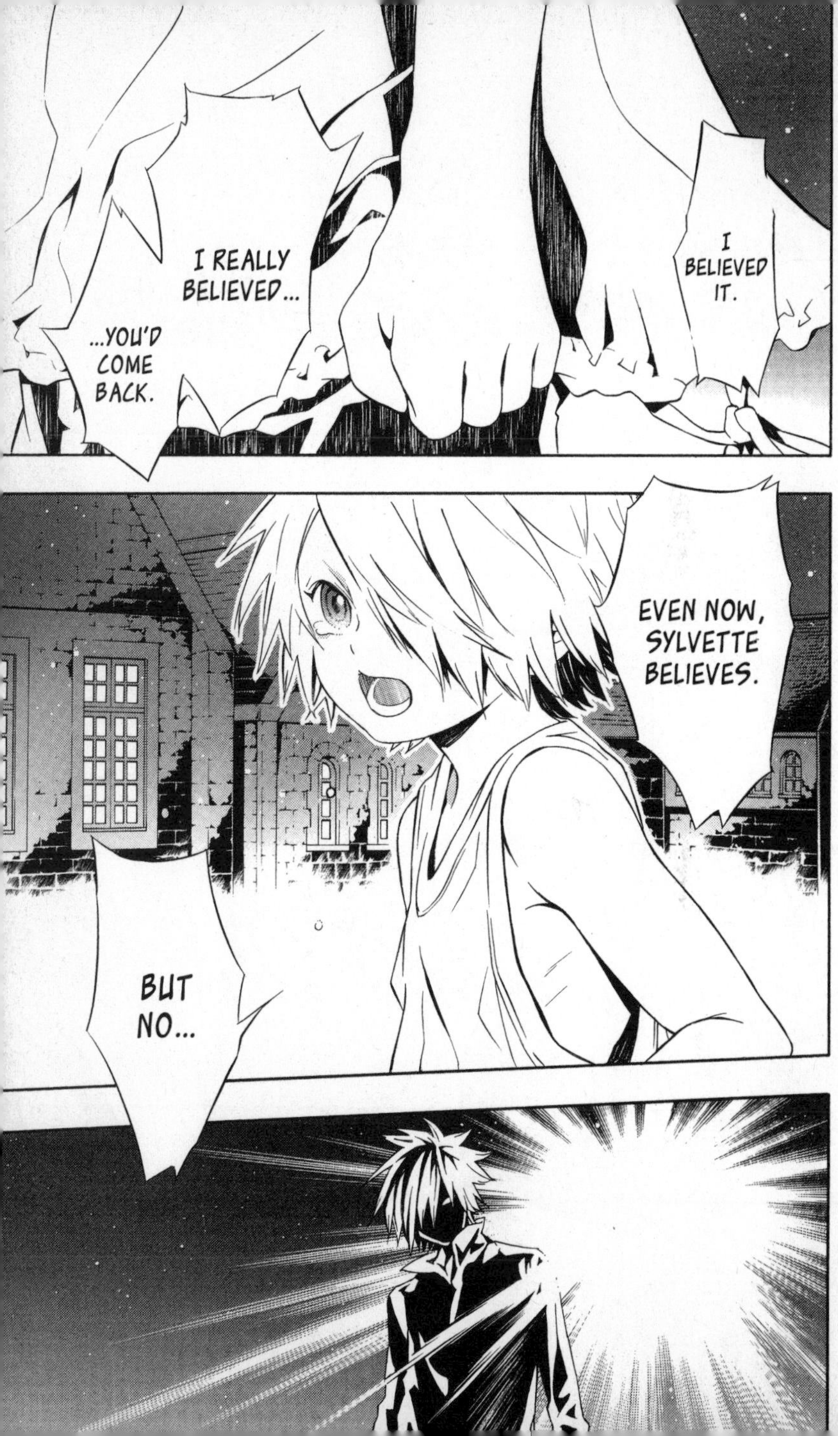
I BELIEVED IT.
I REALLY BELIEVED...
...YOU'D COME BACK.
EVEN NOW, SYLVETTE BELIEVES.
BUT NO...

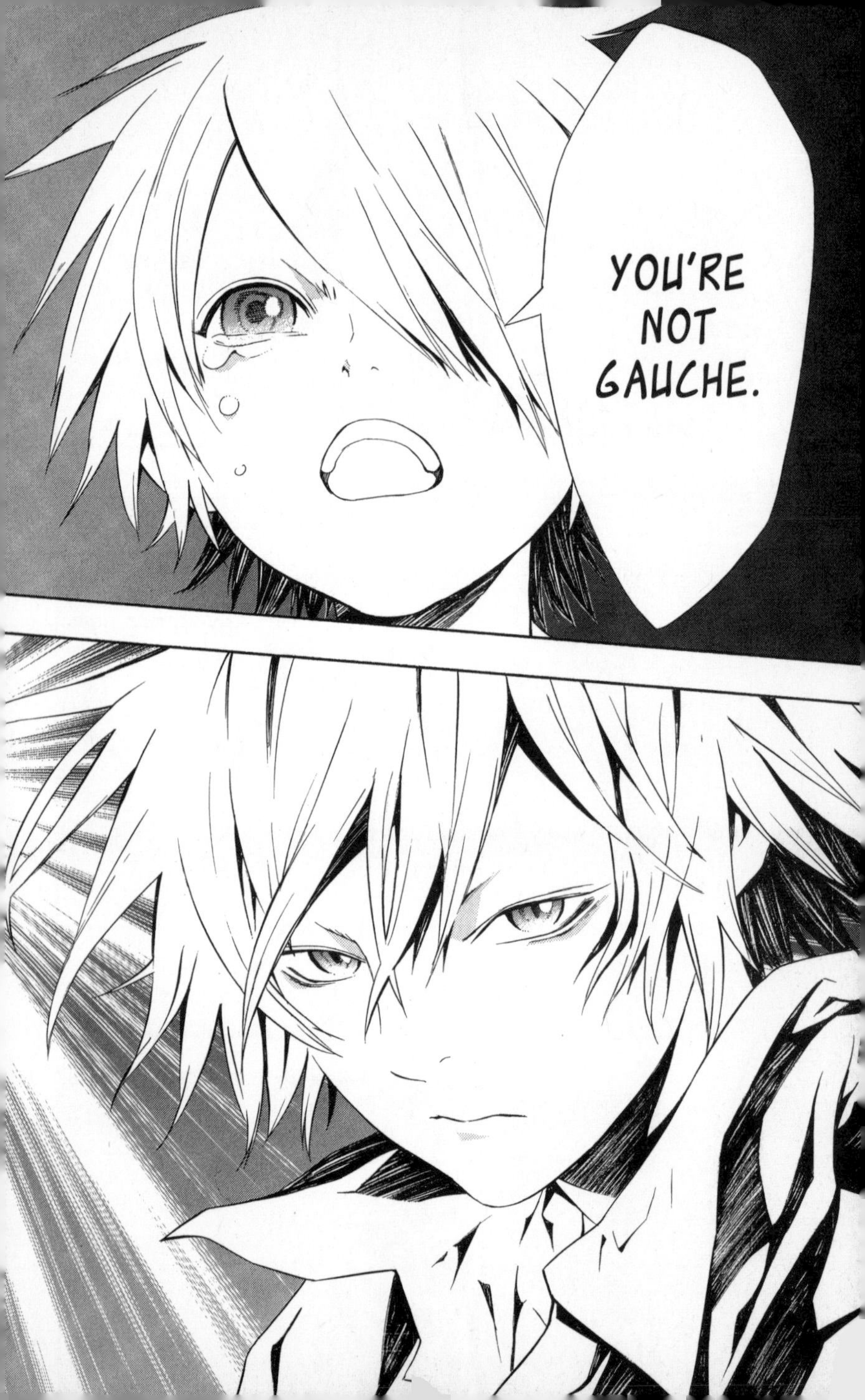
YOU'RE NOT GAUCHE.

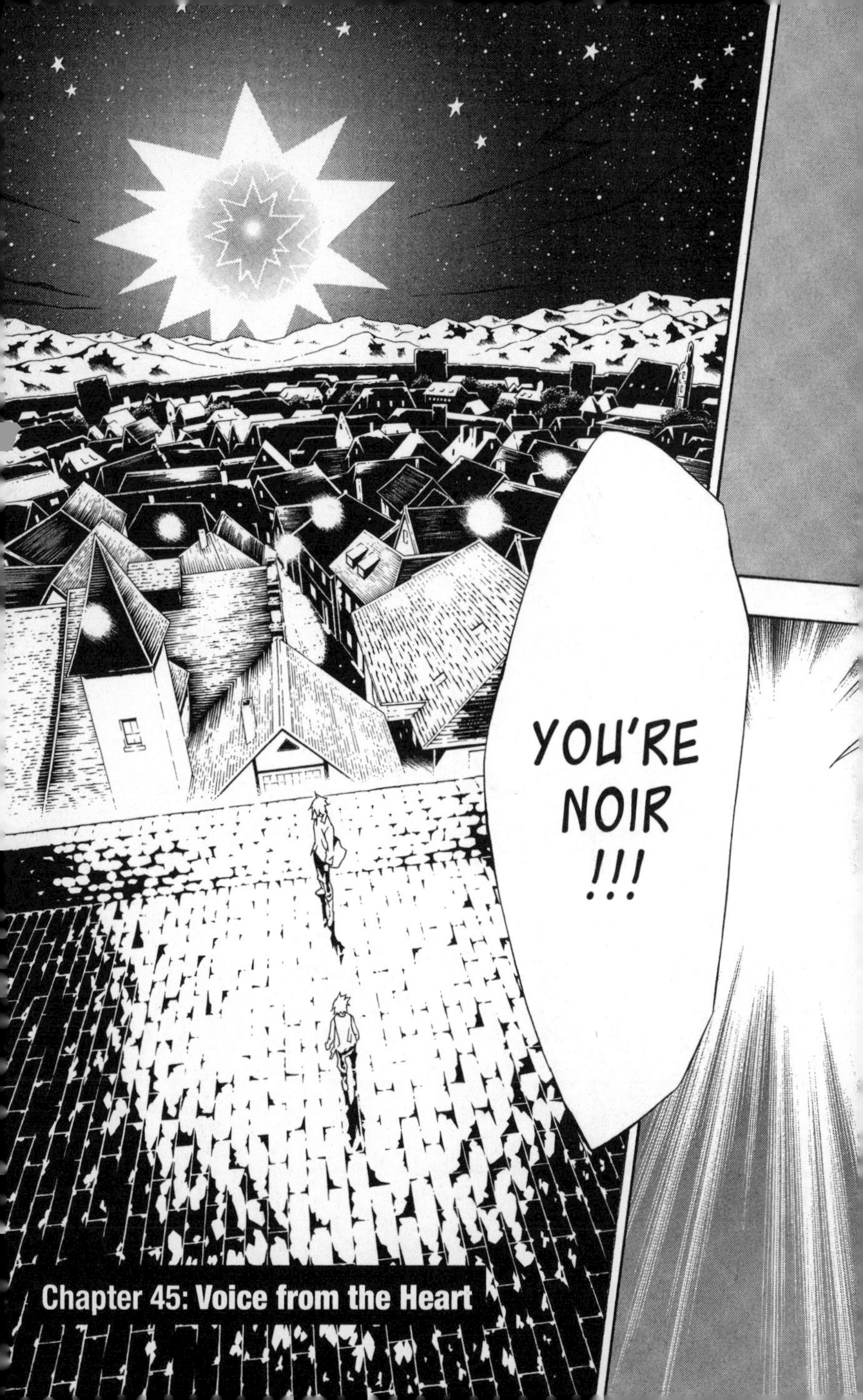
YOU'RE NOIR !!!

Chapter 45: Voice from the Heart

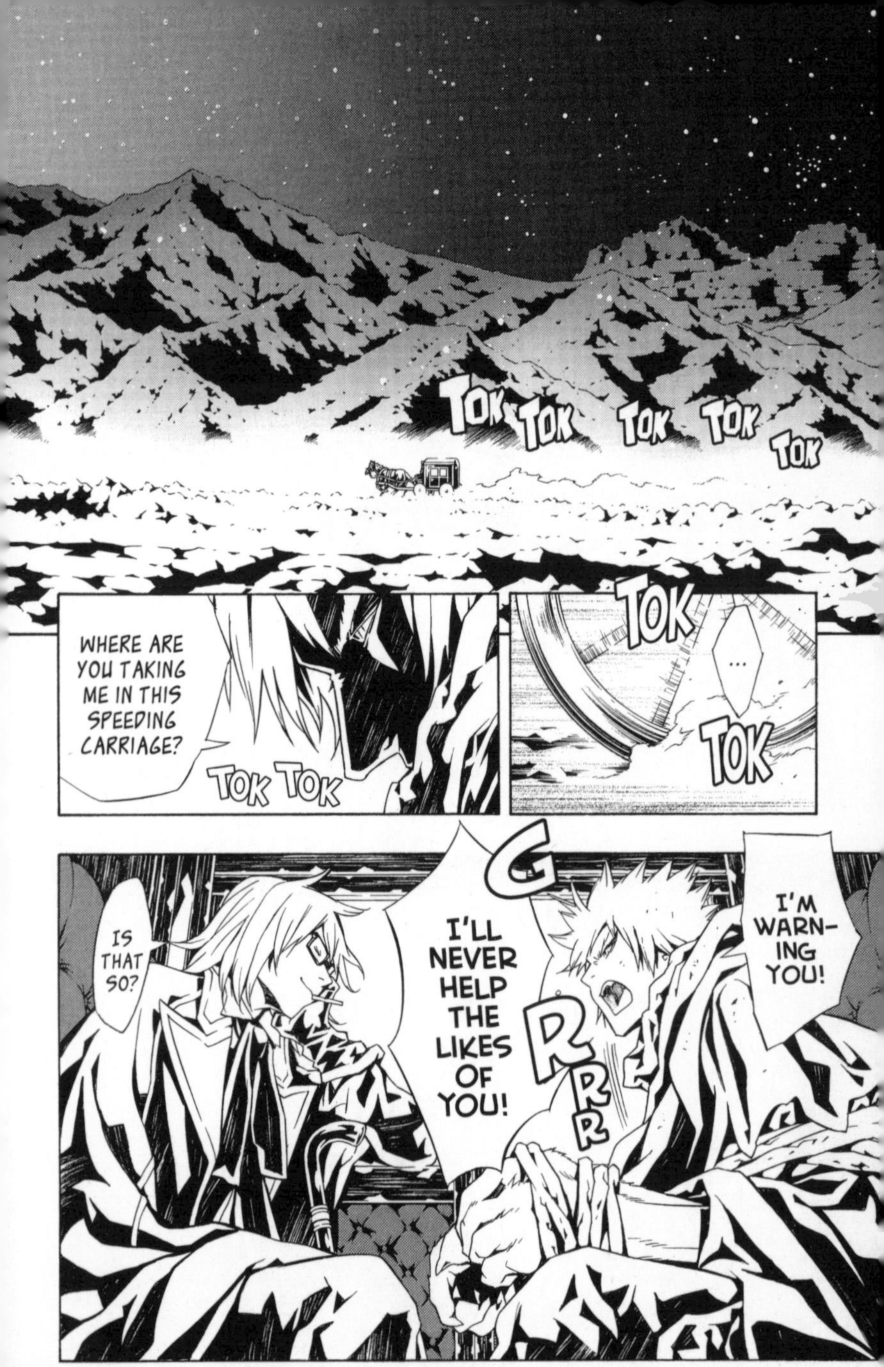
TOK TOK TOK TOK TOK
TOK
...
TOK
WHERE ARE YOU TAKING ME IN THIS SPEEDING CARRIAGE?
TOK TOK
I'M WARNING YOU!
G
I'LL NEVER HELP THE LIKES OF YOU!
RRR
IS THAT SO?

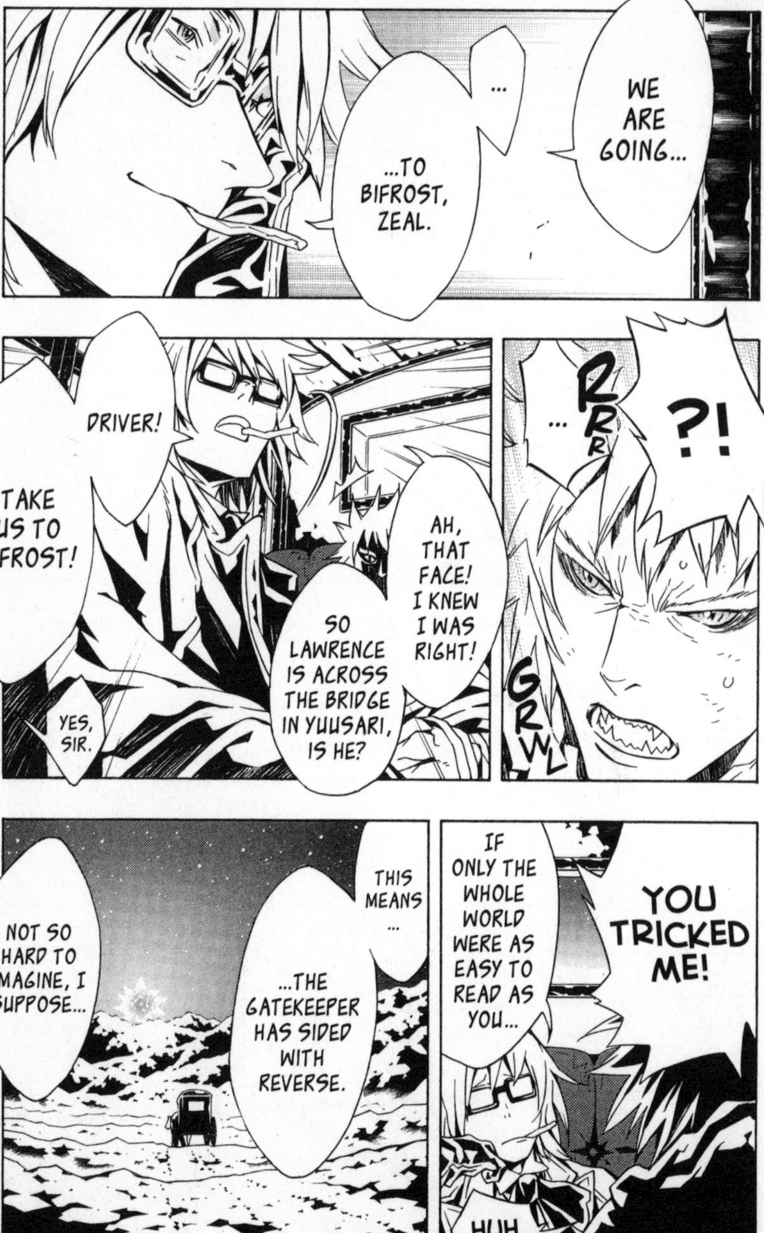
WE ARE GOING...
...
...TO BIFROST, ZEAL.
?!
RRR
...
GRWL
AH, THAT FACE! I KNEW I WAS RIGHT!
SO LAWRENCE IS ACROSS THE BRIDGE IN YUUSARI, IS HE?
DRIVER!
TAKE US TO BIFROST!
YES, SIR.
YOU TRICKED ME!
IF ONLY THE WHOLE WORLD WERE AS EASY TO READ AS YOU...
HUH ?!
THIS MEANS ...
...THE GATEKEEPER HAS SIDED WITH REVERSE.
NOT SO HARD TO IMAGINE, I SUPPOSE...

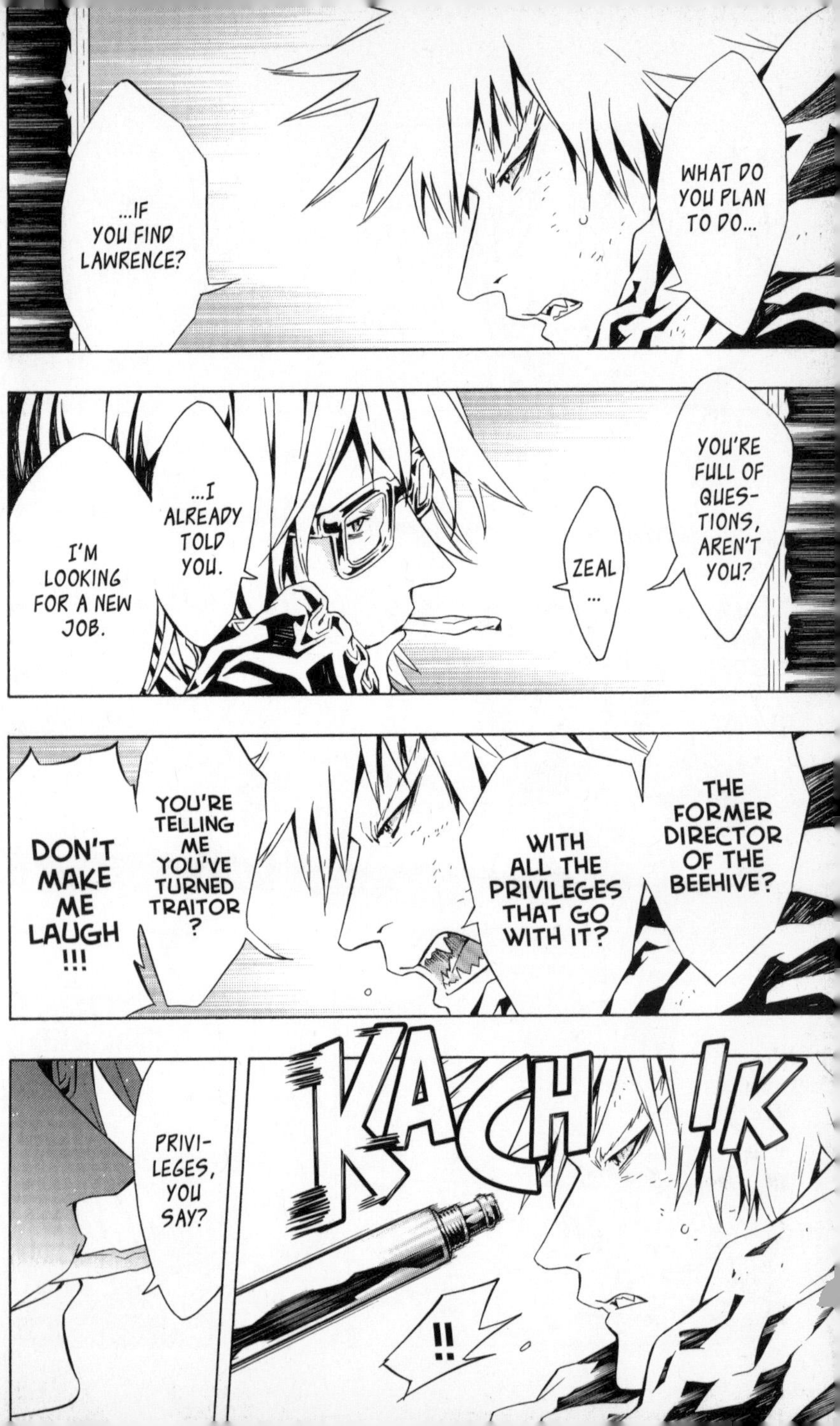
WHAT DO YOU PLAN TO DO...
...IF YOU FIND LAWRENCE?
YOU'RE FULL OF QUES-TIONS, AREN'T YOU?
ZEAL...
...I ALREADY TOLD YOU.
I'M LOOKING FOR A NEW JOB.
THE FORMER DIRECTOR OF THE BEEHIVE?
WITH ALL THE PRIVILEGES THAT GO WITH IT?
YOU'RE TELLING ME YOU'VE TURNED TRAITOR?
DON'T MAKE ME LAUGH!!!
KACH IK
!!
PRIVI-LEGES, YOU SAY?

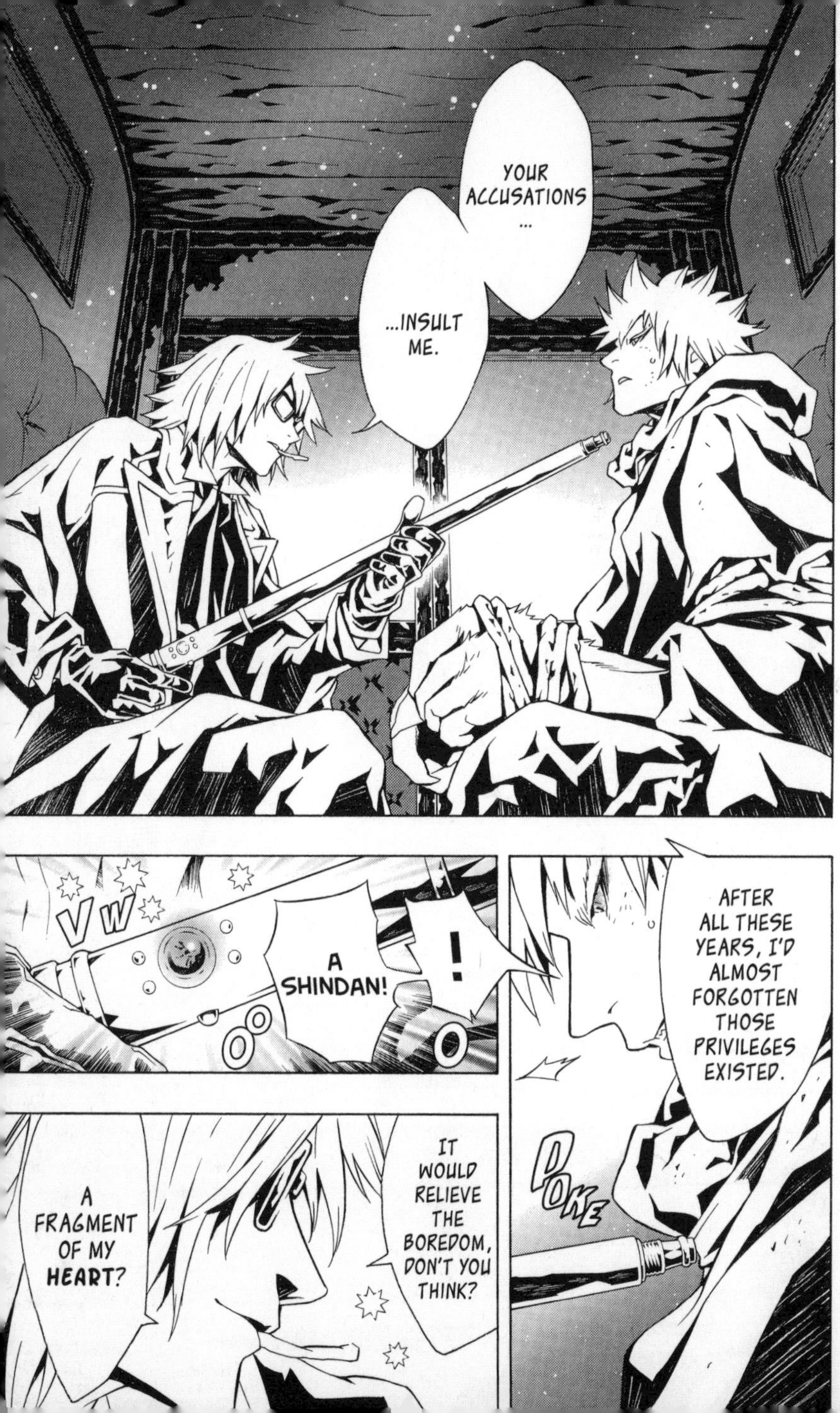
YOUR ACCUSATIONS ...
...INSULT ME.
AFTER ALL THESE YEARS, I'D ALMOST FORGOTTEN THOSE PRIVILEGES EXISTED.
DOKE
!
A SHINDAN!
VW
IT WOULD RELIEVE THE BOREDOM, DON'T YOU THINK?
A FRAGMENT OF MY HEART?

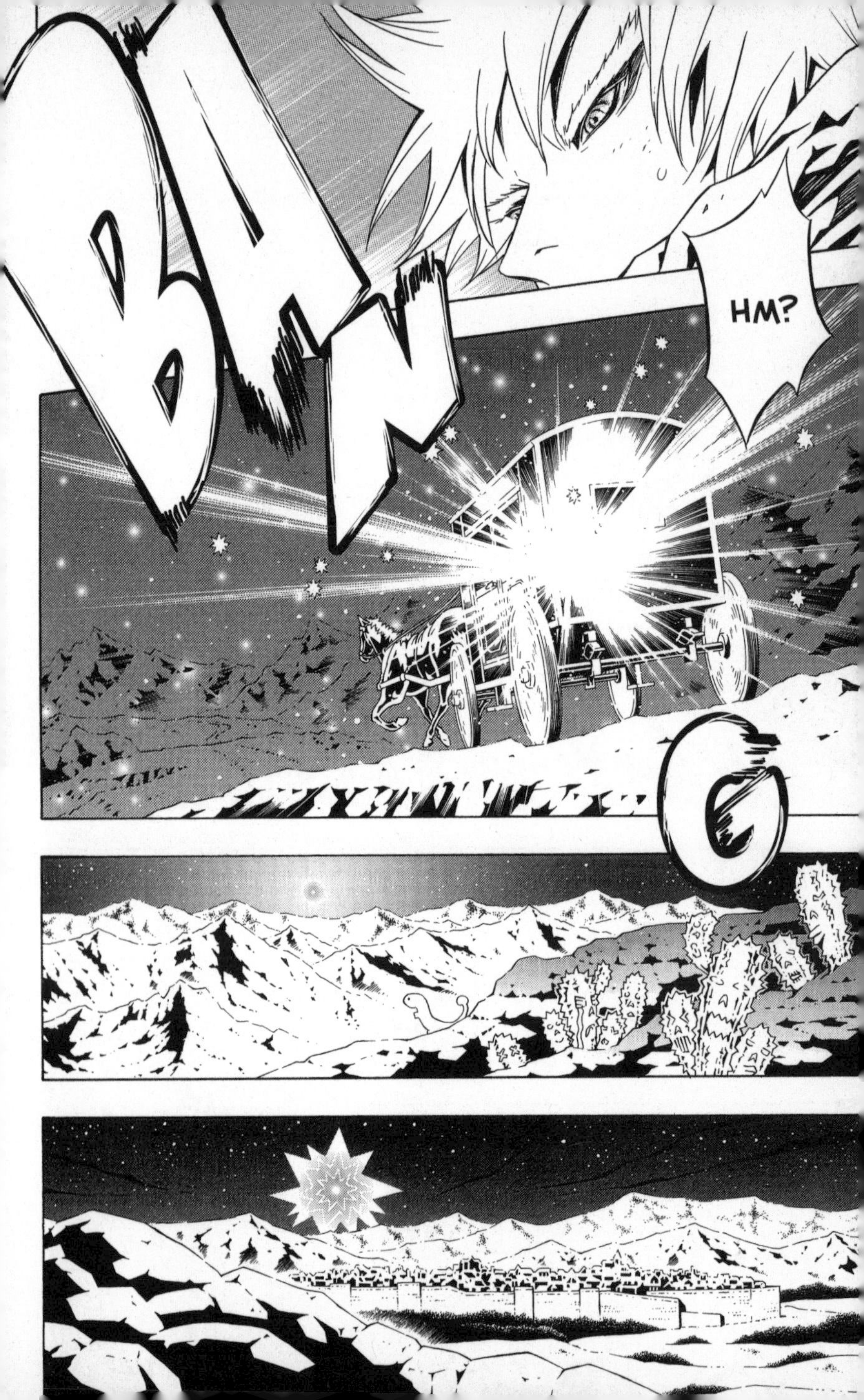
HM?
BANG

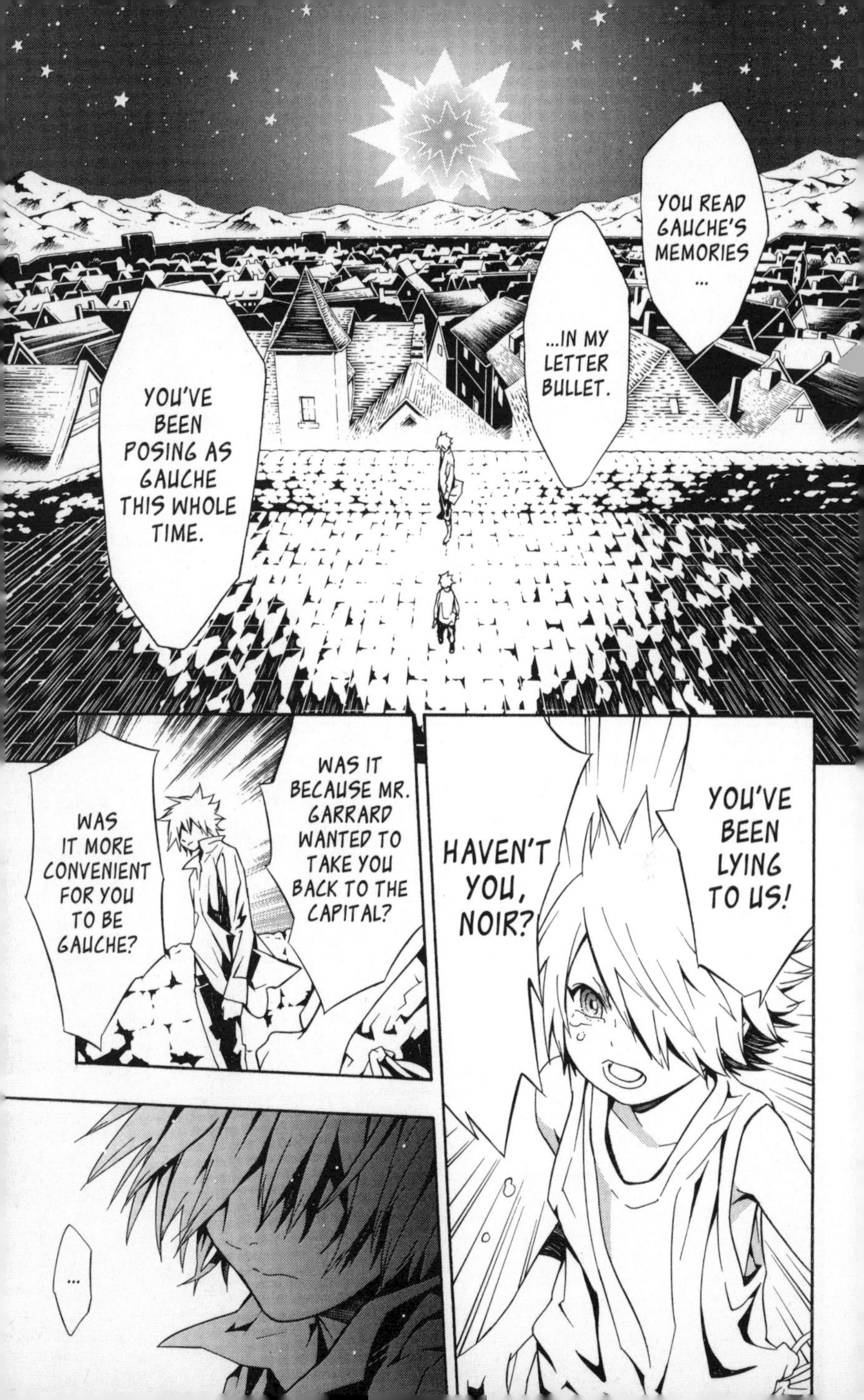
YOU READ GAUCHE'S MEMORIES ...
...IN MY LETTER BULLET.
YOU'VE BEEN POSING AS GAUCHE THIS WHOLE TIME.
YOU'VE BEEN LYING TO US!
HAVEN'T YOU, NOIR?
WAS IT BECAUSE MR. GARRARD WANTED TO TAKE YOU BACK TO THE CAPITAL?
WAS IT MORE CONVENIENT FOR YOU TO BE GAUCHE?
...

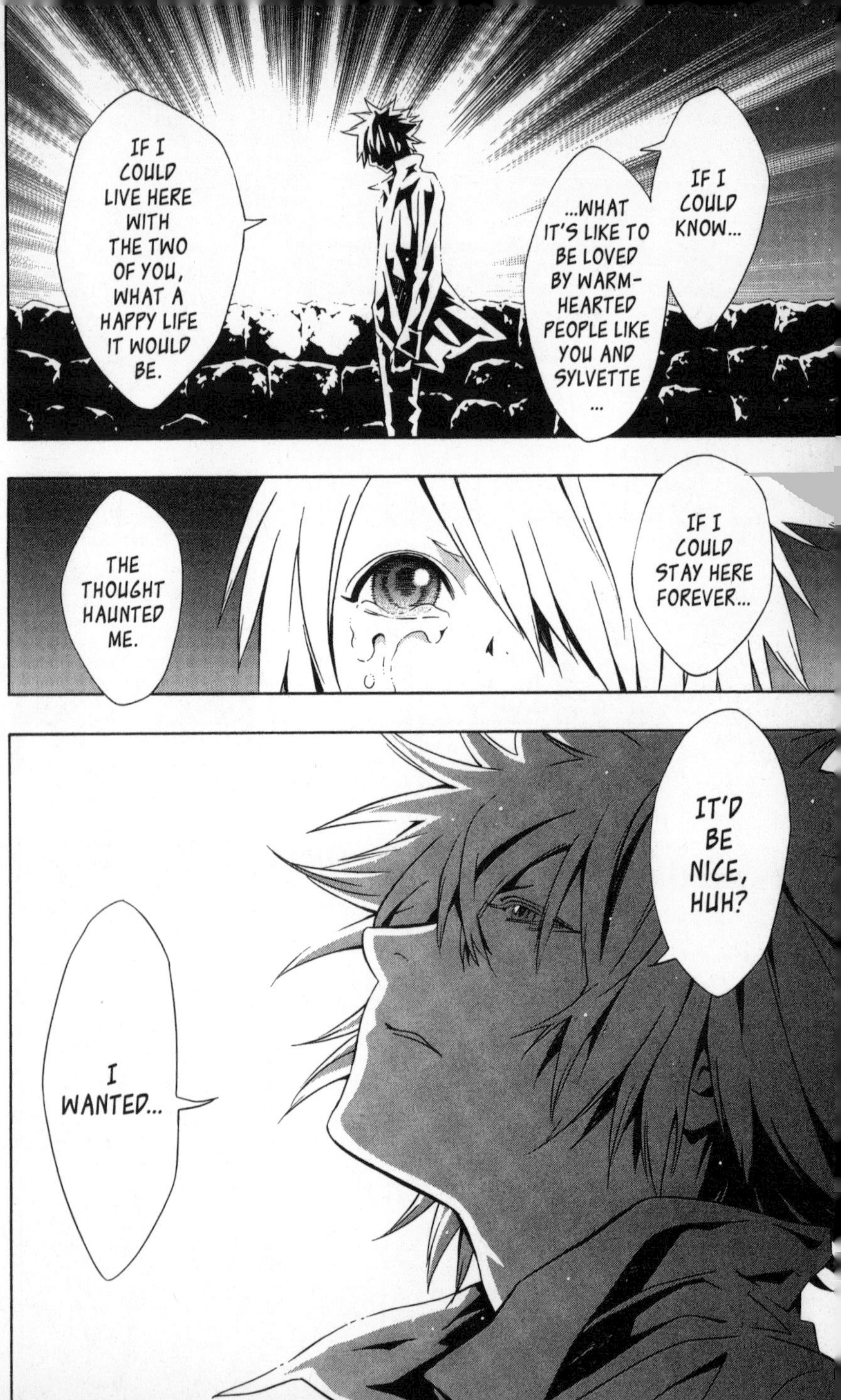
IF I COULD KNOW...
...WHAT IT'S LIKE TO BE LOVED BY WARM-HEARTED PEOPLE LIKE YOU AND SYLVETTE...
IF I COULD LIVE HERE WITH THE TWO OF YOU, WHAT A HAPPY LIFE IT WOULD BE.
IF I COULD STAY HERE FOREVER...
THE THOUGHT HAUNTED ME.
IT'D BE NICE, HUH?
I WANTED...

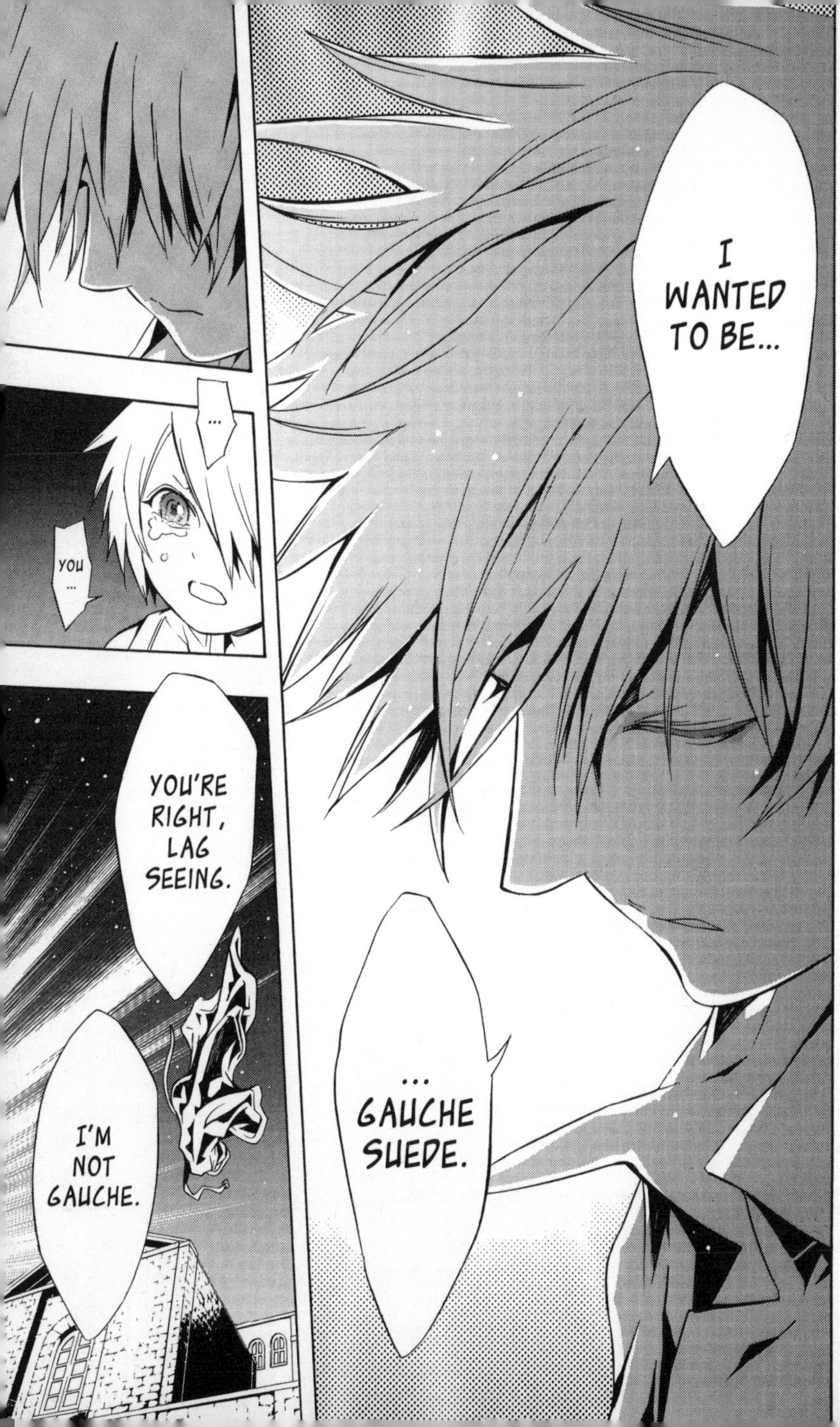
I WANTED TO BE...
...GAUCHE SUEDE.
...
YOU ...
YOU'RE RIGHT, LAG SEEING.
I'M NOT GAUCHE.

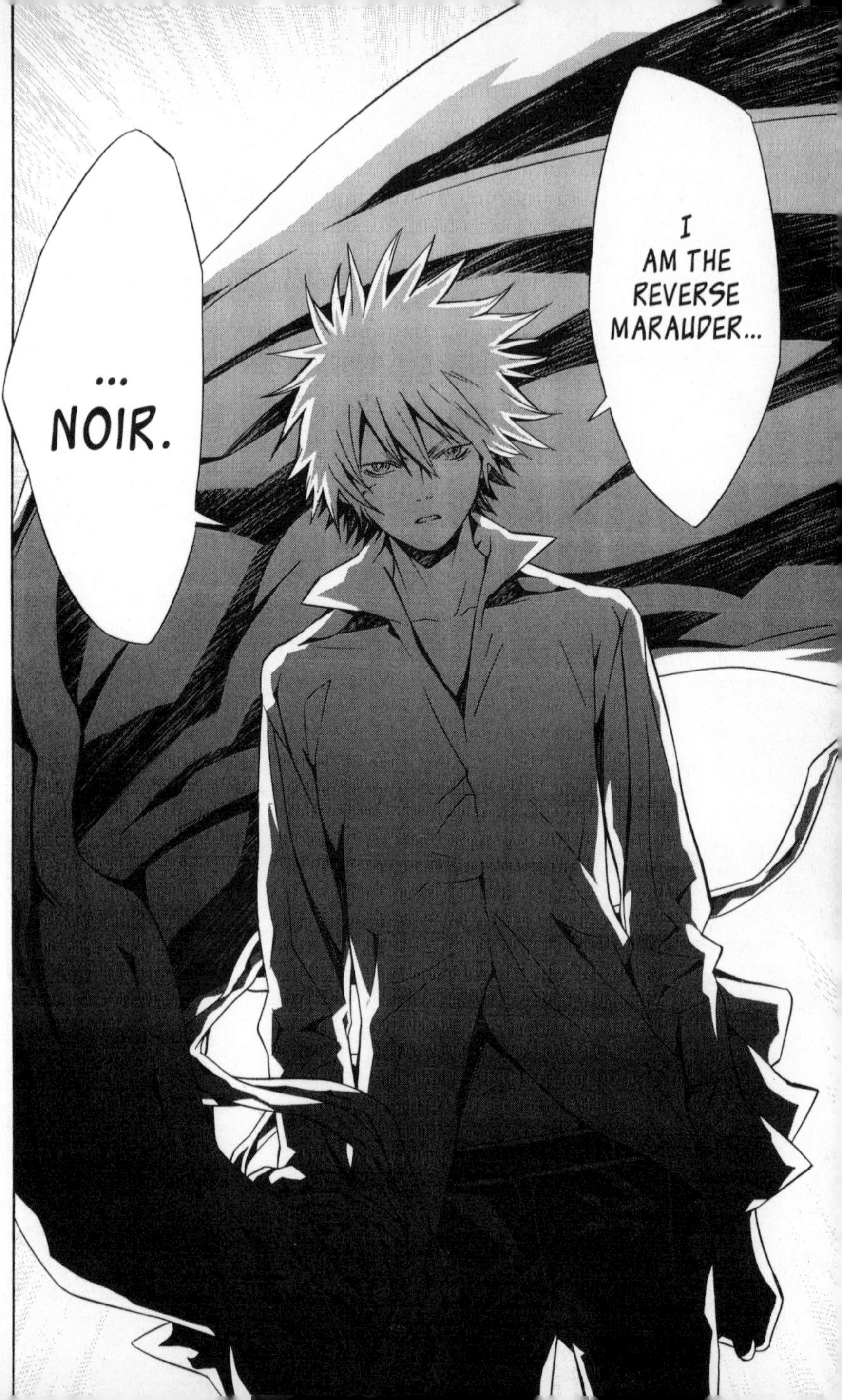
I AM THE REVERSE MARAUDER...
... NOIR.

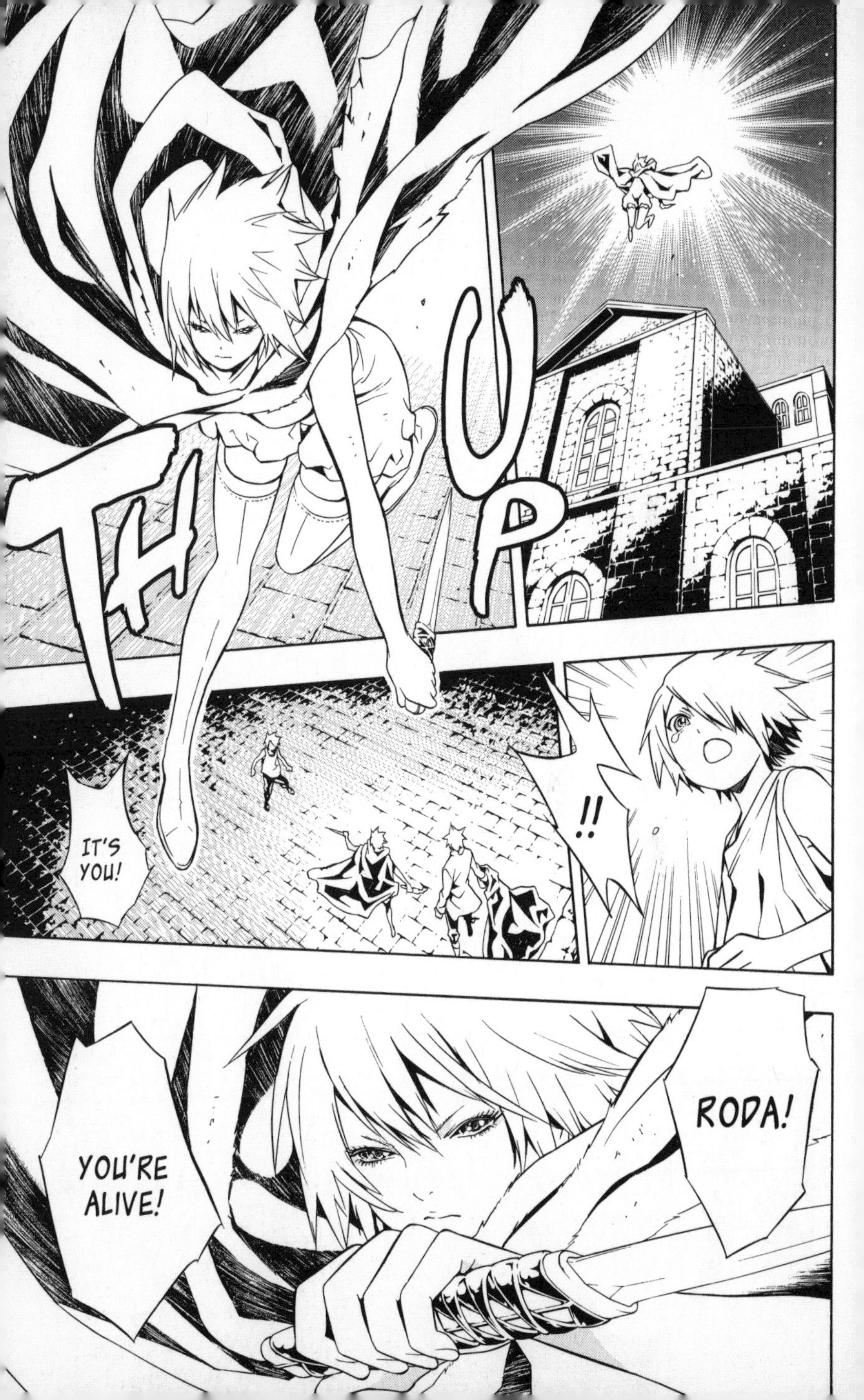

THUP
!!
IT'S YOU!
RODA!
YOU'RE ALIVE!

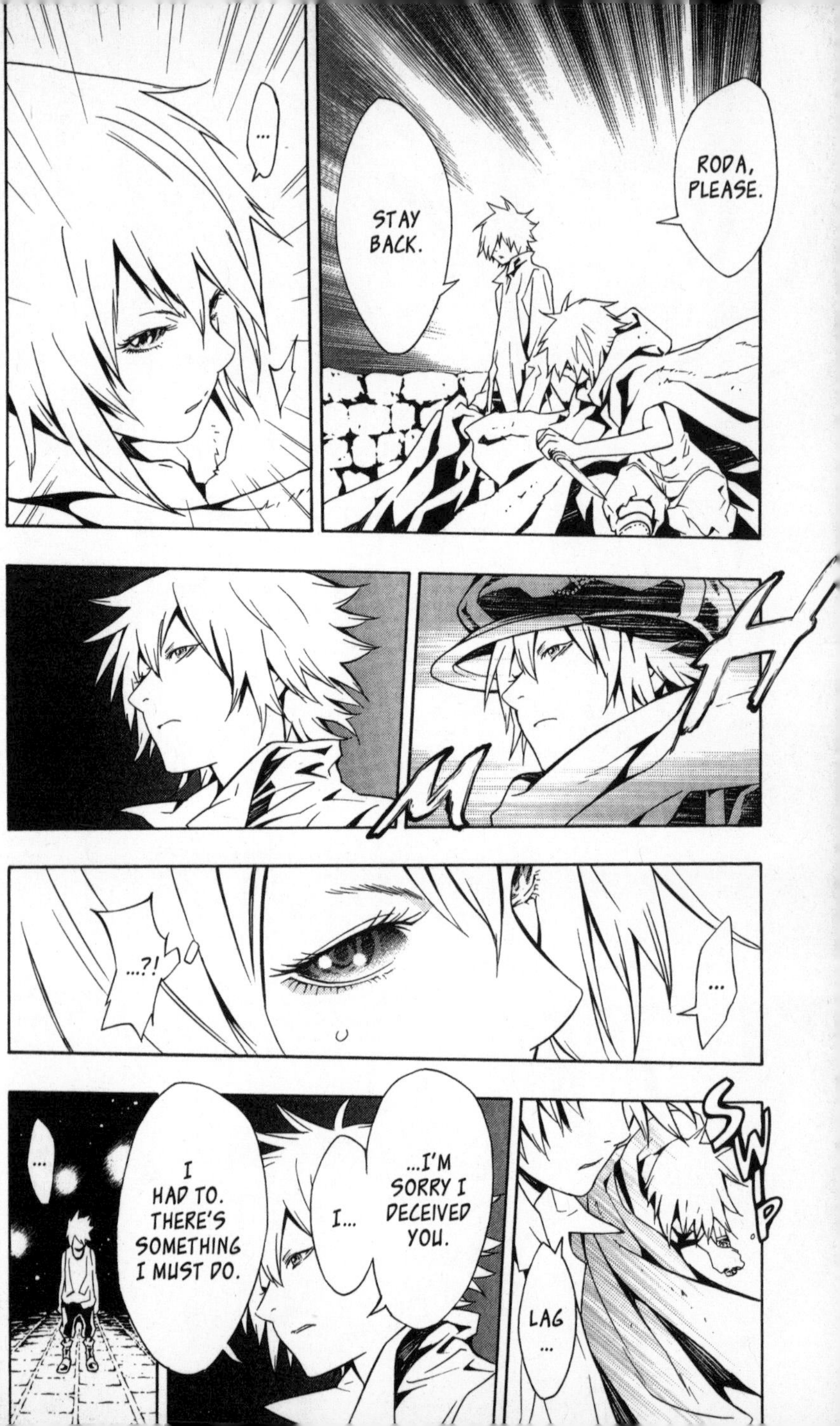
RODA, PLEASE.
STAY BACK.
...
...
...?!
SWP
LAG ...
...I'M SORRY I DECEIVED YOU.
I...
I HAD TO. THERE'S SOMETHING I MUST DO.
...

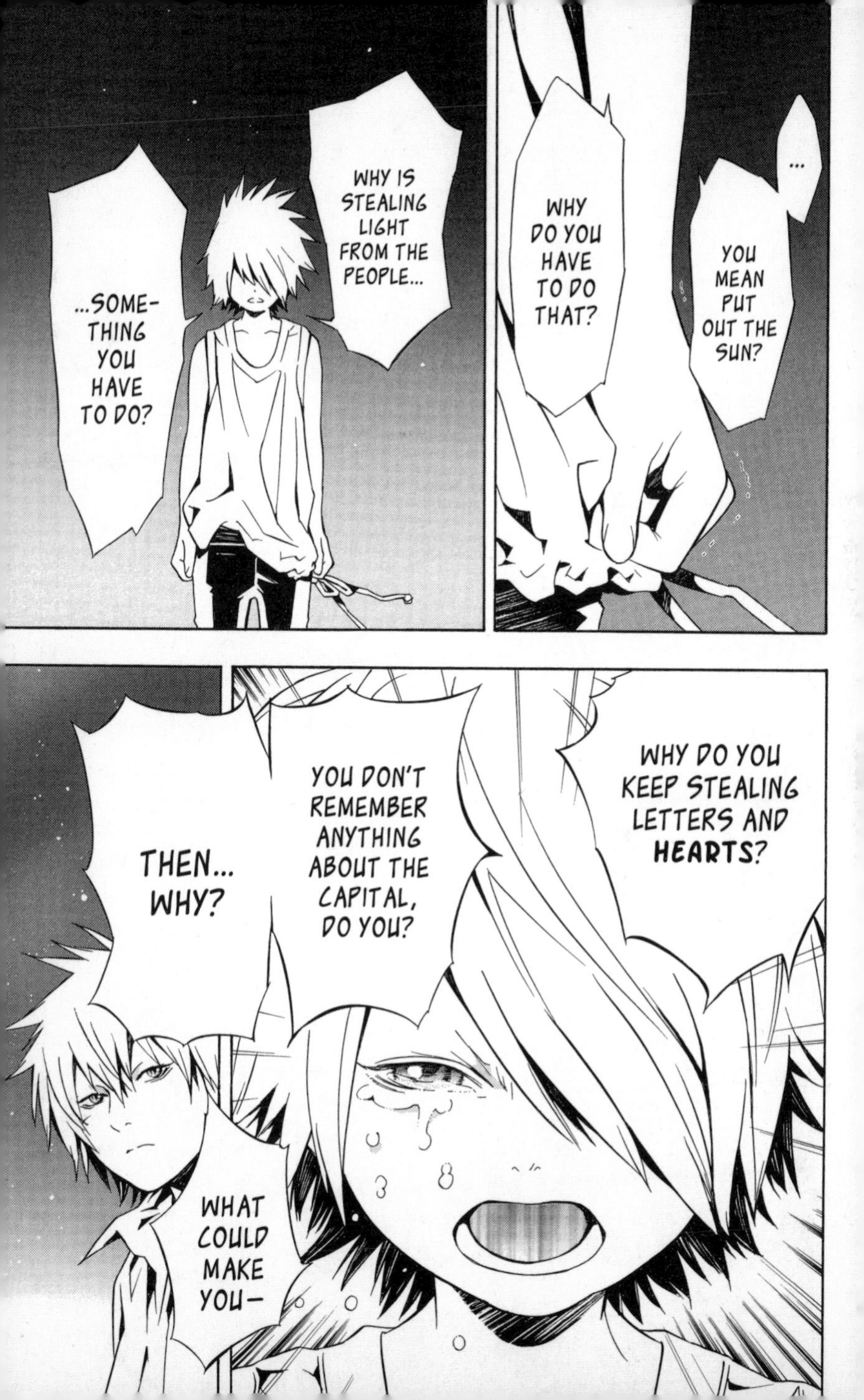
...
YOU MEAN PUT OUT THE SUN?
WHY DO YOU HAVE TO DO THAT?
WHY IS STEALING LIGHT FROM THE PEOPLE...
...SOME-THING YOU HAVE TO DO?
WHY DO YOU KEEP STEALING LETTERS AND **HEARTS**?
YOU DON'T REMEMBER ANYTHING ABOUT THE CAPITAL, DO YOU?
THEN... WHY?
WHAT COULD MAKE YOU—

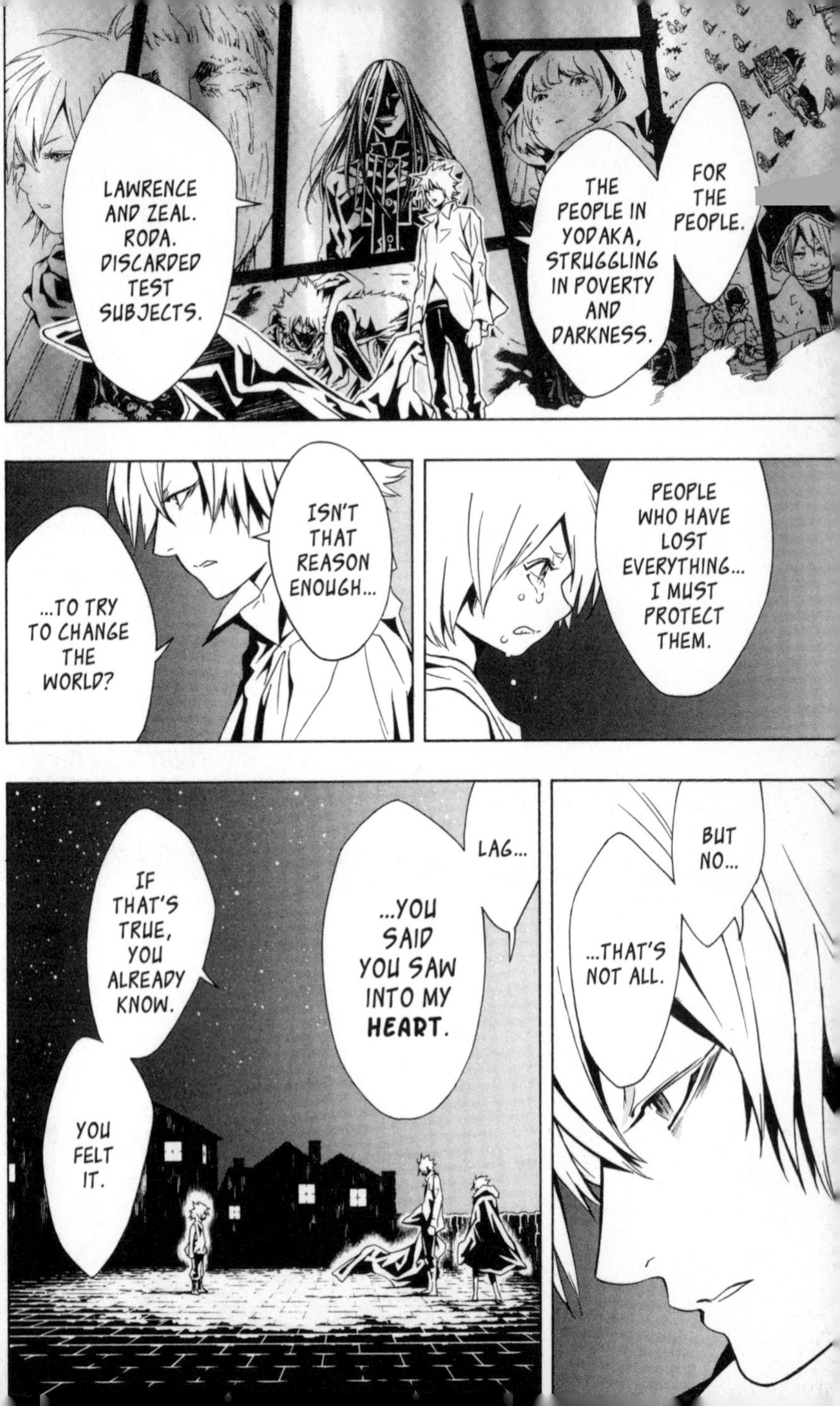
FOR THE PEOPLE.
THE PEOPLE IN YODAKA, STRUGGLING IN POVERTY AND DARKNESS.
LAWRENCE AND ZEAL. RODA. DISCARDED TEST SUBJECTS.
PEOPLE WHO HAVE LOST EVERYTHING... I MUST PROTECT THEM.
ISN'T THAT REASON ENOUGH...
...TO TRY TO CHANGE THE WORLD?
BUT NO...
...THAT'S NOT ALL.
LAG...
...YOU SAID YOU SAW INTO MY **HEART**.
IF THAT'S TRUE, YOU ALREADY KNOW.
YOU FELT IT.

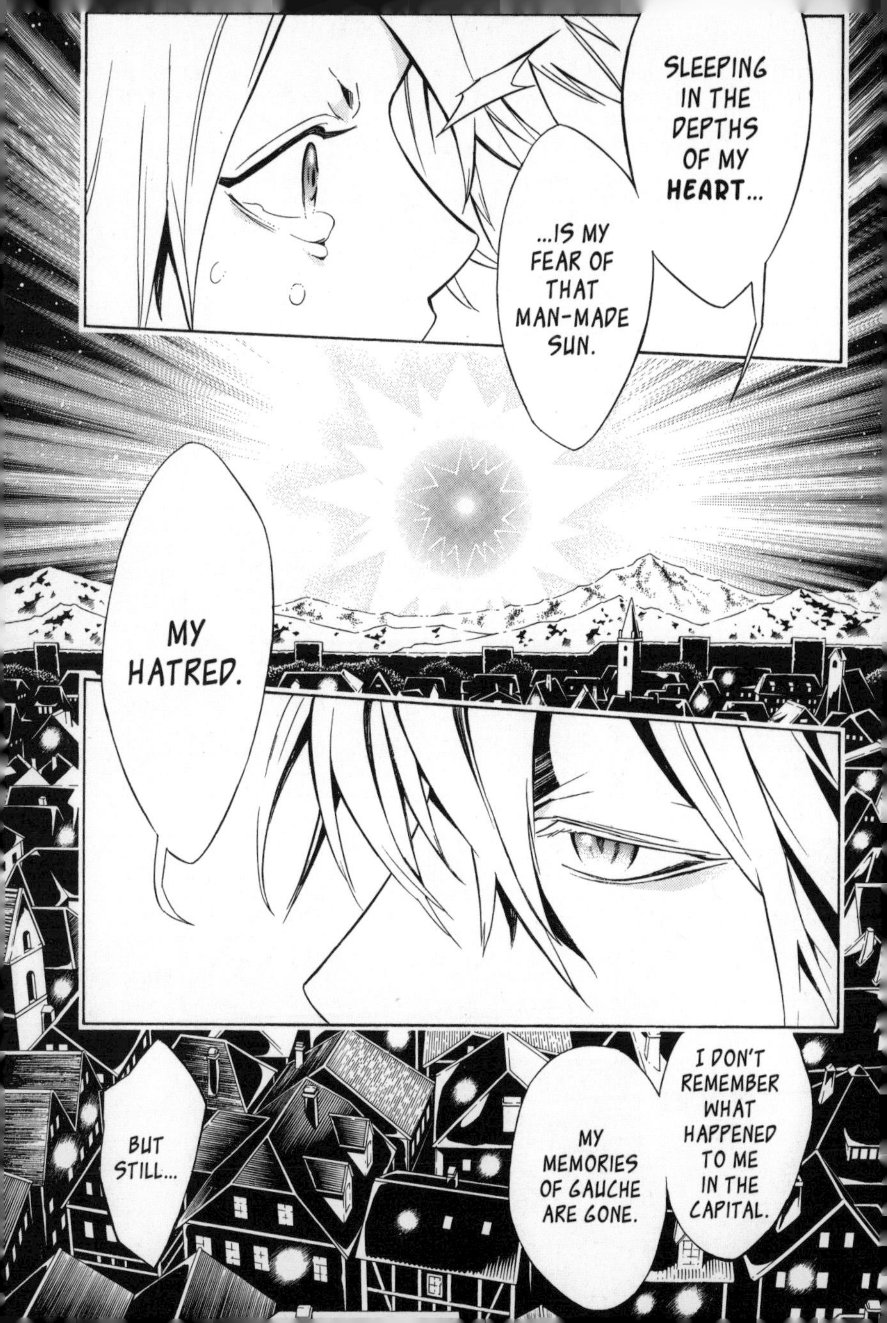
SLEEPING IN THE DEPTHS OF MY HEART...
...IS MY FEAR OF THAT MAN-MADE SUN.
MY HATRED.
I DON'T REMEMBER WHAT HAPPENED TO ME IN THE CAPITAL.
MY MEMORIES OF GAUCHE ARE GONE.
BUT STILL...

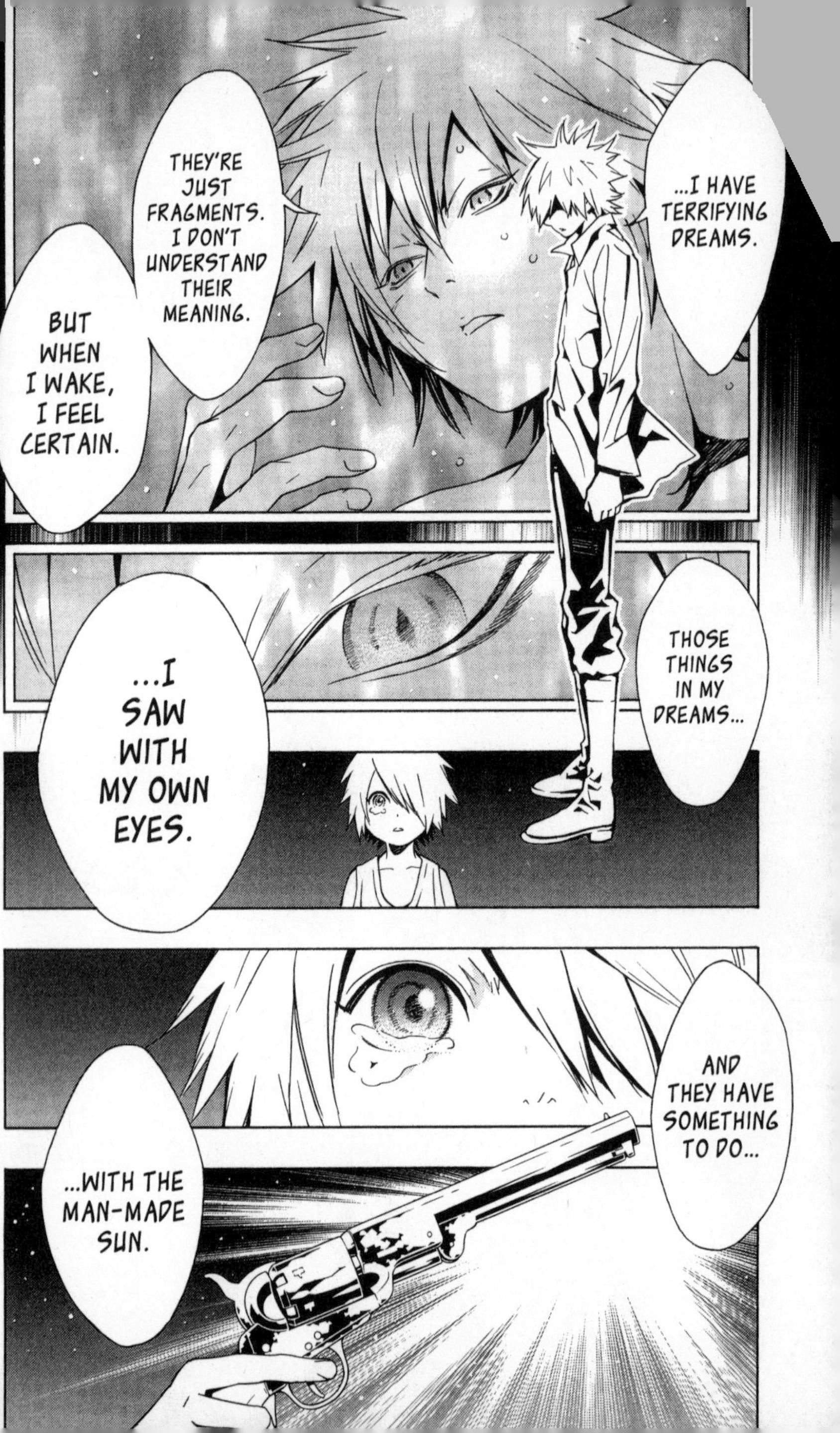
...I HAVE TERRIFYING DREAMS.
THEY'RE JUST FRAGMENTS.
I DON'T UNDERSTAND THEIR MEANING.
BUT WHEN I WAKE, I FEEL CERTAIN.
THOSE THINGS IN MY DREAMS...
...I SAW WITH MY OWN EYES.
AND THEY HAVE SOMETHING TO DO...
...WITH THE MAN-MADE SUN.

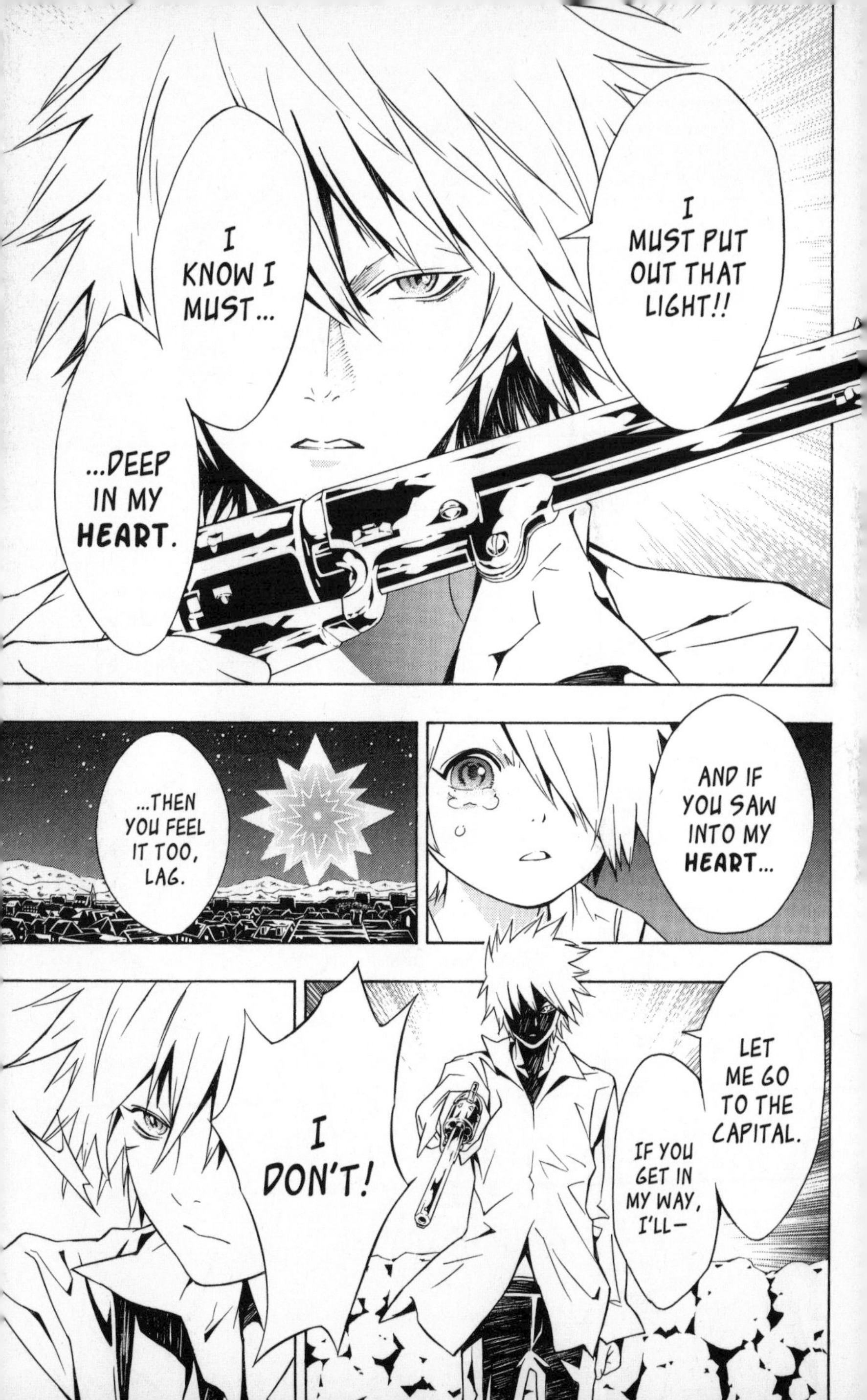
I MUST PUT OUT THAT LIGHT!!
I KNOW I MUST...
...DEEP IN MY HEART.
AND IF YOU SAW INTO MY HEART...
...THEN YOU FEEL IT TOO, LAG.
LET ME GO TO THE CAPITAL.
IF YOU GET IN MY WAY, I'LL—
I DON'T!

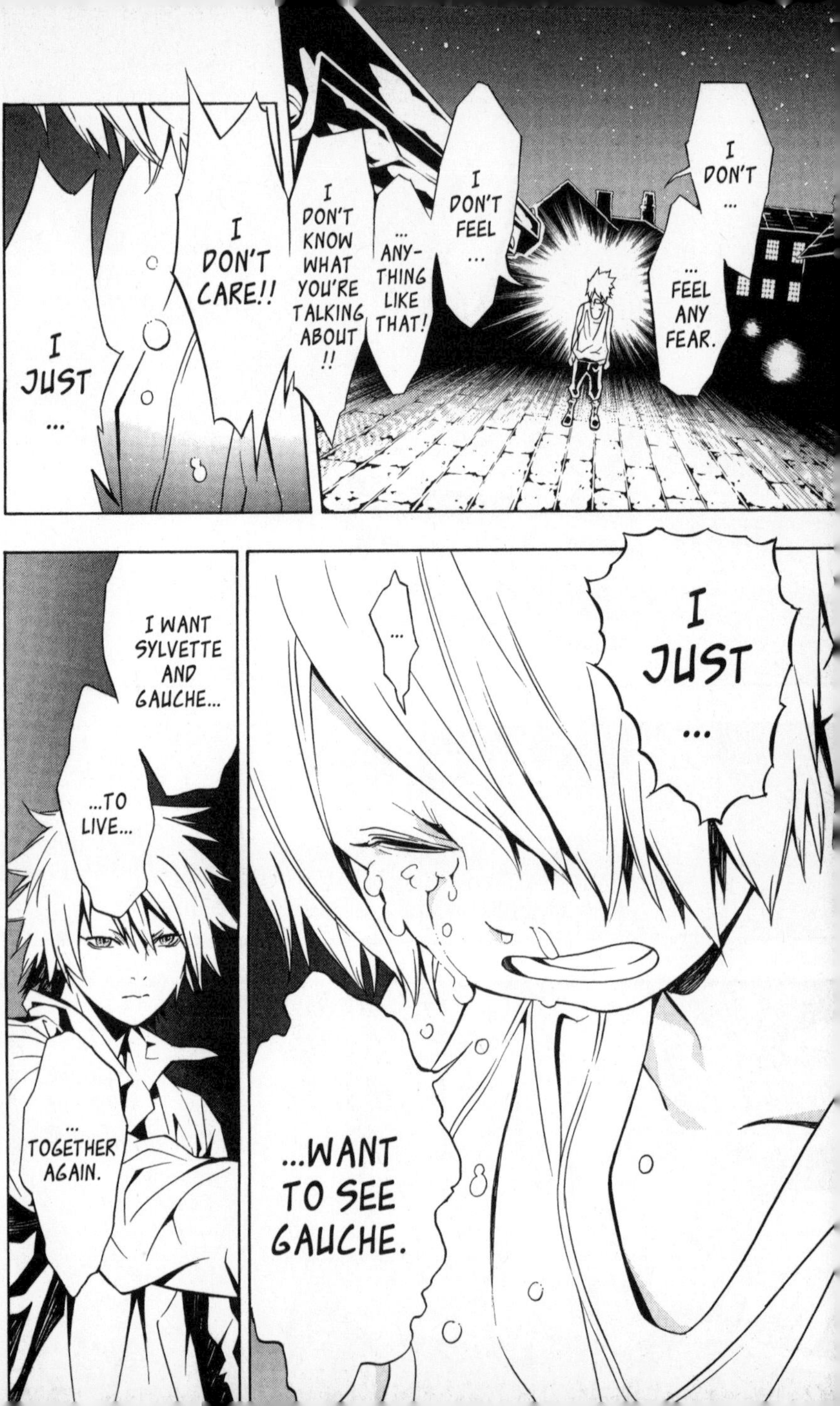
I DON'T ...
... FEEL ANY FEAR.
I DON'T FEEL ...
... ANY-THING LIKE THAT!
I DON'T KNOW WHAT YOU'RE TALKING ABOUT!!
I DON'T CARE!!
I JUST ...
I JUST ...
...
...WANT TO SEE GAUCHE.
I WANT SYLVETTE AND GAUCHE...
...TO LIVE...
... TOGETHER AGAIN.

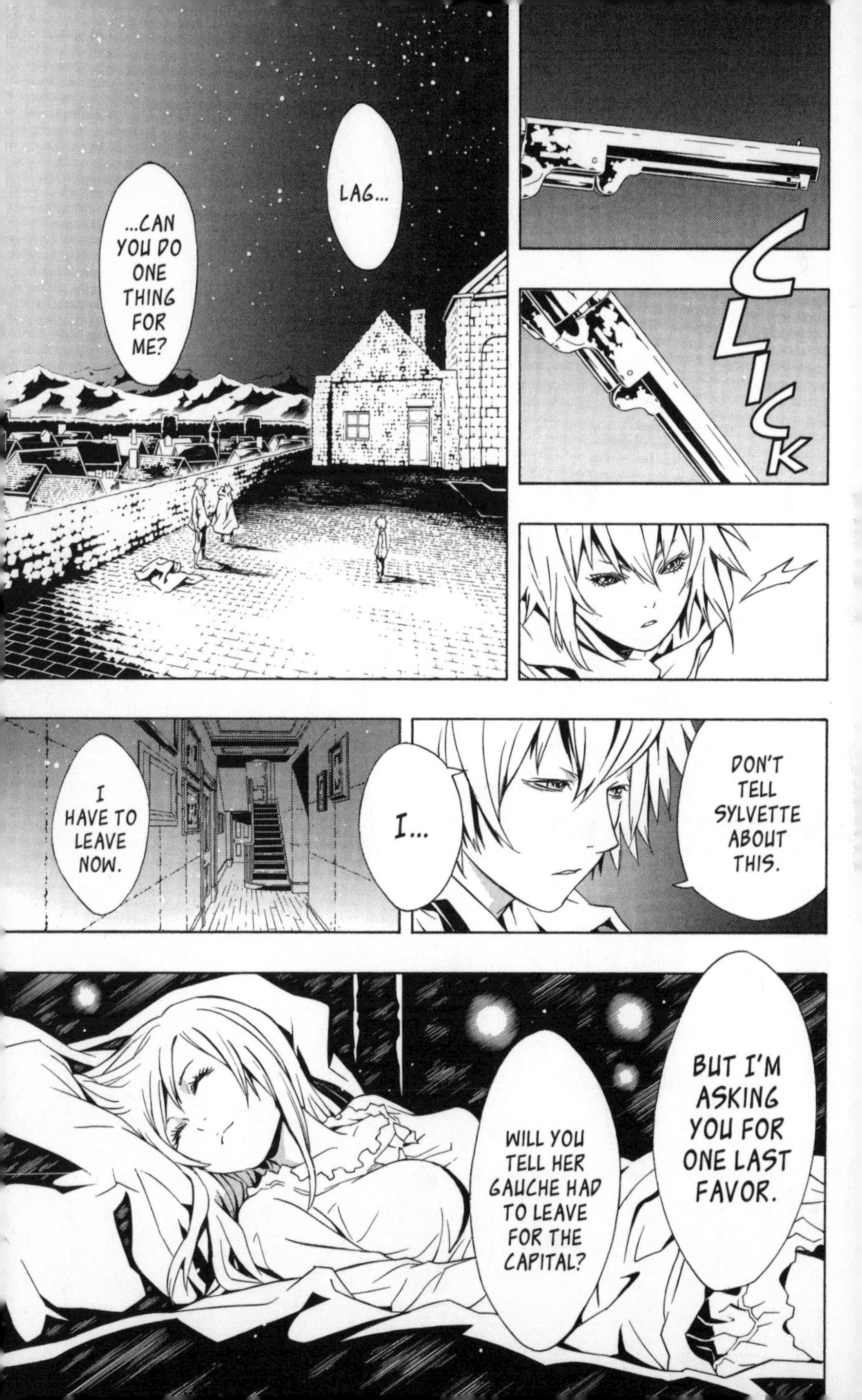
CLICK
LAG...
...CAN YOU DO ONE THING FOR ME?
DON'T TELL SYLVETTE ABOUT THIS.
I...
I HAVE TO LEAVE NOW.
BUT I'M ASKING YOU FOR ONE LAST FAVOR.
WILL YOU TELL HER GAUCHE HAD TO LEAVE FOR THE CAPITAL?

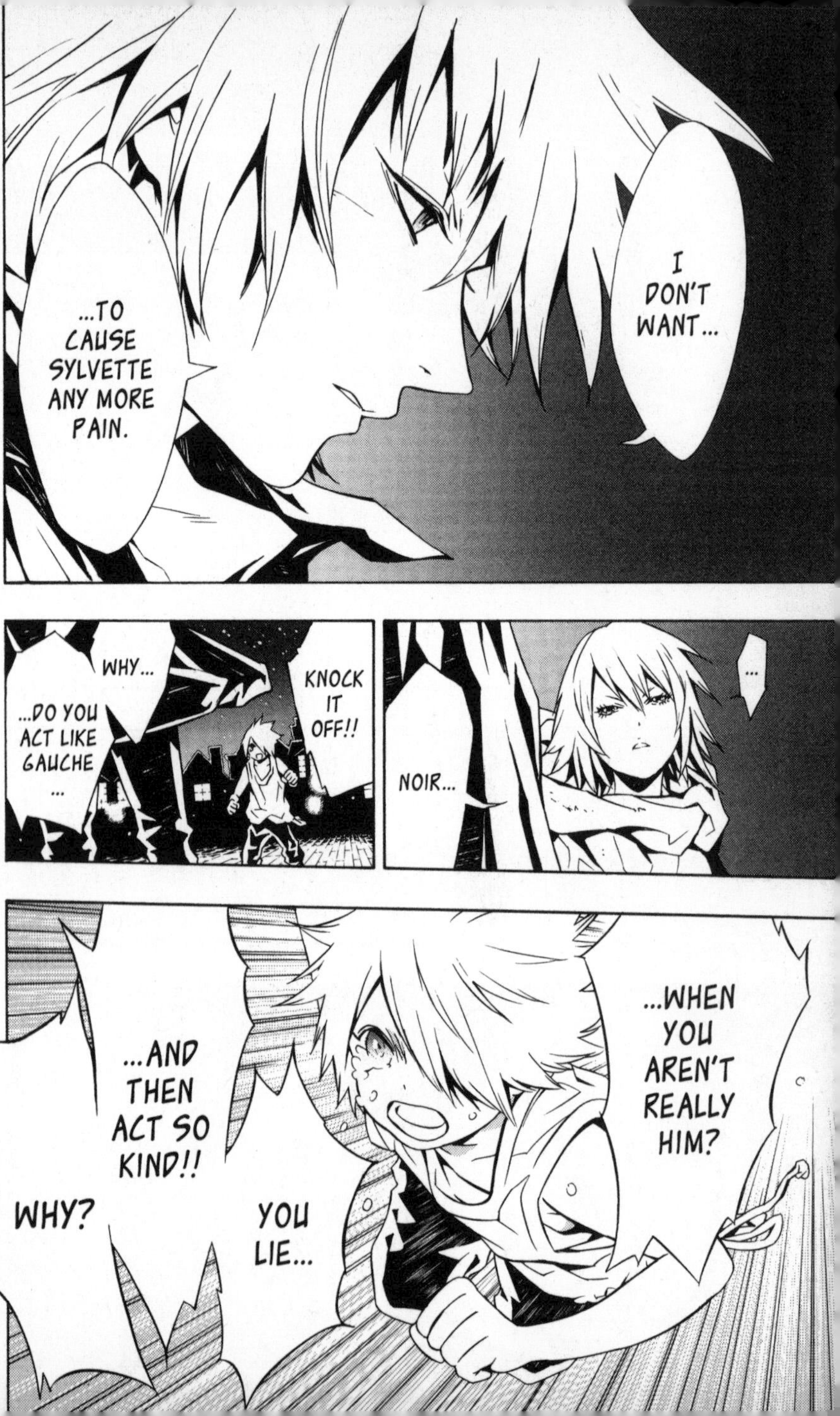
I DON'T WANT...
...TO CAUSE SYLVETTE ANY MORE PAIN.
...
NOIR...
KNOCK IT OFF!!
WHY...
...DO YOU ACT LIKE GAUCHE ...
...WHEN YOU AREN'T REALLY HIM?
...AND THEN ACT SO KIND!!
YOU LIE...
WHY?

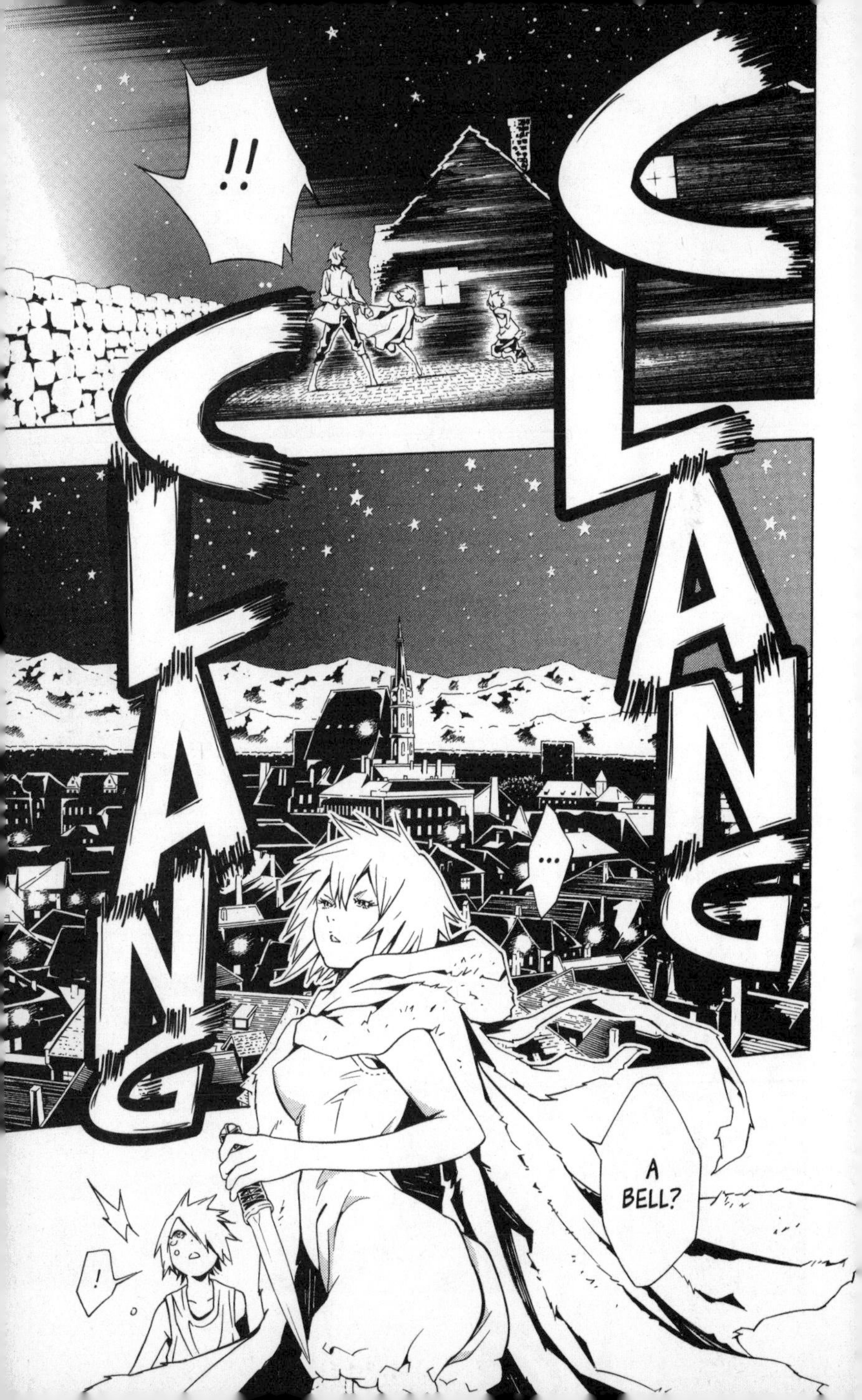
!!
CLANG
CLANG
...
A BELL?
!

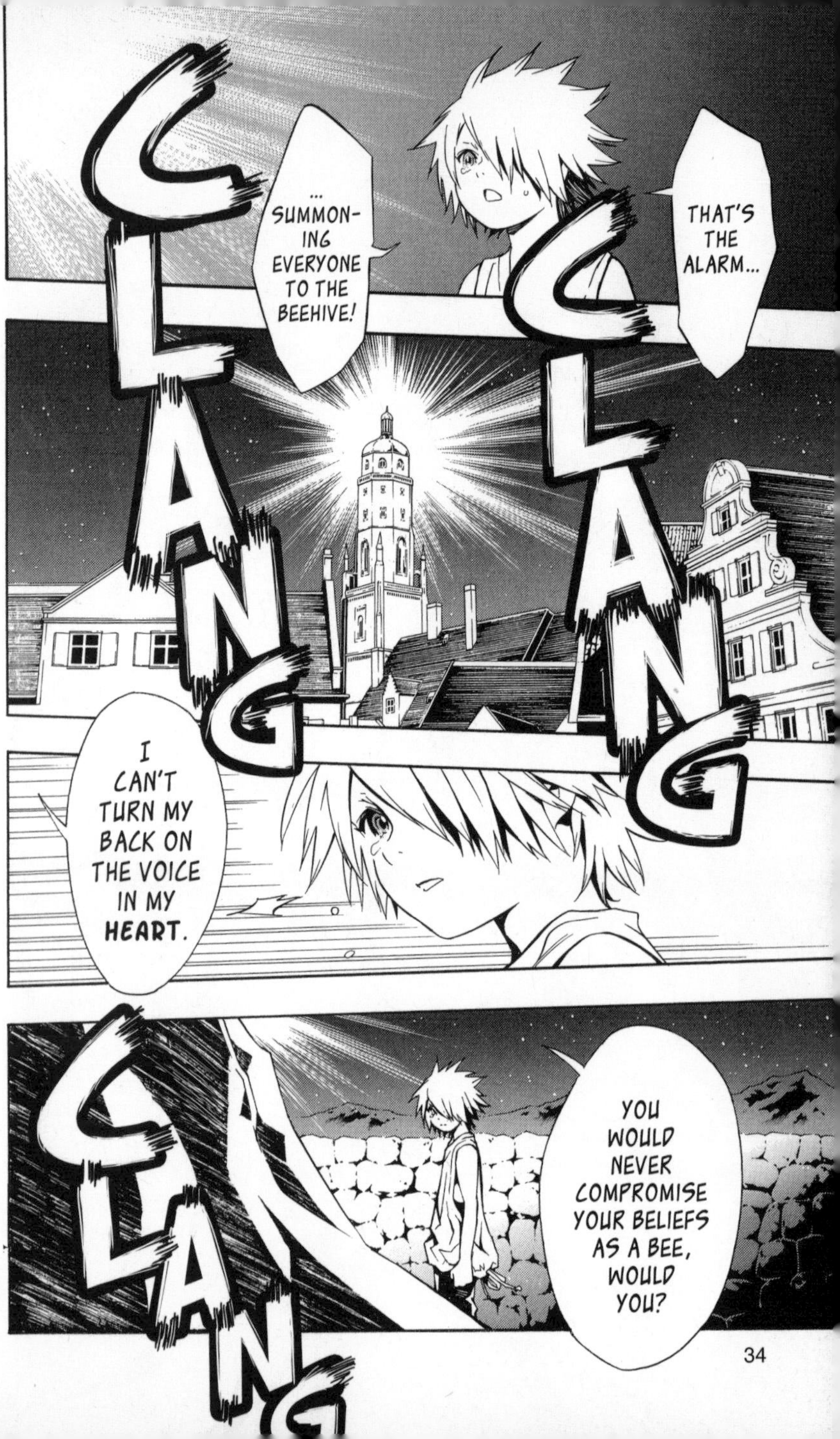
THAT'S THE ALARM...
... SUMMONING EVERYONE TO THE BEEHIVE!
CLANG
CLANG
I CAN'T TURN MY BACK ON THE VOICE IN MY **HEART**.
YOU WOULD NEVER COMPROMISE YOUR BELIEFS AS A BEE, WOULD YOU?
CLANG

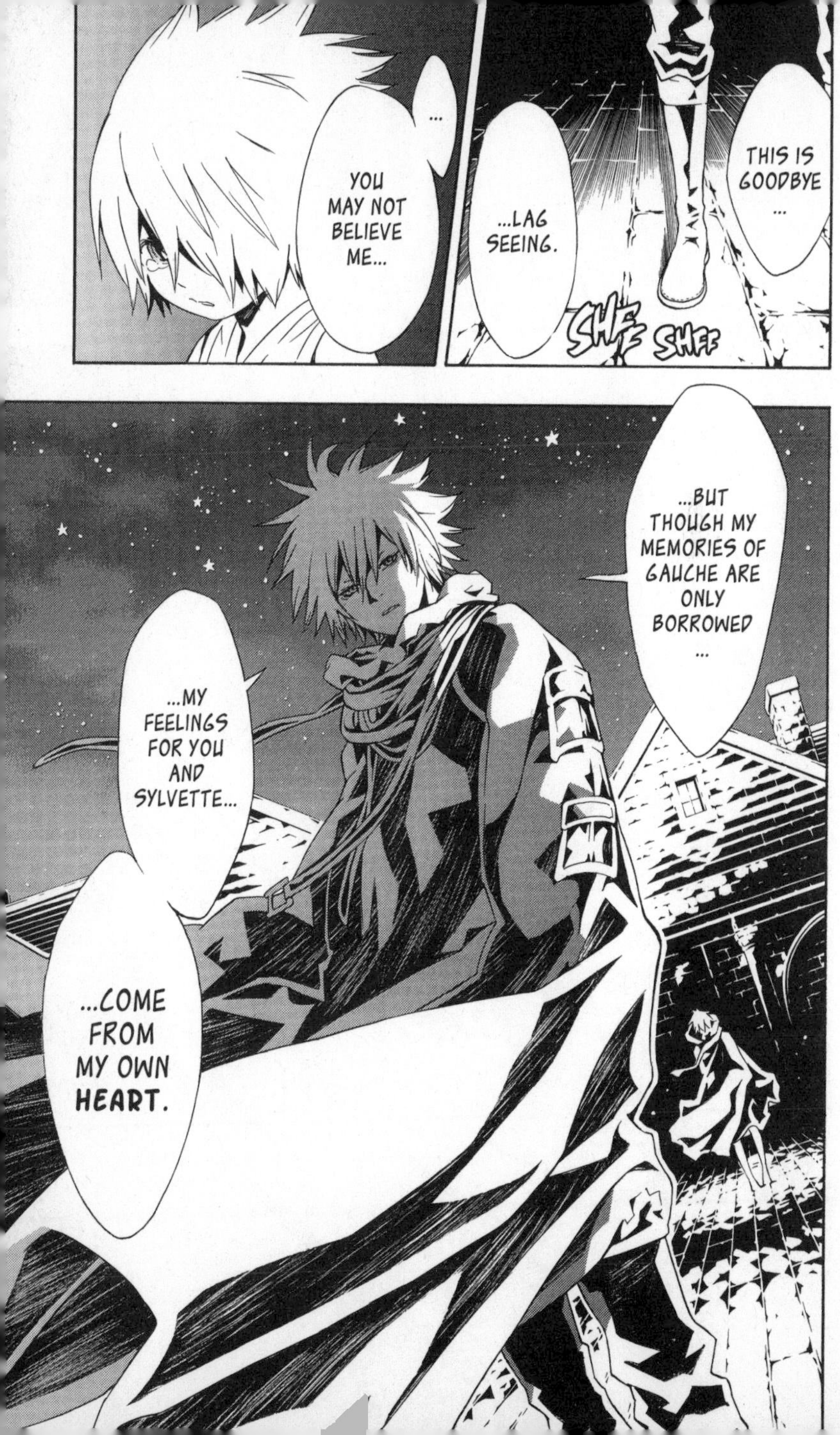
THIS IS GOODBYE...
...LAG SEEING.
SHFF SHFF
...
YOU MAY NOT BELIEVE ME...
...BUT THOUGH MY MEMORIES OF GAUCHE ARE ONLY BORROWED...
...MY FEELINGS FOR YOU AND SYLVETTE...
...COME FROM MY OWN HEART.

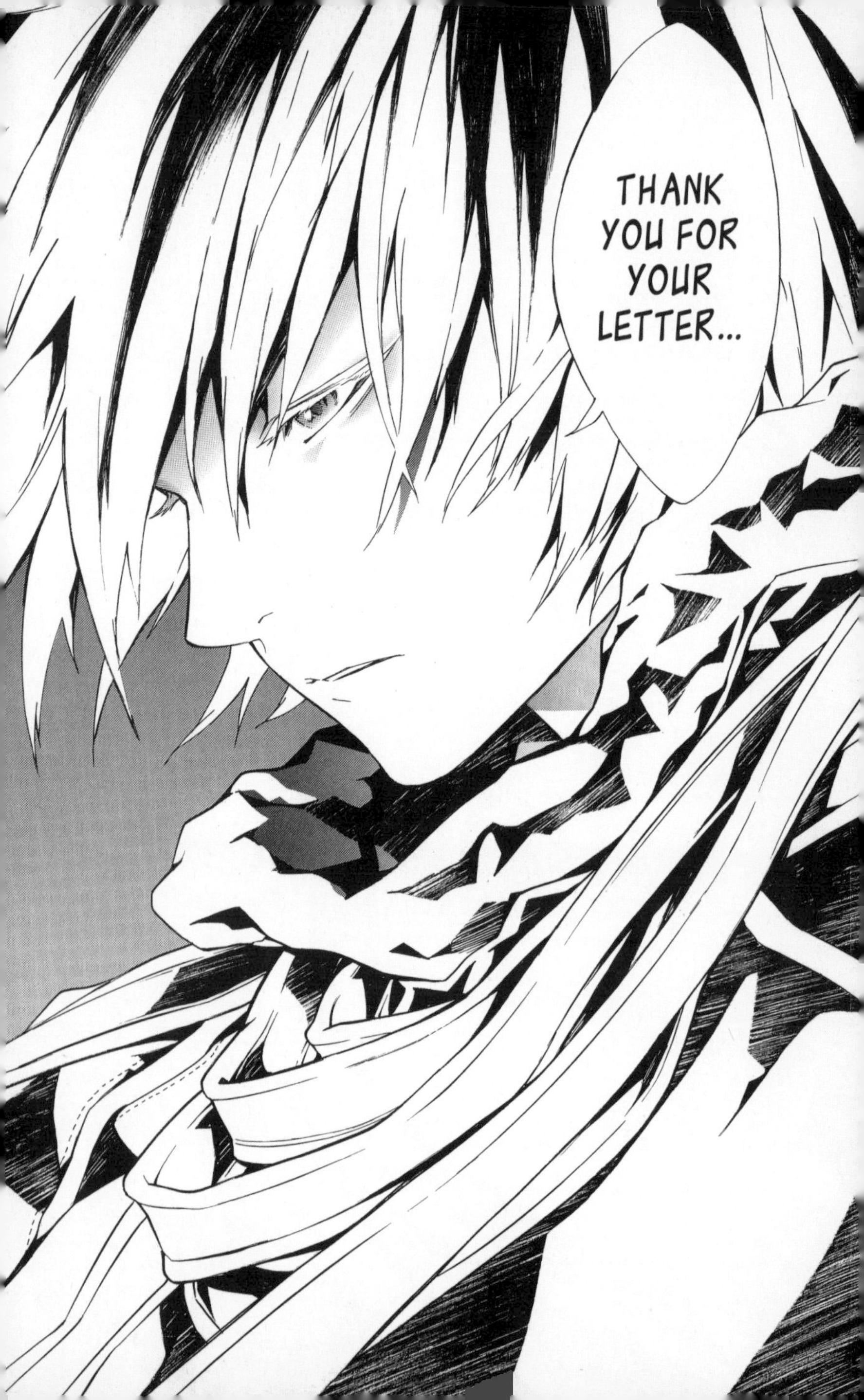
THANK YOU FOR YOUR LETTER...

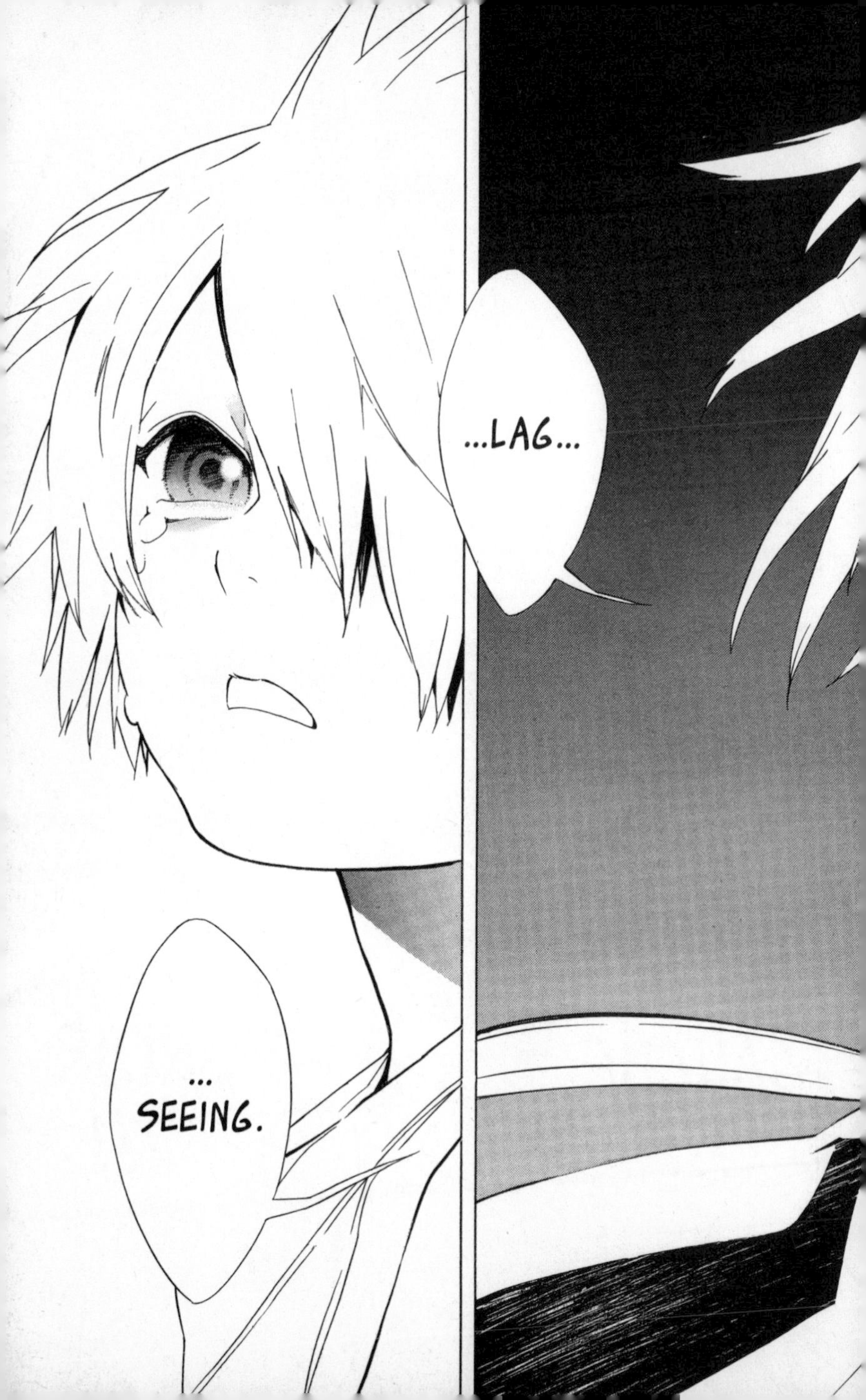
...LAG...
... SEEING.

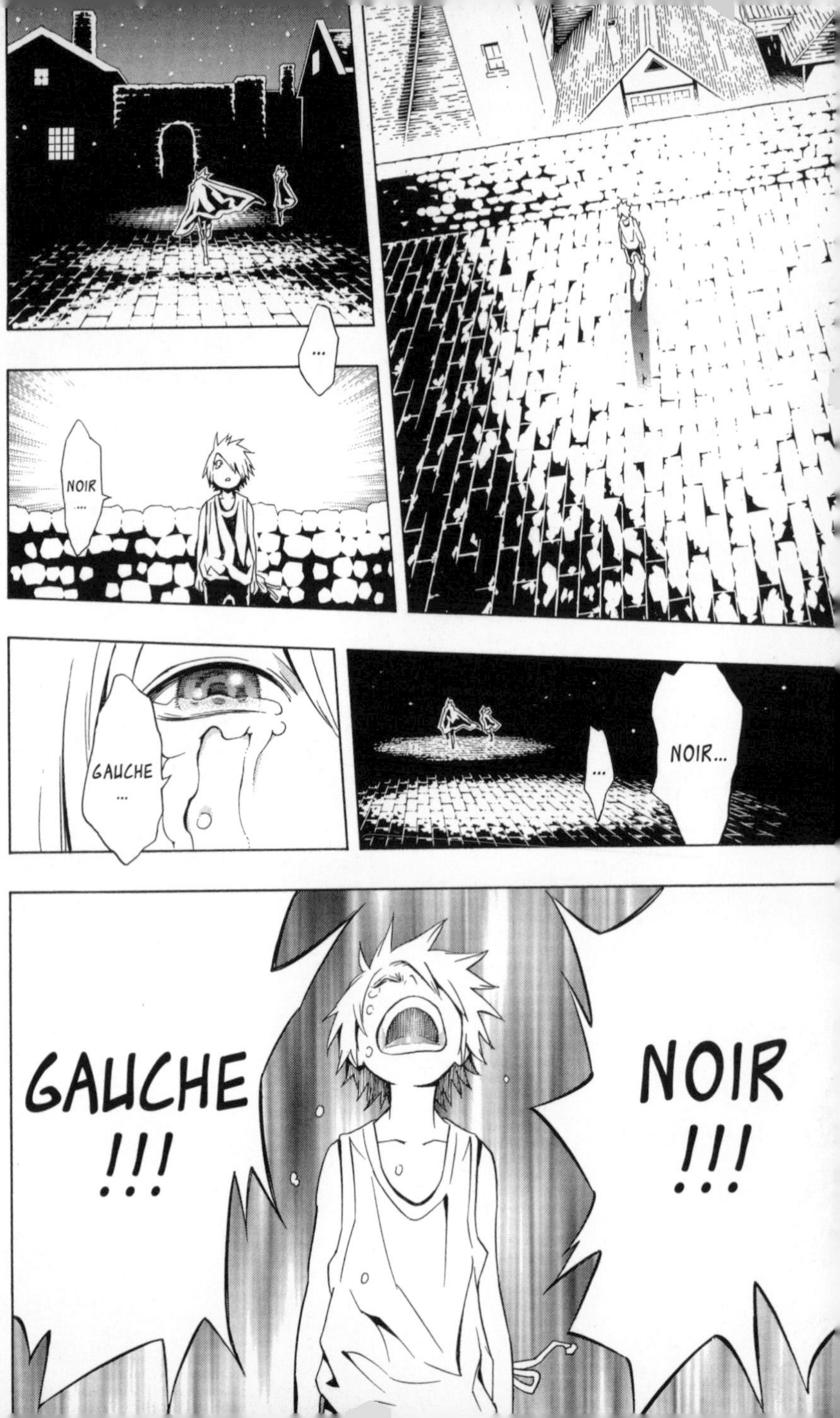
...
NOIR ...
NOIR...
...
GAUCHE ...
NOIR !!!
GAUCHE !!!

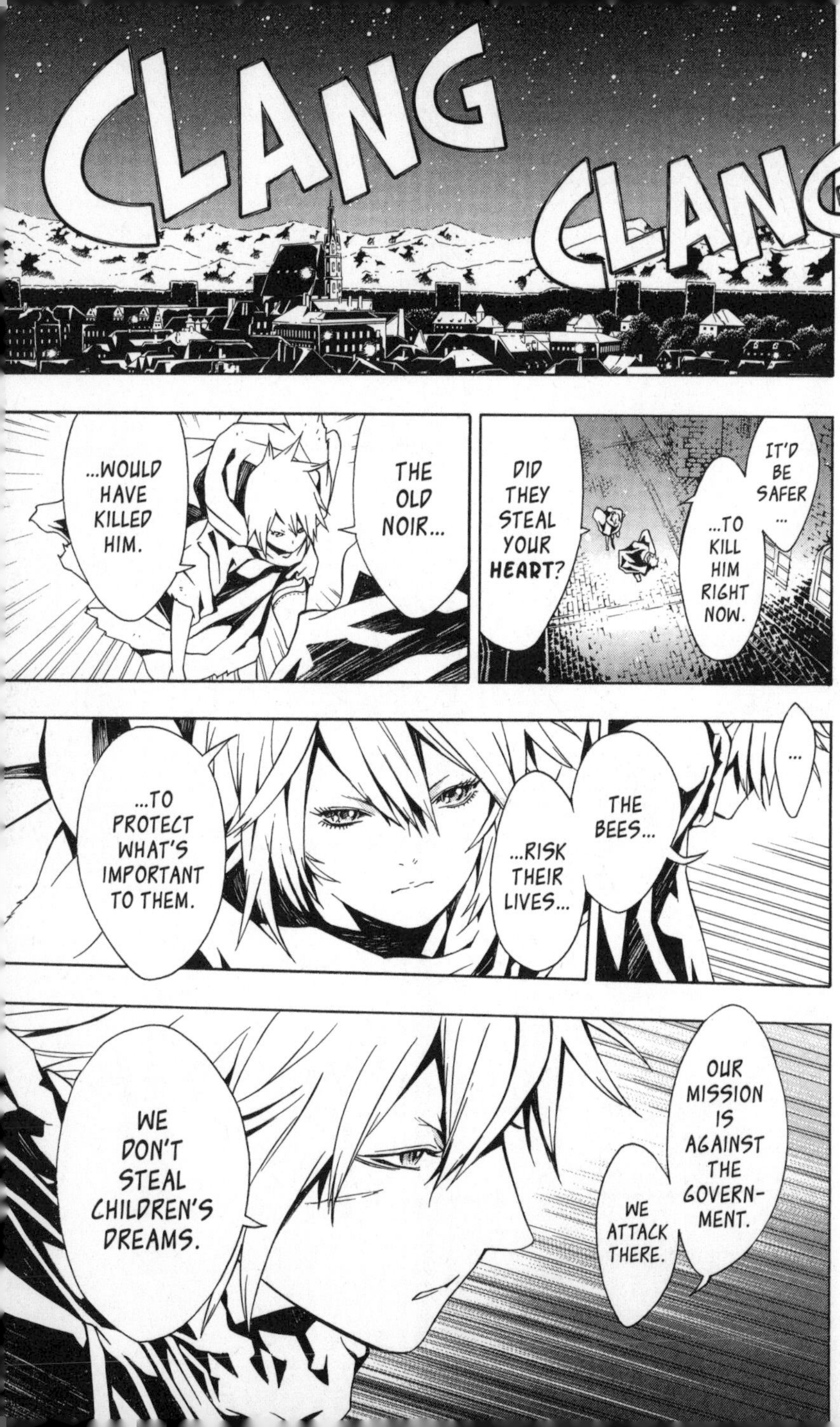
CLANG
CLANG
IT'D BE SAFER...
...TO KILL HIM RIGHT NOW.
DID THEY STEAL YOUR HEART?
THE OLD NOIR...
...WOULD HAVE KILLED HIM.
...
THE BEES...
...RISK THEIR LIVES...
...TO PROTECT WHAT'S IMPORTANT TO THEM.
OUR MISSION IS AGAINST THE GOVERN-MENT.
WE ATTACK THERE.
WE DON'T STEAL CHILDREN'S DREAMS.

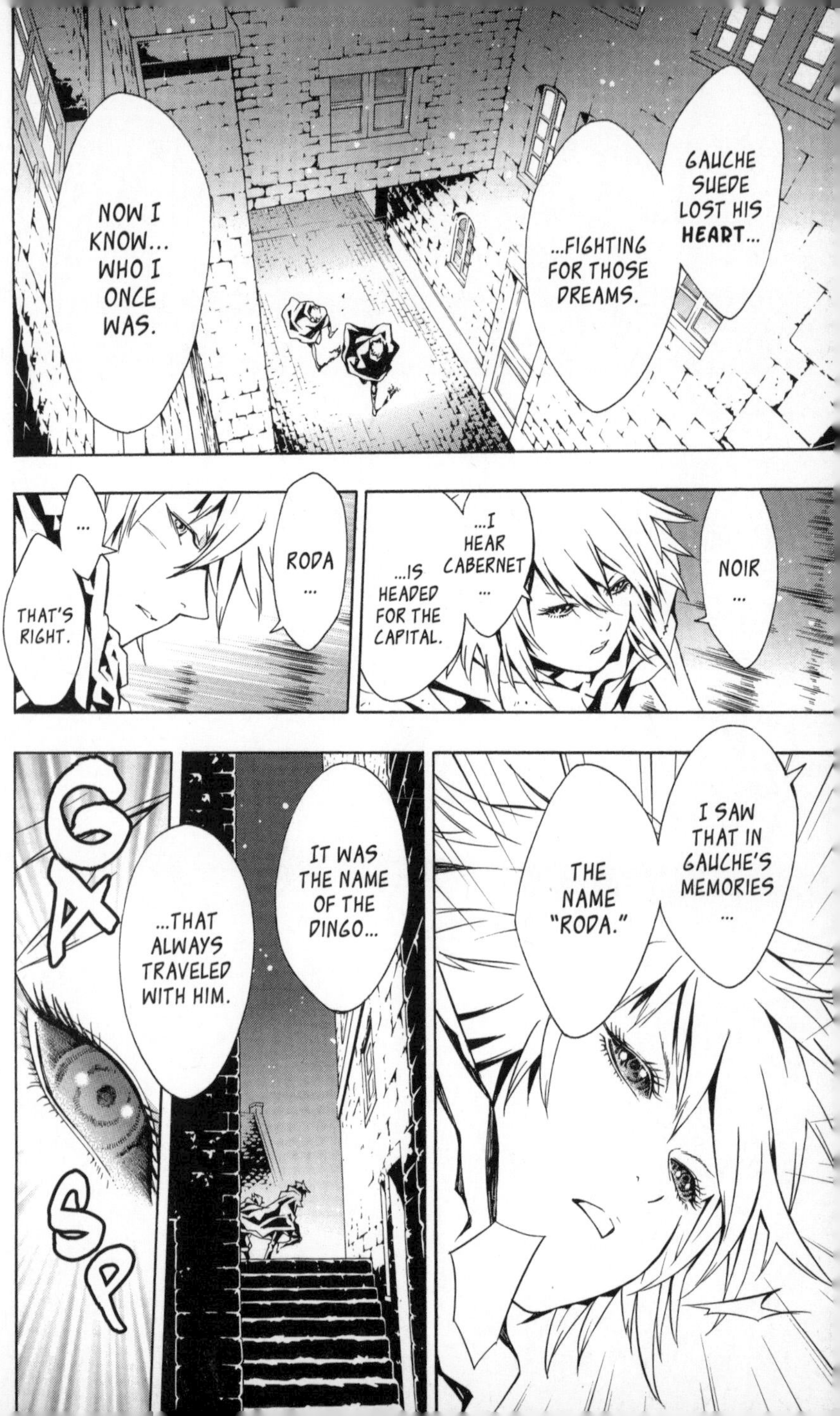
GAUCHE SUEDE LOST HIS **HEART**...
...FIGHTING FOR THOSE DREAMS.
NOW I KNOW... WHO I ONCE WAS.
NOIR ...
...I HEAR CABERNET ...
...IS HEADED FOR THE CAPITAL.
RODA ...
...
THAT'S RIGHT.
I SAW THAT IN GAUCHE'S MEMORIES ...
THE NAME "RODA."
IT WAS THE NAME OF THE DINGO...
...THAT ALWAYS TRAVELED WITH HIM.
GA
SP

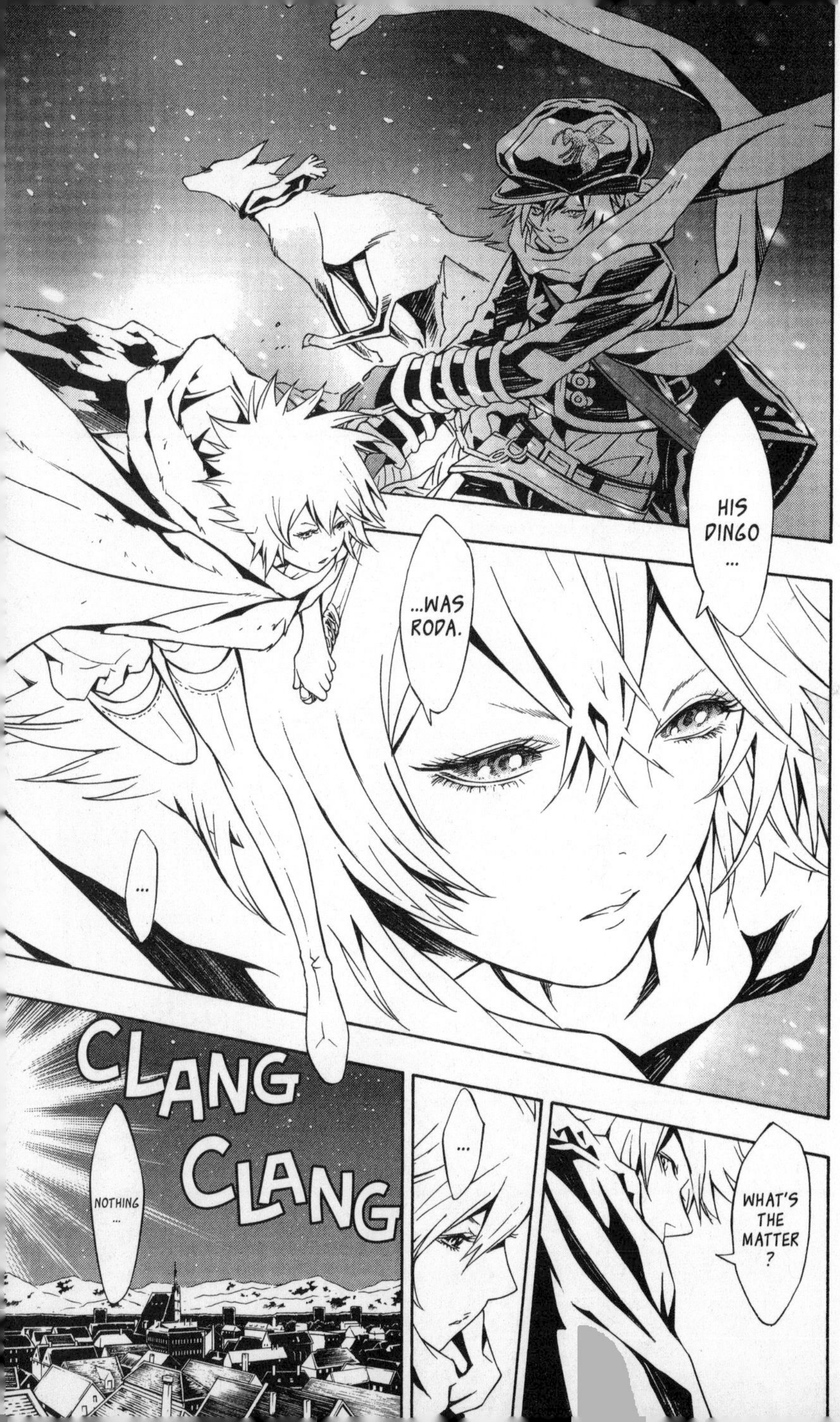
HIS DINGO ...
...WAS RODA.
...
WHAT'S THE MATTER?
...
CLANG
CLANG
NOTHING ...

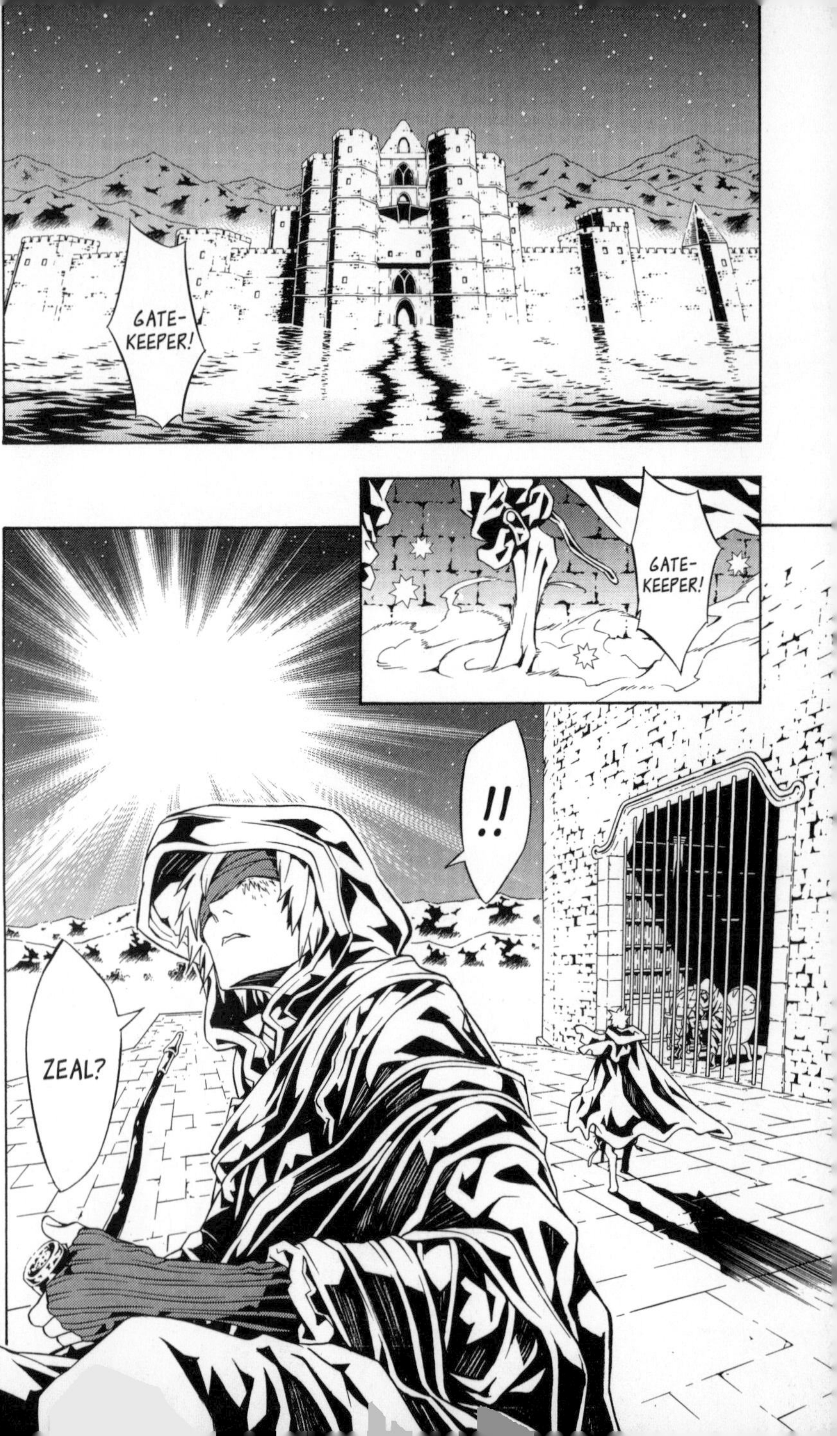
GATE-KEEPER!
GATE-KEEPER!
!!
ZEAL?

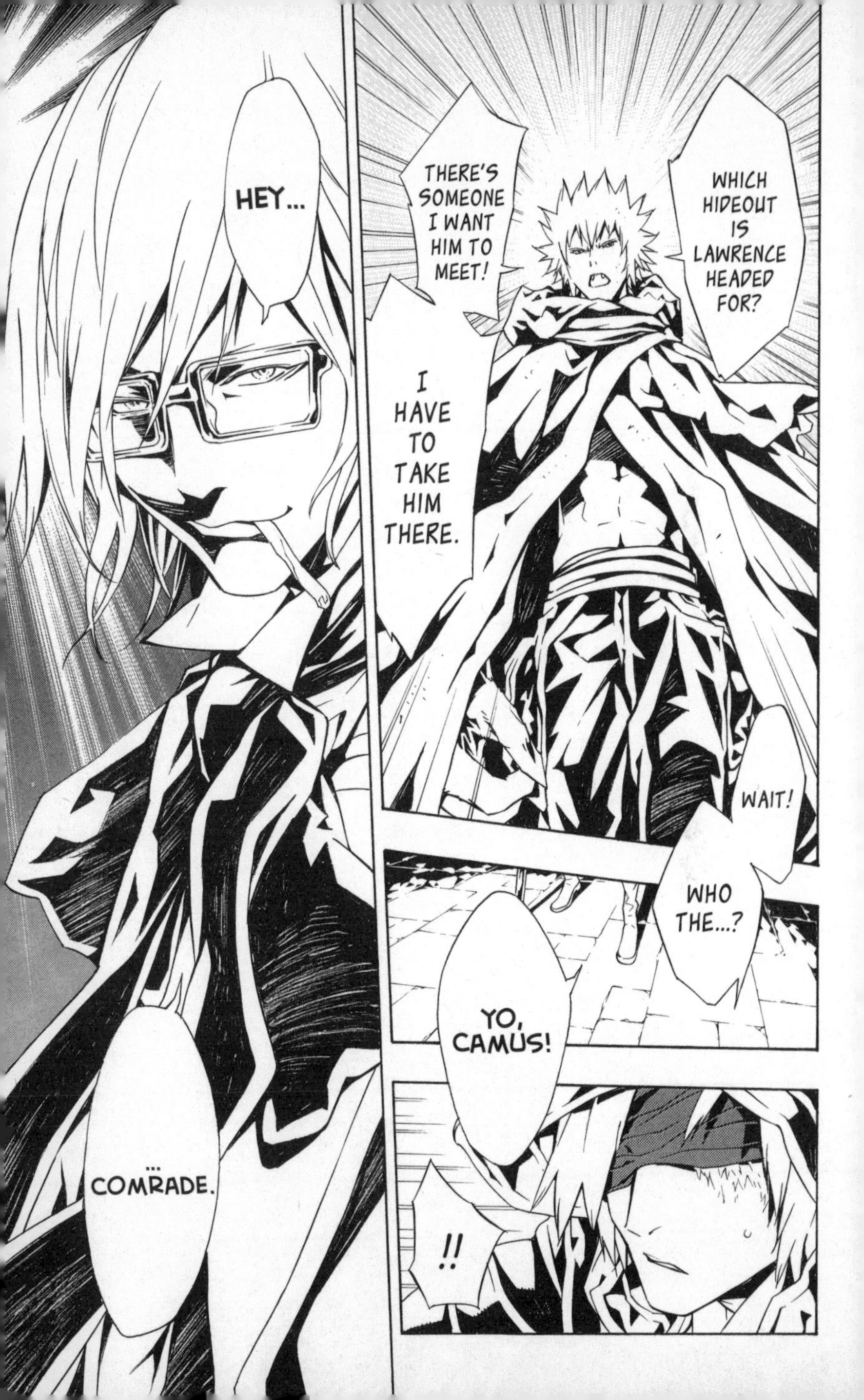
WHICH HIDEOUT IS LAWRENCE HEADED FOR?
THERE'S SOMEONE I WANT HIM TO MEET!
I HAVE TO TAKE HIM THERE.
WAIT!
WHO THE...?
YO, CAMUS!
!!
HEY...
...COMRADE.

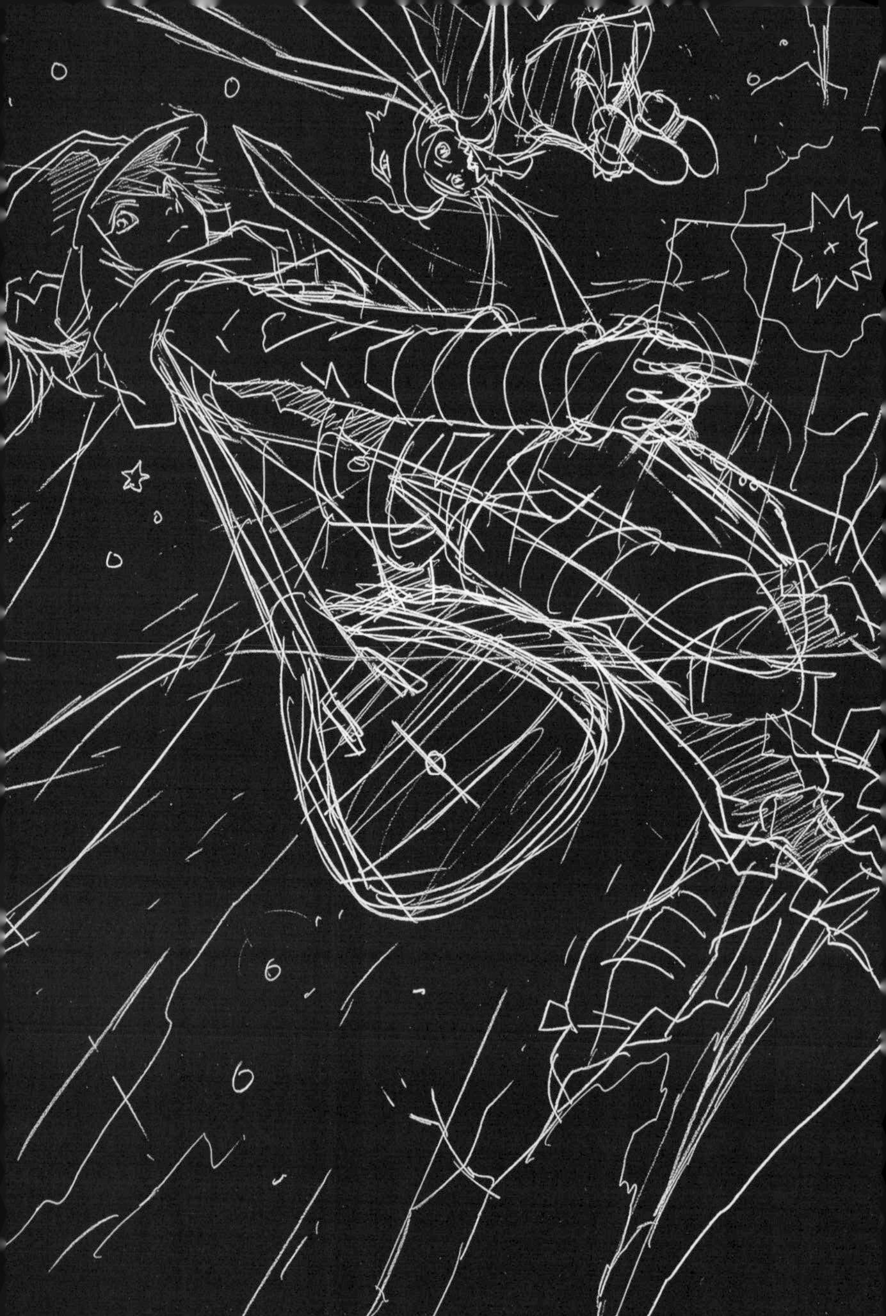

Rough sketch for the cover
to the artbook *Shine*.

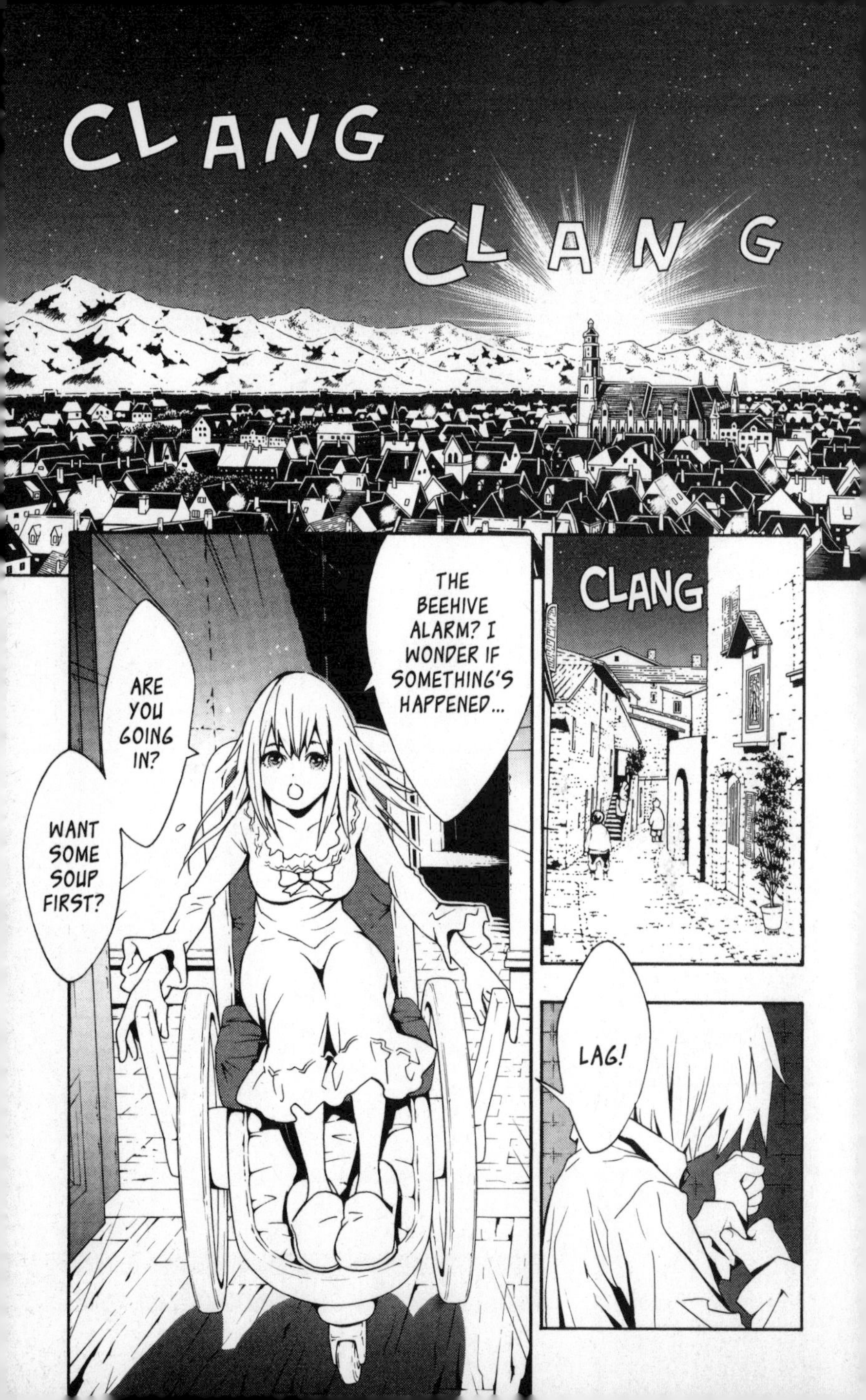
CLANG
CLANG
CLANG
LAG!
THE BEEHIVE ALARM? I WONDER IF SOMETHING'S HAPPENED...
ARE YOU GOING IN?
WANT SOME SOUP FIRST?

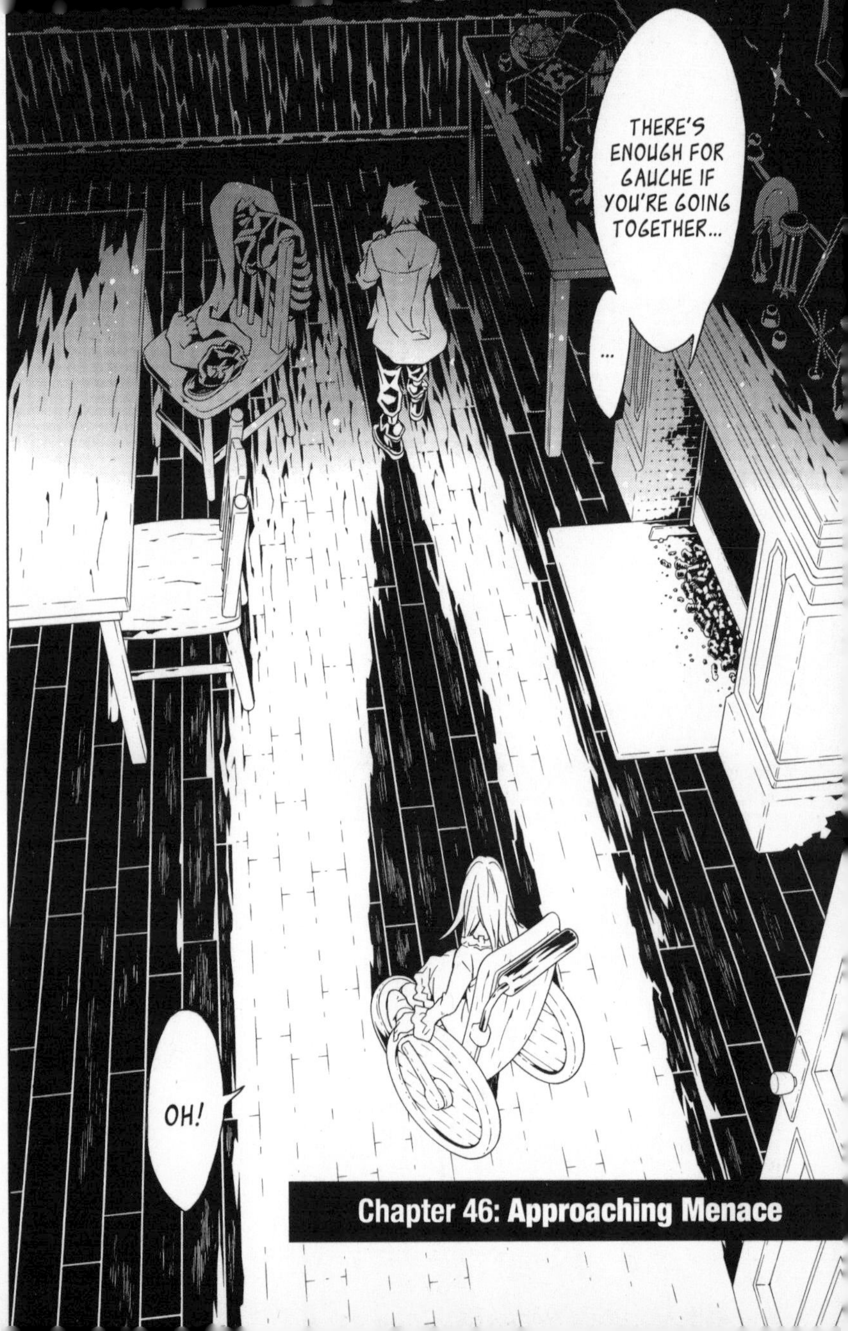
THERE'S ENOUGH FOR GAUCHE IF YOU'RE GOING TOGETHER...
...
OH!

Chapter 46: Approaching Menace

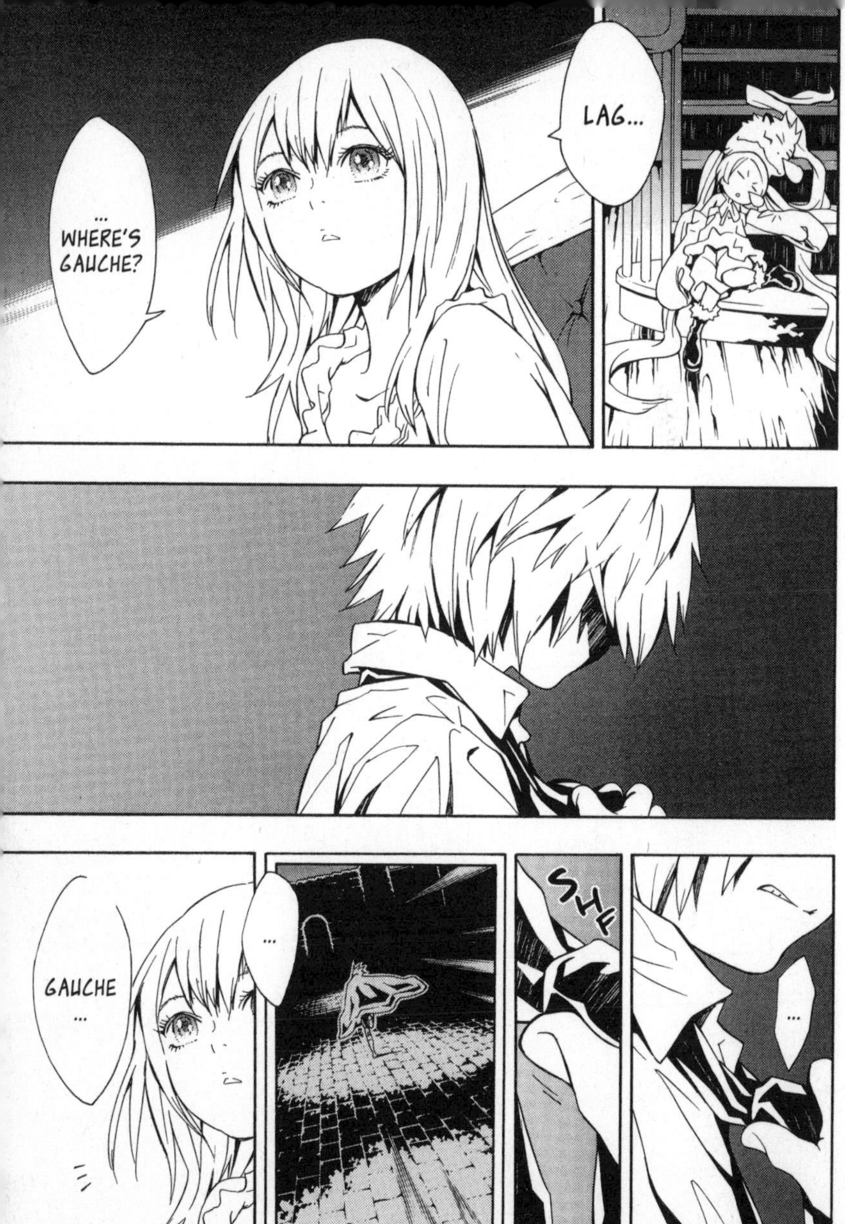
LAG...
...WHERE'S GAUCHE?
...
SHF
...
GAUCHE ...

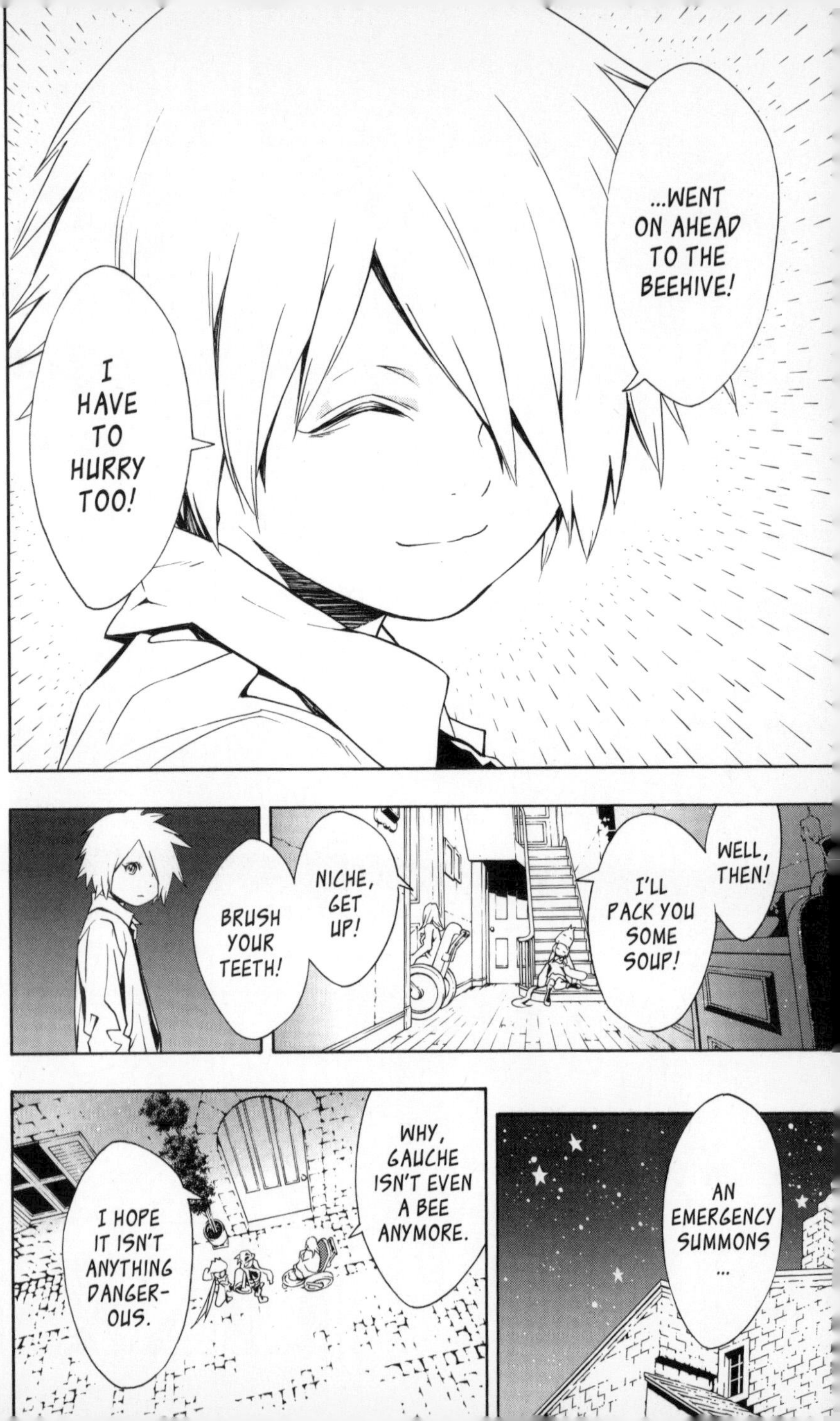
...WENT ON AHEAD TO THE BEEHIVE!
I HAVE TO HURRY TOO!
WELL, THEN!
I'LL PACK YOU SOME SOUP!
NICHE, GET UP!
BRUSH YOUR TEETH!
AN EMERGENCY SUMMONS ...
WHY, GAUCHE ISN'T EVEN A BEE ANYMORE.
I HOPE IT ISN'T ANYTHING DANGER-OUS.

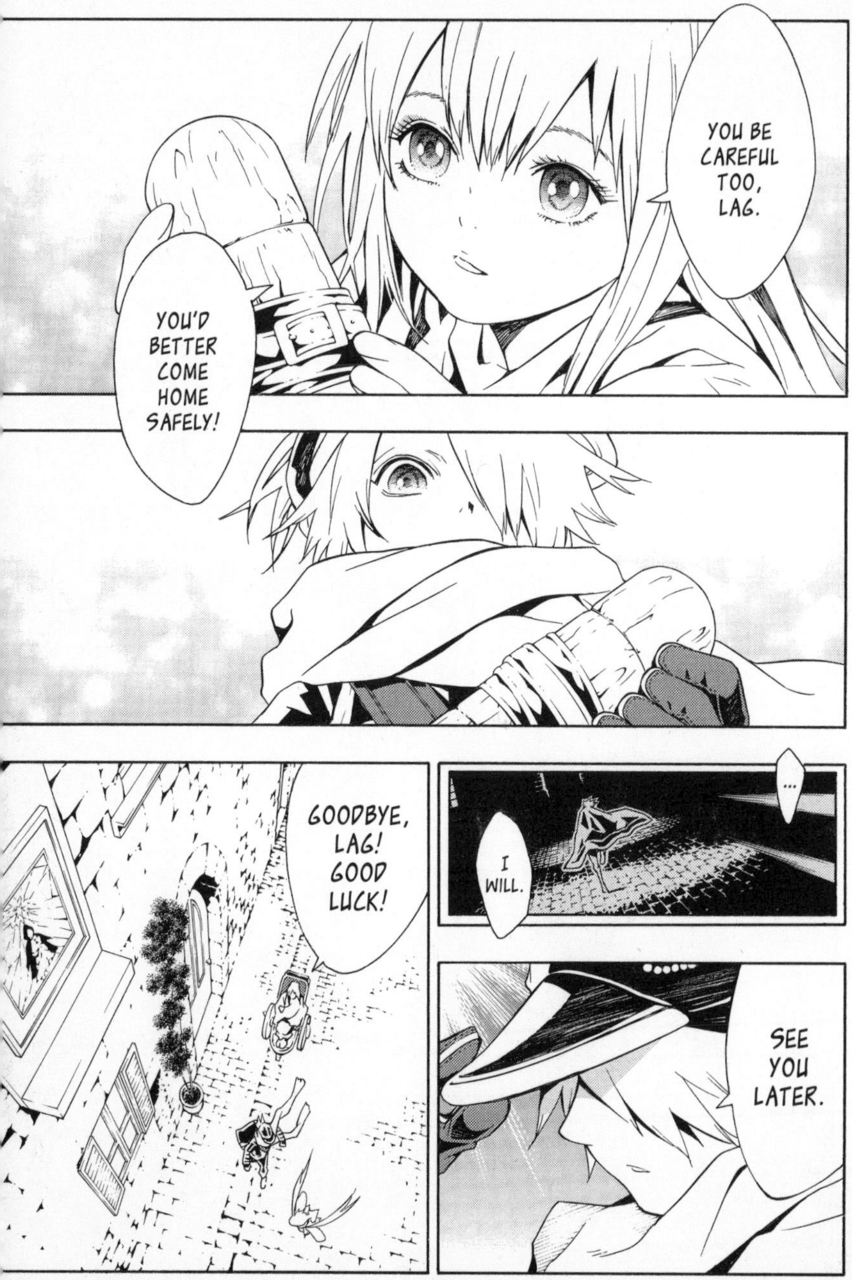
YOU BE CAREFUL TOO, LAG.
YOU'D BETTER COME HOME SAFELY!
...
I WILL.
SEE YOU LATER.
GOODBYE, LAG! GOOD LUCK!

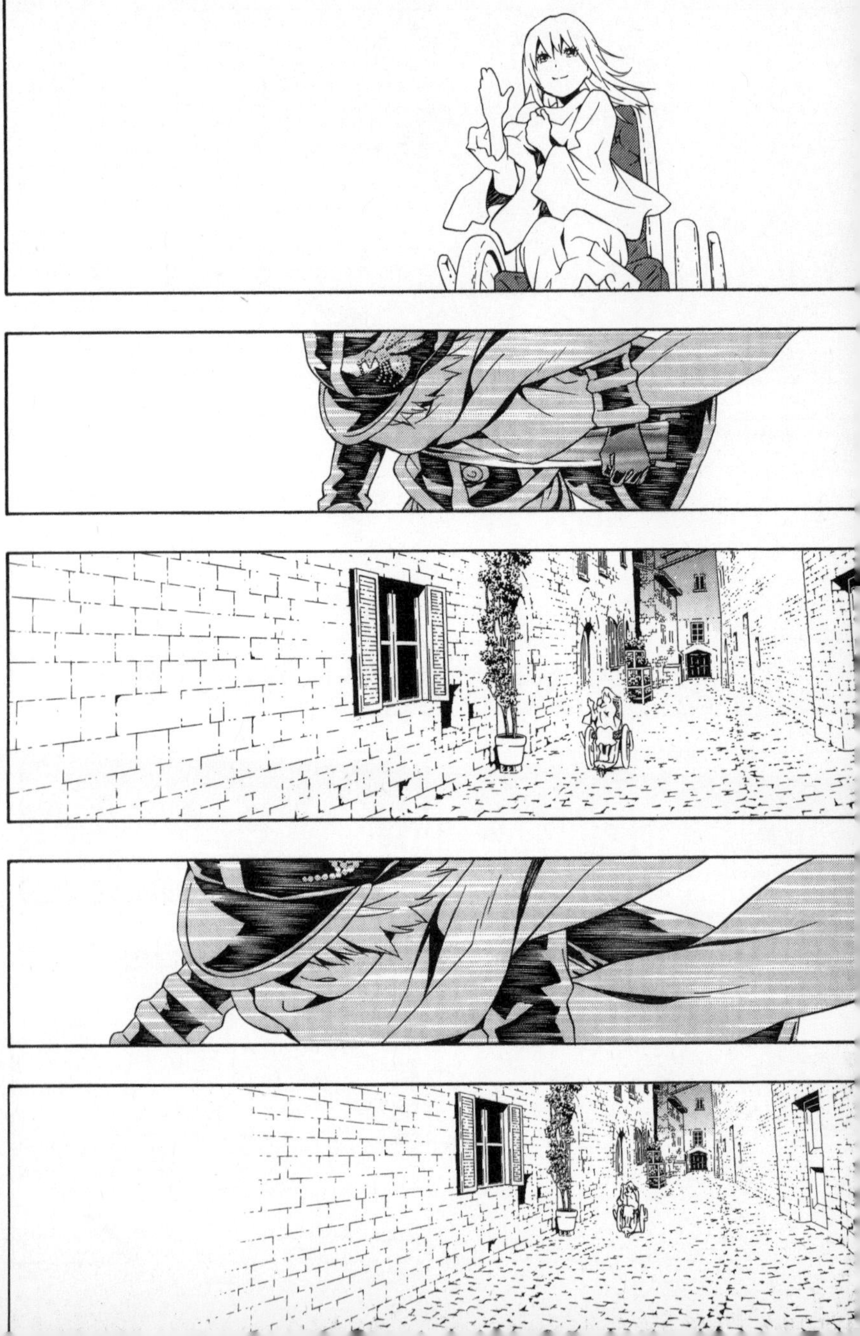

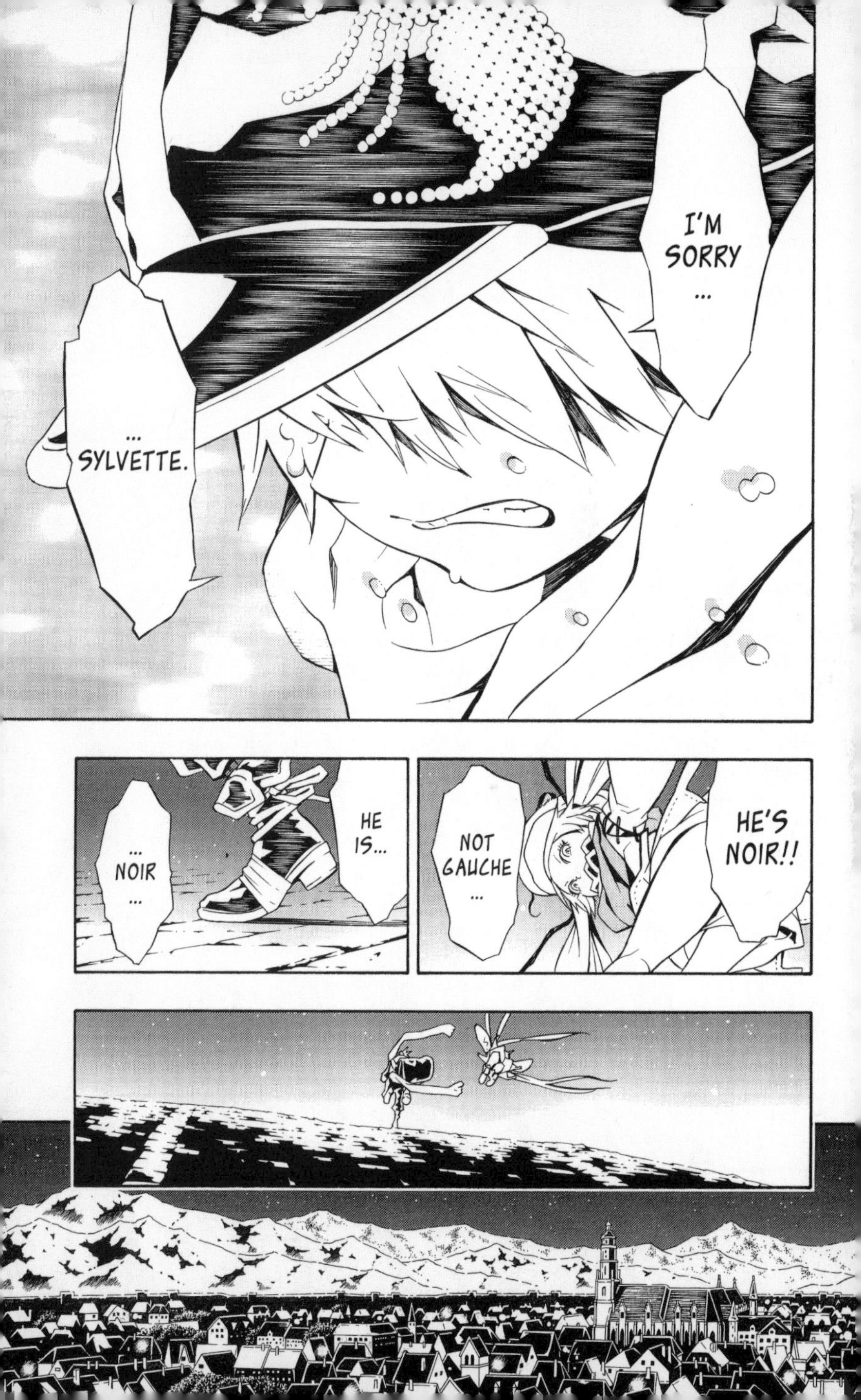
I'M SORRY ...
... SYLVETTE.
HE'S NOIR!!
NOT GAUCHE ...
HE IS...
... NOIR ...

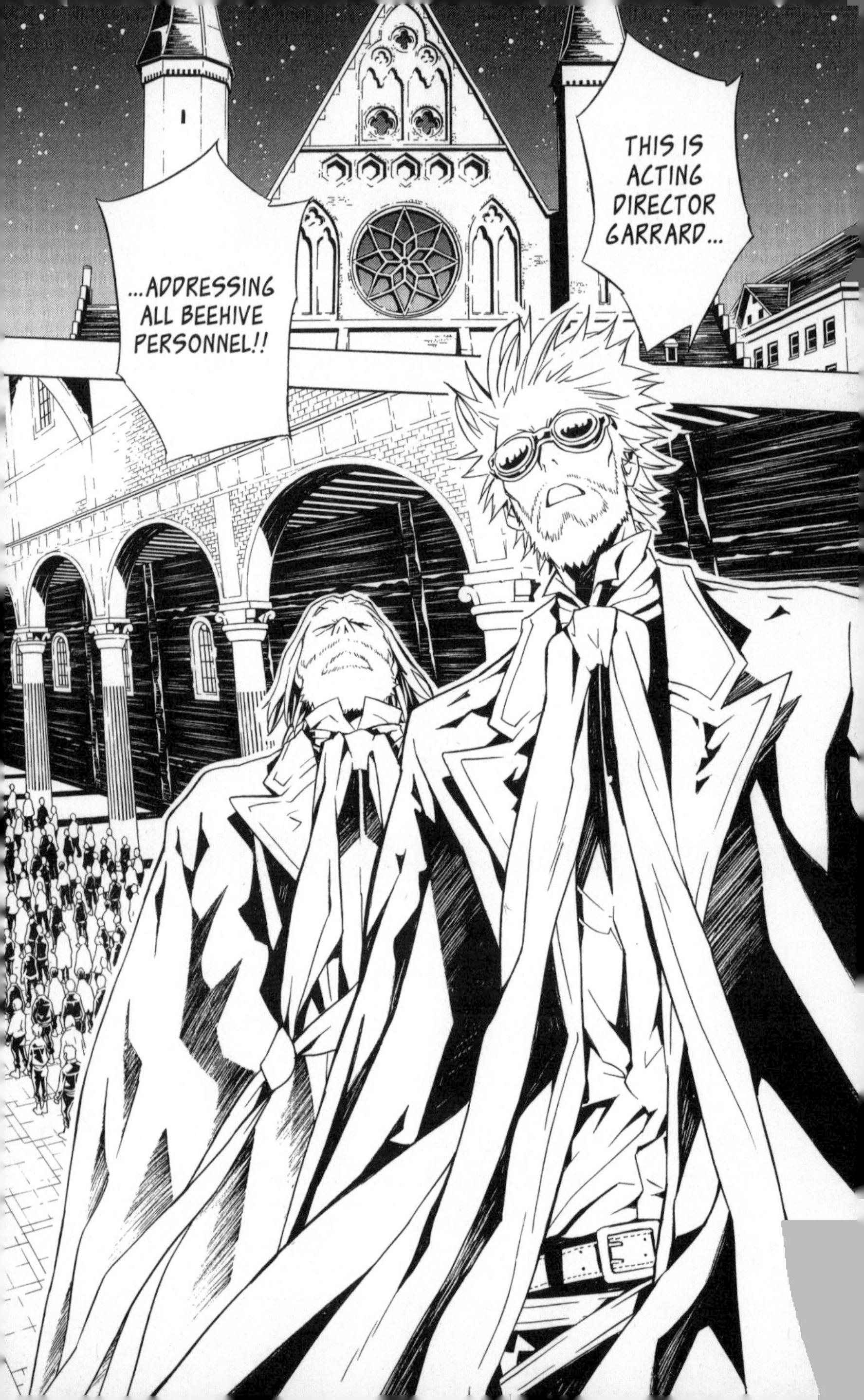
THIS IS ACTING DIRECTOR GARRARD...
...ADDRESSING ALL BEEHIVE PERSONNEL!!

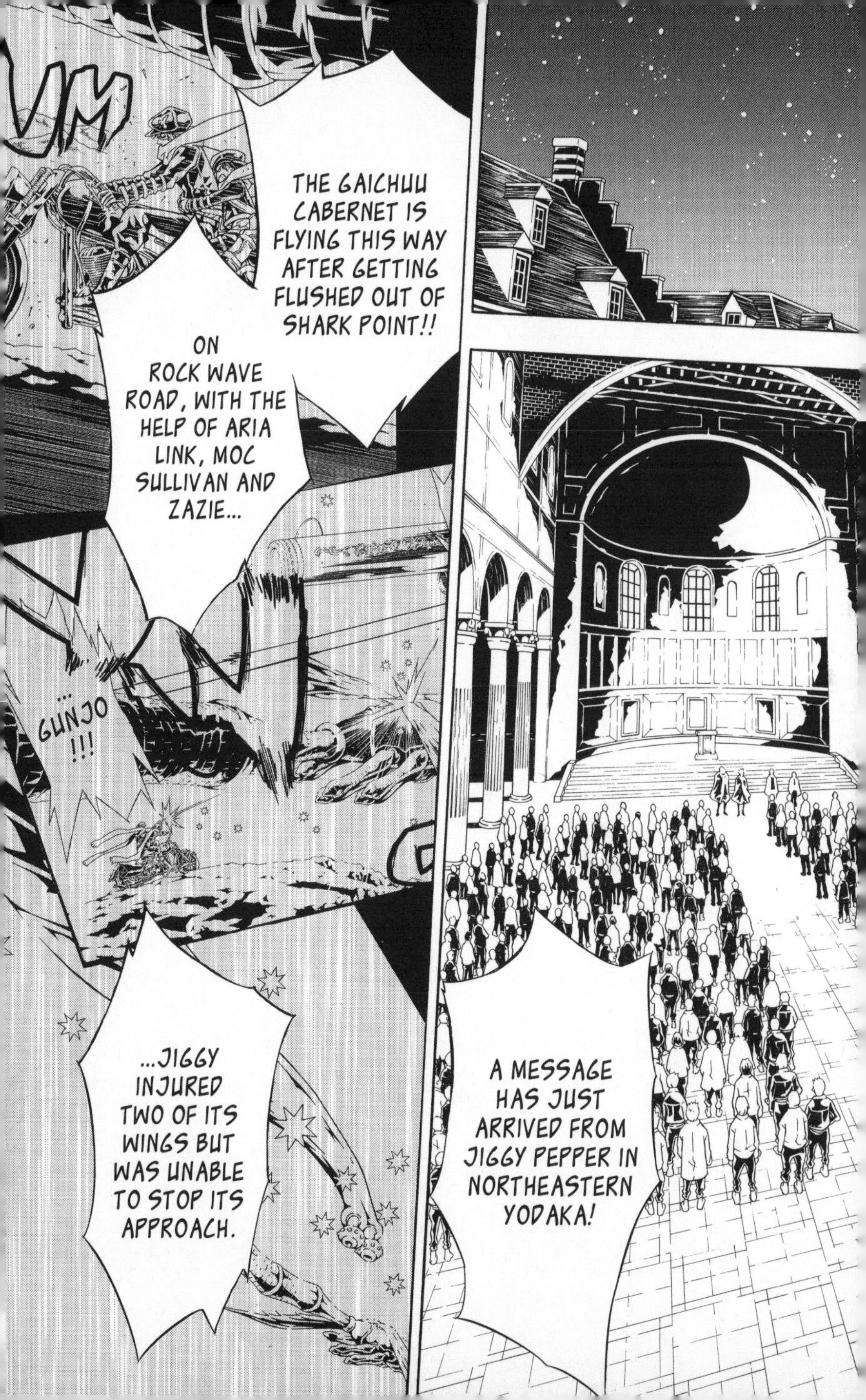
A MESSAGE HAS JUST ARRIVED FROM JIGGY PEPPER IN NORTHEASTERN YODAKA!
THE GAICHUU CABERNET IS FLYING THIS WAY AFTER GETTING FLUSHED OUT OF SHARK POINT!!
VM
ON ROCK WAVE ROAD, WITH THE HELP OF ARIA LINK, MOC SULLIVAN AND ZAZIE...
...GUNJO!!!
...JIGGY INJURED TWO OF ITS WINGS BUT WAS UNABLE TO STOP ITS APPROACH.

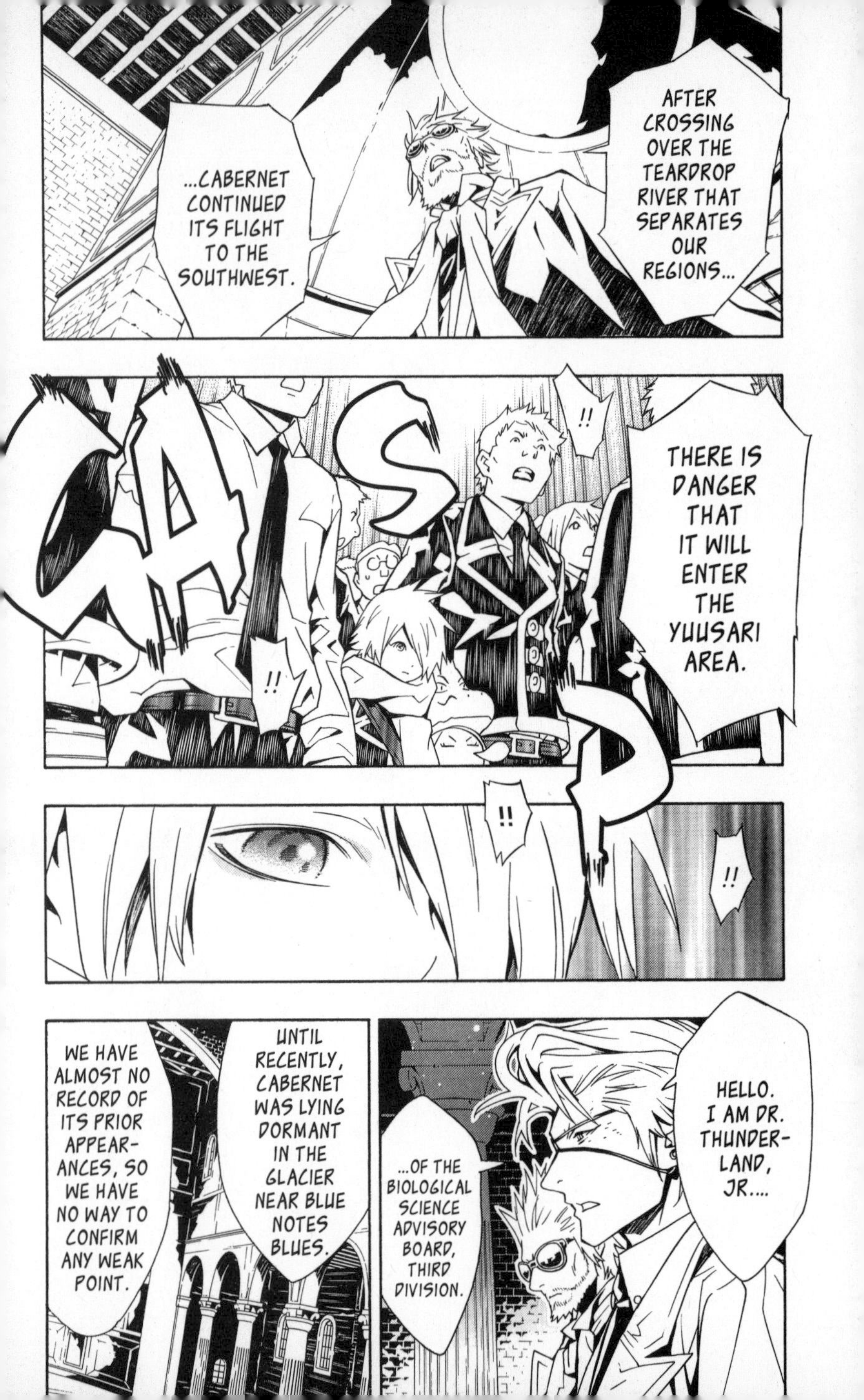
AFTER CROSSING OVER THE TEARDROP RIVER THAT SEPARATES OUR REGIONS...
...CABERNET CONTINUED ITS FLIGHT TO THE SOUTHWEST.
THERE IS DANGER THAT IT WILL ENTER THE YUUSARI AREA.
!!
!!
!!
!!
HELLO. I AM DR. THUNDER-LAND, JR....
...OF THE BIOLOGICAL SCIENCE ADVISORY BOARD, THIRD DIVISION.
UNTIL RECENTLY, CABERNET WAS LYING DORMANT IN THE GLACIER NEAR BLUE NOTES BLUES.
WE HAVE ALMOST NO RECORD OF ITS PRIOR APPEAR-ANCES, SO WE HAVE NO WAY TO CONFIRM ANY WEAK POINT.

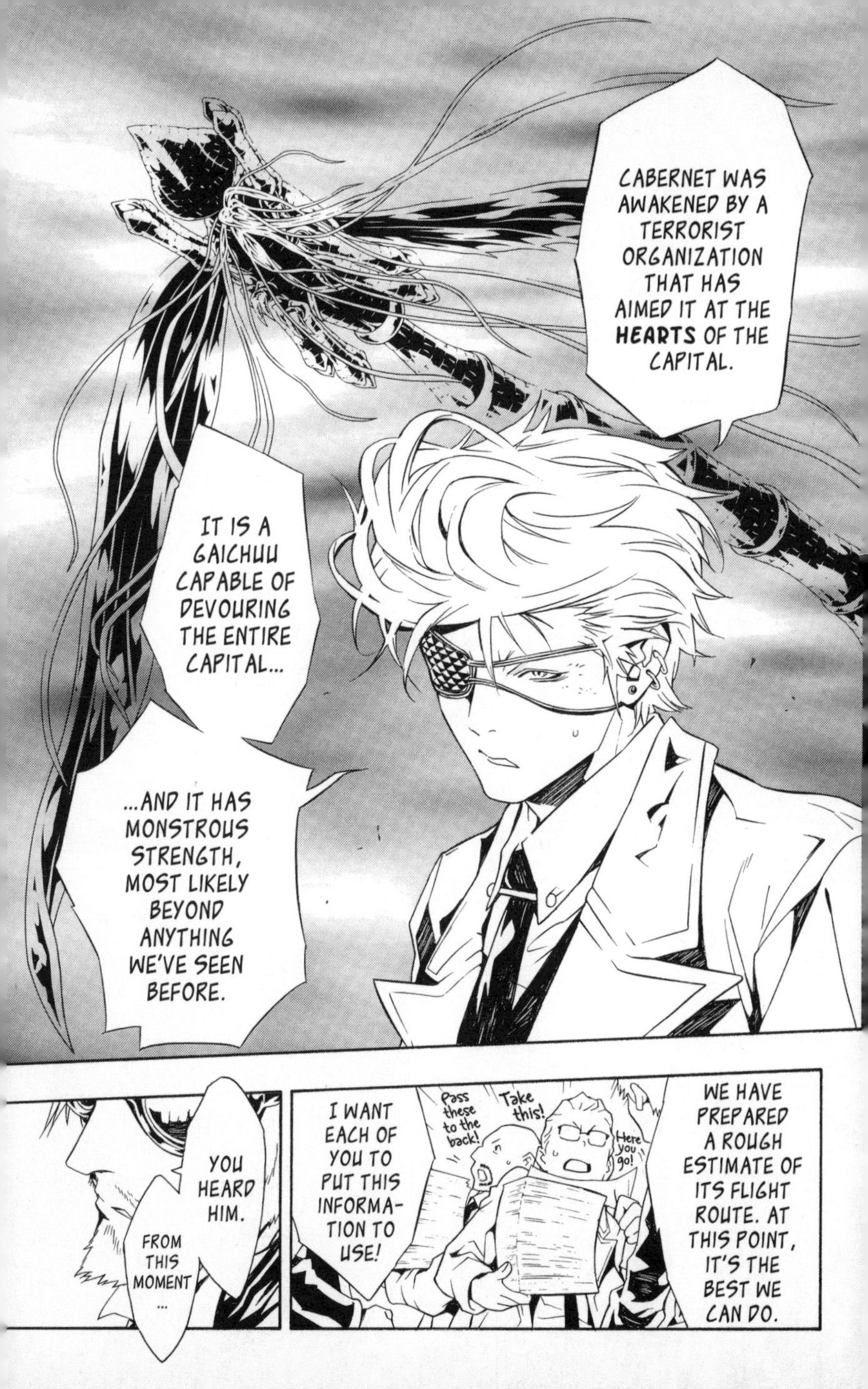
CABERNET WAS AWAKENED BY A TERRORIST ORGANIZATION THAT HAS AIMED IT AT THE **HEARTS** OF THE CAPITAL.
IT IS A GAICHUU CAPABLE OF DEVOURING THE ENTIRE CAPITAL...
...AND IT HAS MONSTROUS STRENGTH, MOST LIKELY BEYOND ANYTHING WE'VE SEEN BEFORE.
WE HAVE PREPARED A ROUGH ESTIMATE OF ITS FLIGHT ROUTE. AT THIS POINT, IT'S THE BEST WE CAN DO.
Take this!
Here you go!
Pass these to the back!
I WANT EACH OF YOU TO PUT THIS INFORMATION TO USE!
YOU HEARD HIM.
FROM THIS MOMENT...

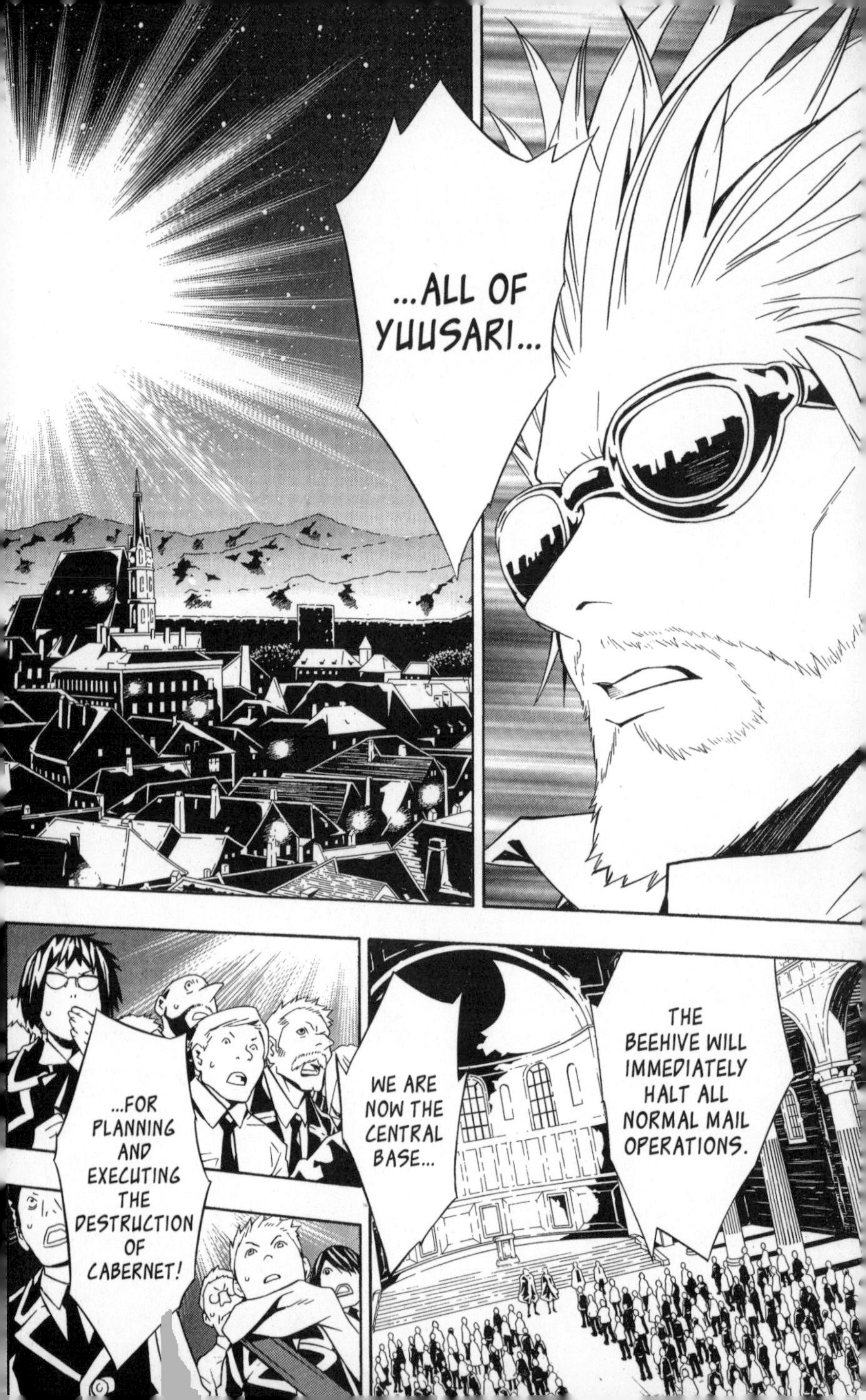
...ALL OF YUUSARI...
THE BEEHIVE WILL IMMEDIATELY HALT ALL NORMAL MAIL OPERATIONS.
WE ARE NOW THE CENTRAL BASE...
...FOR PLANNING AND EXECUTING THE DESTRUCTION OF CABERNET!

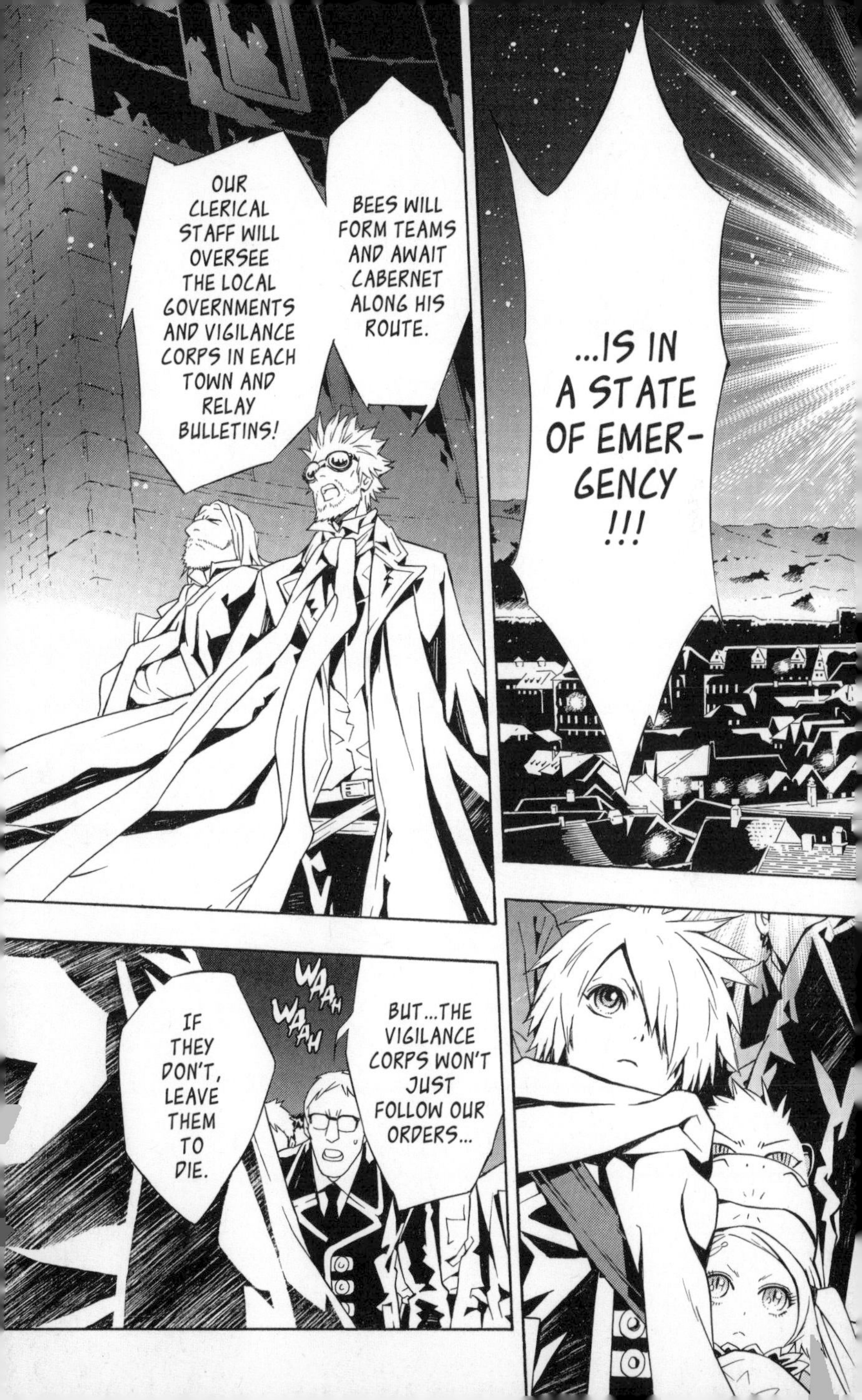
...IS IN A STATE OF EMER-GENCY !!!
BEES WILL FORM TEAMS AND AWAIT CABERNET ALONG HIS ROUTE.
OUR CLERICAL STAFF WILL OVERSEE THE LOCAL GOVERNMENTS AND VIGILANCE CORPS IN EACH TOWN AND RELAY BULLETINS!
BUT...THE VIGILANCE CORPS WON'T JUST FOLLOW OUR ORDERS...
WAAH
WAAH
IF THEY DON'T, LEAVE THEM TO DIE.

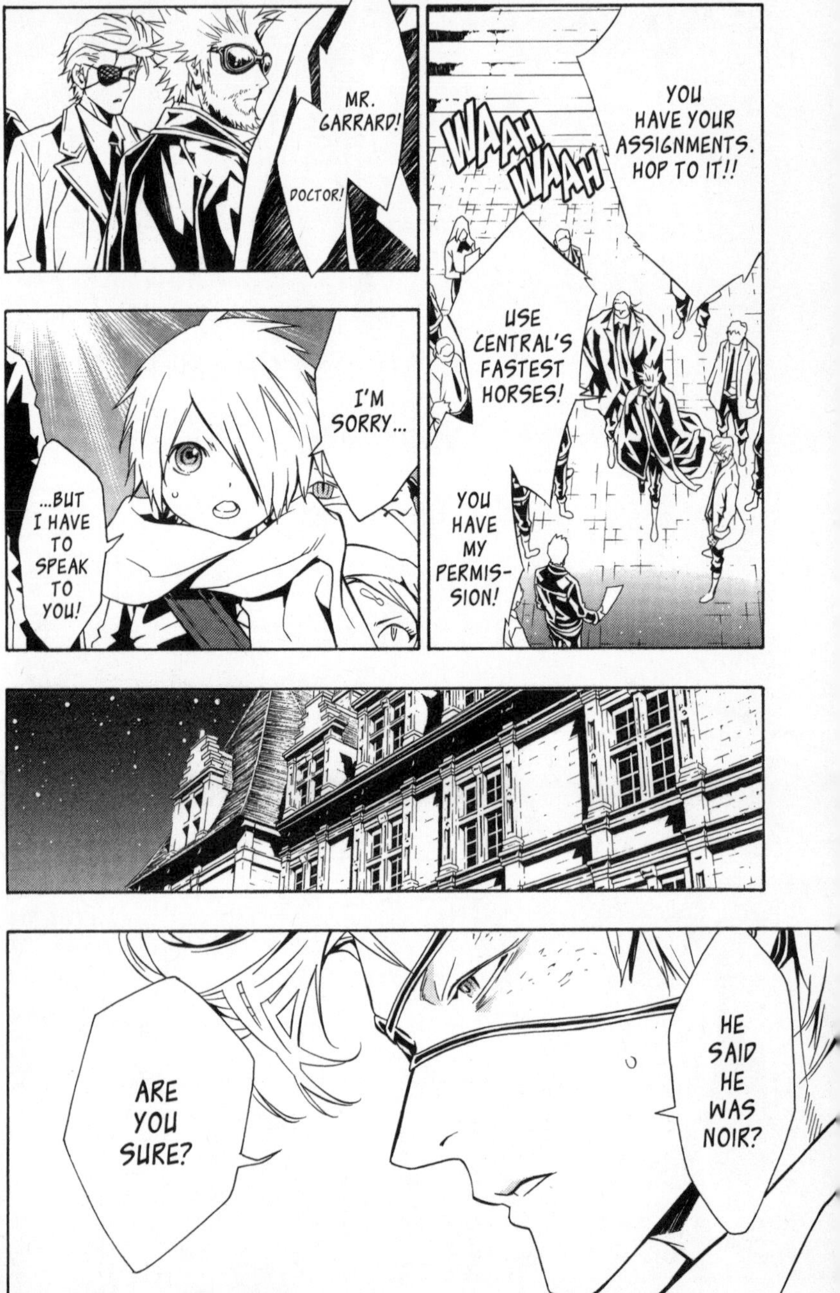
YOU HAVE YOUR ASSIGNMENTS. HOP TO IT!!
WAAH WAAH
USE CENTRAL'S FASTEST HORSES!
YOU HAVE MY PERMIS-SION!
MR. GARRARD!
DOCTOR!
I'M SORRY...
...BUT I HAVE TO SPEAK TO YOU!
HE SAID HE WAS NOIR?
ARE YOU SURE?

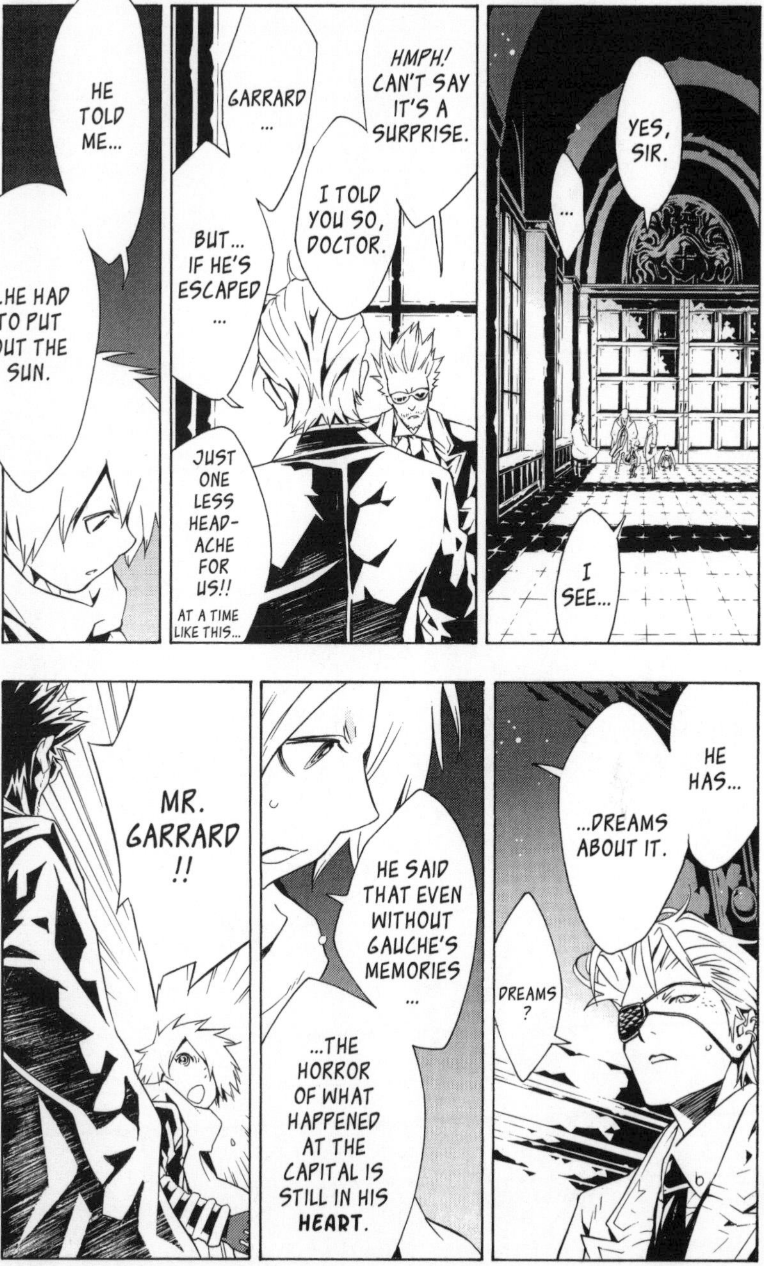
YES, SIR.
...
I SEE...
HMPH! CAN'T SAY IT'S A SURPRISE.
GARRARD...
I TOLD YOU SO, DOCTOR.
BUT... IF HE'S ESCAPED...
JUST ONE LESS HEADACHE FOR US!!
AT A TIME LIKE THIS...
HE TOLD ME...
...HE HAD TO PUT OUT THE SUN.
HE HAS...
...DREAMS ABOUT IT.
DREAMS?
HE SAID THAT EVEN WITHOUT GAUCHE'S MEMORIES...
...THE HORROR OF WHAT HAPPENED AT THE CAPITAL IS STILL IN HIS **HEART**.
MR. GARRARD!!

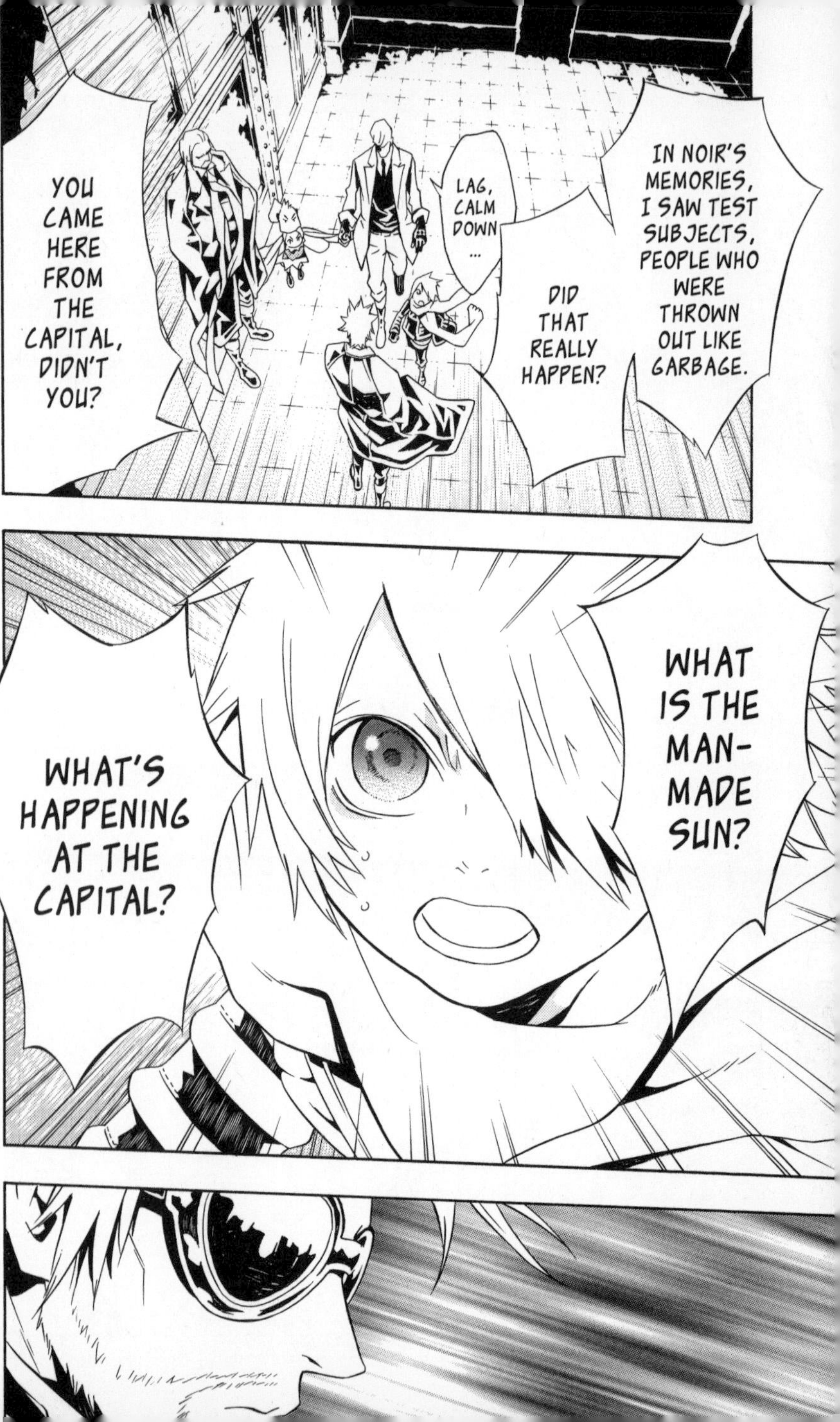

IN NOIR'S MEMORIES, I SAW TEST SUBJECTS, PEOPLE WHO WERE THROWN OUT LIKE GARBAGE.
DID THAT REALLY HAPPEN?
LAG, CALM DOWN...
YOU CAME HERE FROM THE CAPITAL, DIDN'T YOU?
WHAT IS THE MAN-MADE SUN?
WHAT'S HAPPENING AT THE CAPITAL?

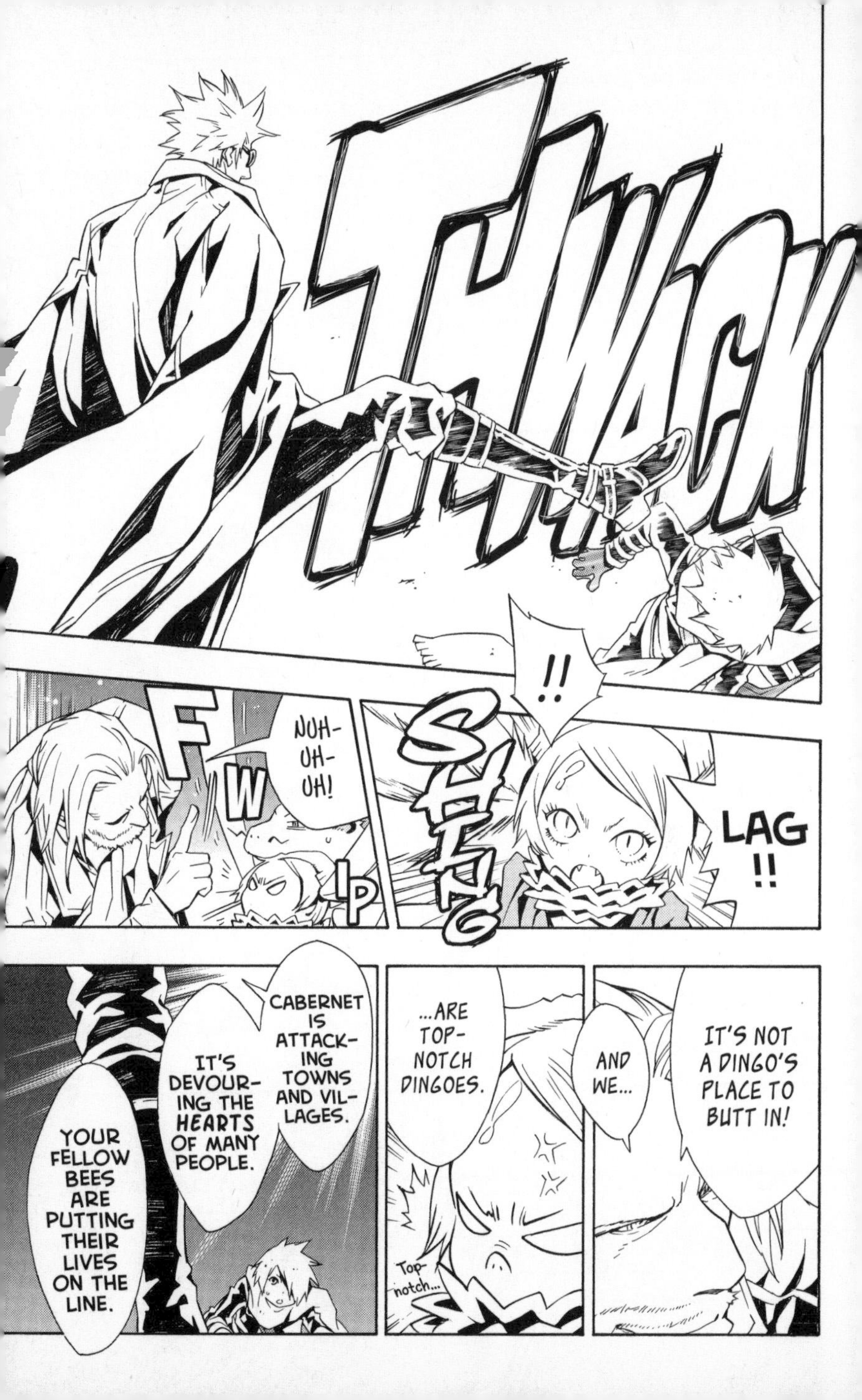
THWACK
!!
SHING
LAG !!
FWIP
NUH-UH-UH!
IT'S NOT A DINGO'S PLACE TO BUTT IN!
AND WE...
...ARE TOP-NOTCH DINGOES.
Top-notch...
CABERNET IS ATTACK-ING TOWNS AND VIL-LAGES.
IT'S DEVOUR-ING THE HEARTS OF MANY PEOPLE.
YOUR FELLOW BEES ARE PUTTING THEIR LIVES ON THE LINE.

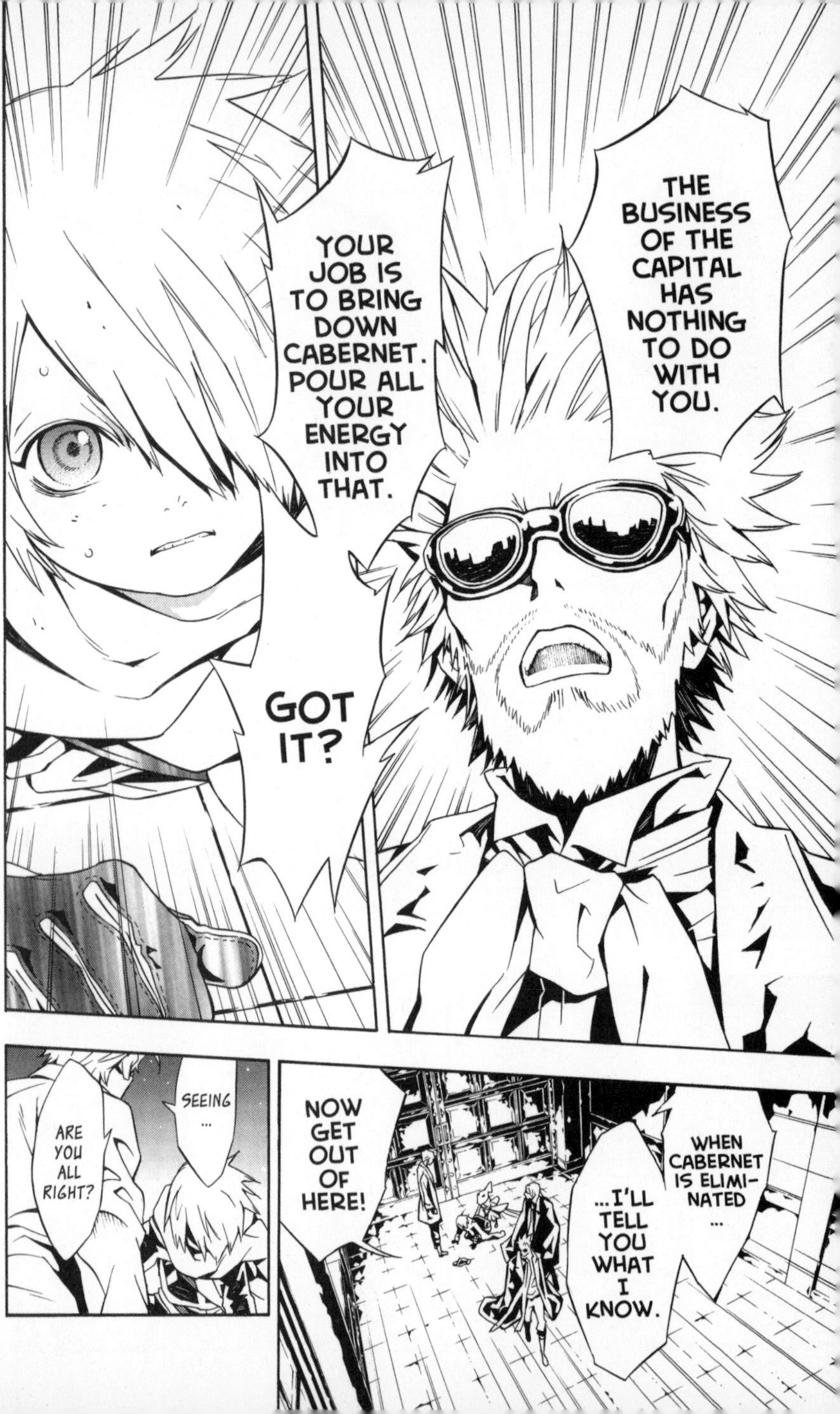
THE BUSINESS OF THE CAPITAL HAS NOTHING TO DO WITH YOU.
YOUR JOB IS TO BRING DOWN CABERNET. POUR ALL YOUR ENERGY INTO THAT.
GOT IT?
WHEN CABERNET IS ELIMINATED ...
...I'LL TELL YOU WHAT I KNOW.
NOW GET OUT OF HERE!
SEEING ...
ARE YOU ALL RIGHT?

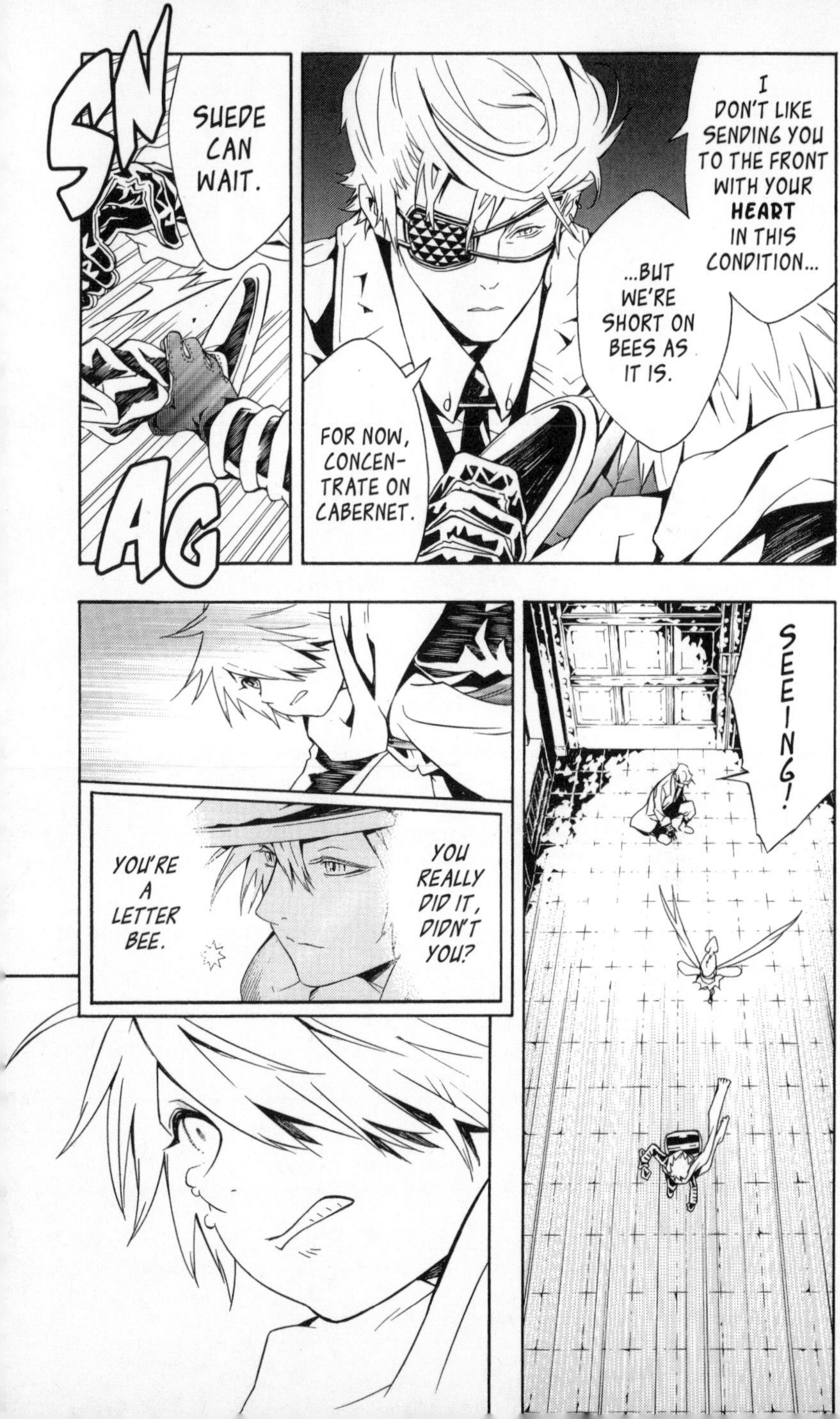
I DON'T LIKE SENDING YOU TO THE FRONT WITH YOUR **HEART** IN THIS CONDITION...
...BUT WE'RE SHORT ON BEES AS IT IS.
FOR NOW, CONCENTRATE ON CABERNET.
SN
SUEDE CAN WAIT.
AG
SEEING!
YOU REALLY DID IT, DIDN'T YOU?
YOU'RE A LETTER BEE.

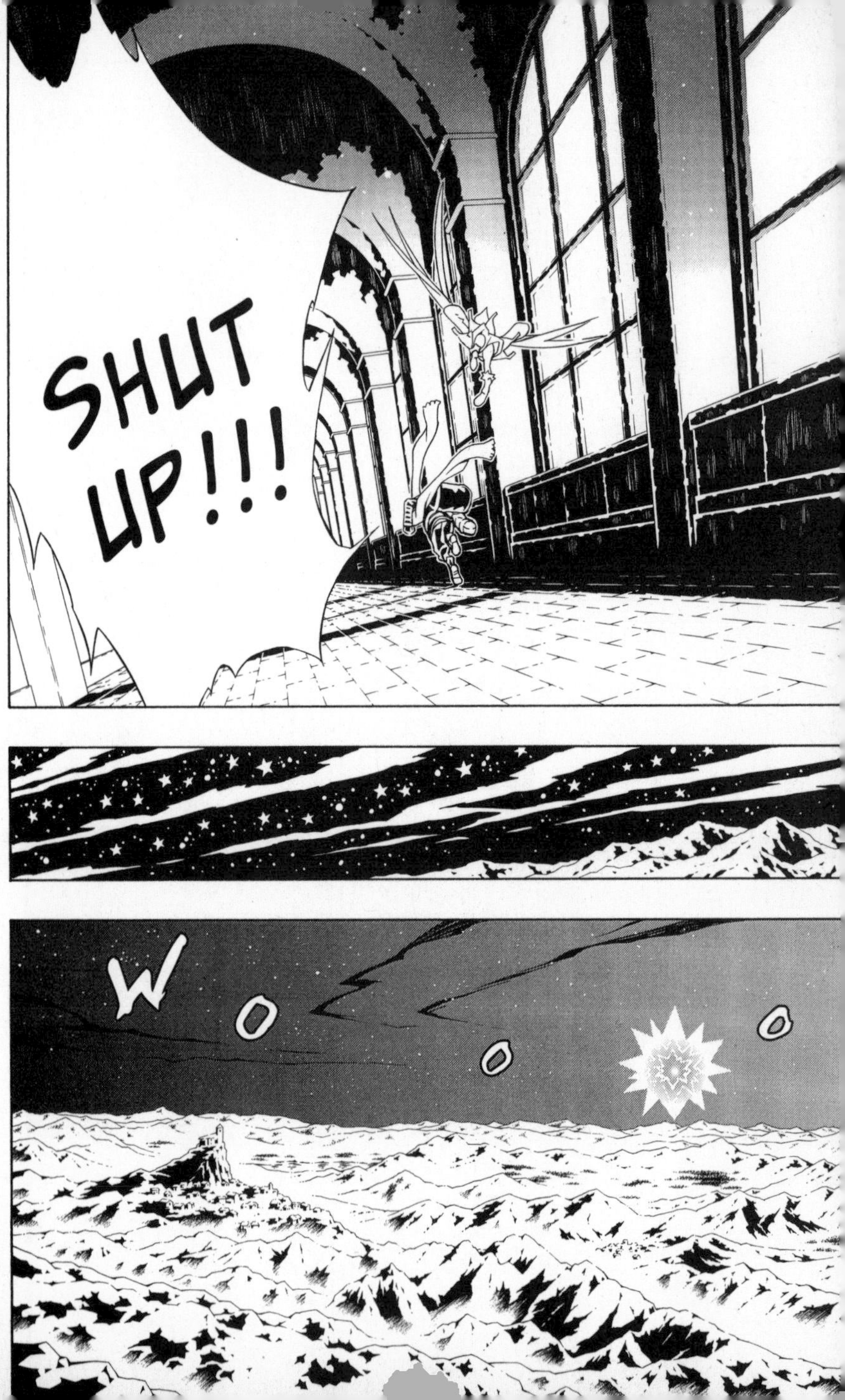
SHUT UP!!!
WOOOO

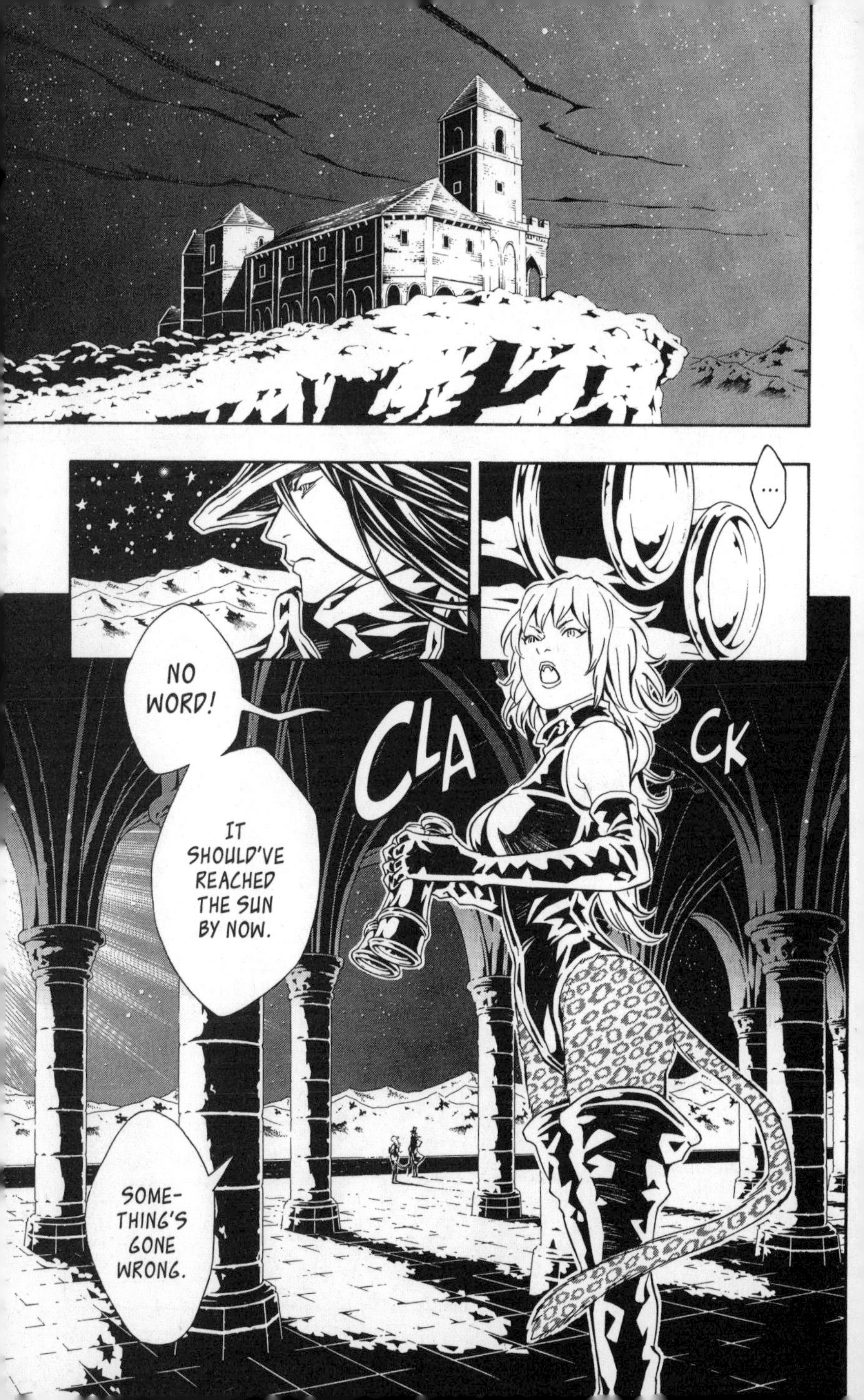
...
NO WORD!
CLACK
IT SHOULD'VE REACHED THE SUN BY NOW.
SOME-THING'S GONE WRONG.

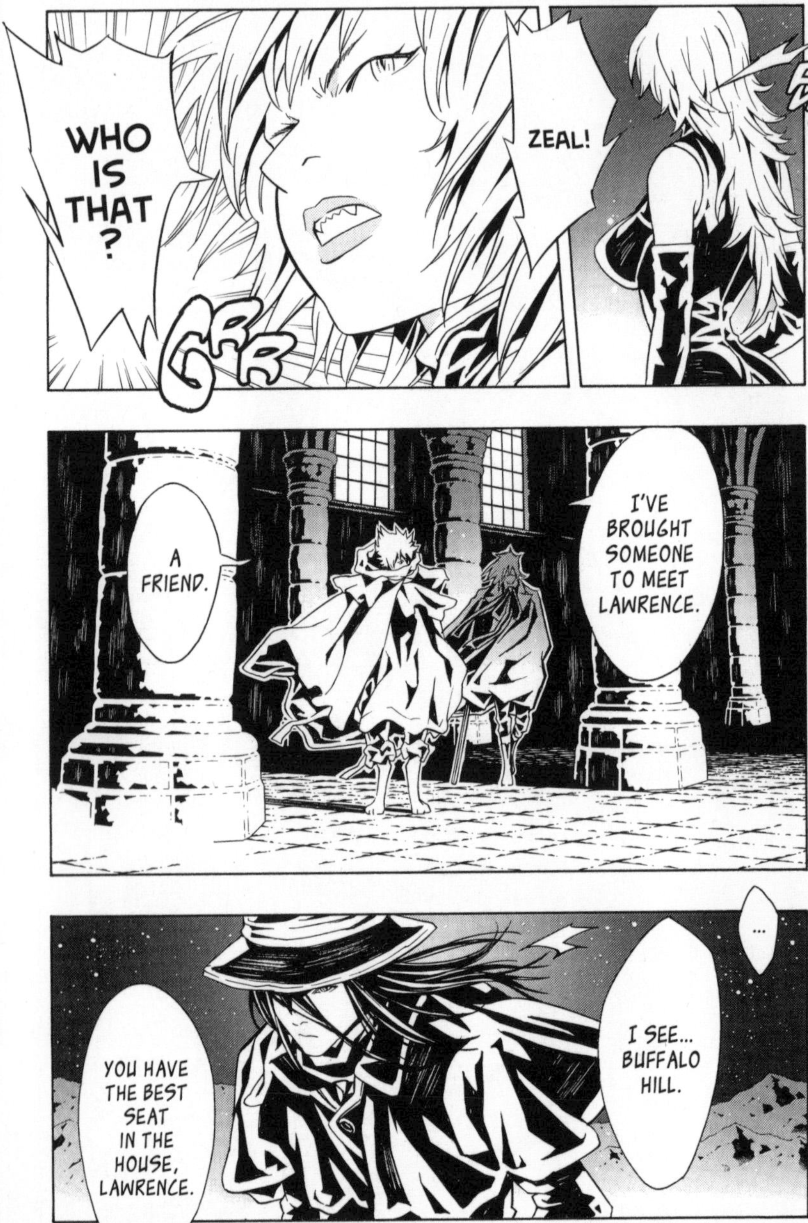

FWP
ZEAL!
WHO IS THAT?
GRR
I'VE BROUGHT SOMEONE TO MEET LAWRENCE.
A FRIEND.
...
I SEE... BUFFALO HILL.
YOU HAVE THE BEST SEAT IN THE HOUSE, LAWRENCE.

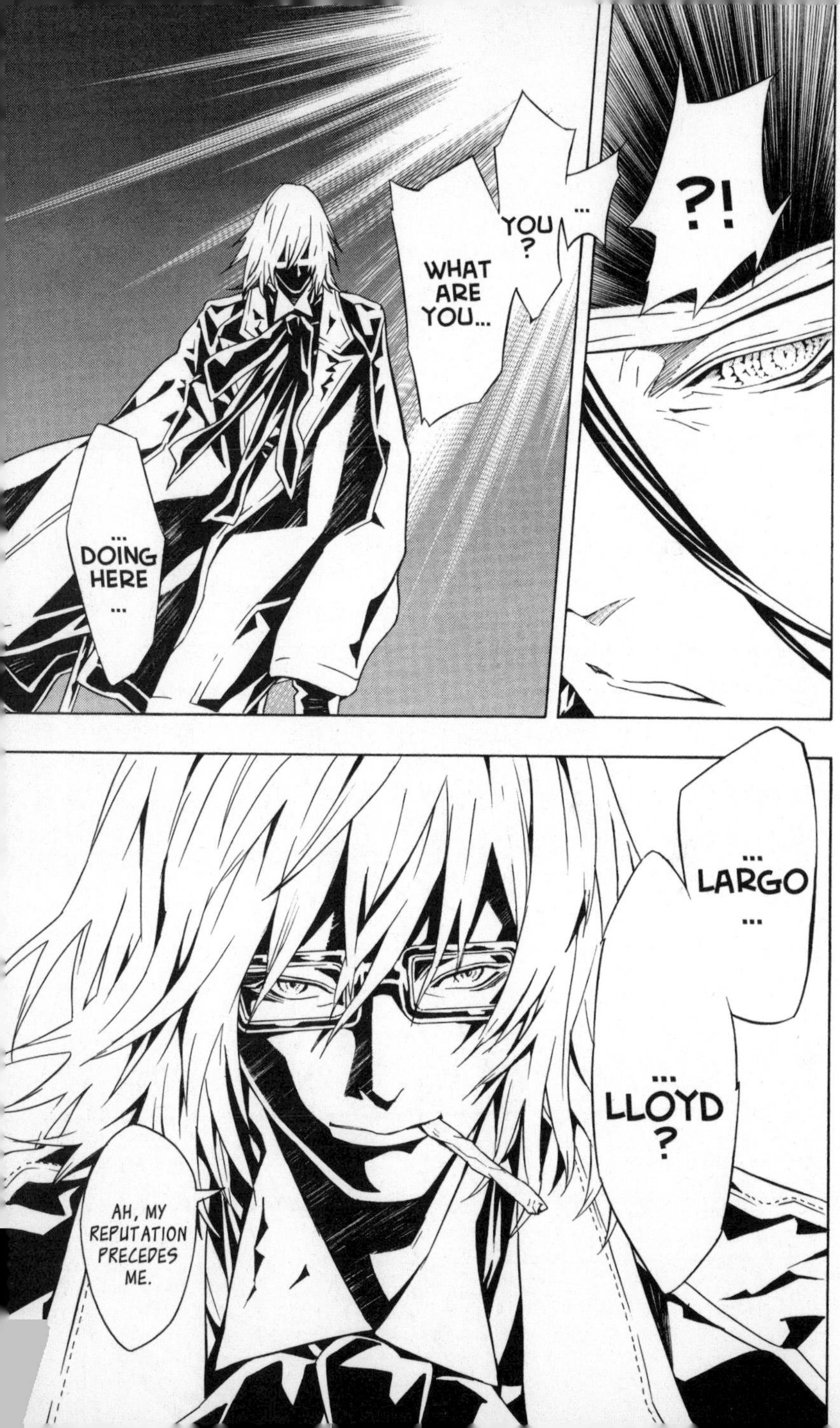
?!
... YOU ?
WHAT ARE YOU...
... DOING HERE ...
... LARGO ...
... LLOYD ?
AH, MY REPUTATION PRECEDES ME.

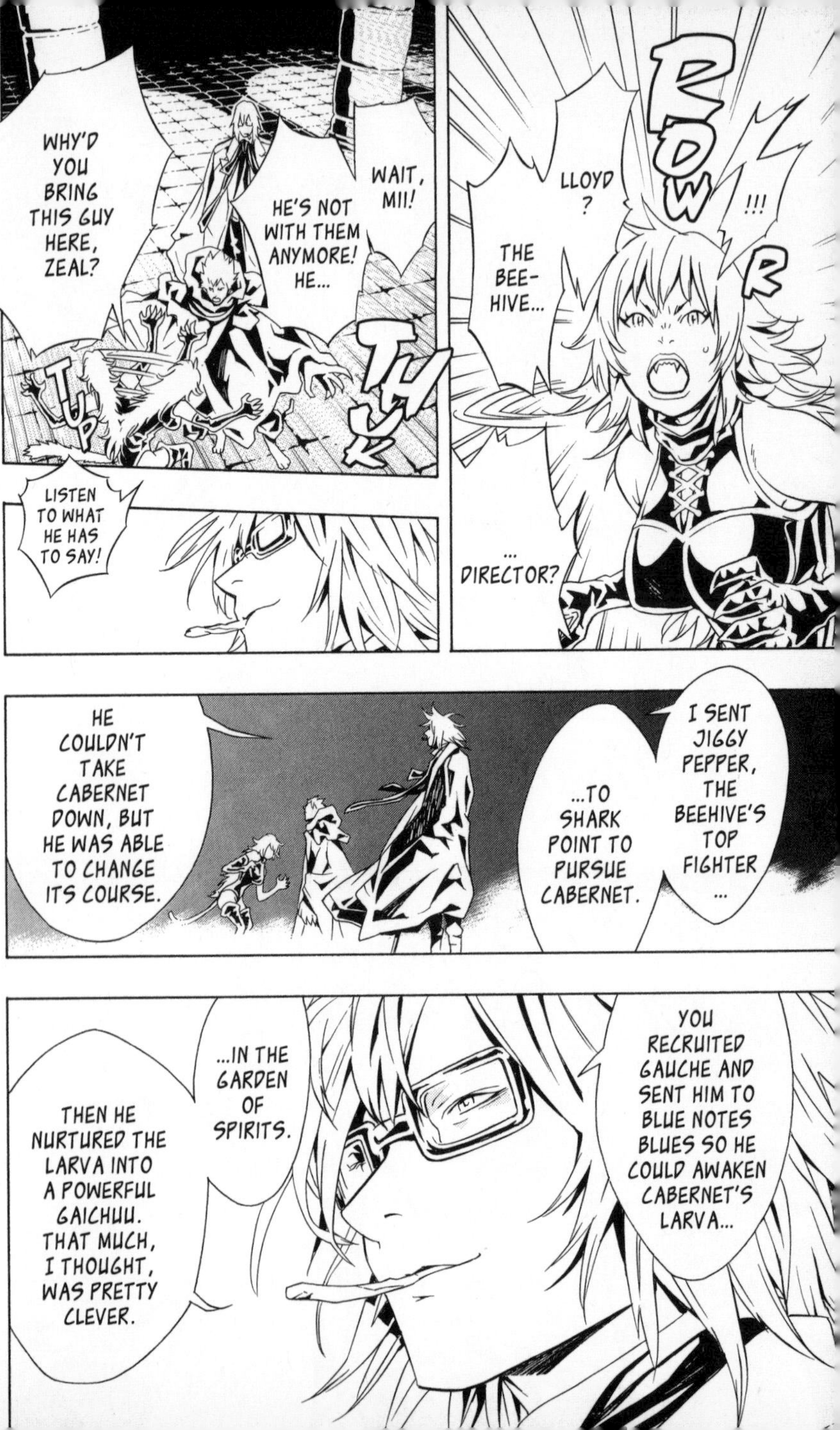
ROWR
!!!
LLOYD?
THE BEEHIVE...
...DIRECTOR?
WAIT, MII!
HE'S NOT WITH THEM ANYMORE! HE...
WHY'D YOU BRING THIS GUY HERE, ZEAL?
TUP
LISTEN TO WHAT HE HAS TO SAY!
I SENT JIGGY PEPPER, THE BEEHIVE'S TOP FIGHTER...
...TO SHARK POINT TO PURSUE CABERNET.
HE COULDN'T TAKE CABERNET DOWN, BUT HE WAS ABLE TO CHANGE ITS COURSE.
YOU RECRUITED GAUCHE AND SENT HIM TO BLUE NOTES BLUES SO HE COULD AWAKEN CABERNET'S LARVA...
...IN THE GARDEN OF SPIRITS.
THEN HE NURTURED THE LARVA INTO A POWERFUL GAICHUU. THAT MUCH, I THOUGHT, WAS PRETTY CLEVER.

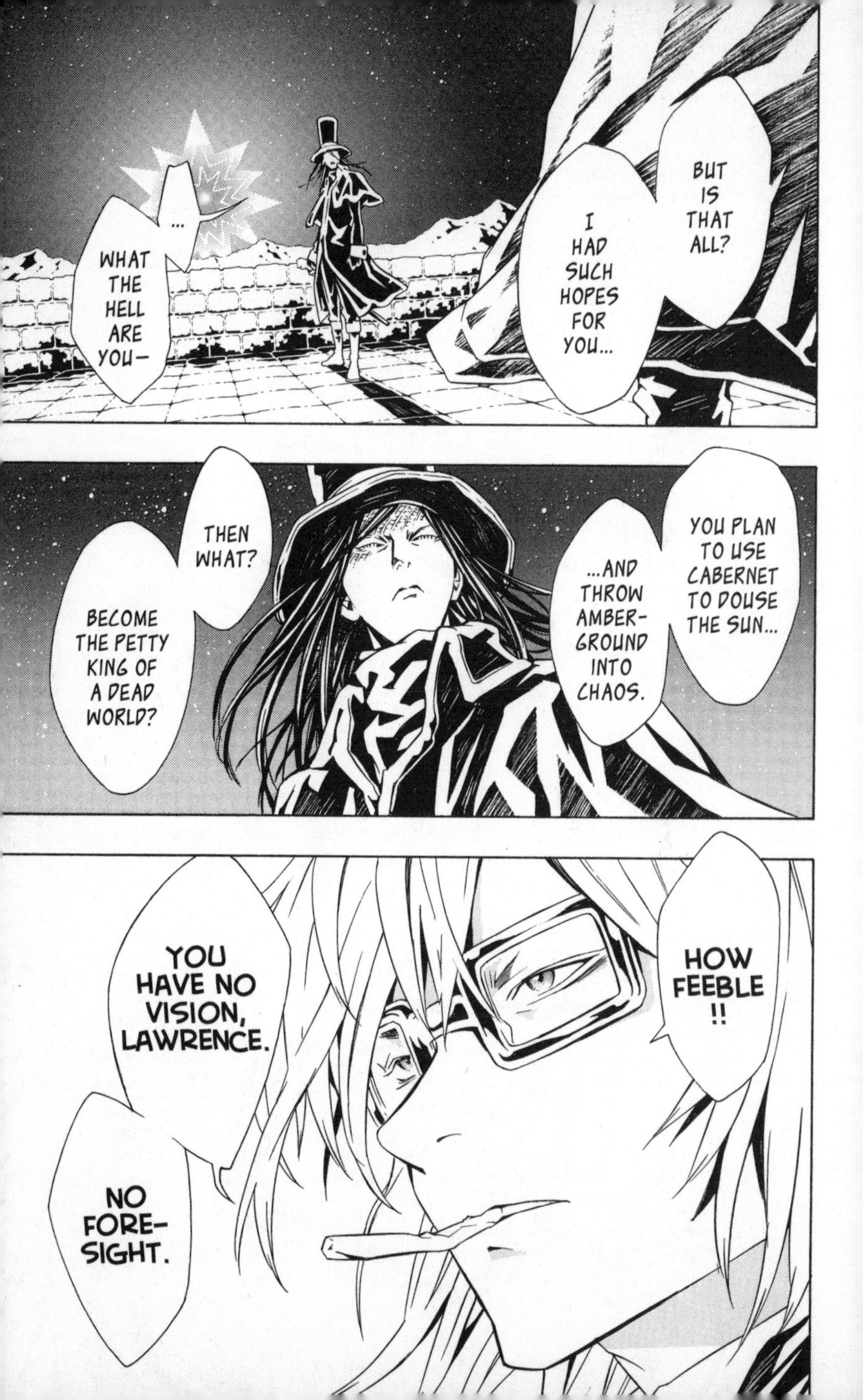
BUT IS THAT ALL?
I HAD SUCH HOPES FOR YOU...
...
WHAT THE HELL ARE YOU—
YOU PLAN TO USE CABERNET TO DOUSE THE SUN...
...AND THROW AMBER-GROUND INTO CHAOS.
THEN WHAT?
BECOME THE PETTY KING OF A DEAD WORLD?
HOW FEEBLE!!
YOU HAVE NO VISION, LAWRENCE.
NO FORE-SIGHT.

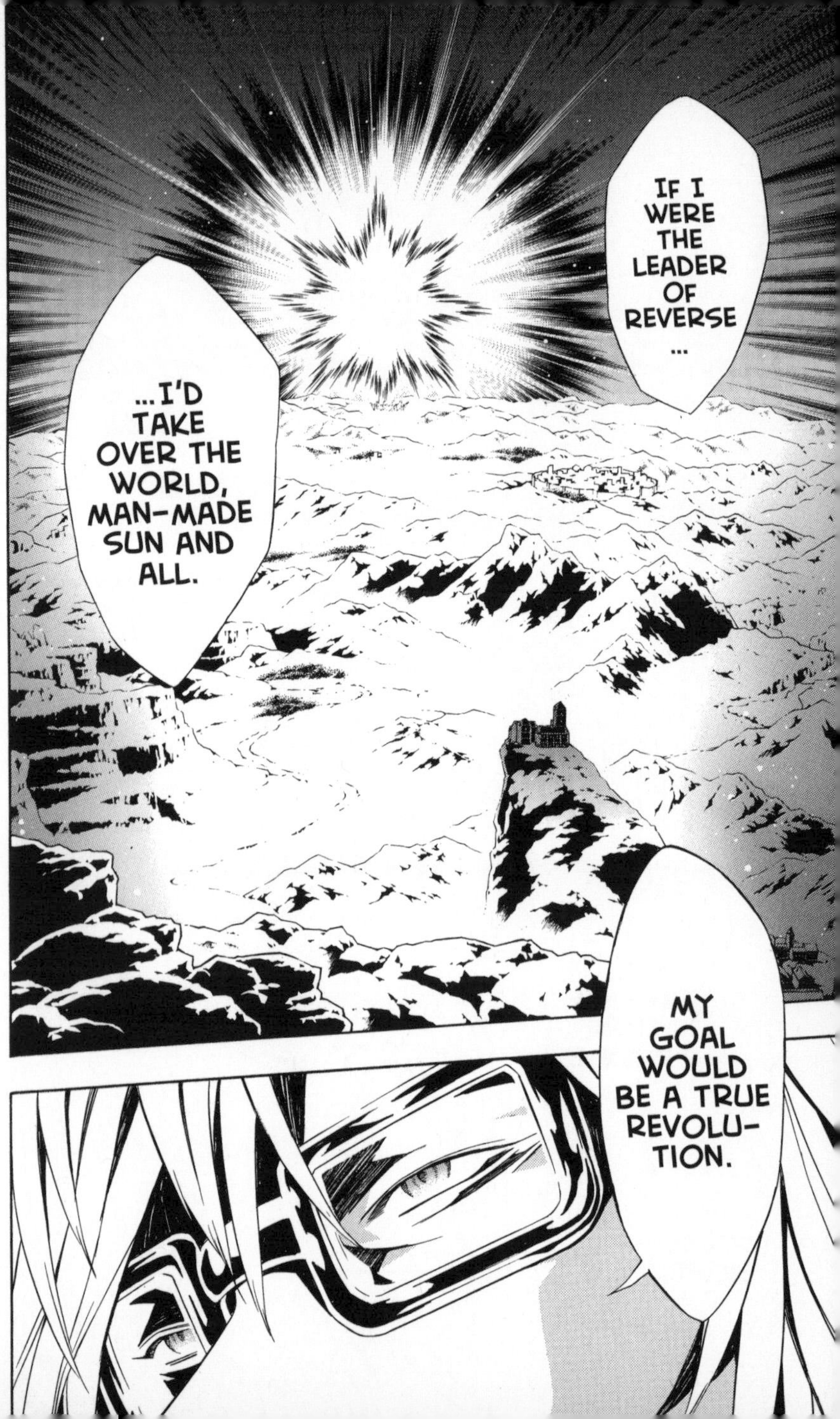
IF I WERE THE LEADER OF REVERSE ...
...I'D TAKE OVER THE WORLD, MAN-MADE SUN AND ALL.
MY GOAL WOULD BE A TRUE REVOLU-TION.

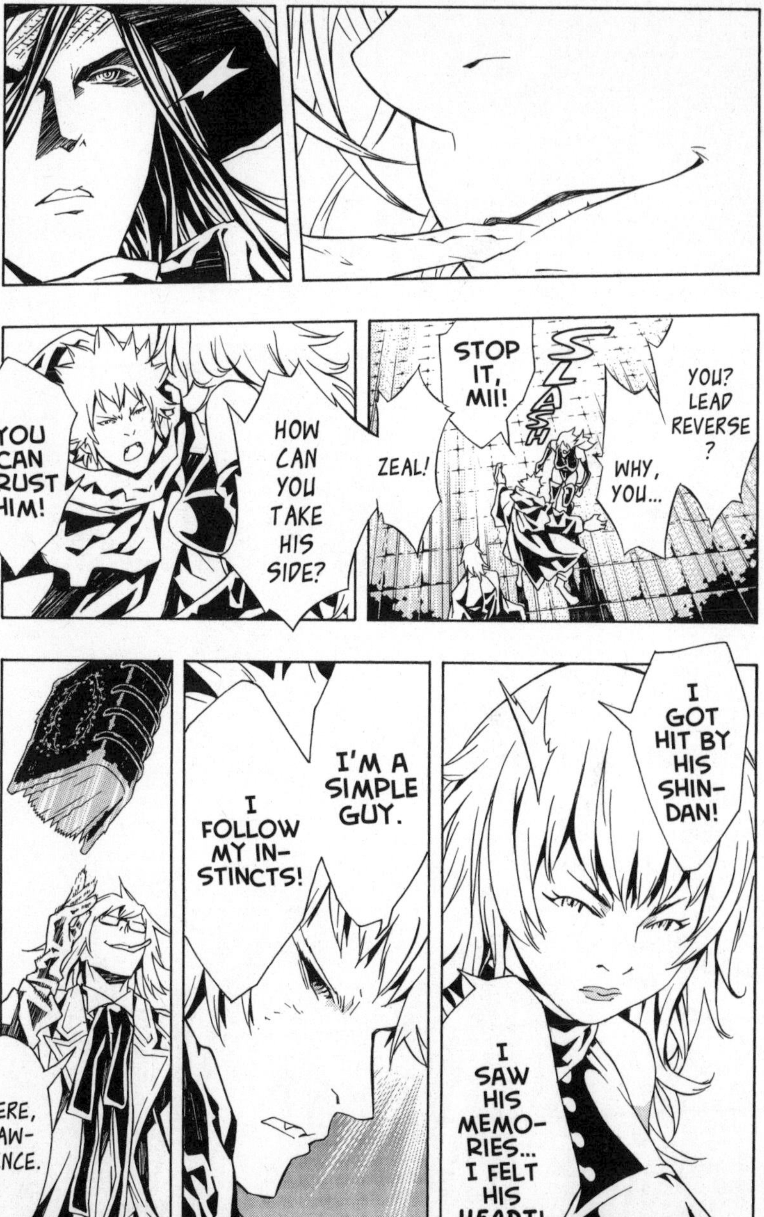
YOU? LEAD REVERSE?
STOP IT, MII!
SLASH
WHY, YOU...
ZEAL!
HOW CAN YOU TAKE HIS SIDE?
YOU CAN TRUST HIM!
I GOT HIT BY HIS SHIN-DAN!
I SAW HIS MEMORIES... I FELT HIS HEART!
I'M A SIMPLE GUY.
I FOLLOW MY IN-STINCTS!
HERE, LAW-RENCE.

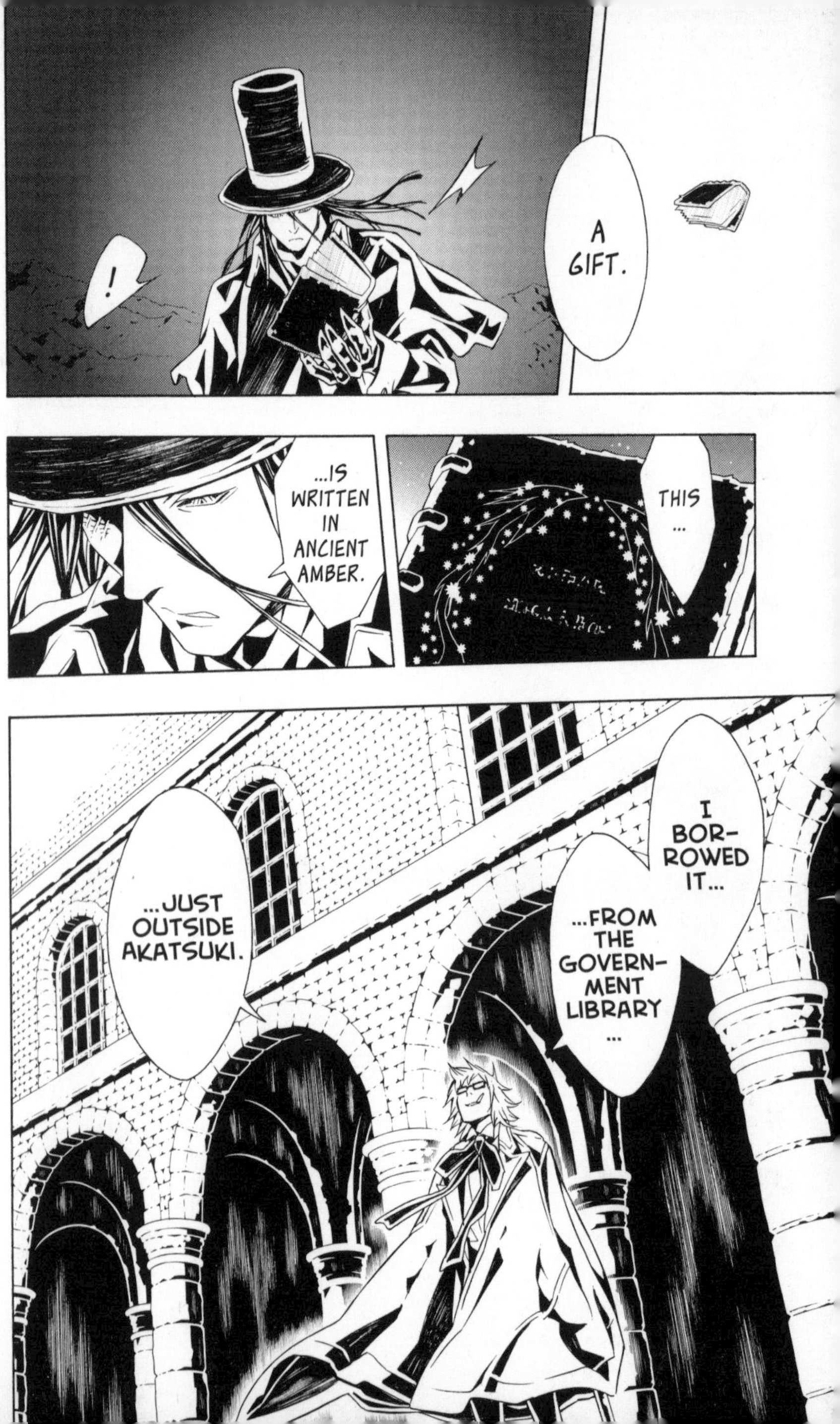
A GIFT.
!
THIS ...
...IS WRITTEN IN ANCIENT AMBER.
I BOR-ROWED IT...
...FROM THE GOVERN-MENT LIBRARY ...
...JUST OUTSIDE AKATSUKI.

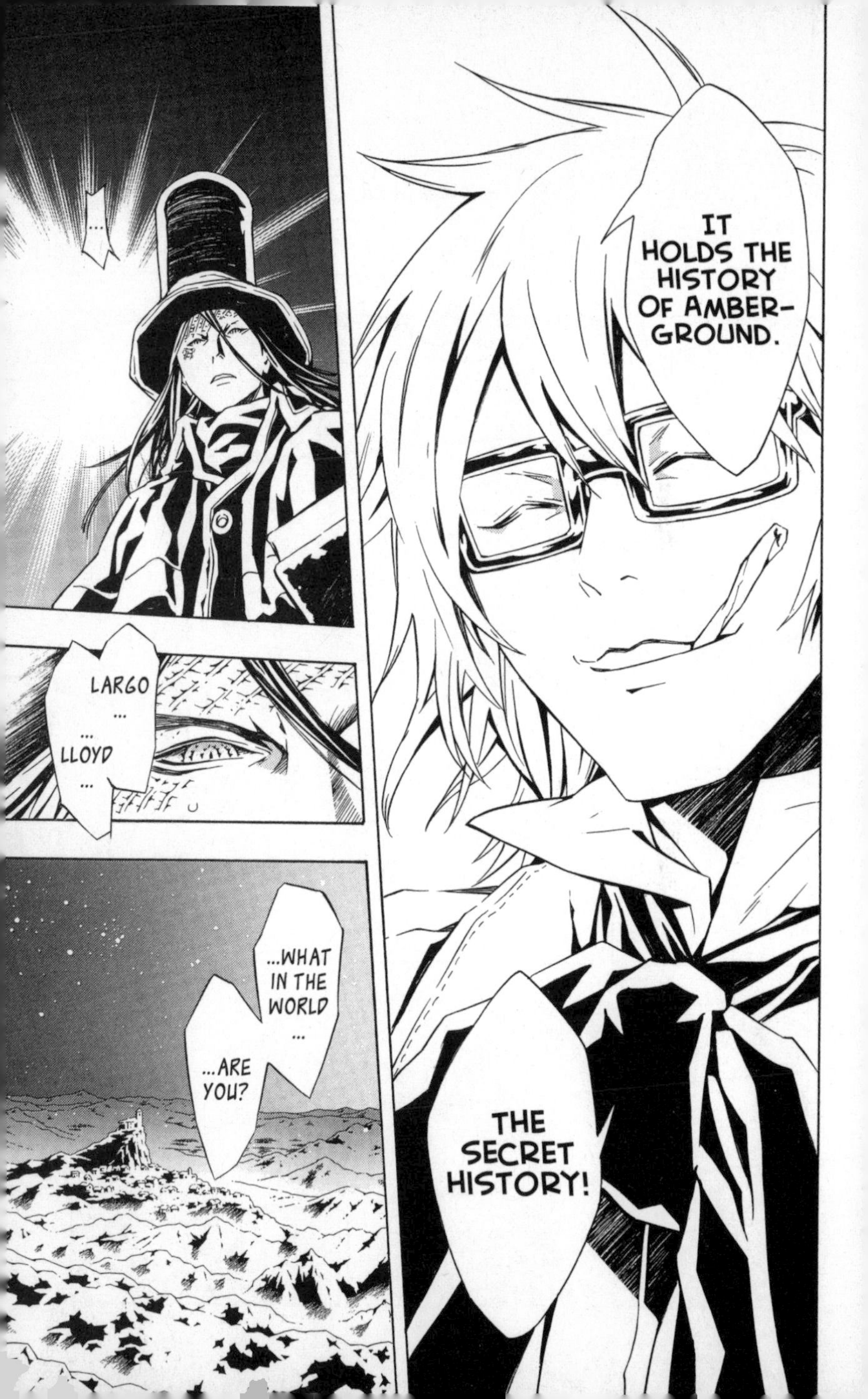
IT HOLDS THE HISTORY OF AMBER-GROUND.
THE SECRET HISTORY!
...
LARGO ... ... LLOYD ...
...WHAT IN THE WORLD ...
...ARE YOU?

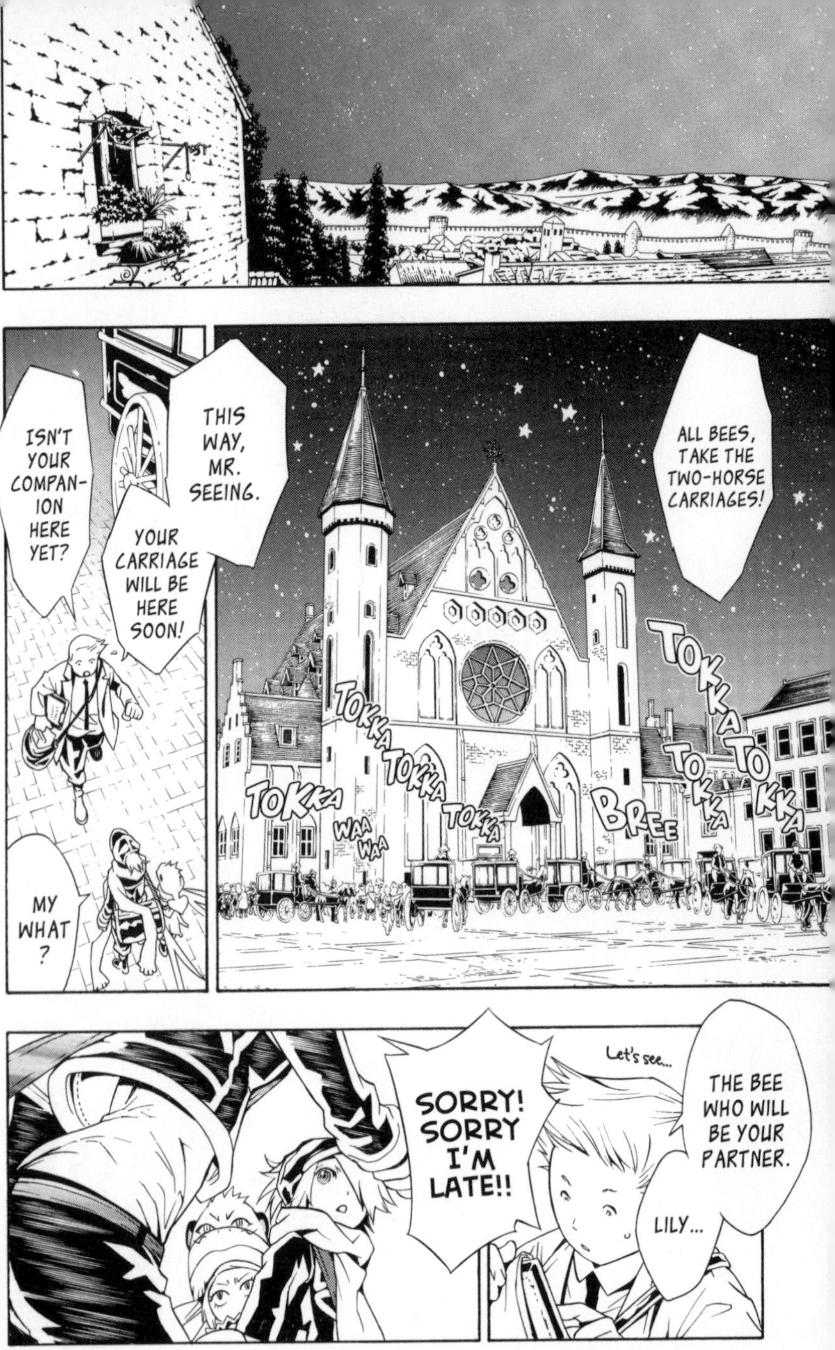
ALL BEES, TAKE THE TWO-HORSE CARRIAGES!
TOKKA TOKKA TOKKA TOKKA
TOKKA TOKKA
BREE
TOKKA TOKKA TOKKA
WAA WAA
TOKKA
THIS WAY, MR. SEEING.
ISN'T YOUR COMPANION HERE YET?
YOUR CARRIAGE WILL BE HERE SOON!
MY WHAT?
Let's see...
THE BEE WHO WILL BE YOUR PARTNER.
LILY...
SORRY! SORRY I'M LATE!!

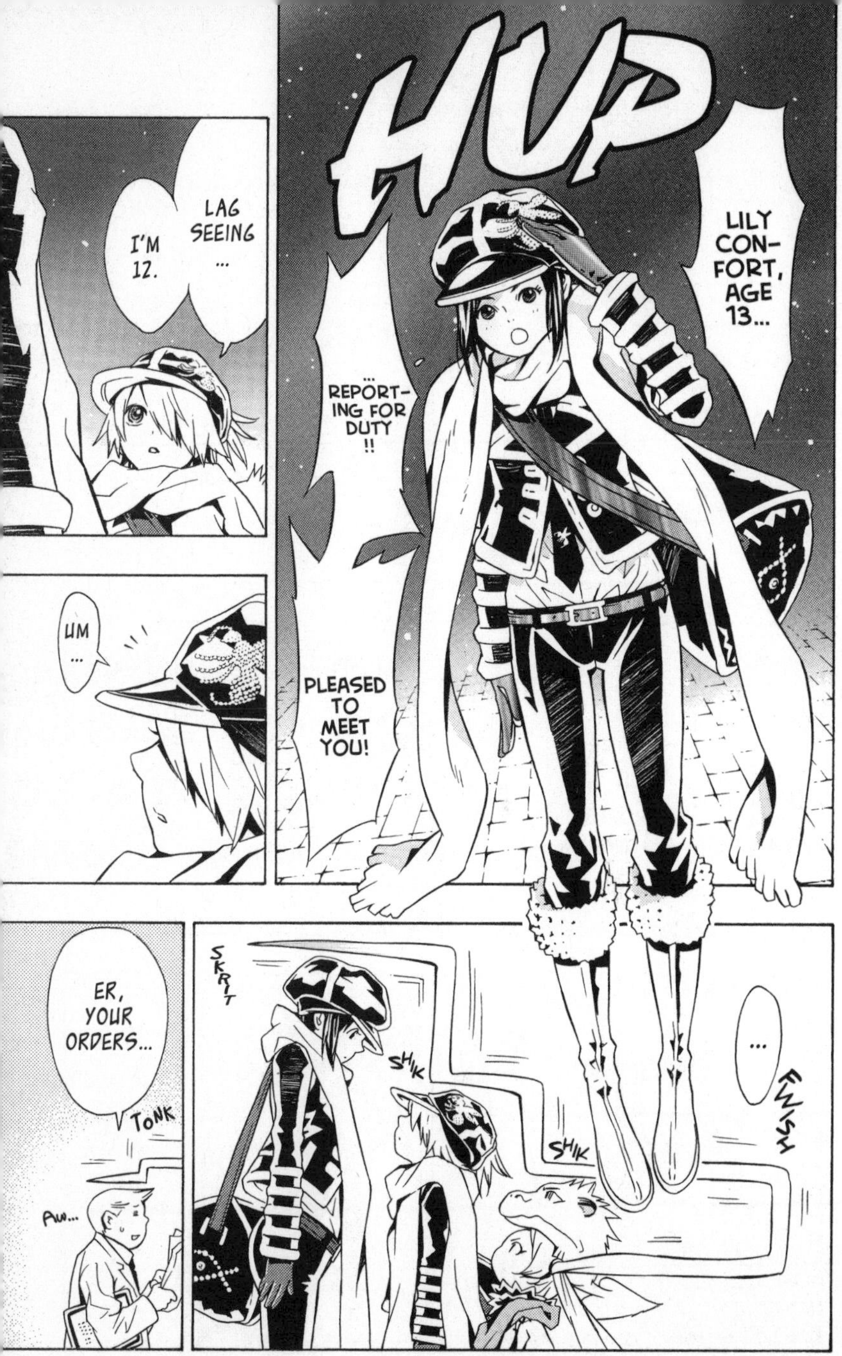
HUP
LILY CONFORT, AGE 13...
...REPORTING FOR DUTY!!
PLEASED TO MEET YOU!
LAG SEEING...
I'M 12.
UM...
...
FWISH
SHIK
SHIK
SKRIT
ER, YOUR ORDERS...
TONK
AW...

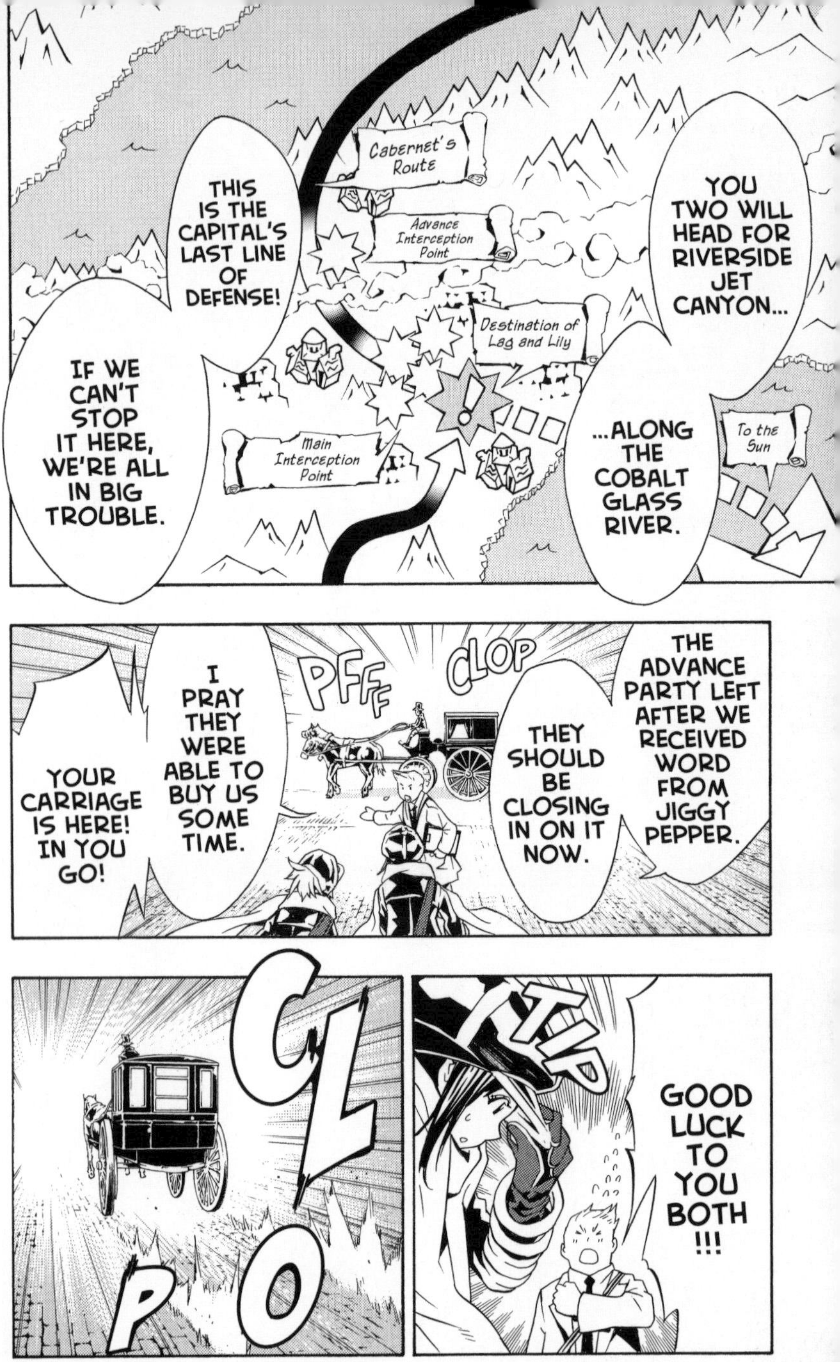

YOU TWO WILL HEAD FOR RIVERSIDE JET CANYON...
...ALONG THE COBALT GLASS RIVER.
To the Sun
Destination of Lag and Lily
Cabernet's Route
Advance Interception Point
THIS IS THE CAPITAL'S LAST LINE OF DEFENSE!
Main Interception Point
IF WE CAN'T STOP IT HERE, WE'RE ALL IN BIG TROUBLE.
THE ADVANCE PARTY LEFT AFTER WE RECEIVED WORD FROM JIGGY PEPPER.
THEY SHOULD BE CLOSING IN ON IT NOW.
CLOP
PFFF
I PRAY THEY WERE ABLE TO BUY US SOME TIME.
YOUR CARRIAGE IS HERE! IN YOU GO!
TIP
GOOD LUCK TO YOU BOTH!!!
CLOP

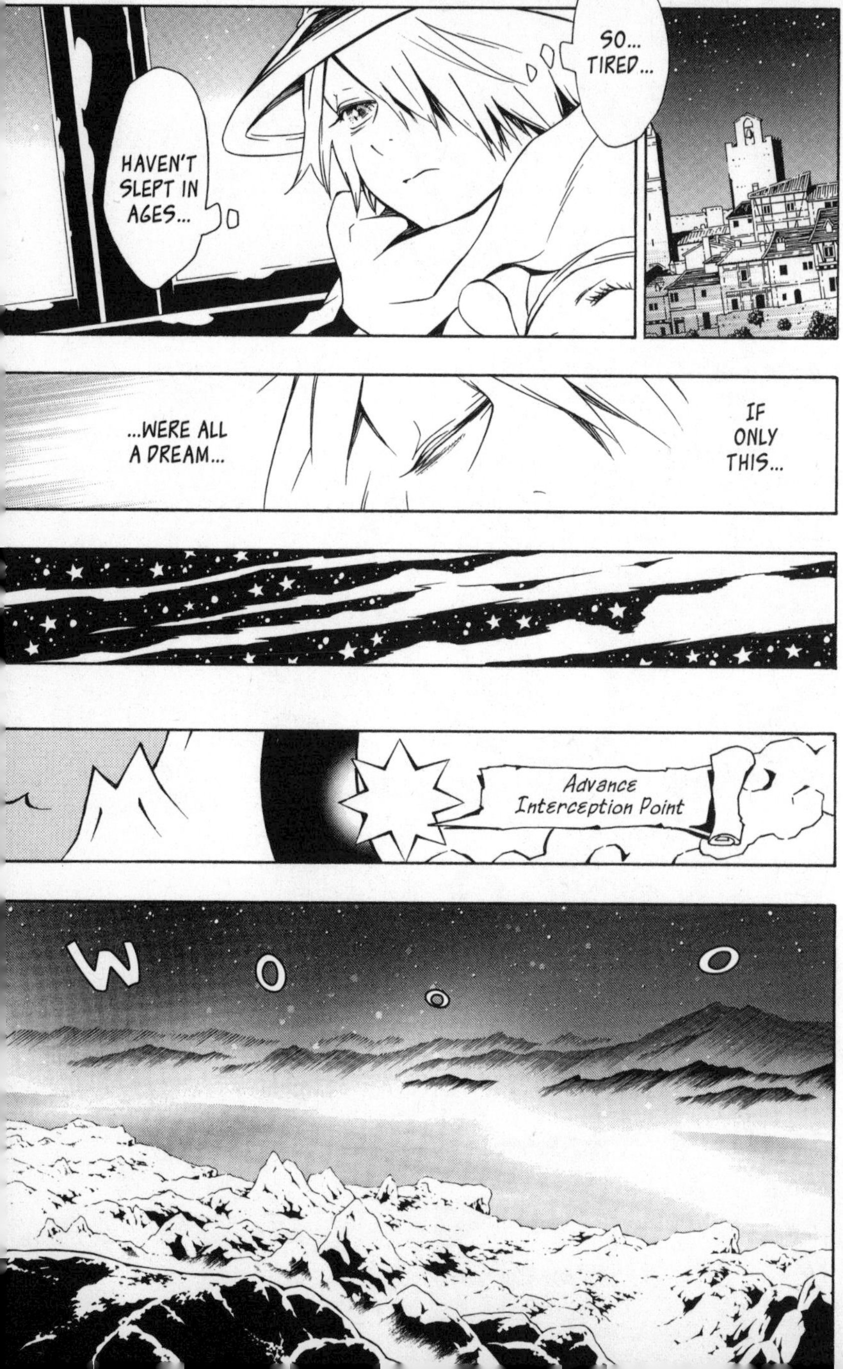
SO... TIRED...
HAVEN'T SLEPT IN AGES...
IF ONLY THIS...
...WERE ALL A DREAM...
Advance Interception Point
WOOO

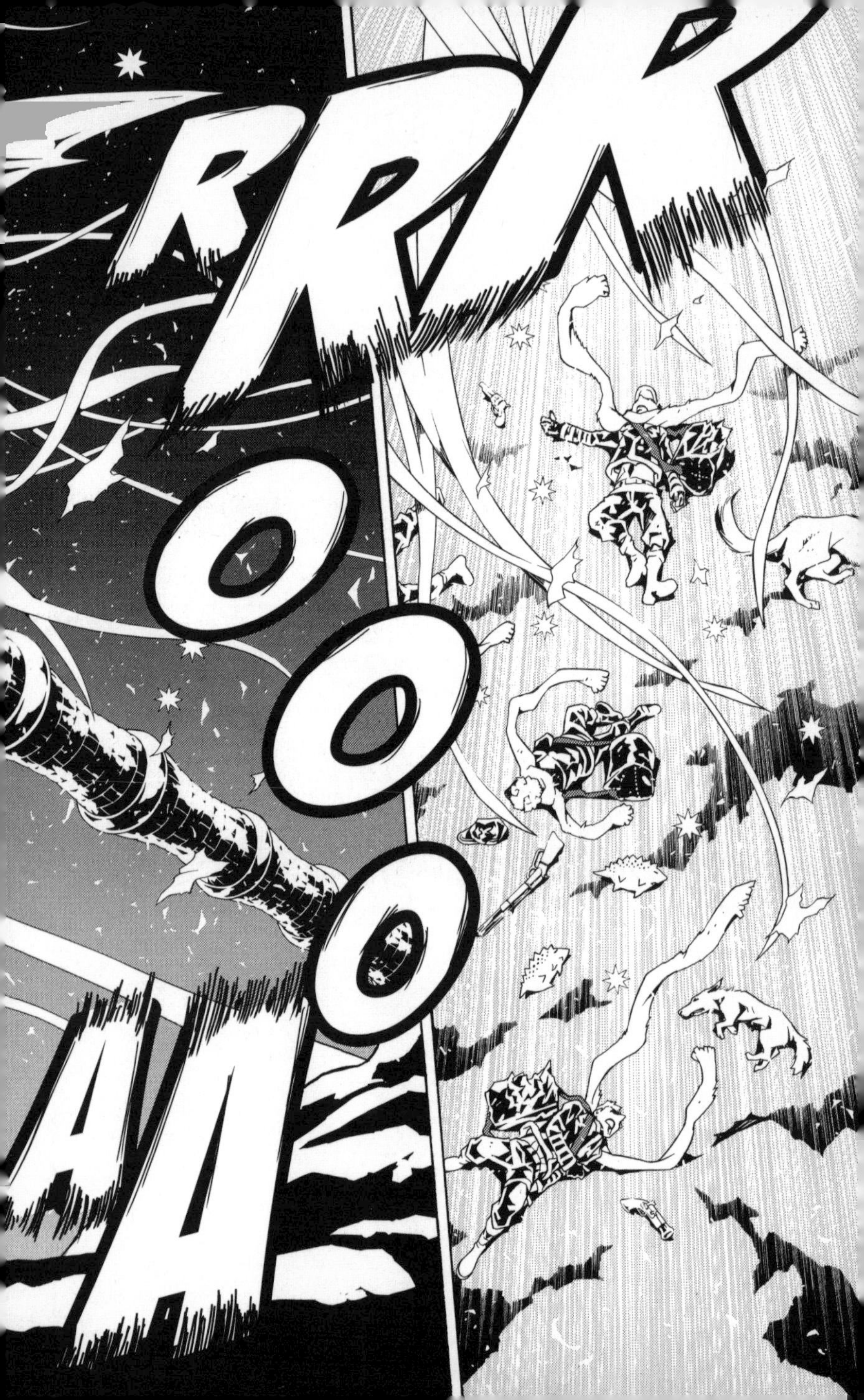
RRROOOAA

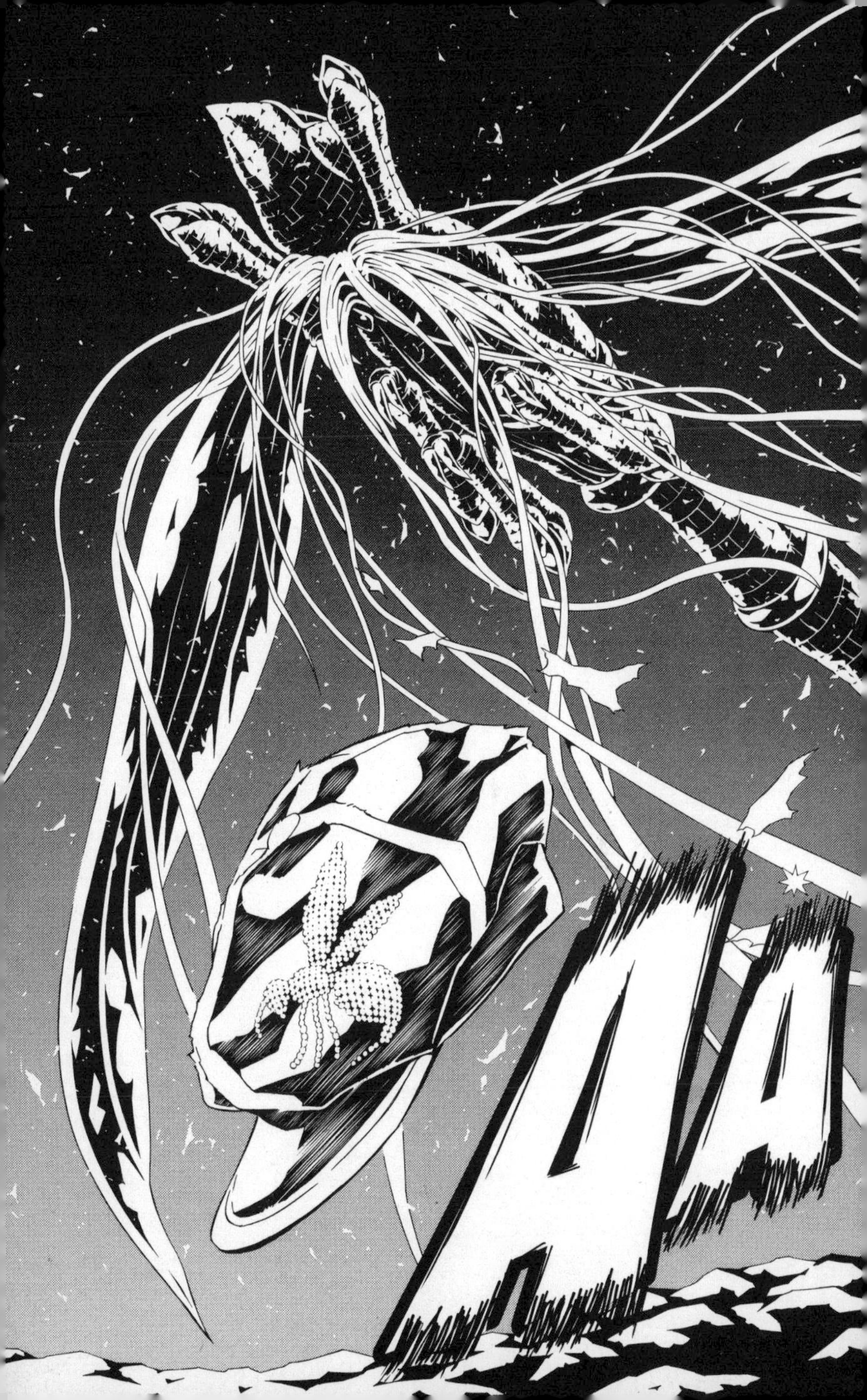
AA

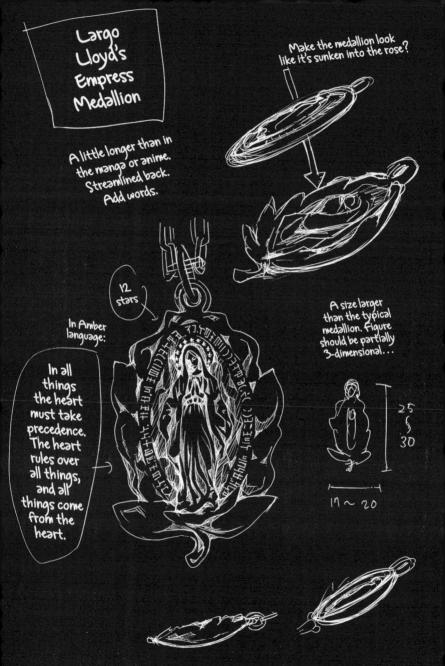

Largo Lloyd's Empress Medallion

Make the medallion look like it's sunken into the rose?

A little longer than in the manga or anime. Streamlined back. Add words.

12 stars

In Amber language:

In all things the heart must take precedence. The heart rules over all things, and all things come from the heart.

A size larger than the typical medallion. Figure should be partially 3-dimensional...

25 ⌇ 30

17 ~ 20

Rough sketches of the Empress Medallion for merchandising.

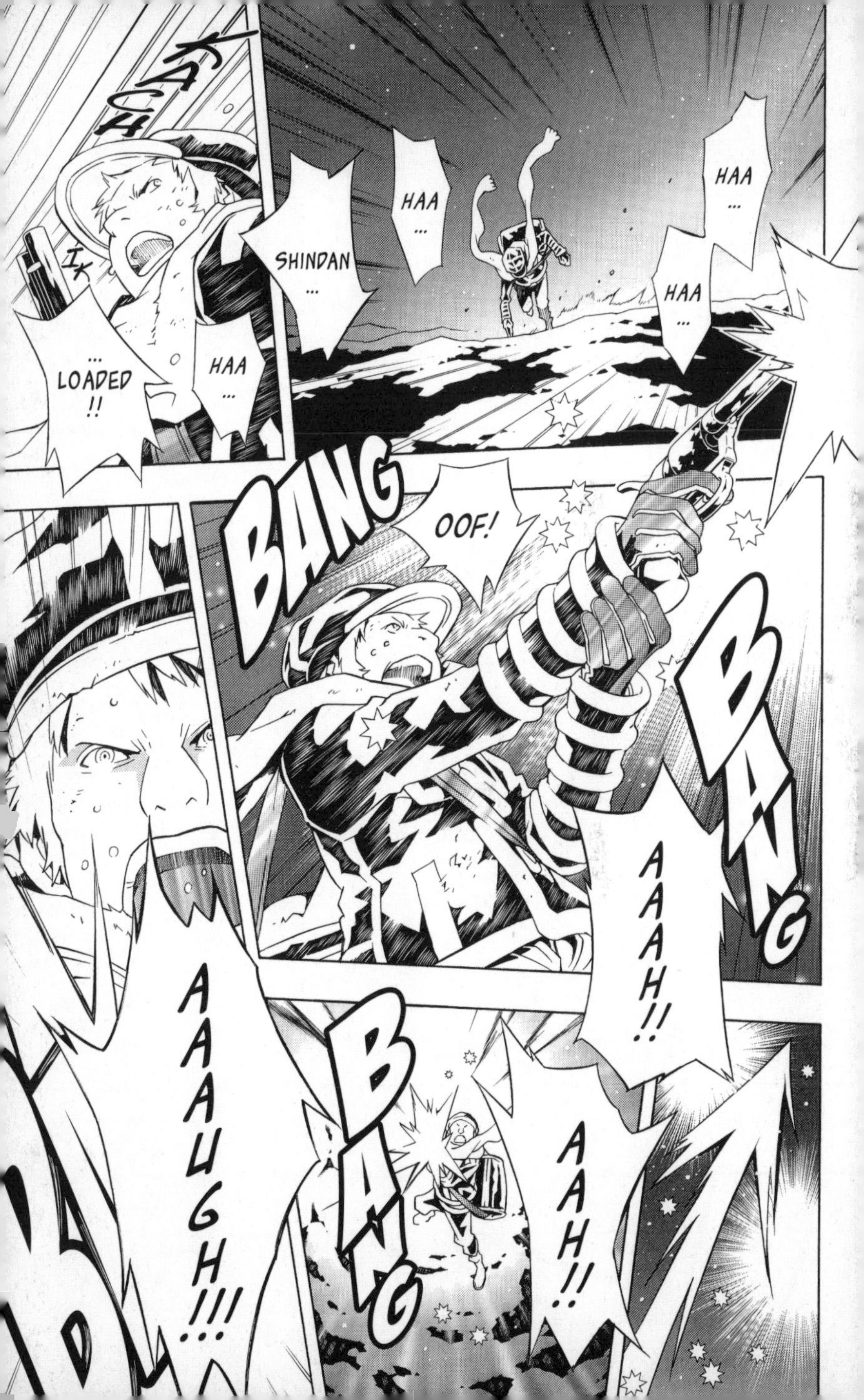
HAA ...
HAA ...
HAA ...
SHINDAN ...
KACH
IK
HAA ...
... LOADED !!
BANG
BANG
OOF!
AAAAH!!
AAAAUGH!!!...
BANG
AAAH!!

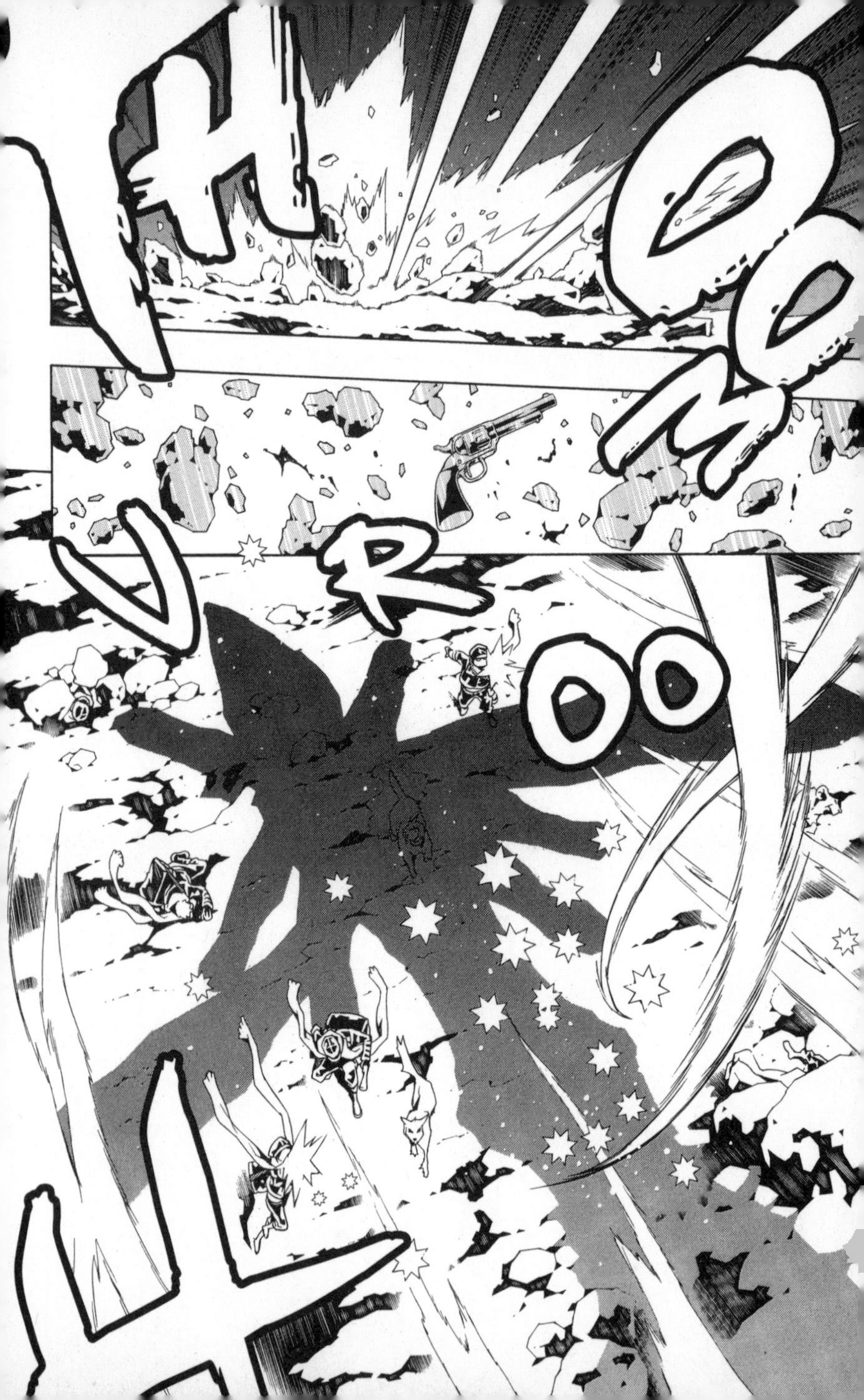
VROO

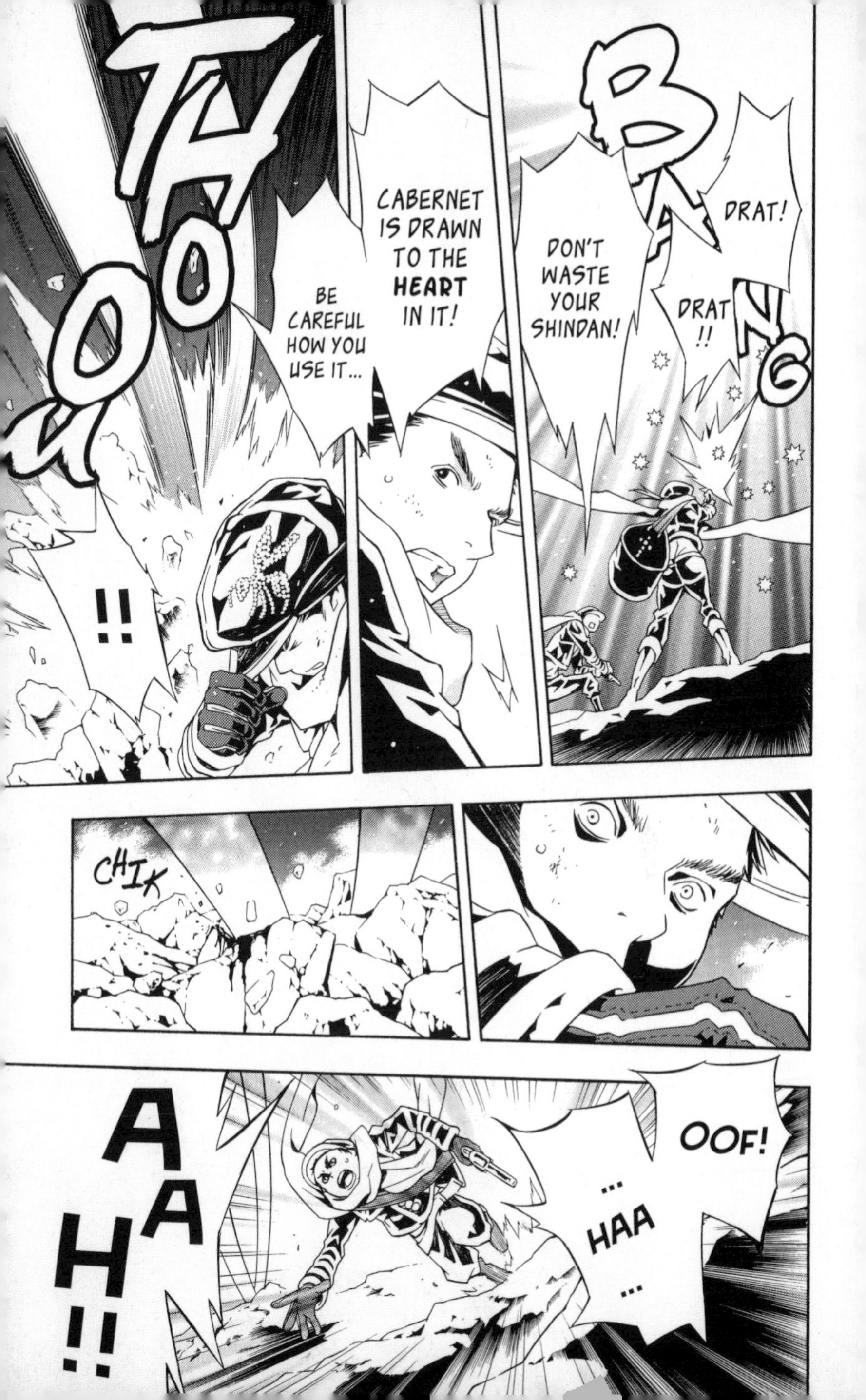

BANG
DRAT!
DRAT!!
DON'T WASTE YOUR SHINDAN!
CABERNET IS DRAWN TO THE **HEART** IN IT!
BE CAREFUL HOW YOU USE IT...
THOO
!!
CHIK
OOF!
...HAA...
AAH!!

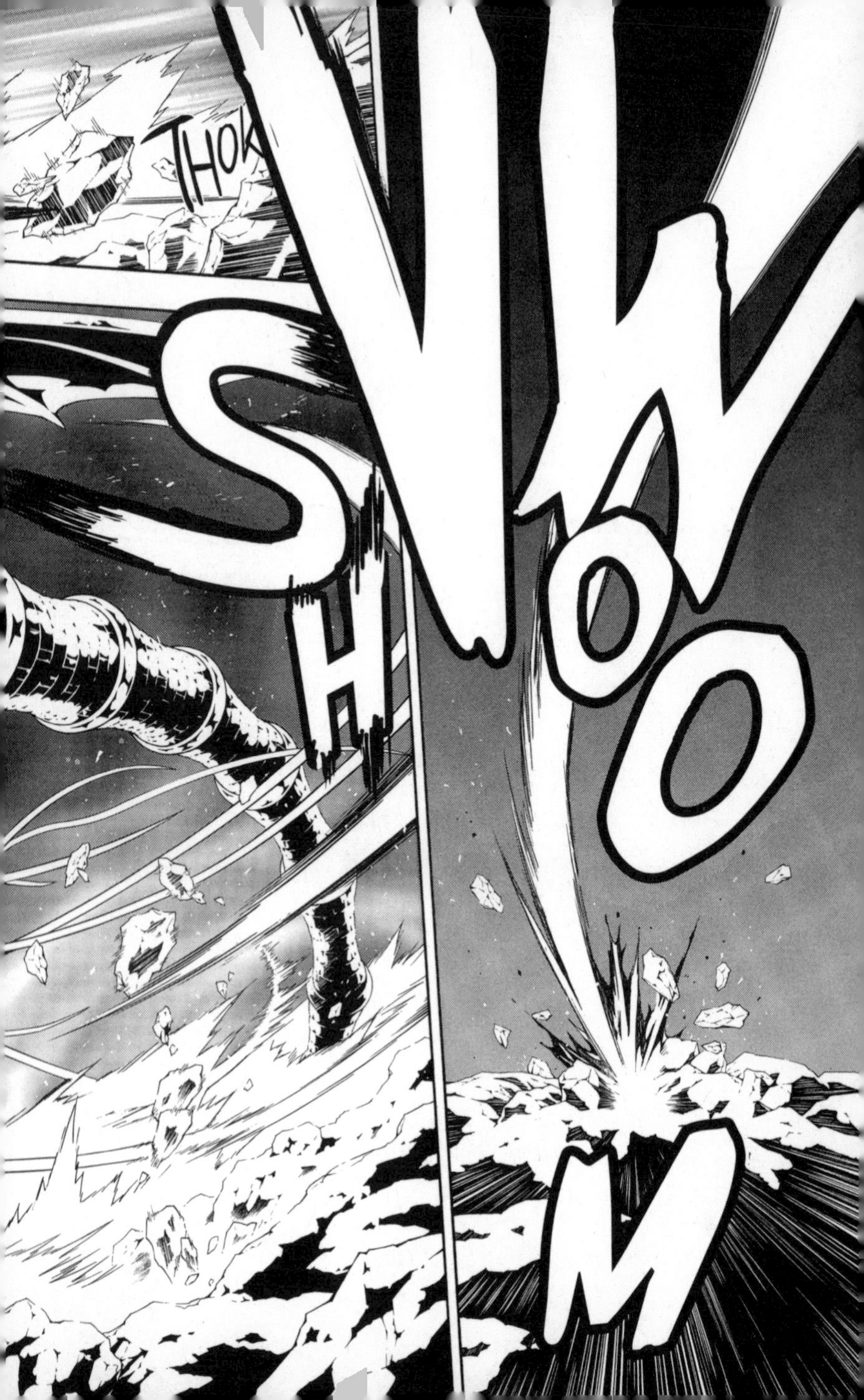
THOK
SWHOOOM

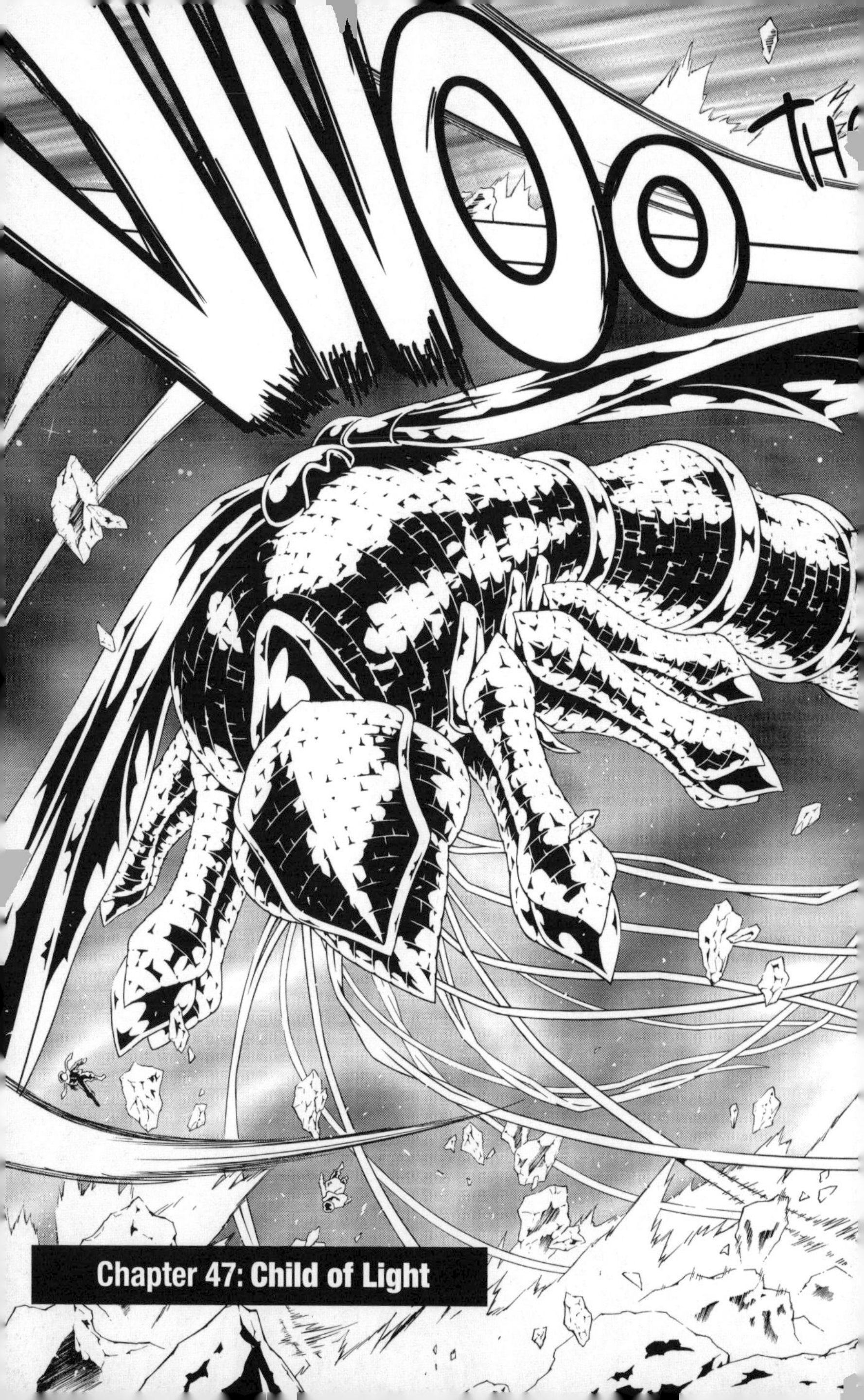
VWOO
THO
Chapter 47: Child of Light

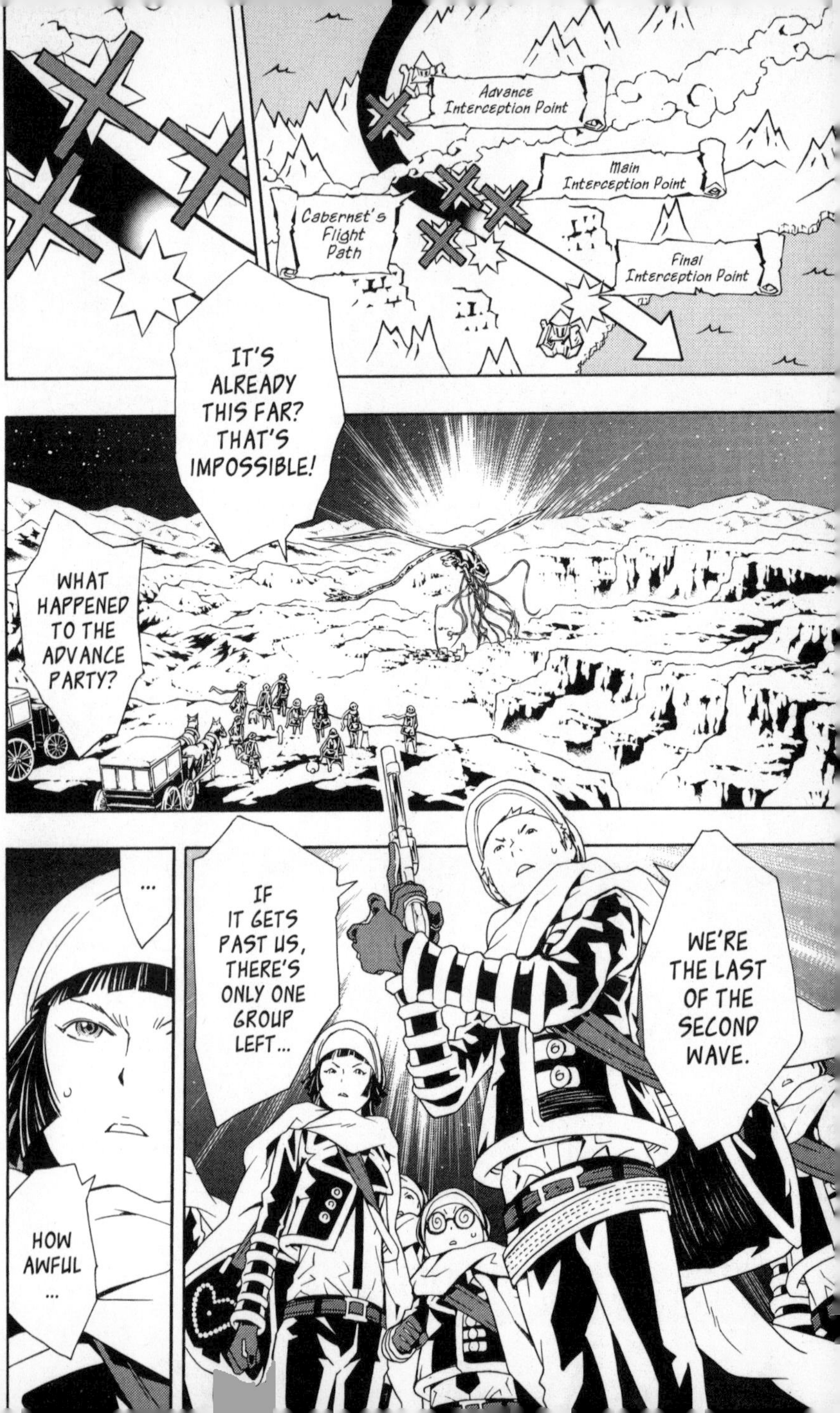
Advance Interception Point
Main Interception Point
Final Interception Point
Cabernet's Flight Path
IT'S ALREADY THIS FAR? THAT'S IMPOSSIBLE!
WHAT HAPPENED TO THE ADVANCE PARTY?
WE'RE THE LAST OF THE SECOND WAVE.
IF IT GETS PAST US, THERE'S ONLY ONE GROUP LEFT...
...
HOW AWFUL ...

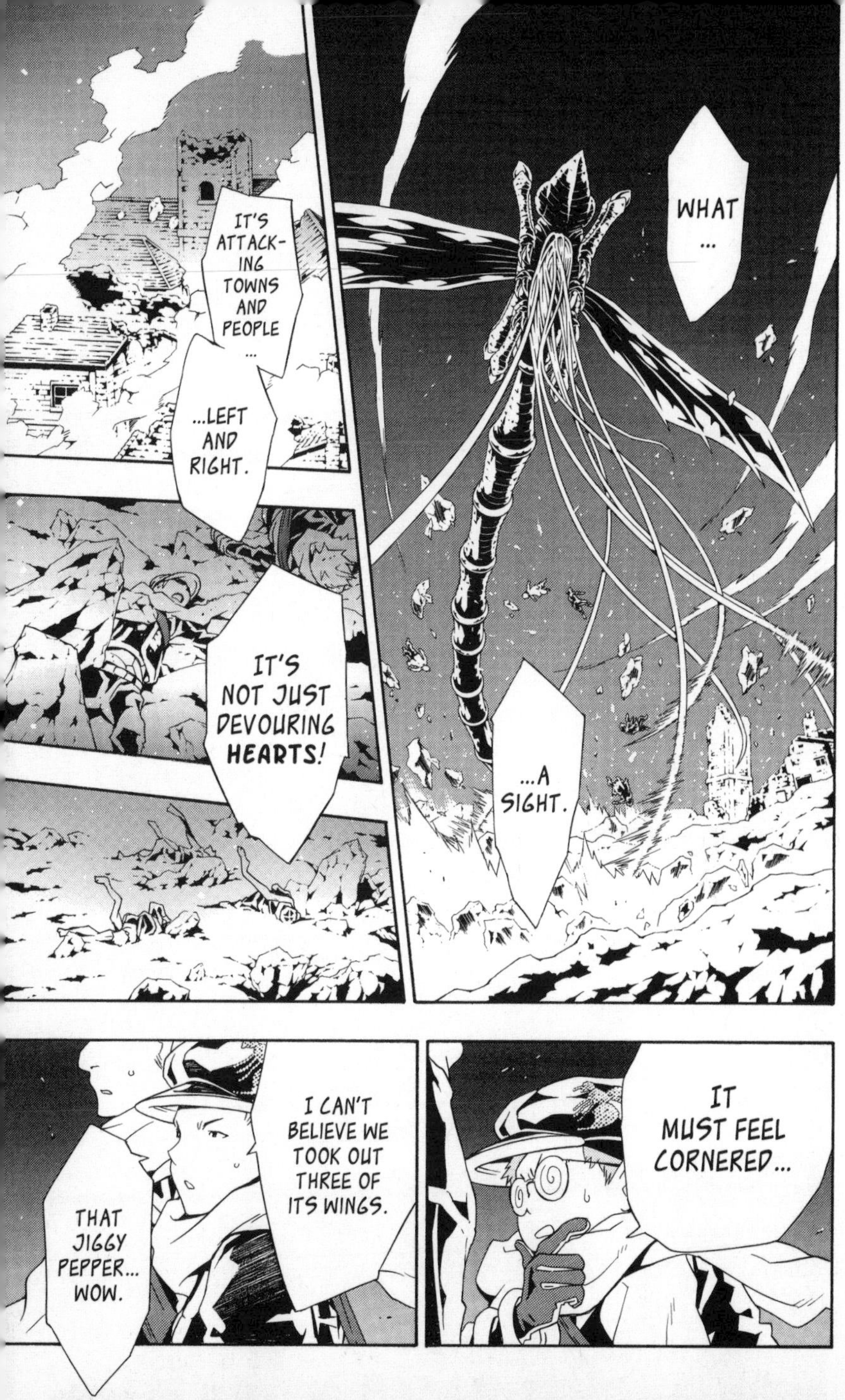
WHAT...
...A SIGHT.
IT'S ATTACKING TOWNS AND PEOPLE...
...LEFT AND RIGHT.
IT'S NOT JUST DEVOURING HEARTS!
IT MUST FEEL CORNERED...
I CAN'T BELIEVE WE TOOK OUT THREE OF ITS WINGS.
THAT JIGGY PEPPER... WOW.

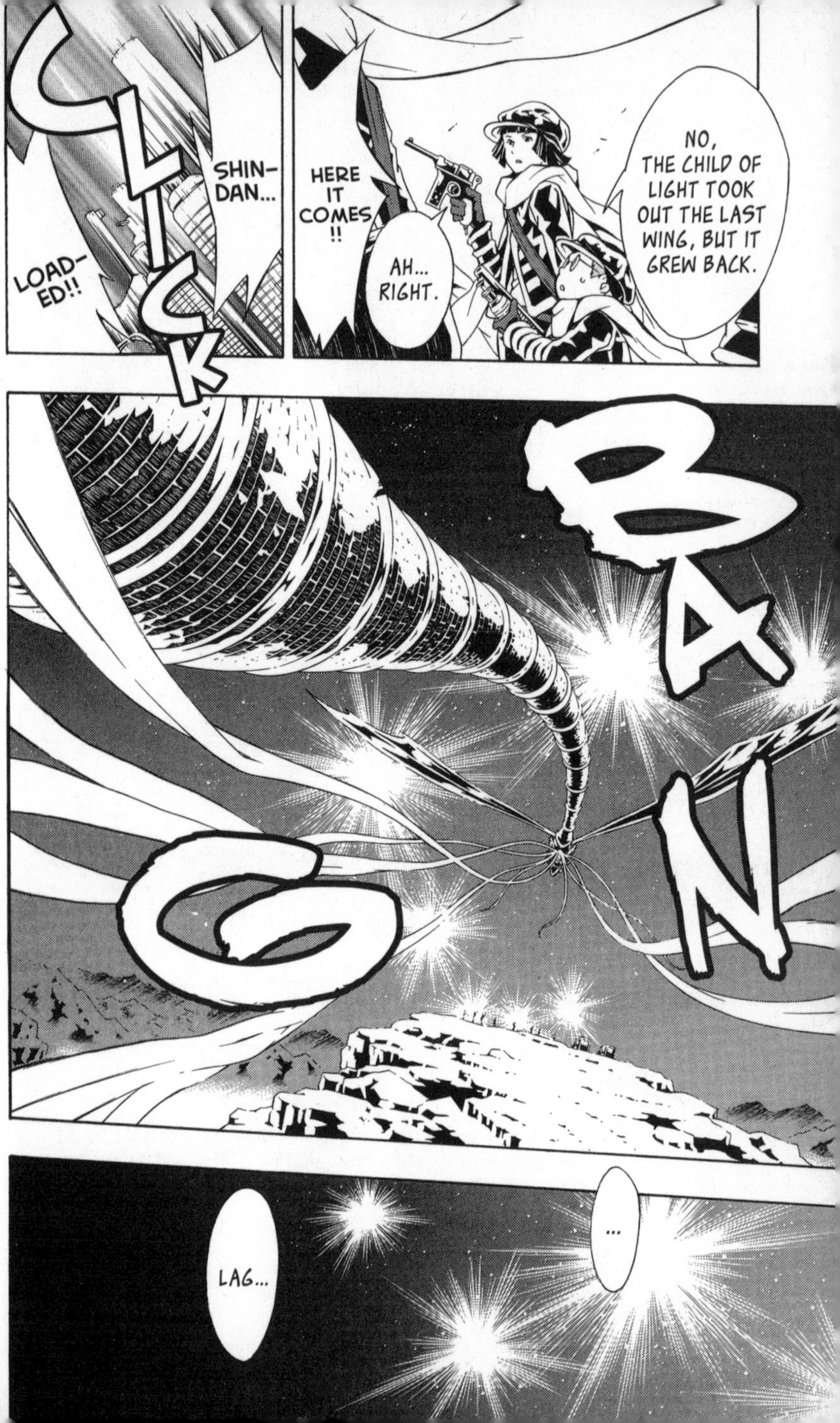
NO, THE CHILD OF LIGHT TOOK OUT THE LAST WING, BUT IT GREW BACK.
AH... RIGHT.
HERE IT COMES!!
SHIN-DAN...
LOADED!!
CLICK
BANG
...
LAG...

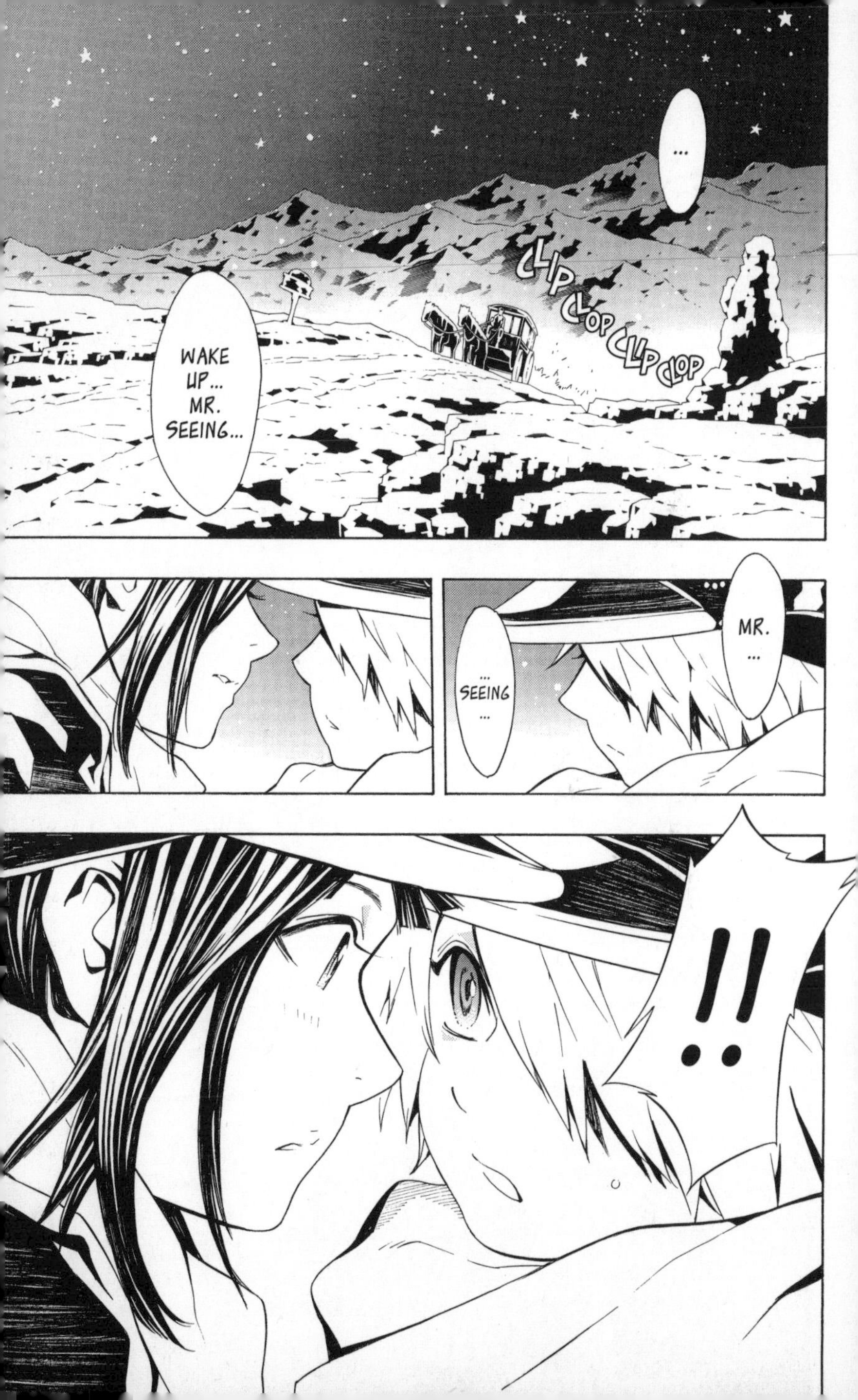
...
CLIP CLOP CLIP CLOP
WAKE UP... MR. SEEING...
MR. ...
... SEEING ...
!!

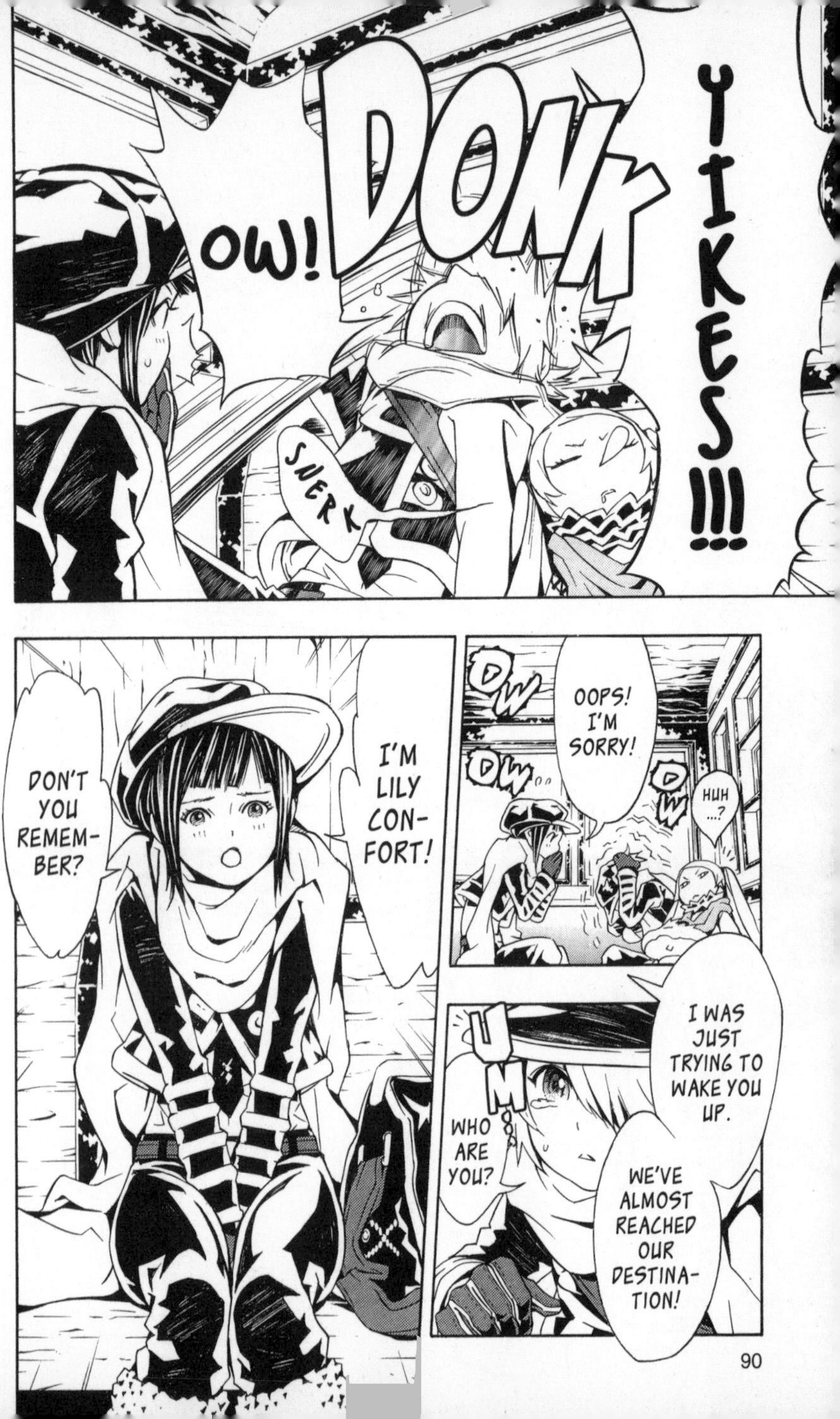
YIKES!!!
DONK
OW!
SNERK
OOPS! I'M SORRY!
HUH ...?
OW OW OW
I WAS JUST TRYING TO WAKE YOU UP.
WE'VE ALMOST REACHED OUR DESTINATION!
UM...
WHO ARE YOU?
I'M LILY CONFORT!
DON'T YOU REMEMBER?

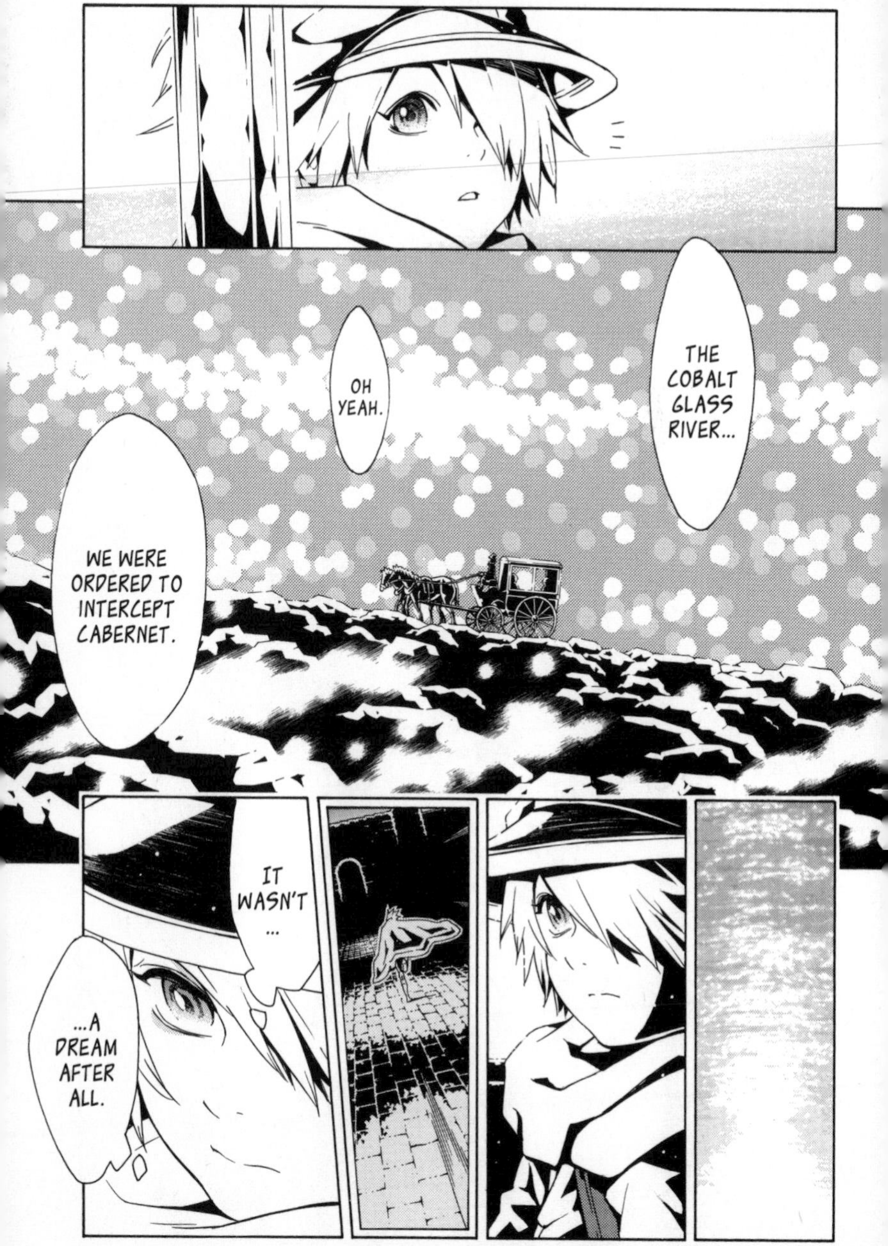
THE COBALT GLASS RIVER...
OH YEAH.
WE WERE ORDERED TO INTERCEPT CABERNET.
IT WASN'T ...
...A DREAM AFTER ALL.

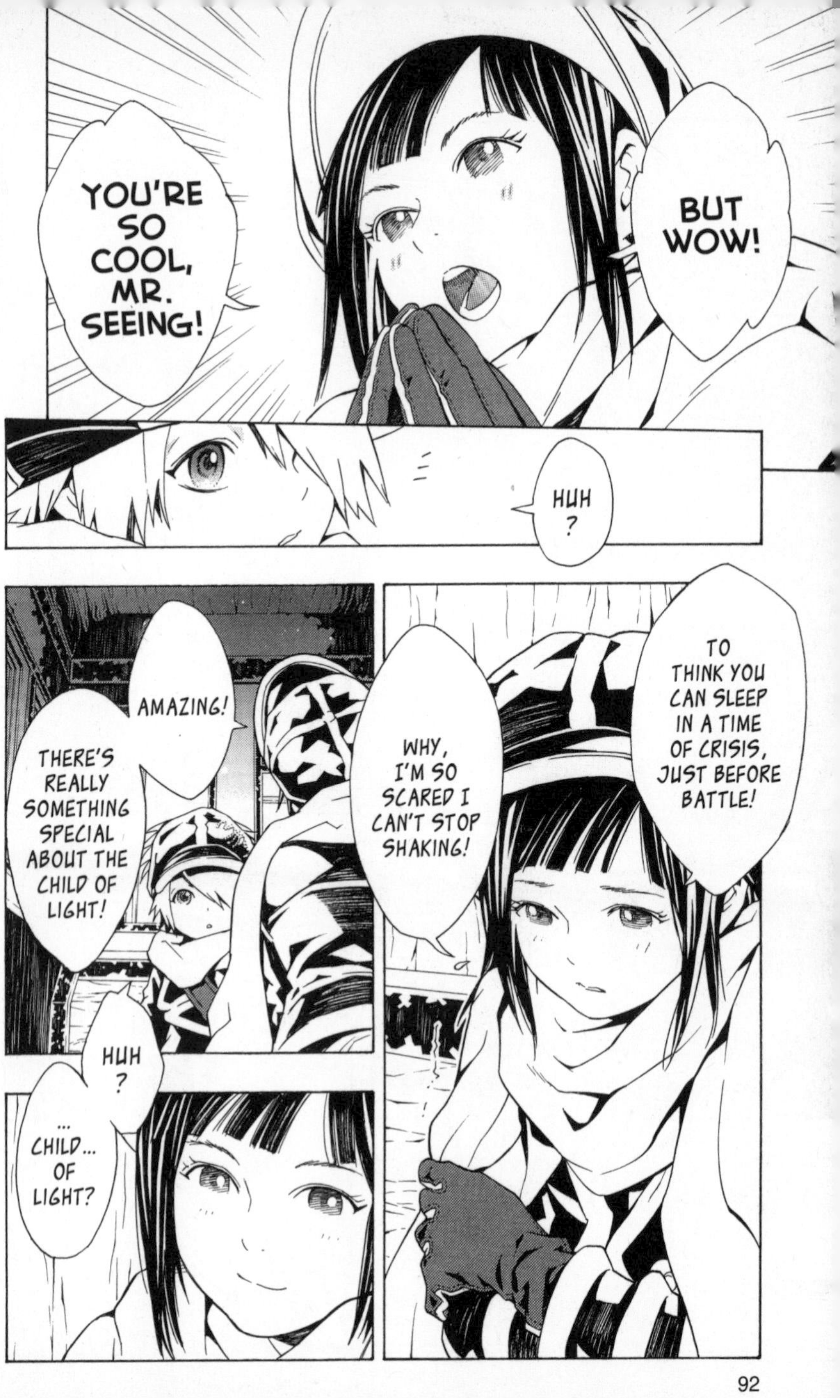
BUT WOW!
YOU'RE SO COOL, MR. SEEING!
HUH?
TO THINK YOU CAN SLEEP IN A TIME OF CRISIS, JUST BEFORE BATTLE!
WHY, I'M SO SCARED I CAN'T STOP SHAKING!
AMAZING!
THERE'S REALLY SOMETHING SPECIAL ABOUT THE CHILD OF LIGHT!
HUH?
... CHILD... OF LIGHT?

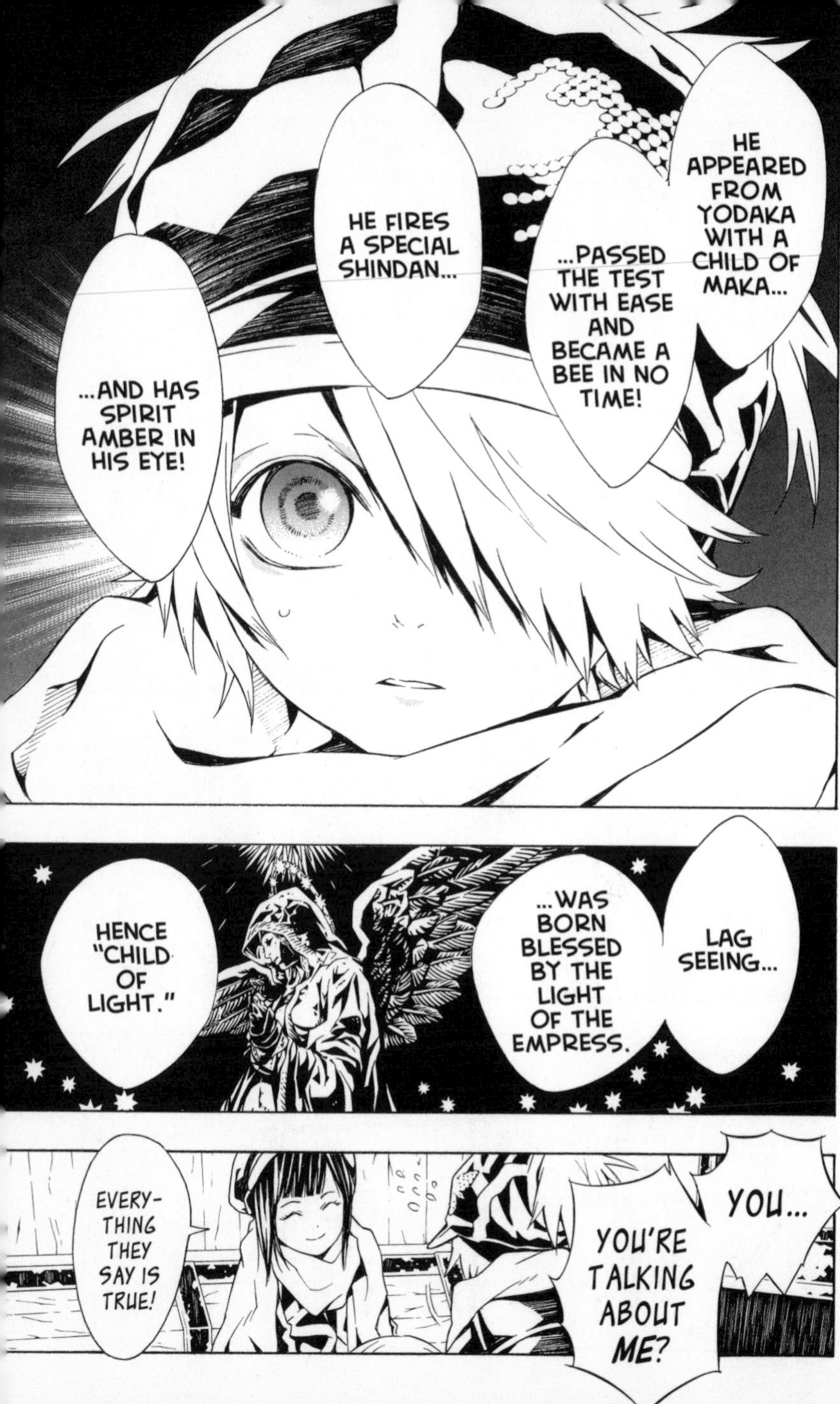
HE APPEARED FROM YODAKA WITH A CHILD OF MAKA...
...PASSED THE TEST WITH EASE AND BECAME A BEE IN NO TIME!
HE FIRES A SPECIAL SHINDAN...
...AND HAS SPIRIT AMBER IN HIS EYE!
LAG SEEING...
...WAS BORN BLESSED BY THE LIGHT OF THE EMPRESS.
HENCE "CHILD OF LIGHT."
YOU...
YOU'RE TALKING ABOUT *ME*?
EVERY-THING THEY SAY IS TRUE!

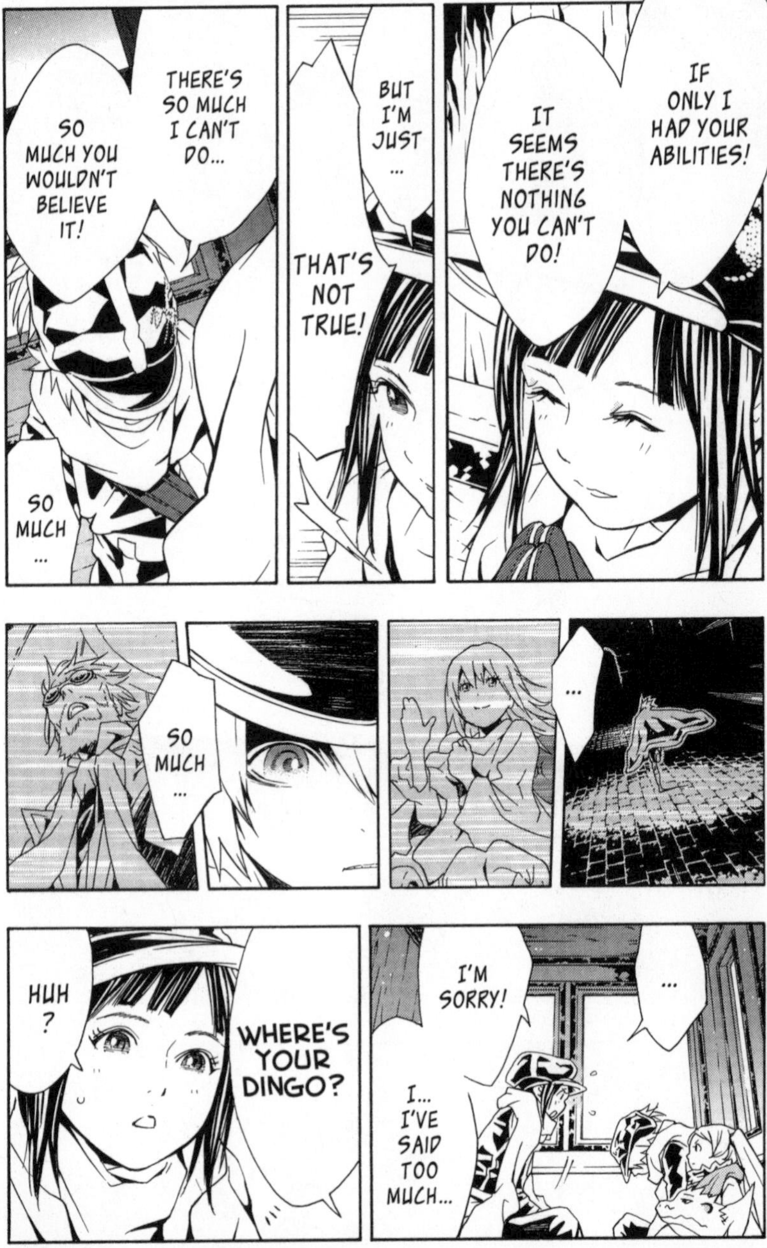
IF ONLY I HAD YOUR ABILITIES!
IT SEEMS THERE'S NOTHING YOU CAN'T DO!
BUT I'M JUST ...
THAT'S NOT TRUE!
THERE'S SO MUCH I CAN'T DO...
SO MUCH YOU WOULDN'T BELIEVE IT!
SO MUCH ...
...
SO MUCH ...
...
I'M SORRY!
I... I'VE SAID TOO MUCH...
WHERE'S YOUR DINGO?
HUH ?

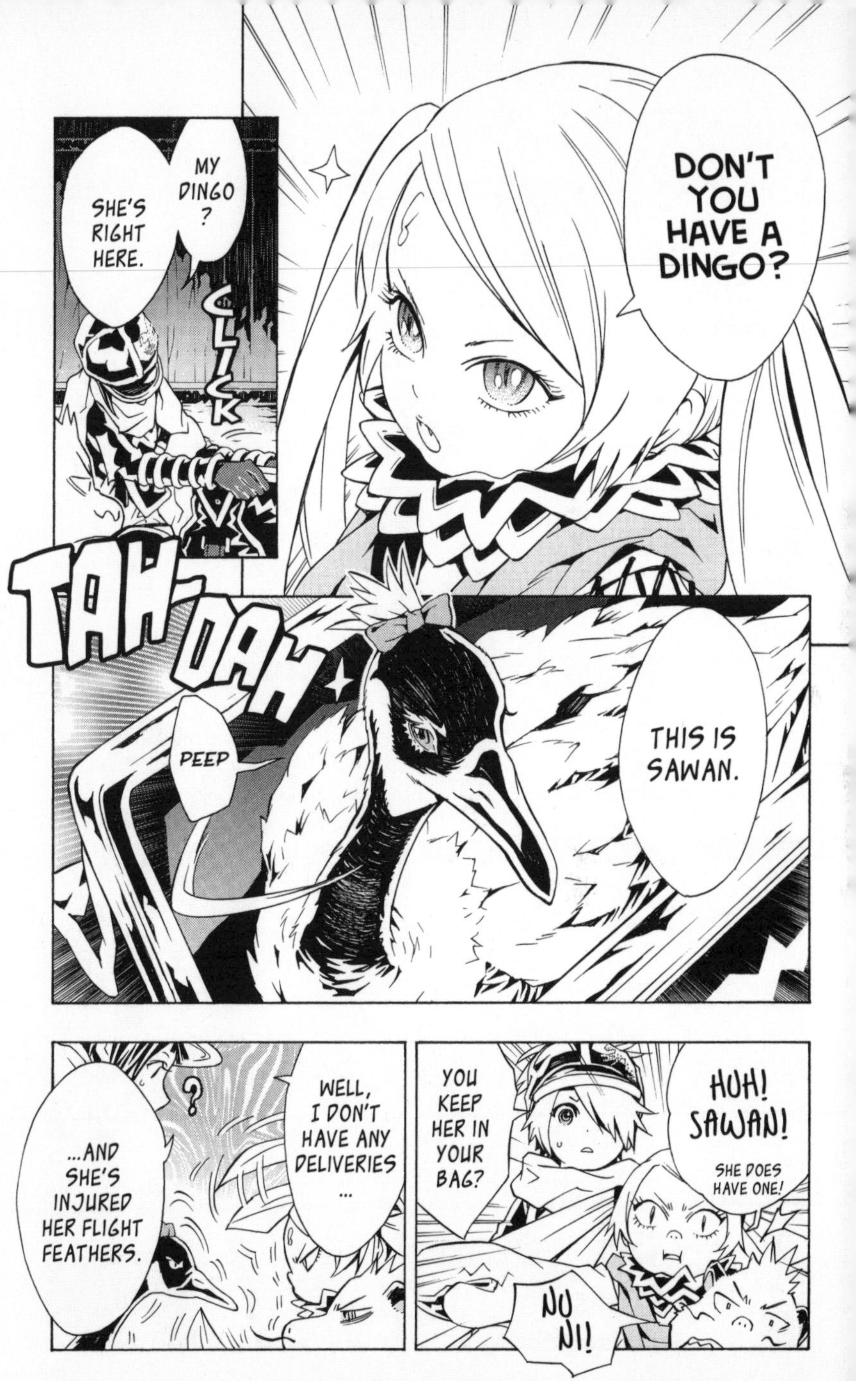
DON'T YOU HAVE A DINGO?
MY DINGO?
SHE'S RIGHT HERE.
CLICK
TAH-DAH
THIS IS SAWAN.
PEEP
HUH! SAWAN!
SHE DOES HAVE ONE!
YOU KEEP HER IN YOUR BAG?
NU NI!
WELL, I DON'T HAVE ANY DELIVERIES...
...AND SHE'S INJURED HER FLIGHT FEATHERS.

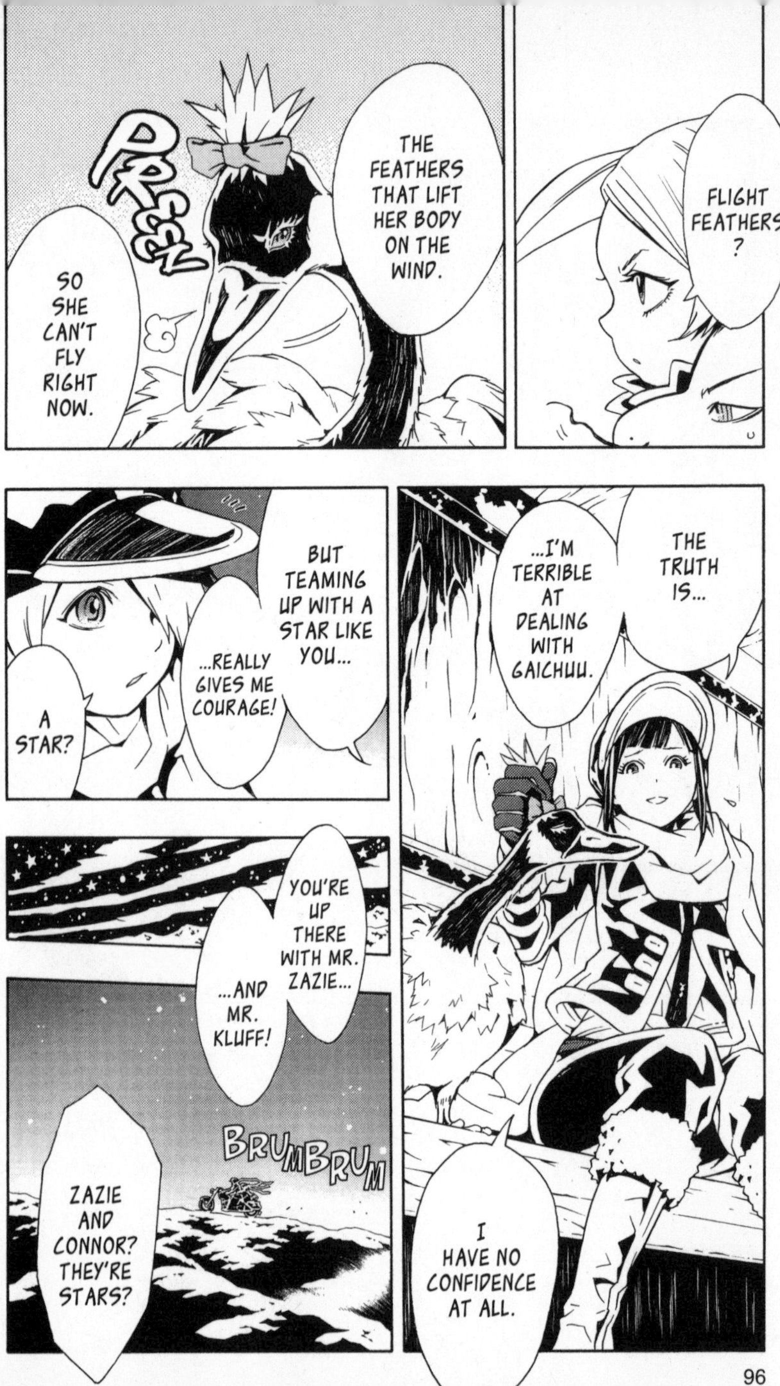
FLIGHT FEATHERS?
THE FEATHERS THAT LIFT HER BODY ON THE WIND.
PREEN
SO SHE CAN'T FLY RIGHT NOW.
THE TRUTH IS...
...I'M TERRIBLE AT DEALING WITH GAICHUU.
I HAVE NO CONFIDENCE AT ALL.
BUT TEAMING UP WITH A STAR LIKE YOU...
...REALLY GIVES ME COURAGE!
A STAR?
YOU'RE UP THERE WITH MR. ZAZIE...
...AND MR. KLUFF!
BRUMBRUM
ZAZIE AND CONNOR? THEY'RE STARS?

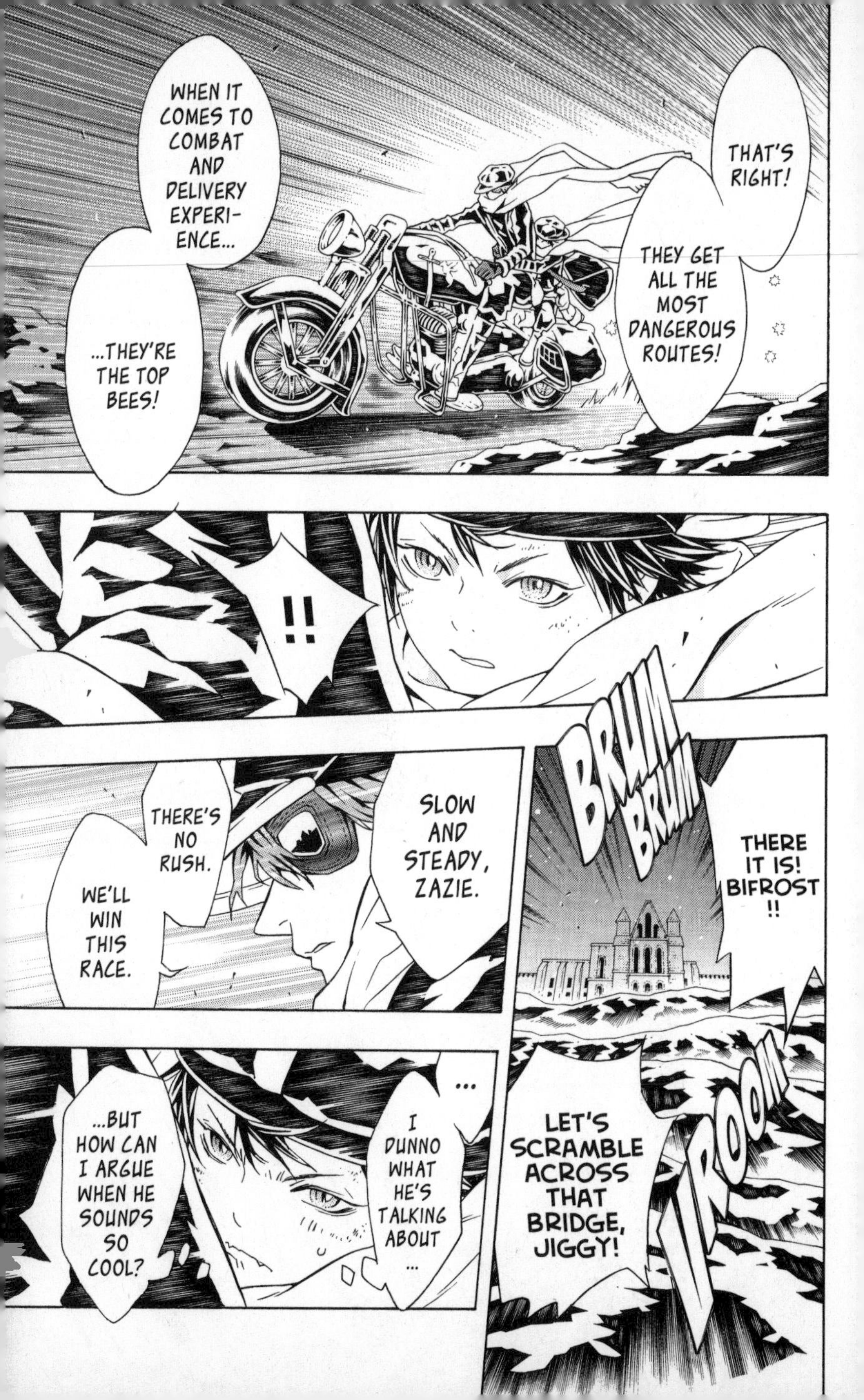
THAT'S RIGHT!
THEY GET ALL THE MOST DANGEROUS ROUTES!
WHEN IT COMES TO COMBAT AND DELIVERY EXPERI- ENCE...
...THEY'RE THE TOP BEES!
!!
BRUM BRUM
THERE IT IS! BIFROST !!
VROOM
LET'S SCRAMBLE ACROSS THAT BRIDGE, JIGGY!
SLOW AND STEADY, ZAZIE.
THERE'S NO RUSH.
WE'LL WIN THIS RACE.
...
I DUNNO WHAT HE'S TALKING ABOUT ...
...BUT HOW CAN I ARGUE WHEN HE SOUNDS SO COOL?

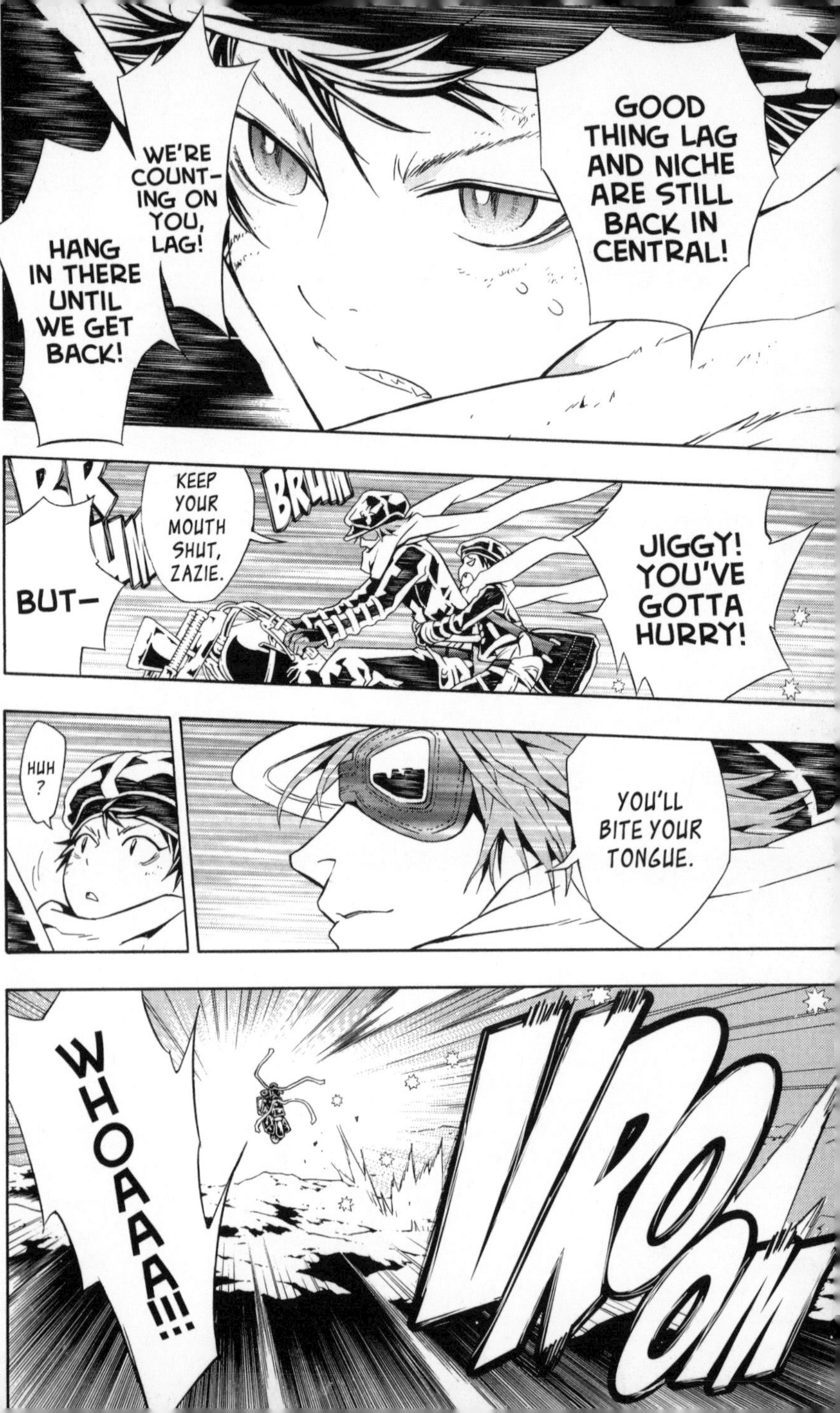
GOOD THING LAG AND NICHE ARE STILL BACK IN CENTRAL!
WE'RE COUNTING ON YOU, LAG!
HANG IN THERE UNTIL WE GET BACK!
JIGGY! YOU'VE GOTTA HURRY!
BRUM
KEEP YOUR MOUTH SHUT, ZAZIE.
BUT—
YOU'LL BITE YOUR TONGUE.
HUH?
WHOAAAA!!!

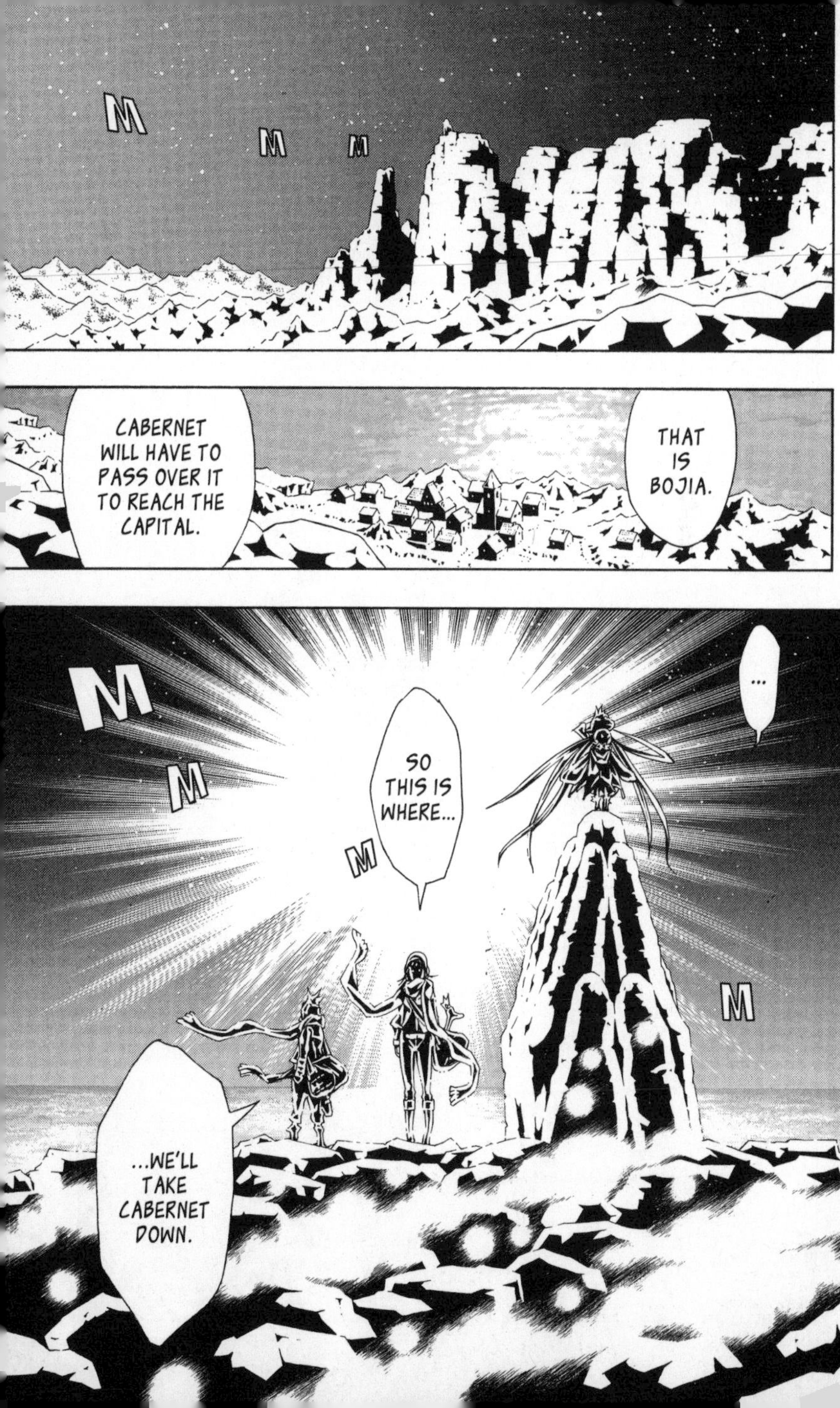
M
M
M
THAT IS BOJIA.
CABERNET WILL HAVE TO PASS OVER IT TO REACH THE CAPITAL.
...
M
M
M
M
SO THIS IS WHERE...
...WE'LL TAKE CABERNET DOWN.

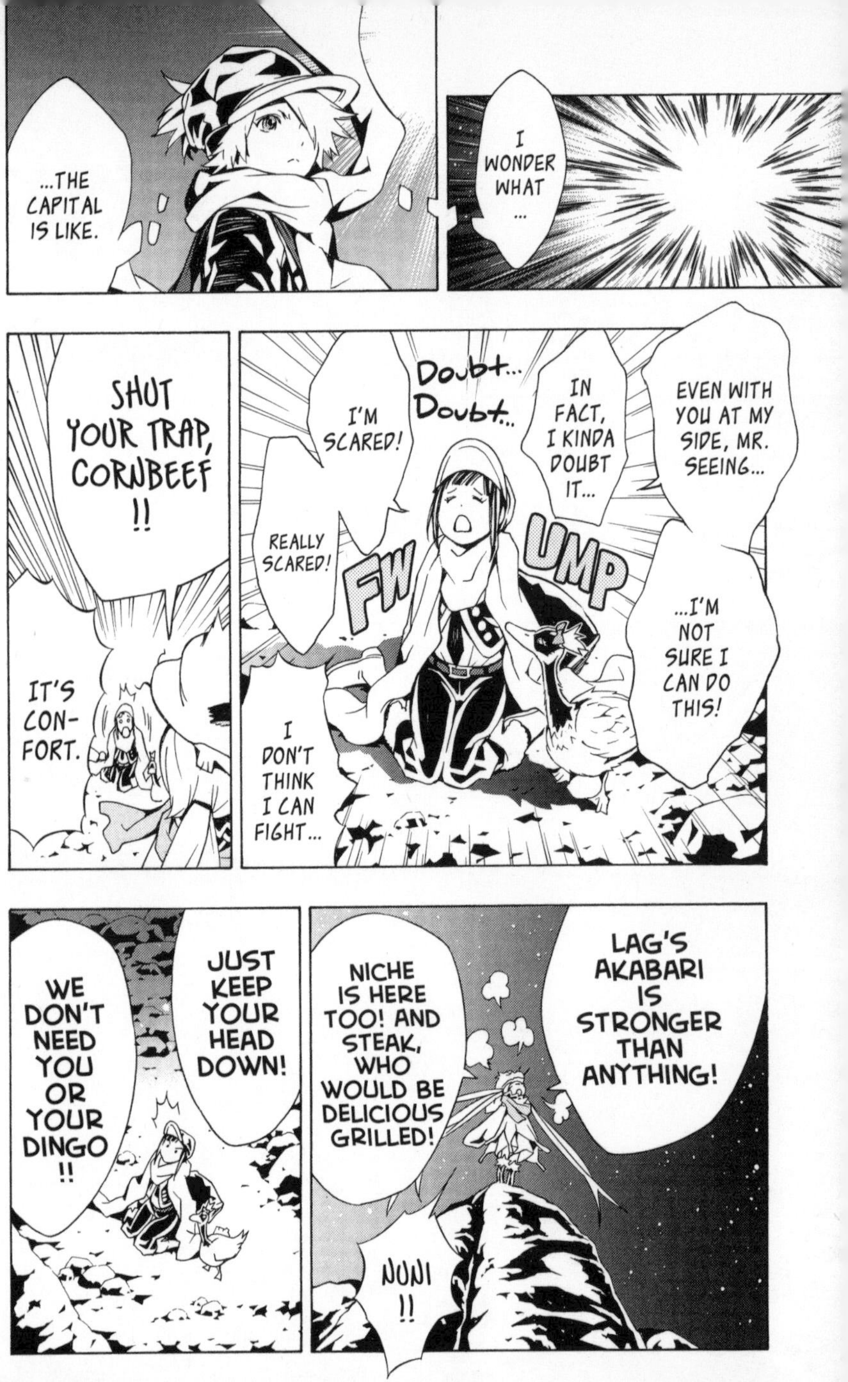

I WONDER WHAT ...
...THE CAPITAL IS LIKE.
EVEN WITH YOU AT MY SIDE, MR. SEEING...
IN FACT, I KINDA DOUBT IT...
Doubt... Doubt...
I'M SCARED!
...I'M NOT SURE I CAN DO THIS!
FWUMP
REALLY SCARED!
I DON'T THINK I CAN FIGHT...
SHUT YOUR TRAP, CORNBEEF !!
IT'S CONFORT.
LAG'S AKABARI IS STRONGER THAN ANYTHING!
NICHE IS HERE TOO! AND STEAK, WHO WOULD BE DELICIOUS GRILLED!
NUNI !!
JUST KEEP YOUR HEAD DOWN!
WE DON'T NEED YOU OR YOUR DINGO !!

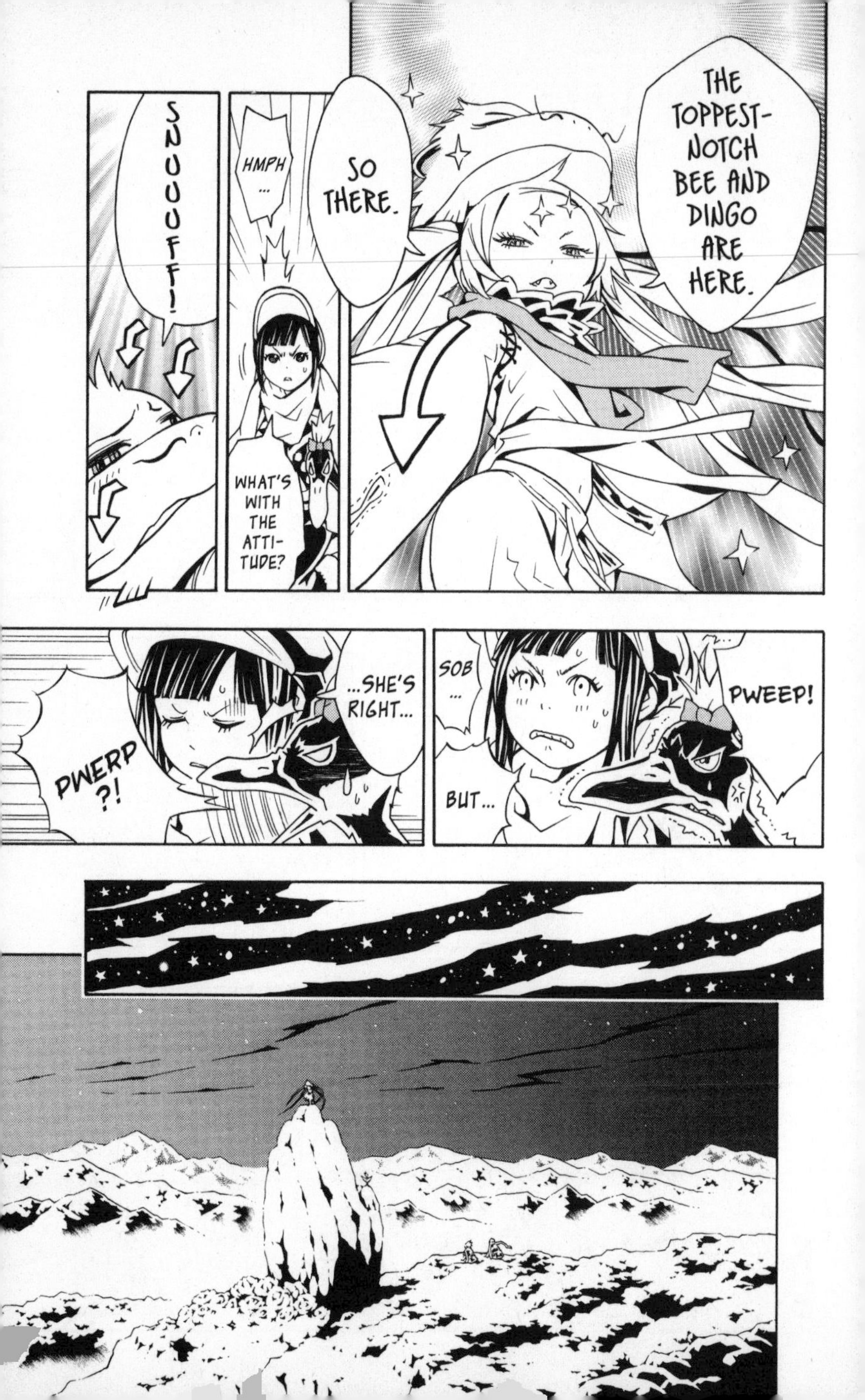
THE TOPPEST-NOTCH BEE AND DINGO ARE HERE.
SO THERE.
HMPH ...
WHAT'S WITH THE ATTITUDE?
SNUUUFF!
PWEEP!
SOB ...
BUT...
...SHE'S RIGHT...
PWERP ?!

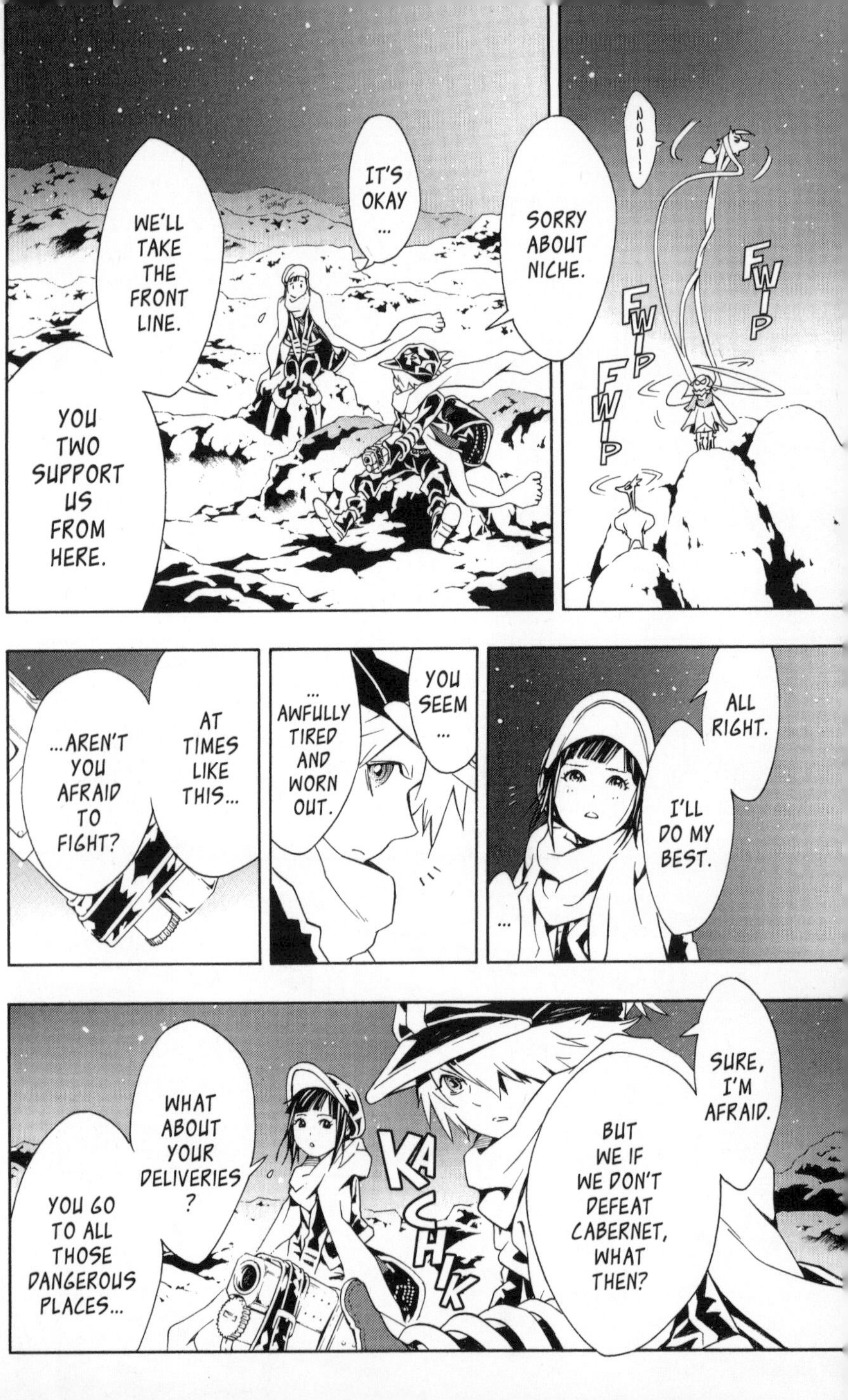
NUNI!!
FWIP
FWIP
FWIP
SORRY ABOUT NICHE.
IT'S OKAY ...
WE'LL TAKE THE FRONT LINE.
YOU TWO SUPPORT US FROM HERE.
ALL RIGHT.
I'LL DO MY BEST.
...
YOU SEEM ...
... AWFULLY TIRED AND WORN OUT.
AT TIMES LIKE THIS...
...AREN'T YOU AFRAID TO FIGHT?
SURE, I'M AFRAID.
BUT WE IF WE DON'T DEFEAT CABERNET, WHAT THEN?
KACHIK
WHAT ABOUT YOUR DELIVERIES?
YOU GO TO ALL THOSE DANGEROUS PLACES...

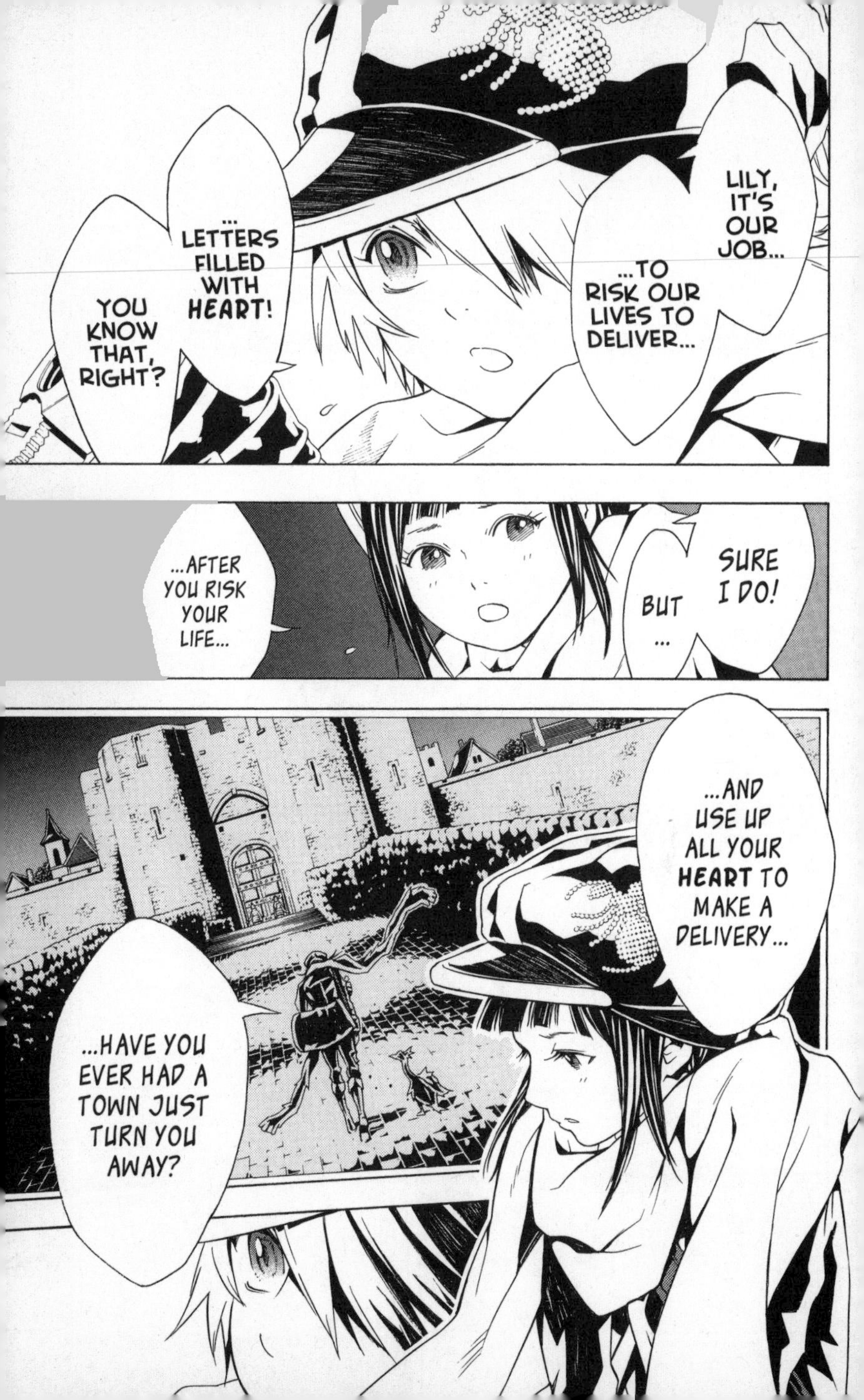

LILY, IT'S OUR JOB...
...TO RISK OUR LIVES TO DELIVER...
... LETTERS FILLED WITH **HEART**!
YOU KNOW THAT, RIGHT?
SURE I DO!
BUT ...
...AFTER YOU RISK YOUR LIFE...
...AND USE UP ALL YOUR **HEART** TO MAKE A DELIVERY...
...HAVE YOU EVER HAD A TOWN JUST TURN YOU AWAY?

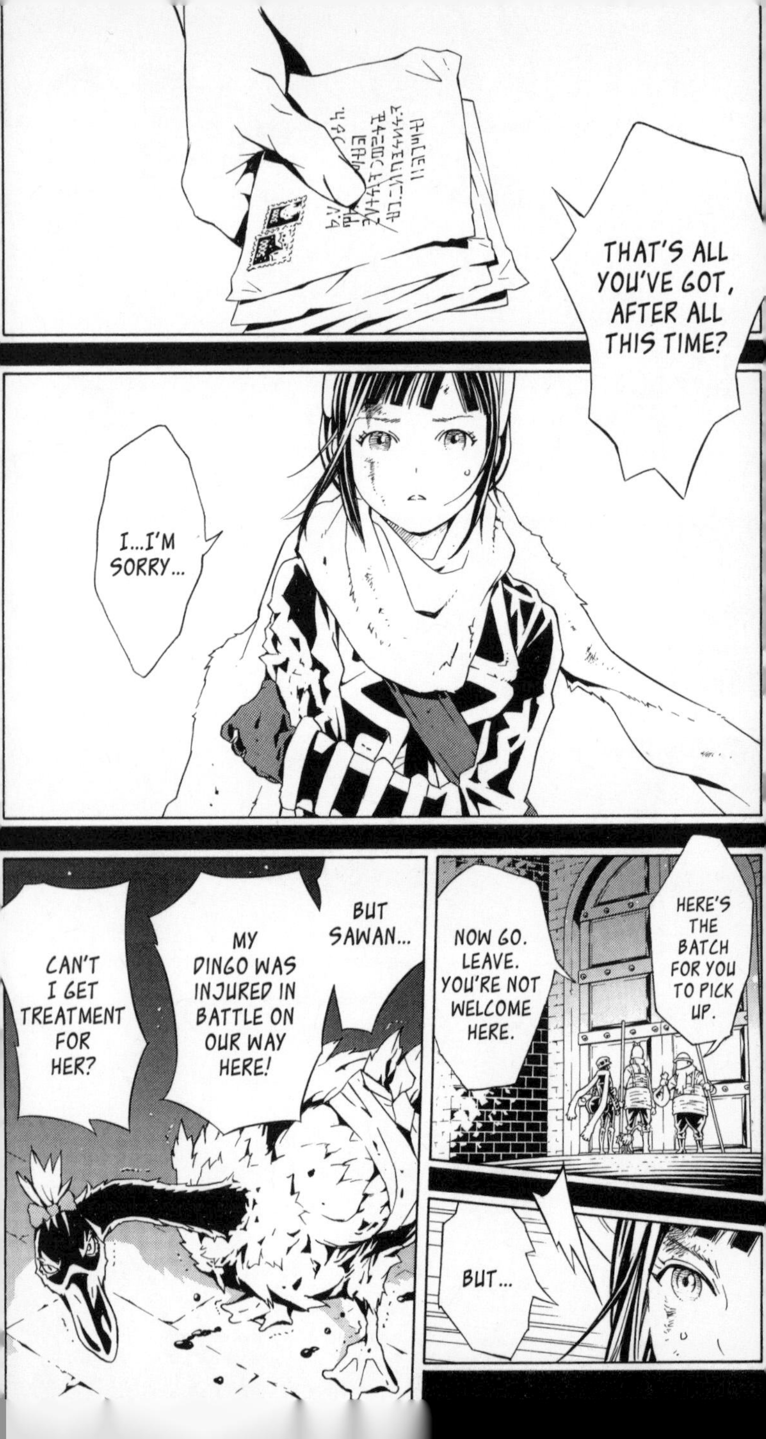
THAT'S ALL YOU'VE GOT, AFTER ALL THIS TIME?
I...I'M SORRY...
HERE'S THE BATCH FOR YOU TO PICK UP.
NOW GO. LEAVE. YOU'RE NOT WELCOME HERE.
BUT...
BUT SAWAN...
MY DINGO WAS INJURED IN BATTLE ON OUR WAY HERE!
CAN'T I GET TREATMENT FOR HER?

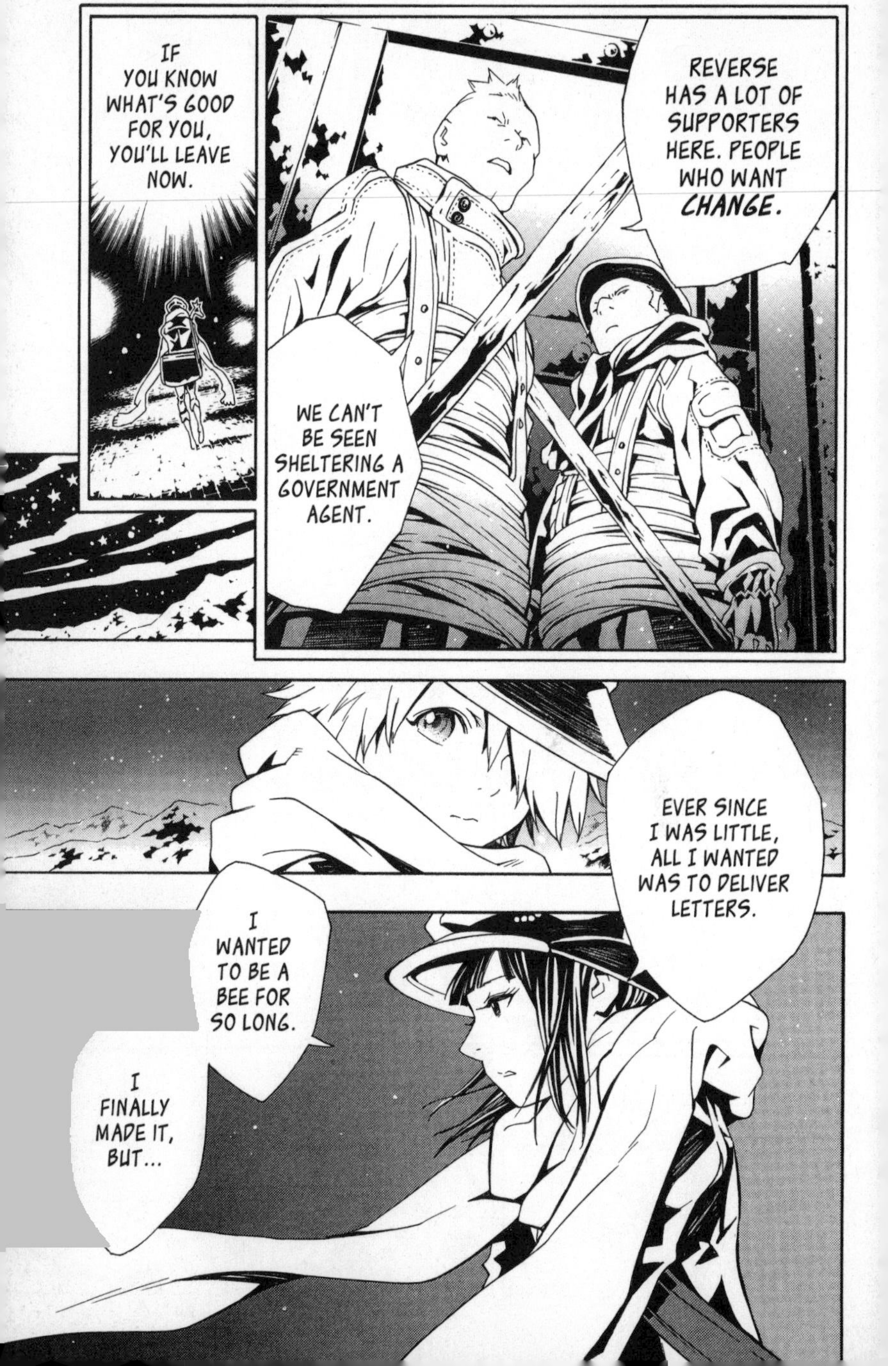
REVERSE HAS A LOT OF SUPPORTERS HERE. PEOPLE WHO WANT CHANGE.
WE CAN'T BE SEEN SHELTERING A GOVERNMENT AGENT.
IF YOU KNOW WHAT'S GOOD FOR YOU, YOU'LL LEAVE NOW.
EVER SINCE I WAS LITTLE, ALL I WANTED WAS TO DELIVER LETTERS.
I WANTED TO BE A BEE FOR SO LONG.
I FINALLY MADE IT, BUT...

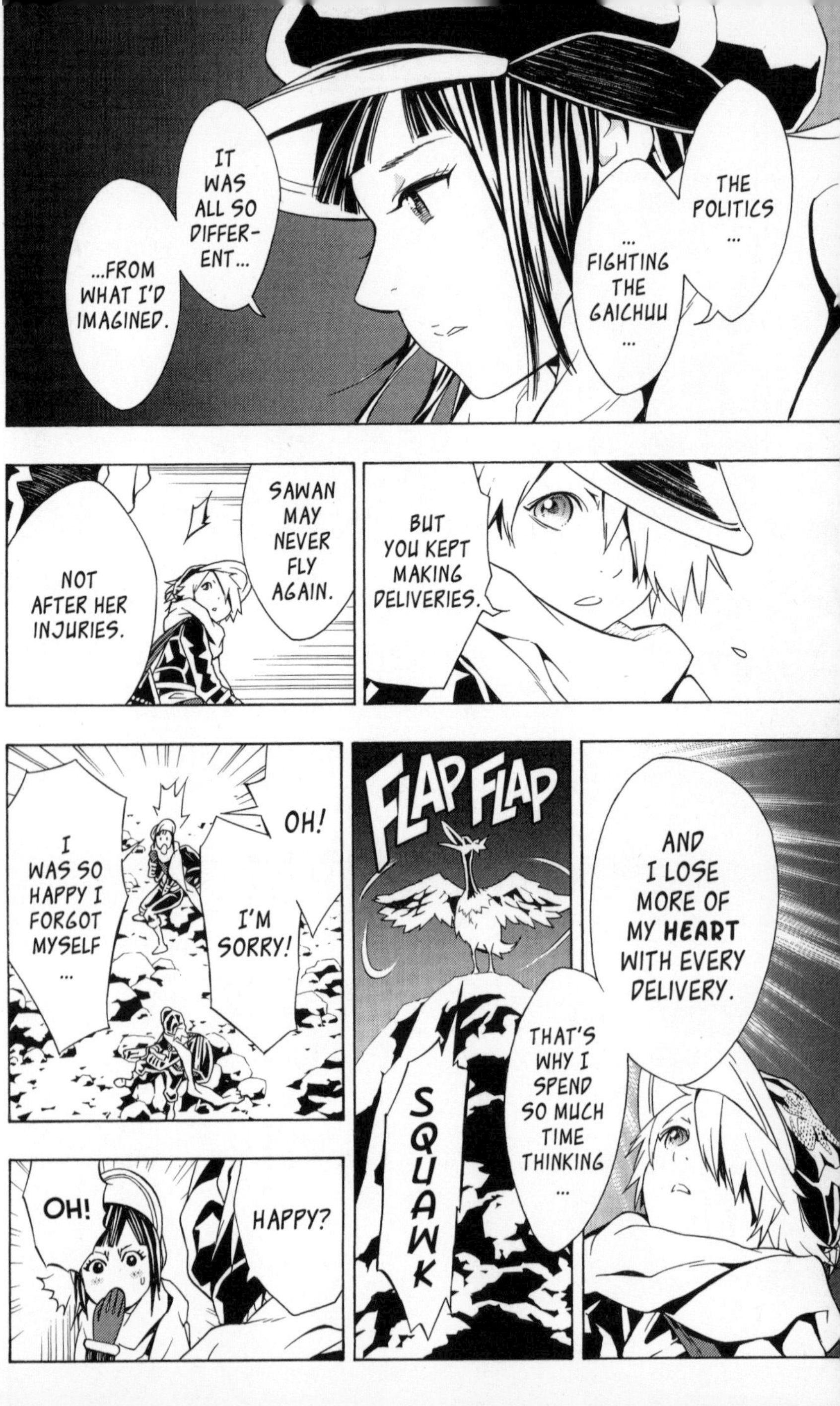
THE POLITICS ...
... FIGHTING THE GAICHUU ...
IT WAS ALL SO DIFFER-ENT...
...FROM WHAT I'D IMAGINED.
BUT YOU KEPT MAKING DELIVERIES.
SAWAN MAY NEVER FLY AGAIN.
NOT AFTER HER INJURIES.
AND I LOSE MORE OF MY **HEART** WITH EVERY DELIVERY.
THAT'S WHY I SPEND SO MUCH TIME THINKING ...
FLAP FLAP
SQUAWK
OH!
I'M SORRY!
I WAS SO HAPPY I FORGOT MYSELF ...
HAPPY?
OH!

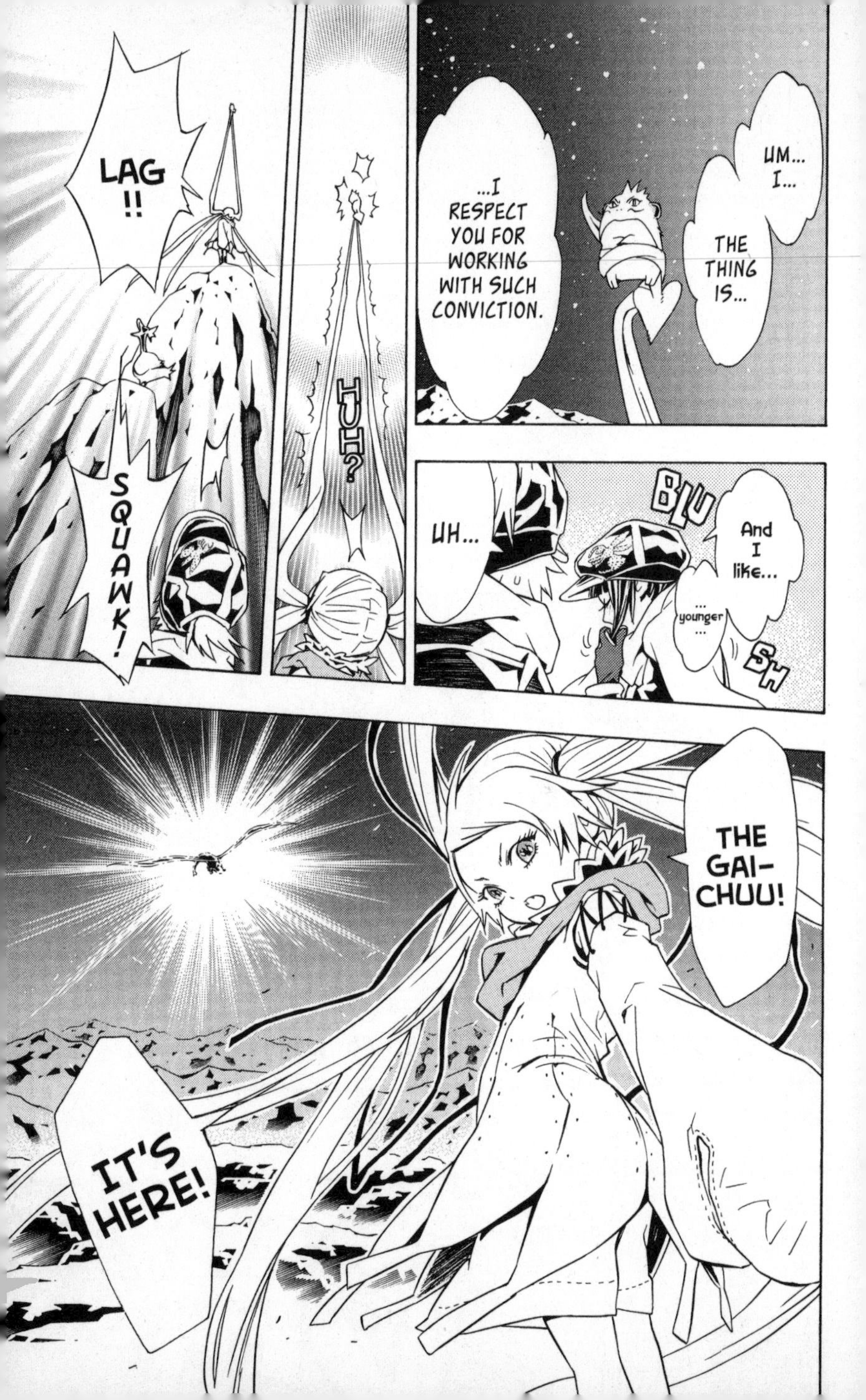
UM... I...
THE THING IS...
...I RESPECT YOU FOR WORKING WITH SUCH CONVICTION.
And I like...
...younger...
BLU
SH
UH...
HUH?
LAG!!
SQUAWK!
THE GAI-CHUU!
IT'S HERE!

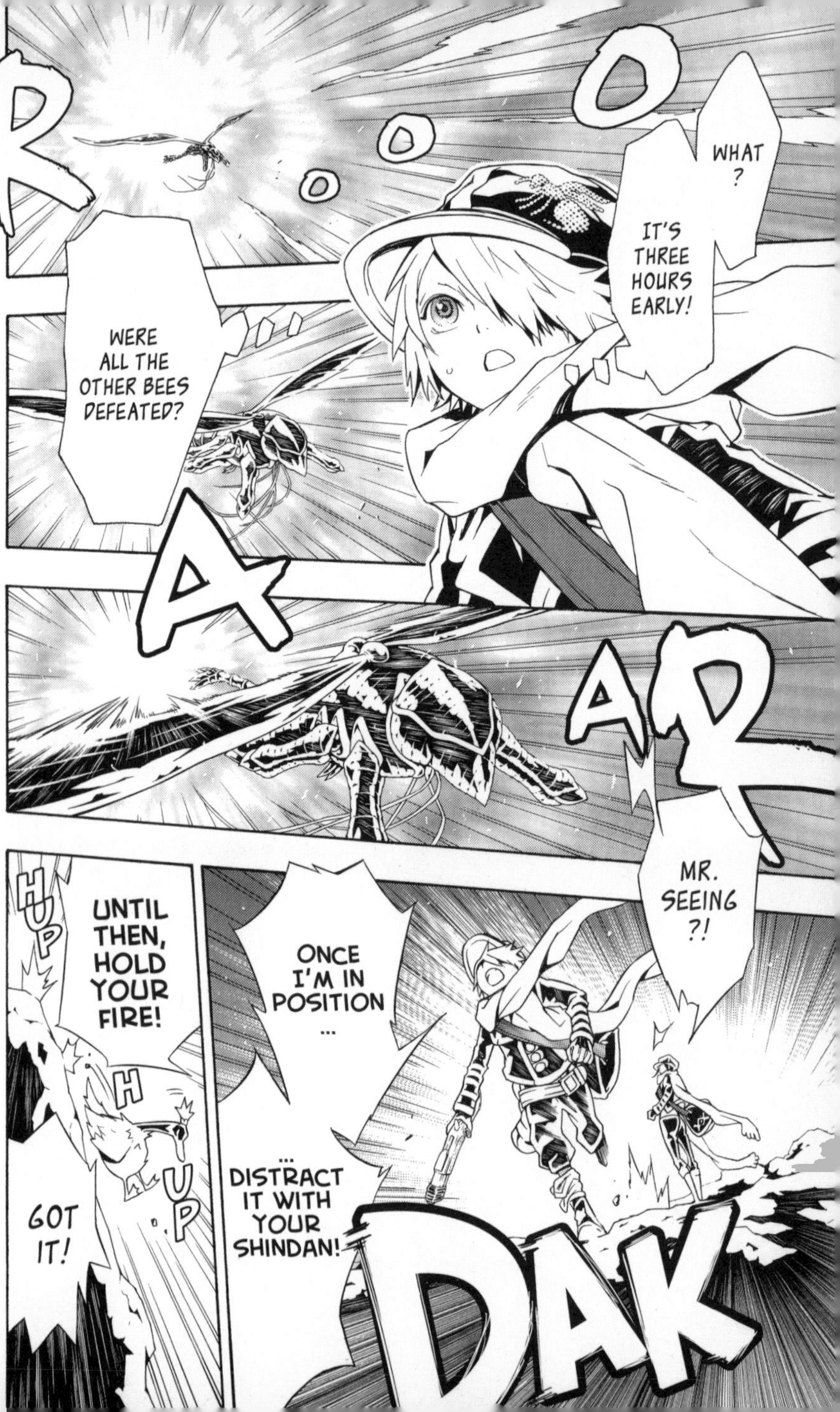
R O O O
WHAT? IT'S THREE HOURS EARLY!
...!
WERE ALL THE OTHER BEES DEFEATED?
A
AR
MR. SEEING?!
ONCE I'M IN POSITION ...
... DISTRACT IT WITH YOUR SHINDAN!
DAK
UNTIL THEN, HOLD YOUR FIRE!
HUP
HUP
GOT IT!

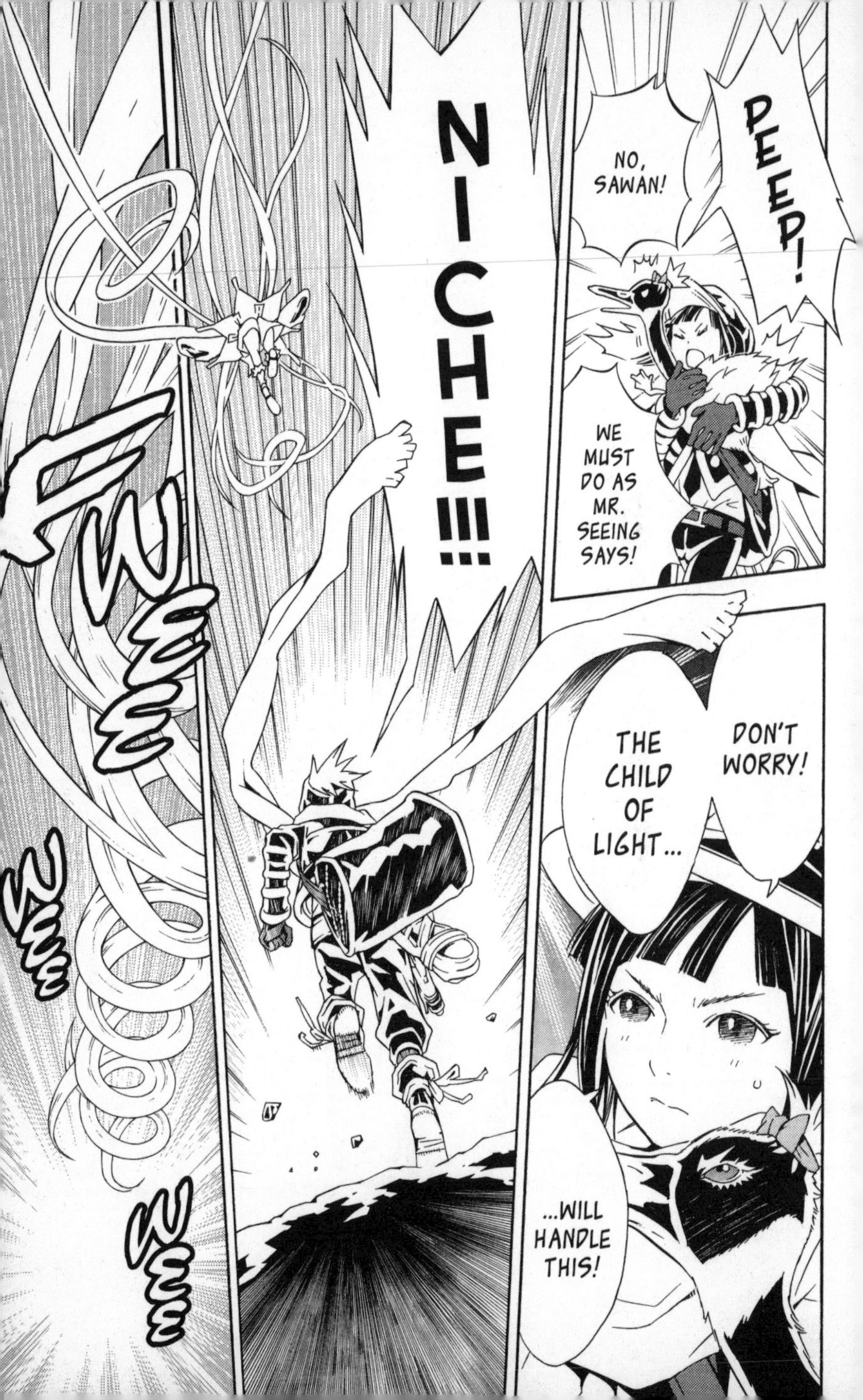
PEEP!
NO, SAWAN!
WE MUST DO AS MR. SEEING SAYS!
DON'T WORRY!
THE CHILD OF LIGHT...
...WILL HANDLE THIS!
NICHE!!!

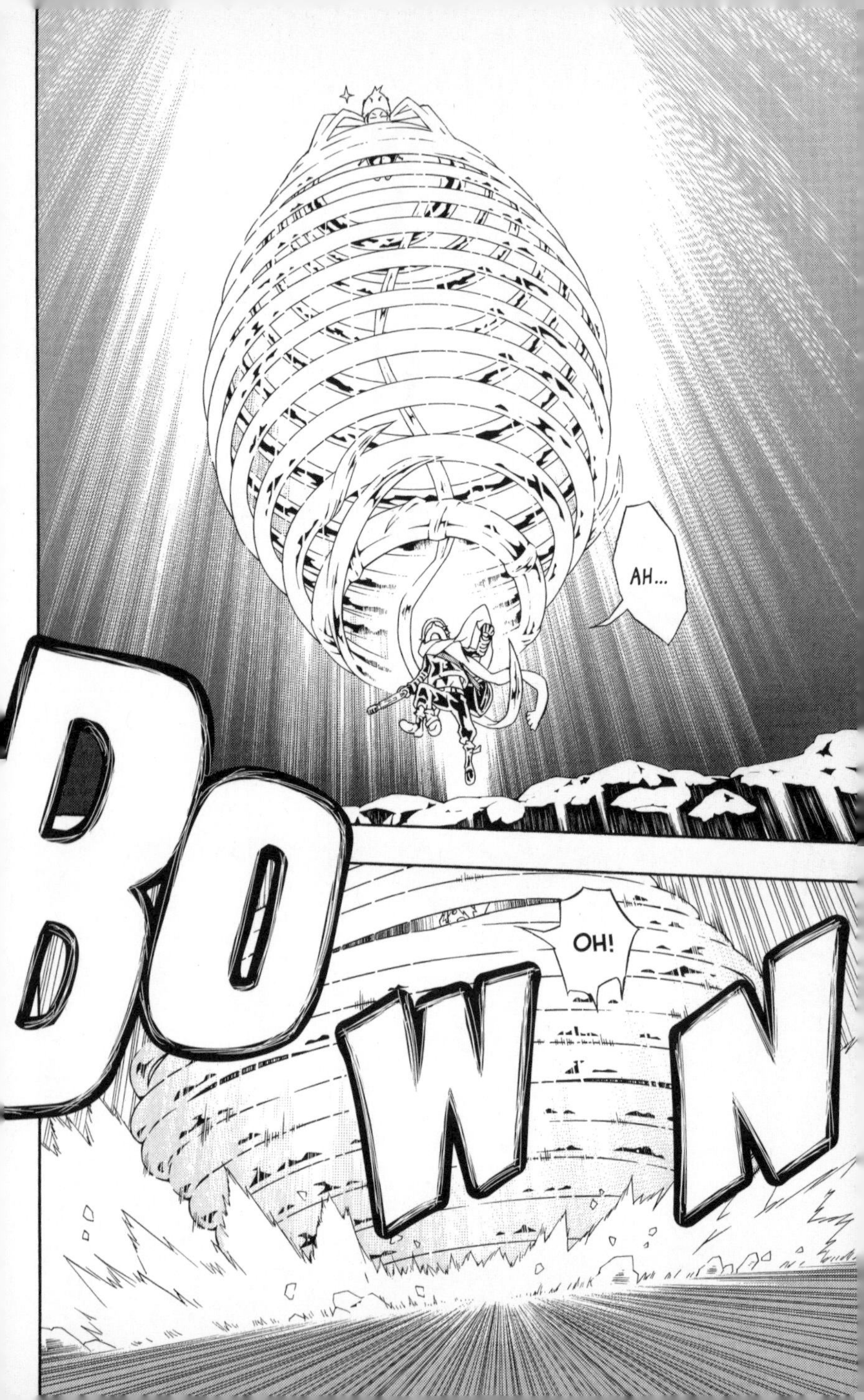
AH...
OH!
BOWN

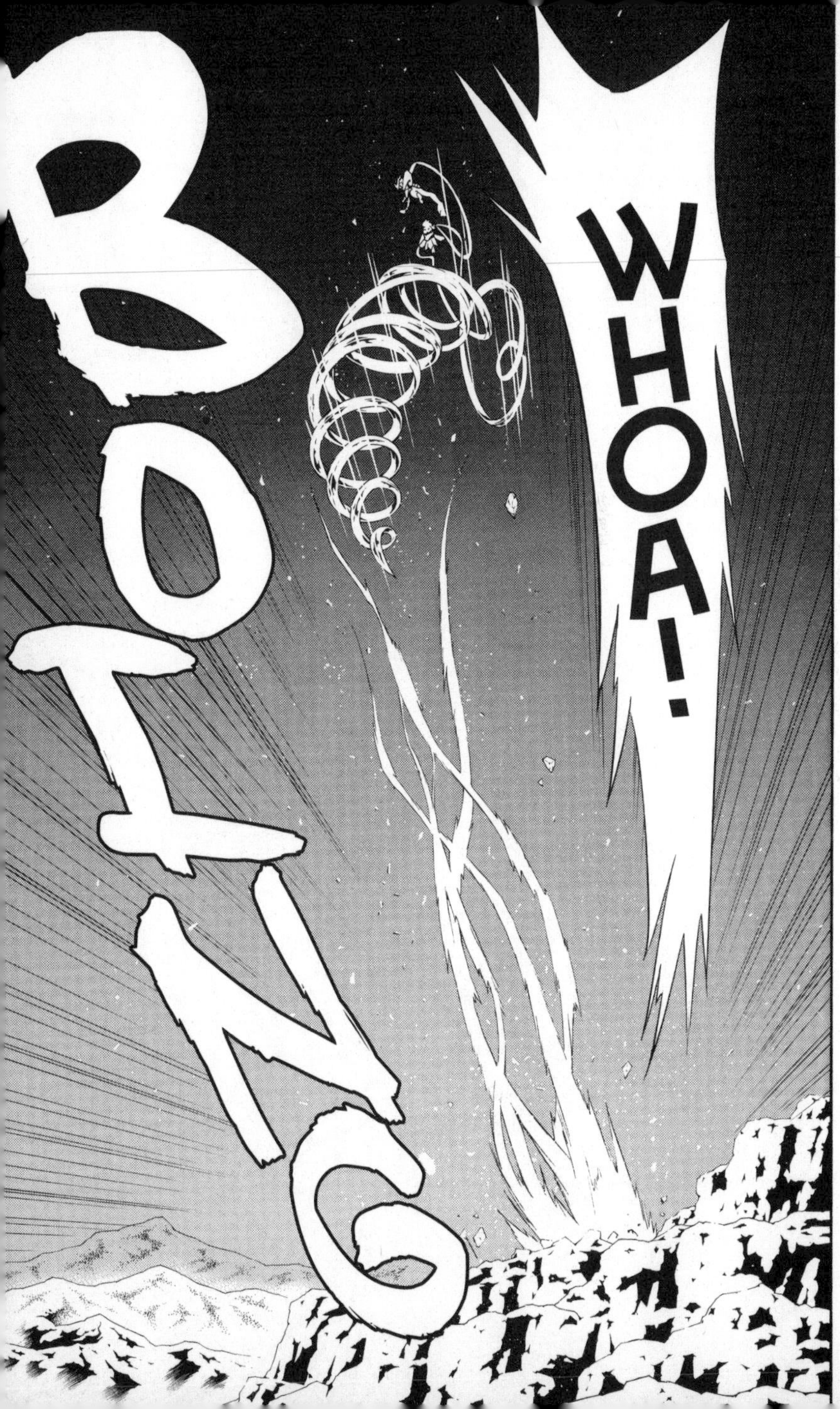
WHOA!
BOING

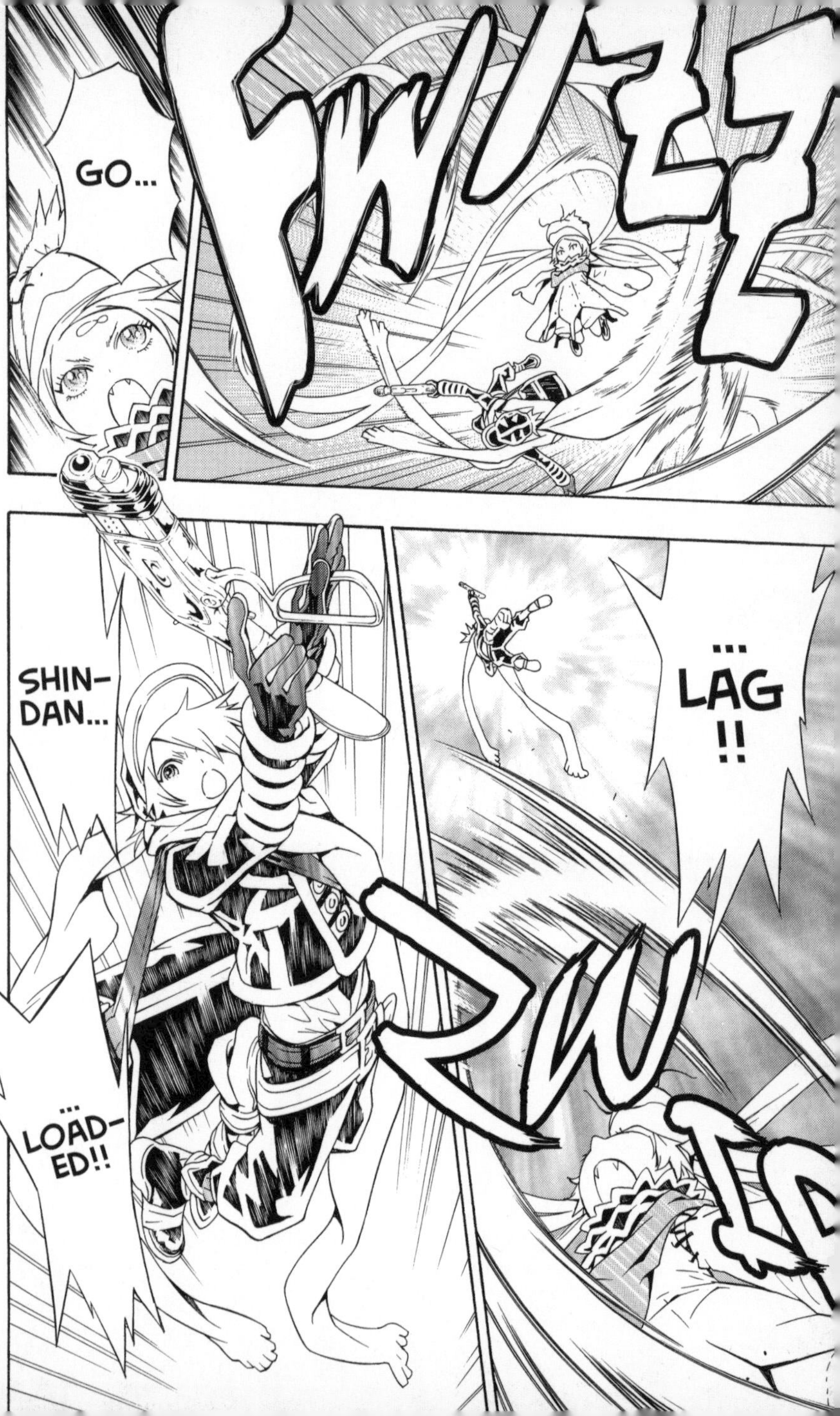
GO...
...LAG!!
SHIN-DAN...
...LOAD-ED!!

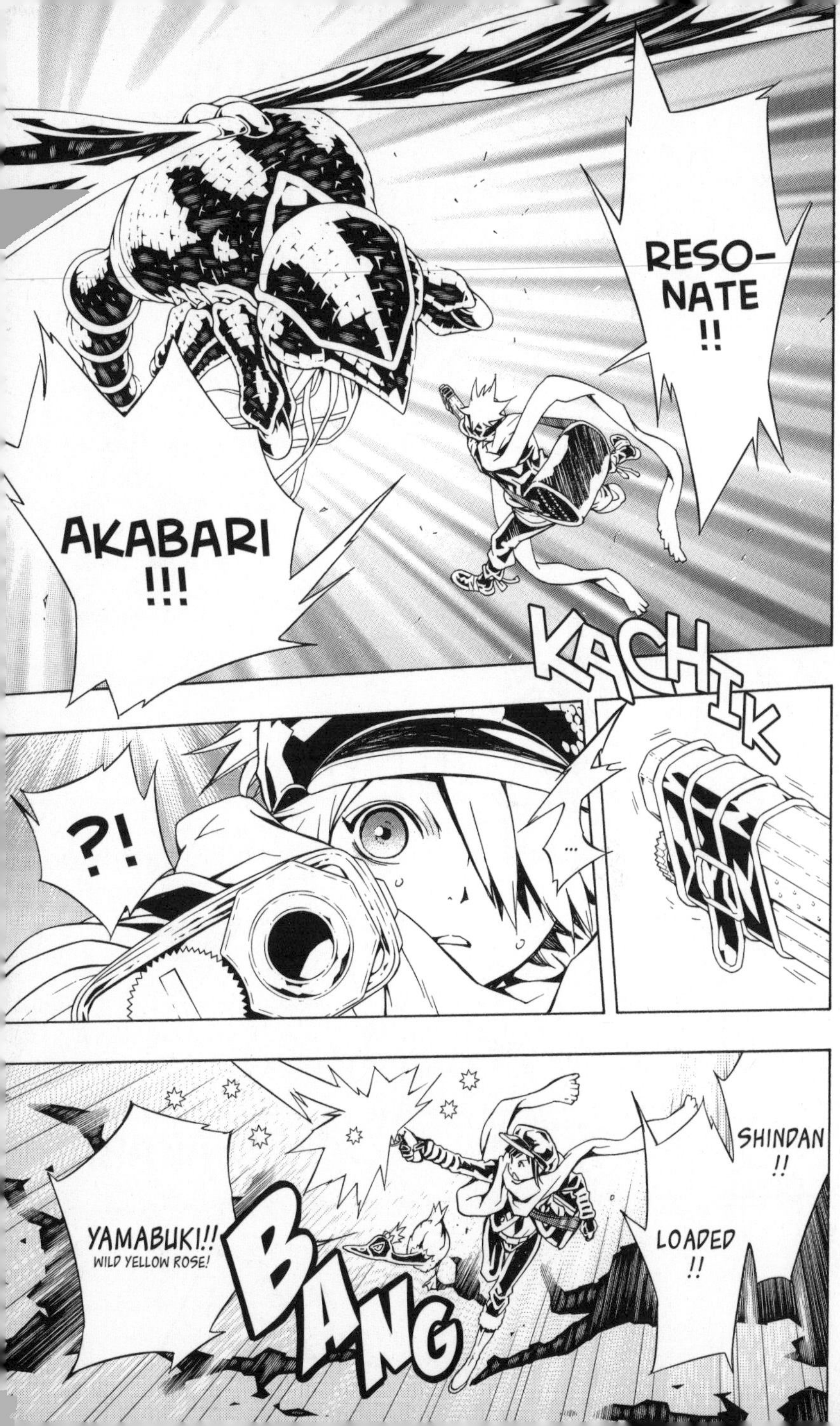
RESO-
NATE
!!
AKABARI
!!!
KACHIK
...
?!
SHINDAN
!!
LOADED
!!
BANG
YAMABUKI!!!
WILD YELLOW ROSE!

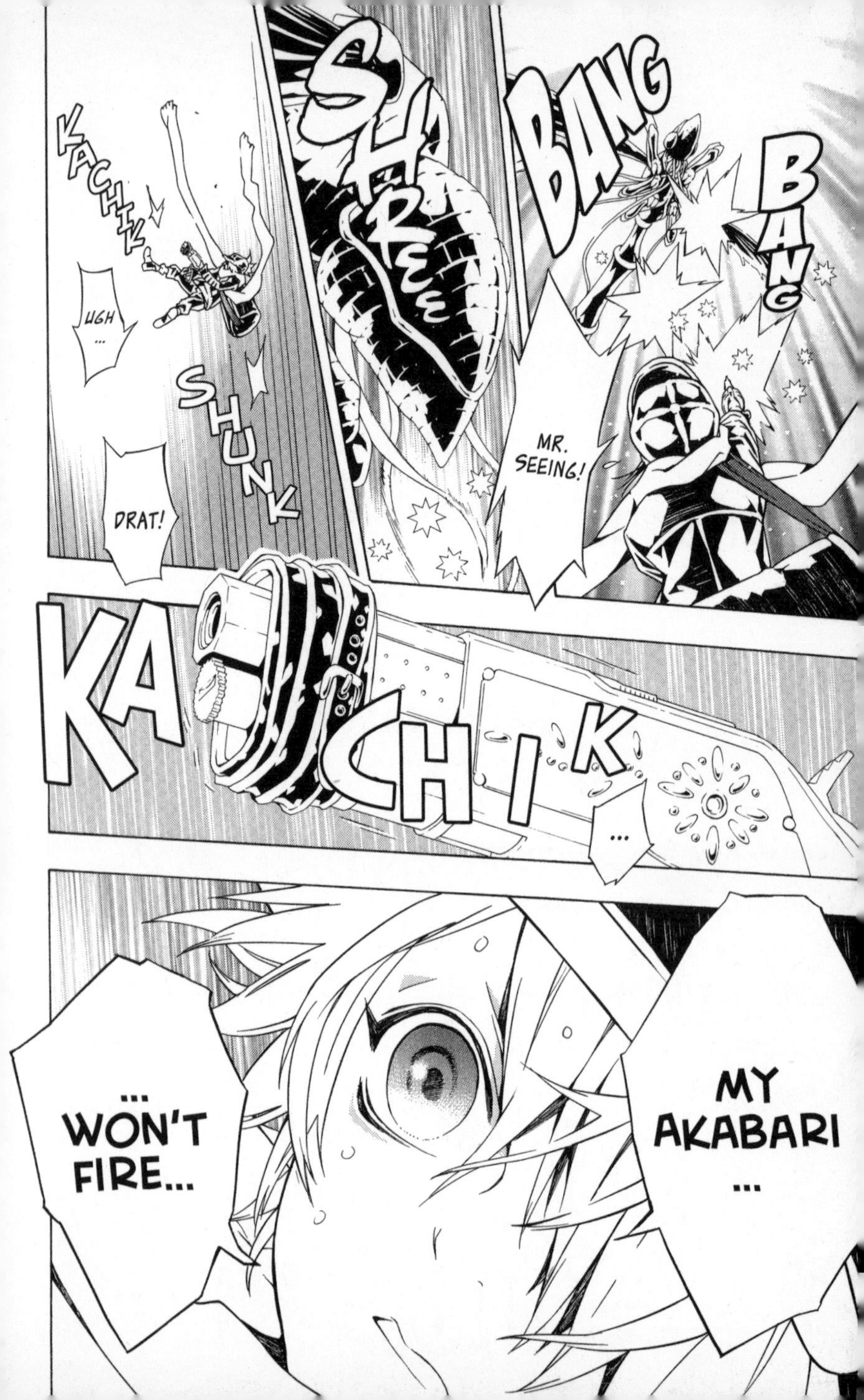
BANG
BANG
SHREE
MR. SEEING!
KACHIK
UGH ...
SHUNK
DRAT!
KACHIK
...
MY AKABARI ...
... WON'T FIRE...

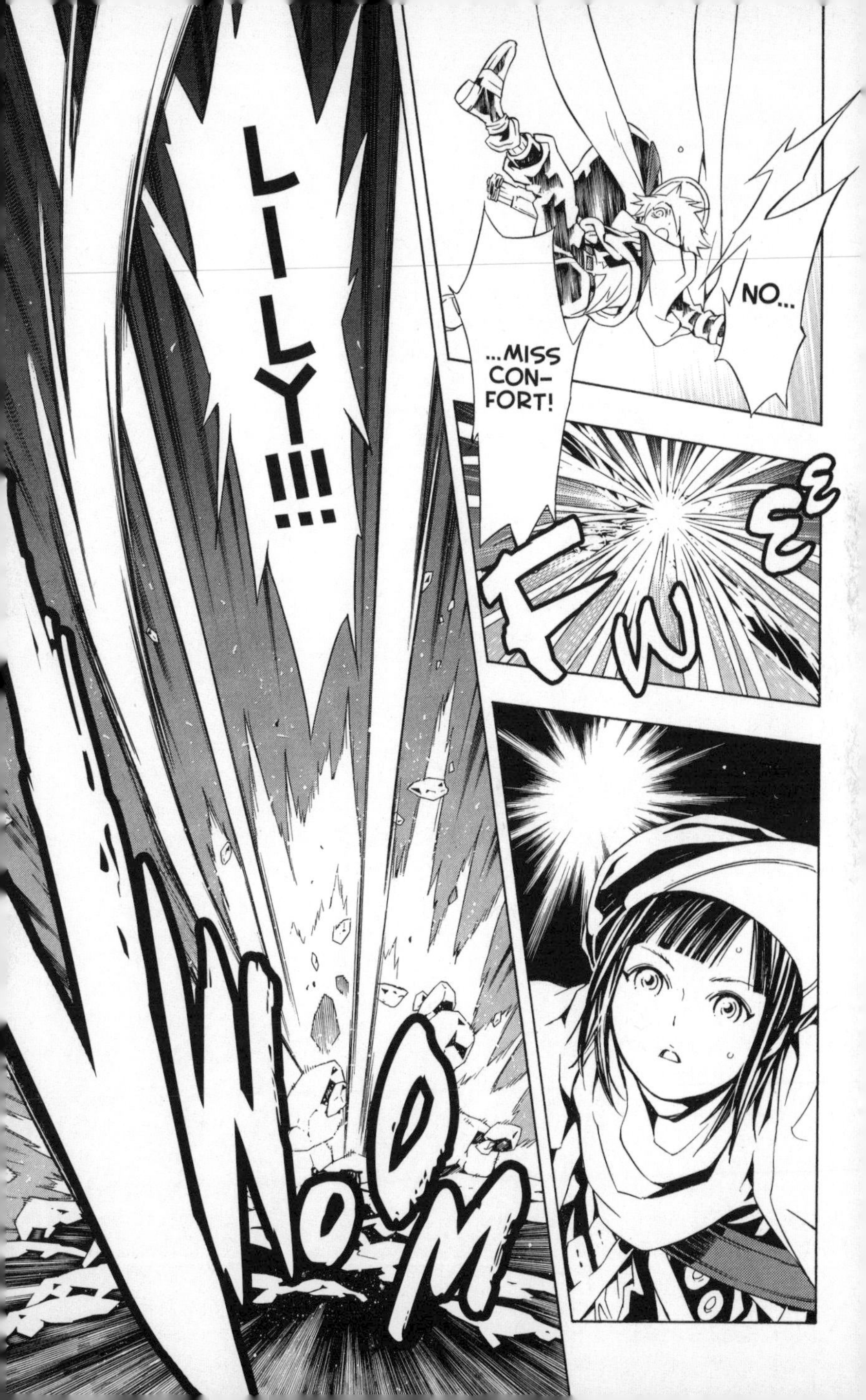
NO...
...MISS CON-FORT!
LILY!!!
WHOOM

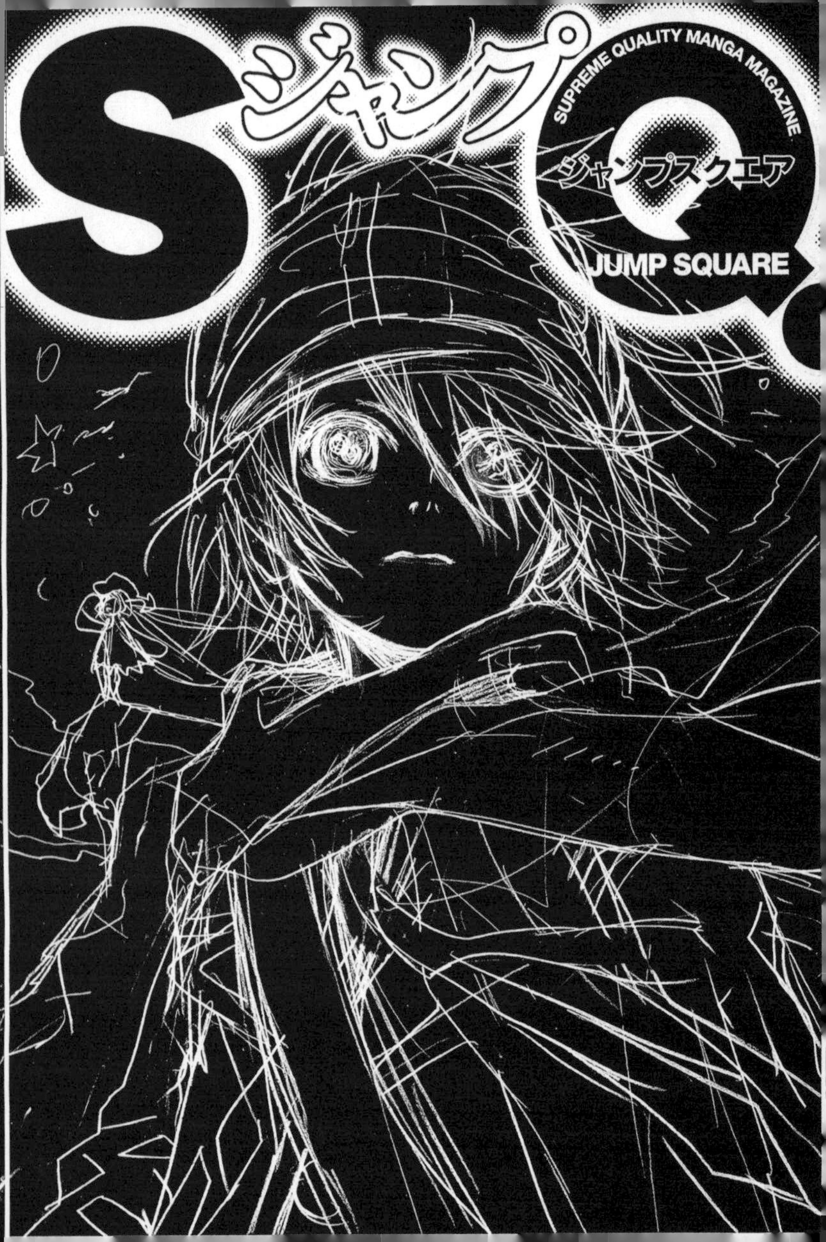
Sジャンプ
SUPREME QUALITY MANGA MAGAZINE
Q.
ジャンプスクエア
JUMP SQUARE

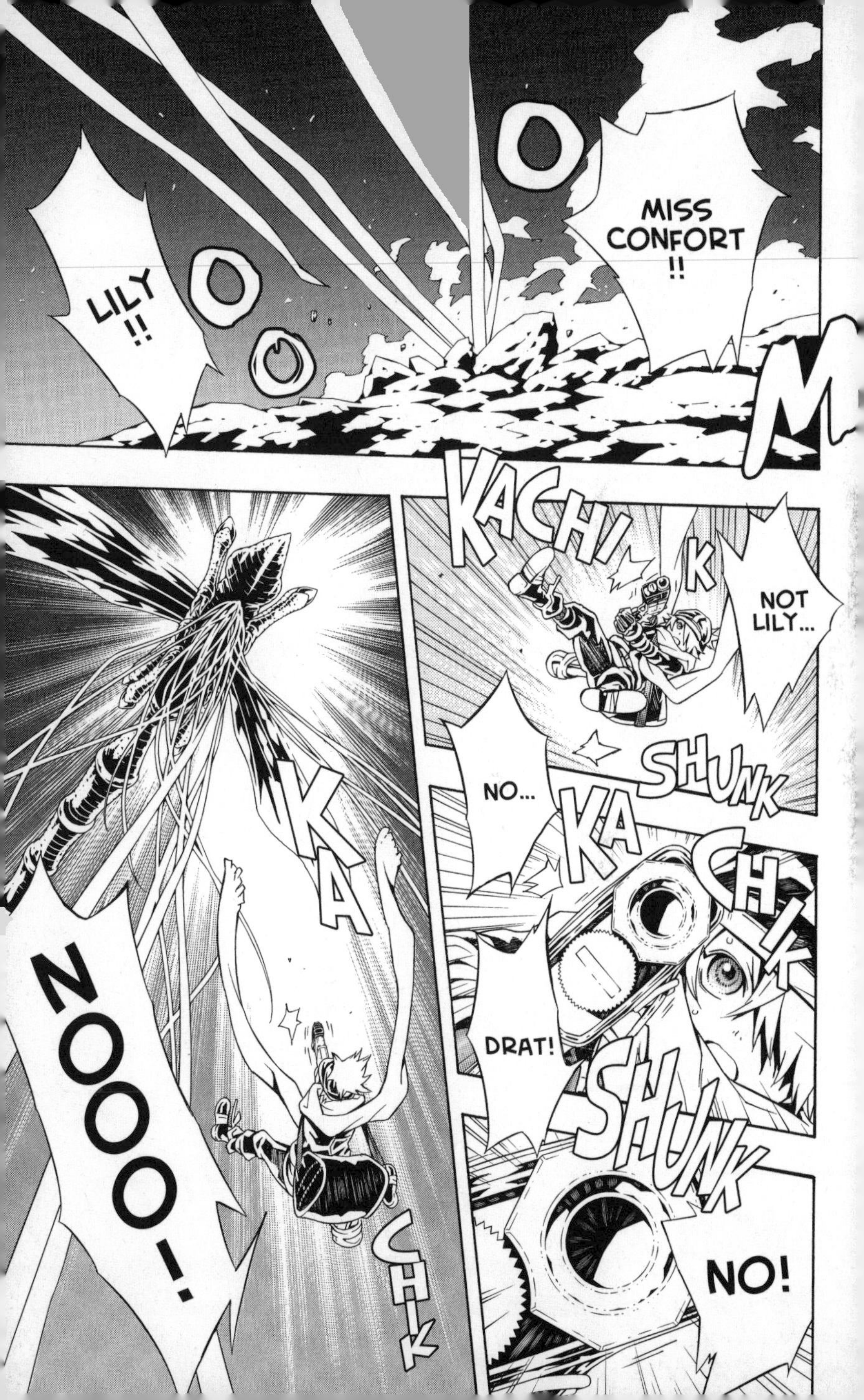
MISS CONFORT !!
LILY !!
KACHIK
NOT LILY...
NO...
SHUNK
KA CHIK
DRAT!
SHUNK
NO!
KA
CHIK
NOOO!!

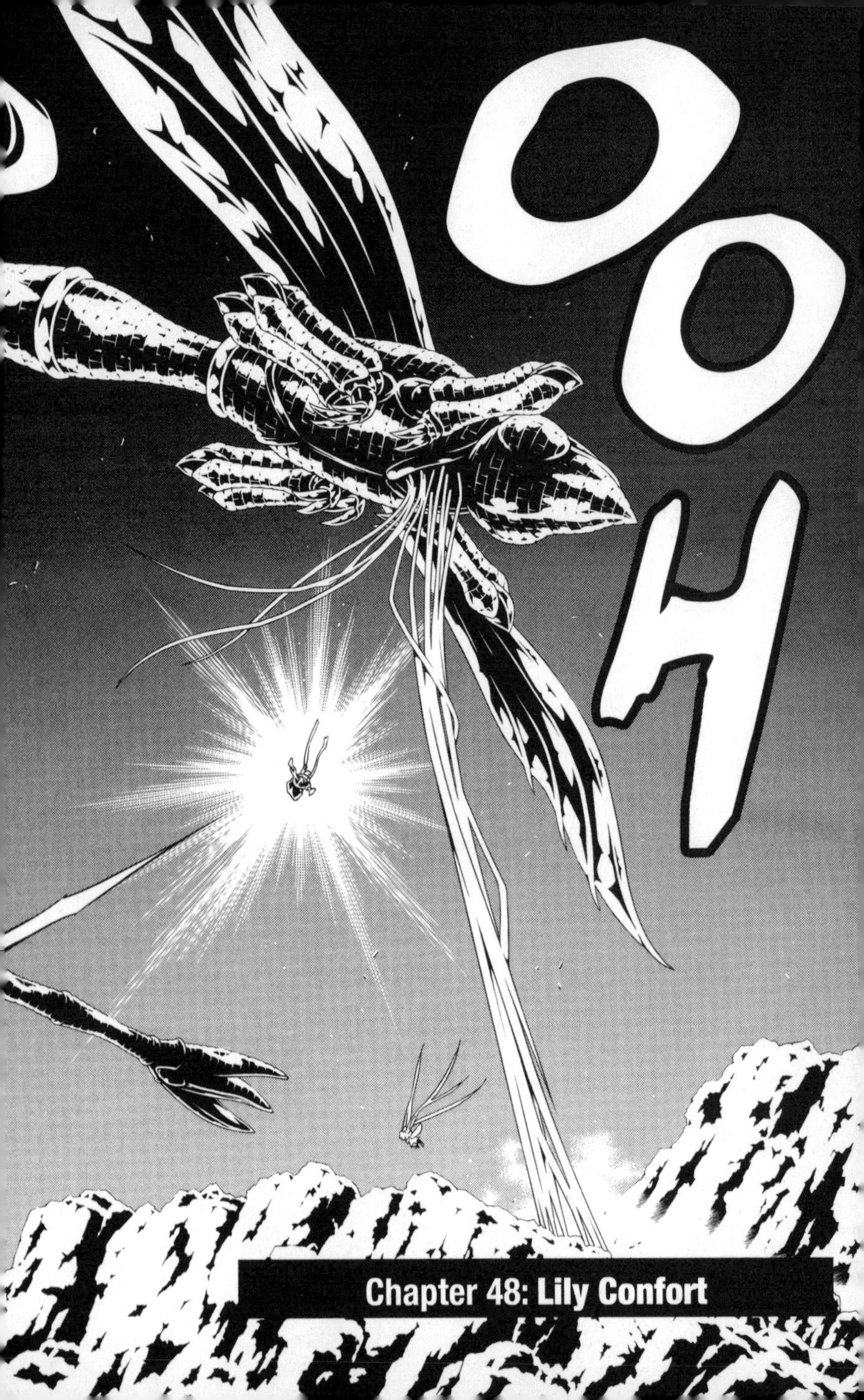
OOH

Chapter 48: Lily Confort

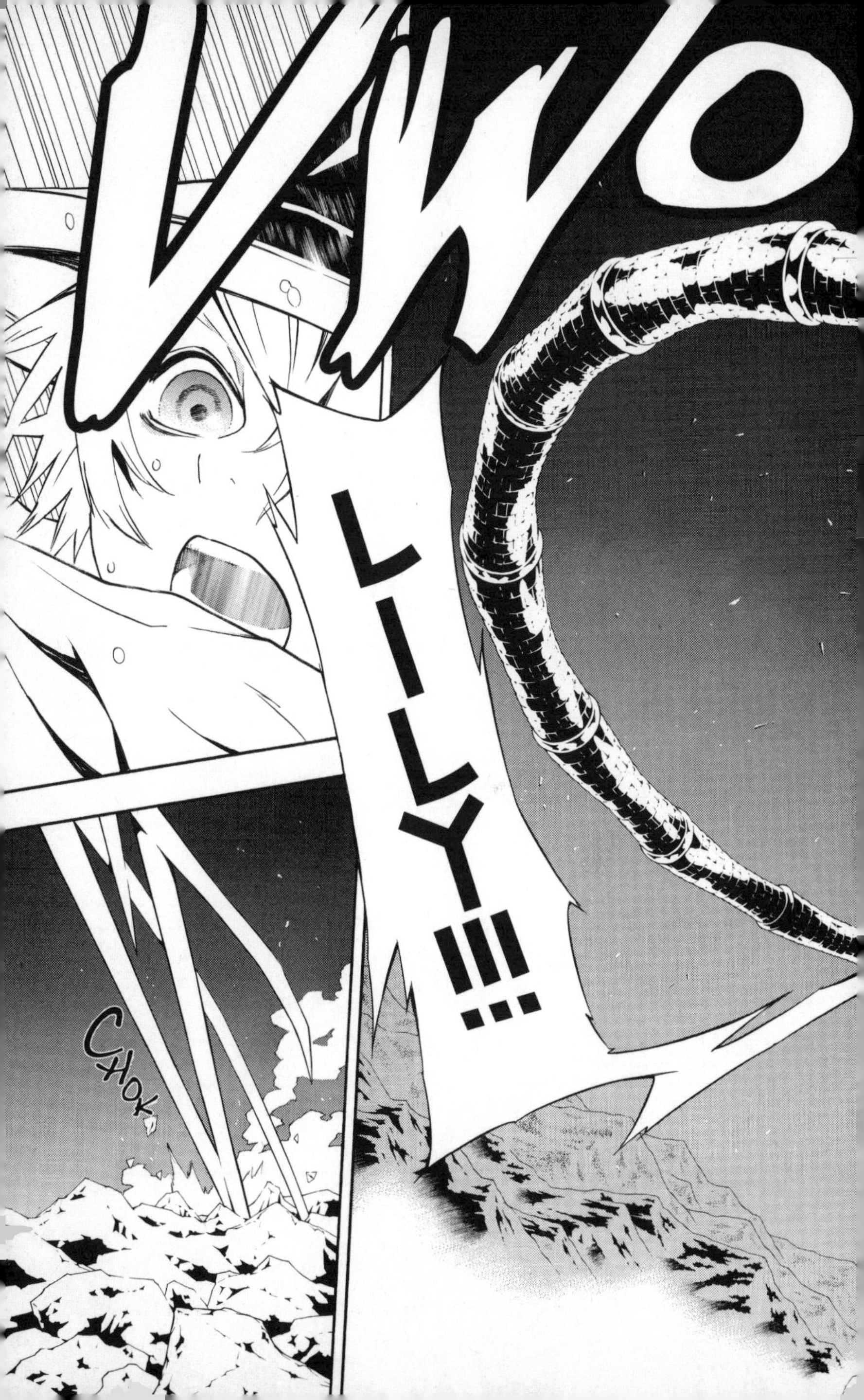
VWO
LILLY!!!
CHOK

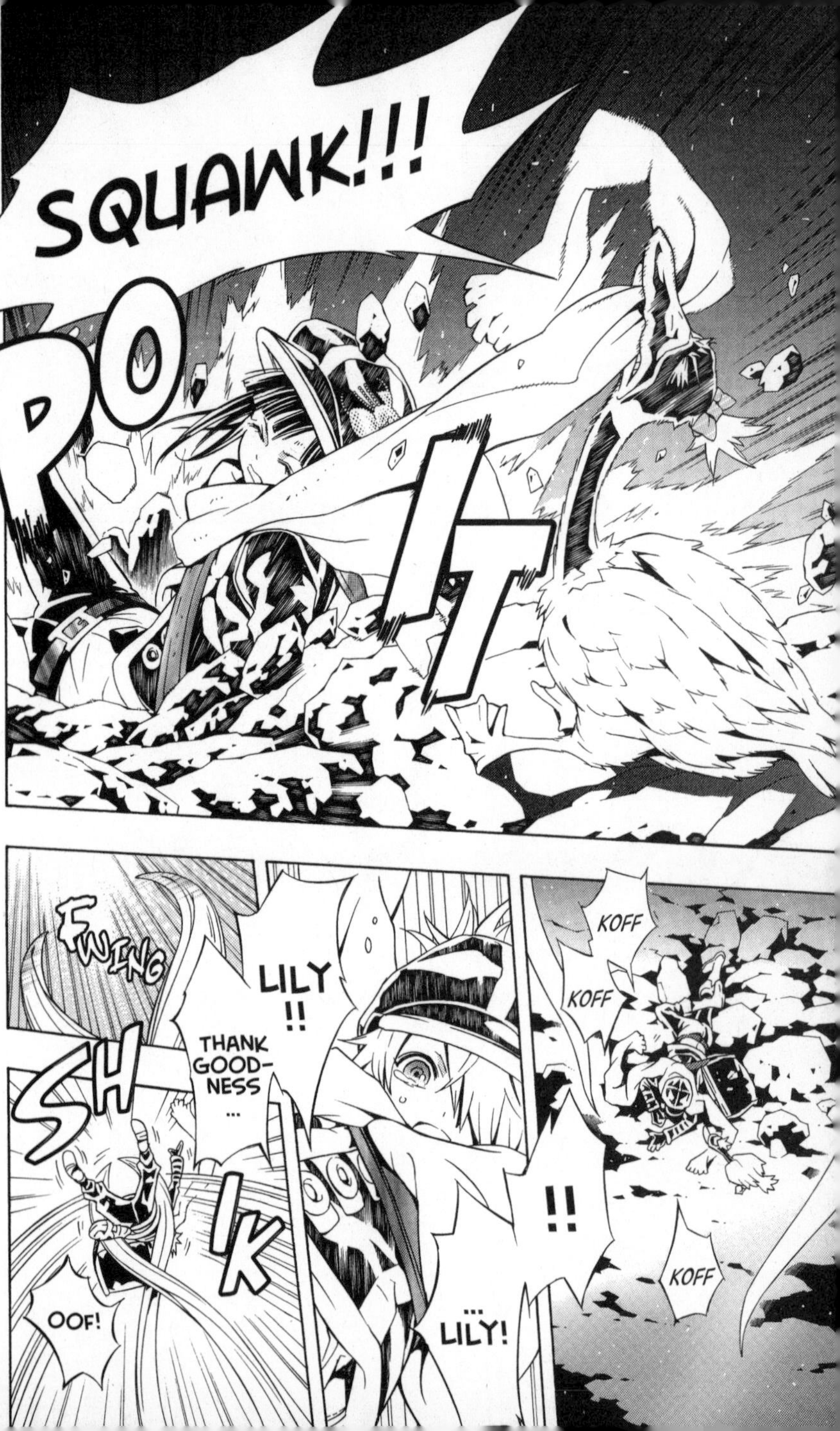
SQUAWK!!!
PO
IT
KOFF
KOFF
LILY !!
THANK GOODNESS ...
FWING
SH
IK
!!
KOFF
... LILY!
OOF!

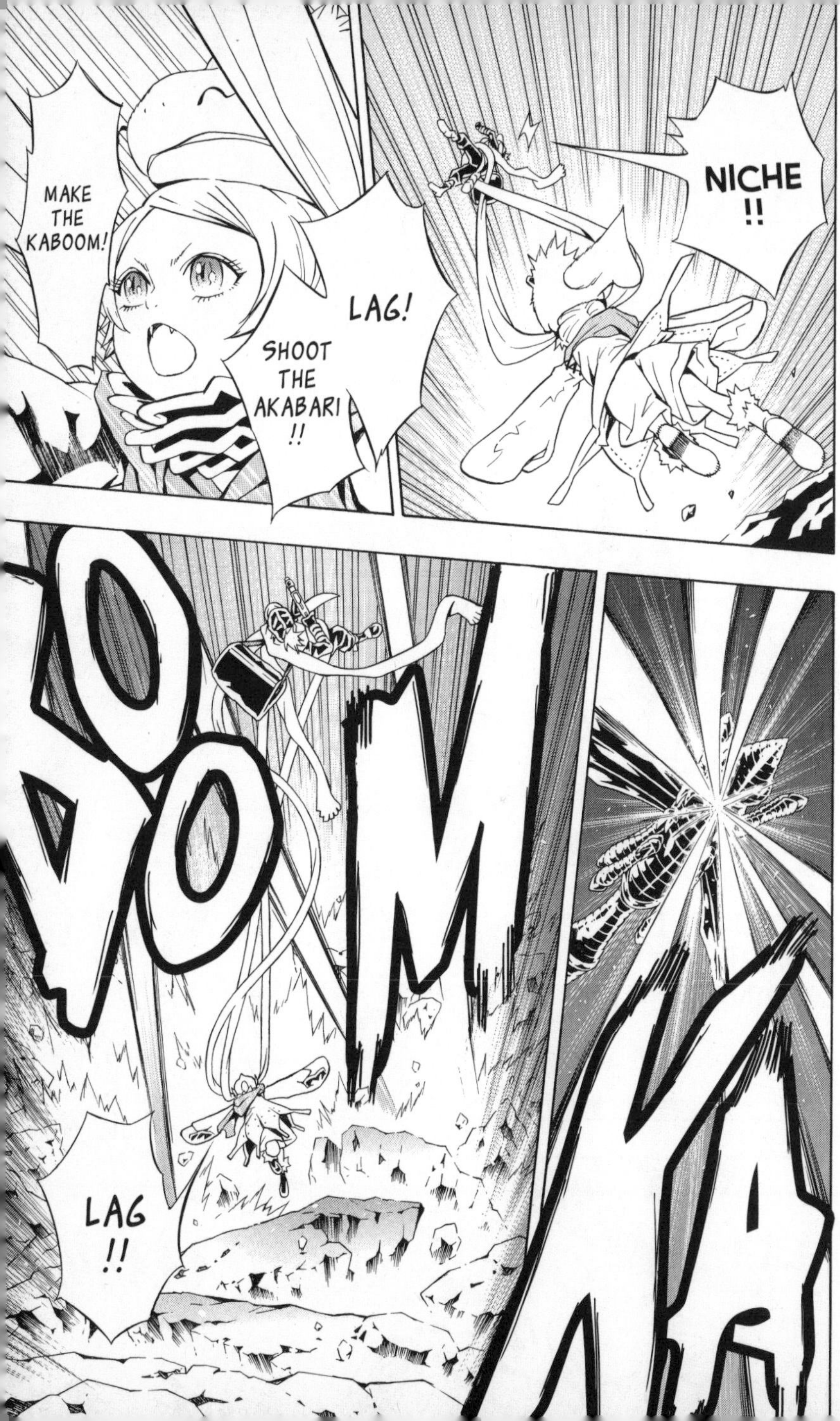
NICHE !!
LAG!
SHOOT THE AKABARI !!
MAKE THE KABOOM!
DOOM
LAG !!

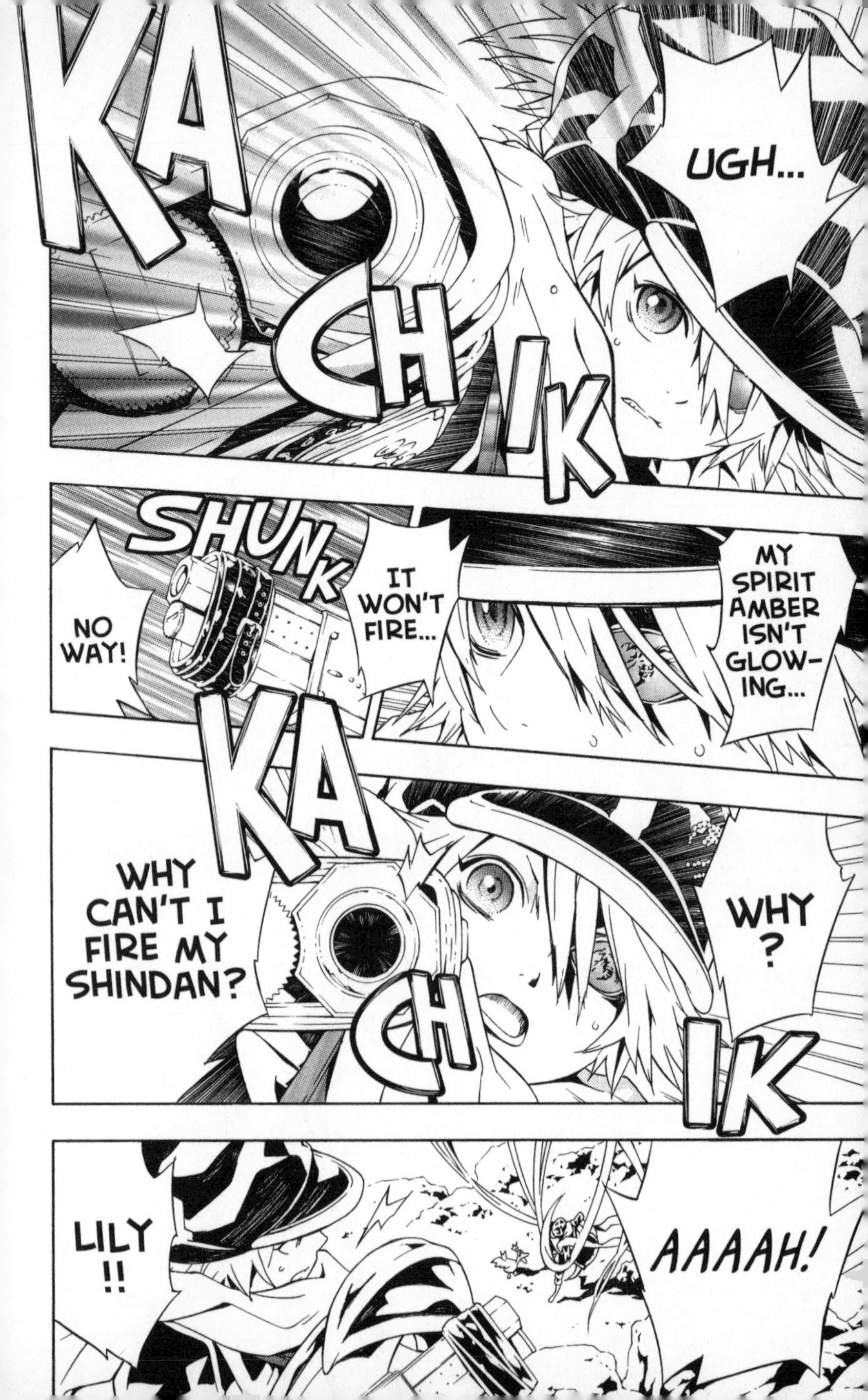
UGH...
KACHIK
MY SPIRIT AMBER ISN'T GLOWING...
IT WON'T FIRE...
SHUNK
NO WAY!
WHY?
KACHIK
WHY CAN'T I FIRE MY SHINDAN?
AAAAH!
LILY !!

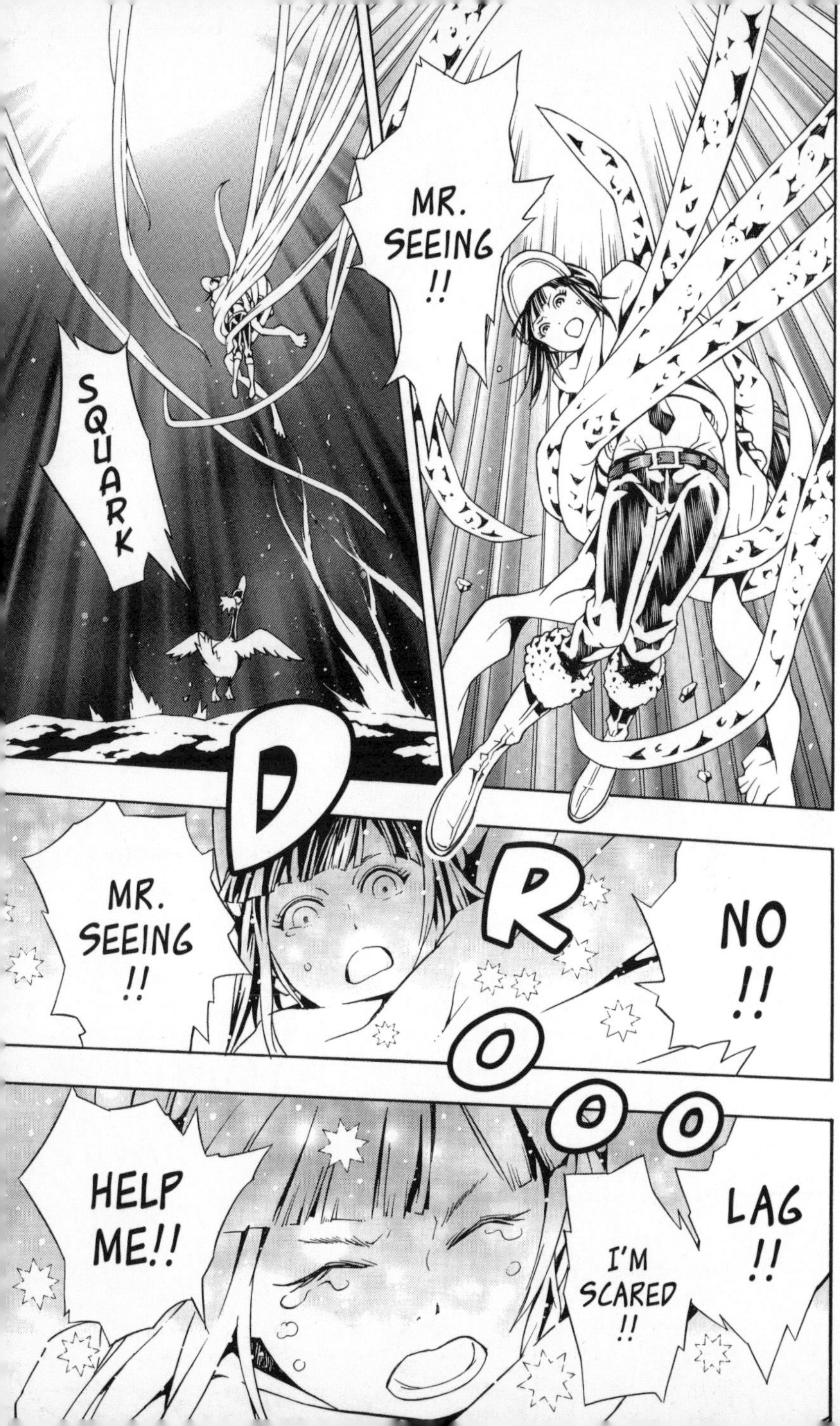
MR. SEEING !!
SQUARK
DROOOO
NO !!
MR. SEEING !!
LAG !!
I'M SCARED !!
HELP ME!!

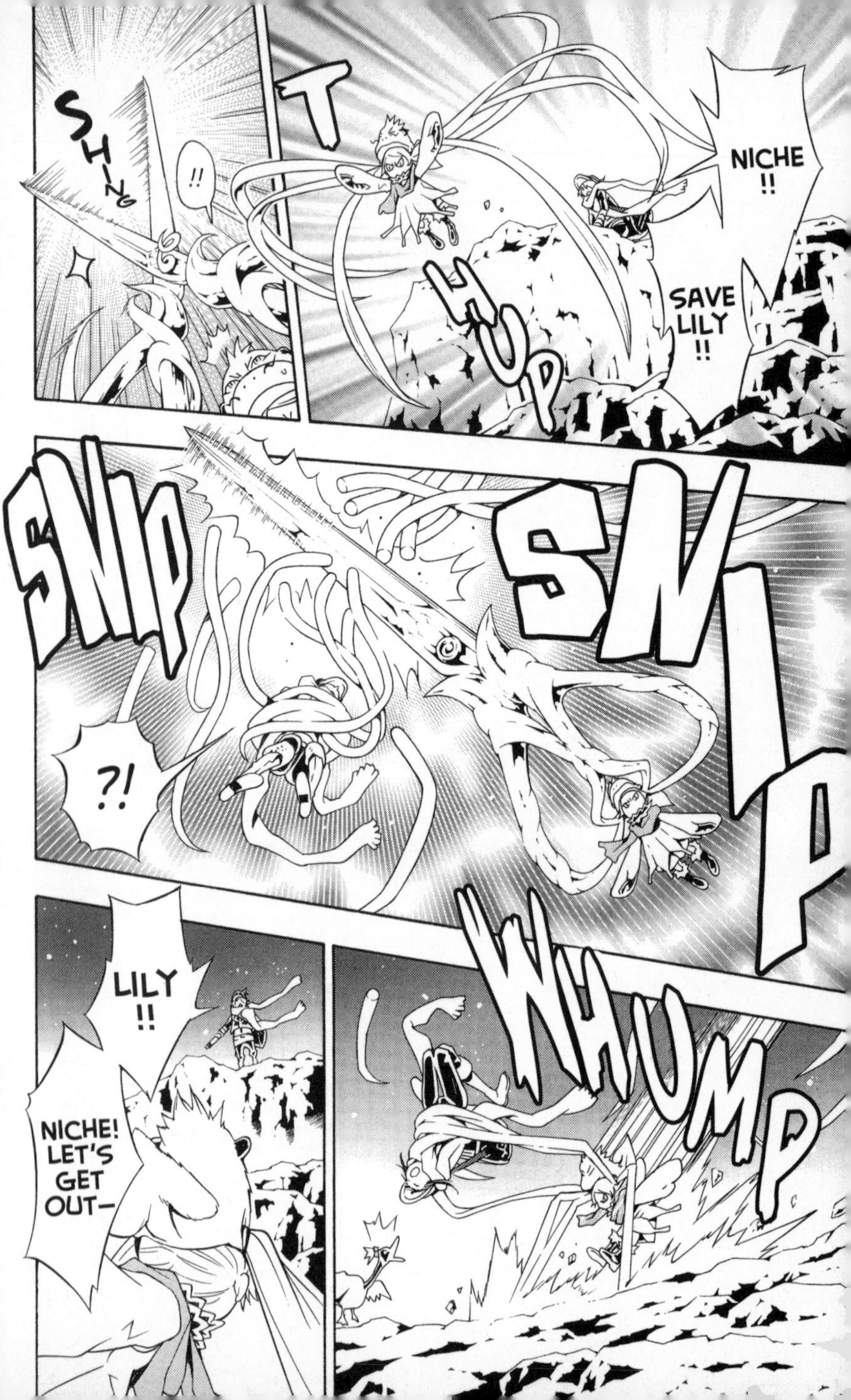
T
NICHE !!
SAVE LILY !!
HUP
SHING
!!
SNIP
SNIP
?!
WHUMP
LILY !!
NICHE! LET'S GET OUT—

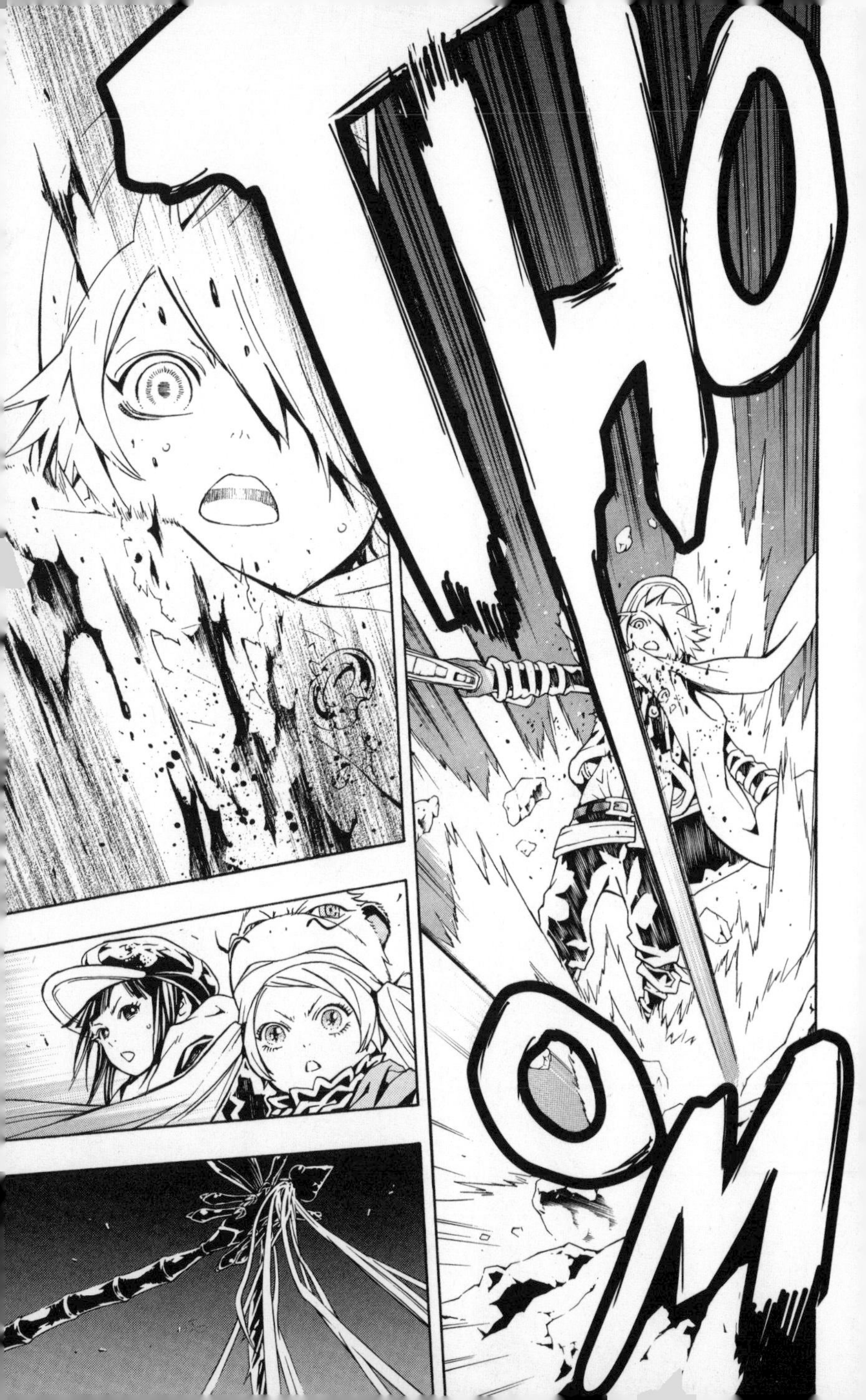
WHOOM

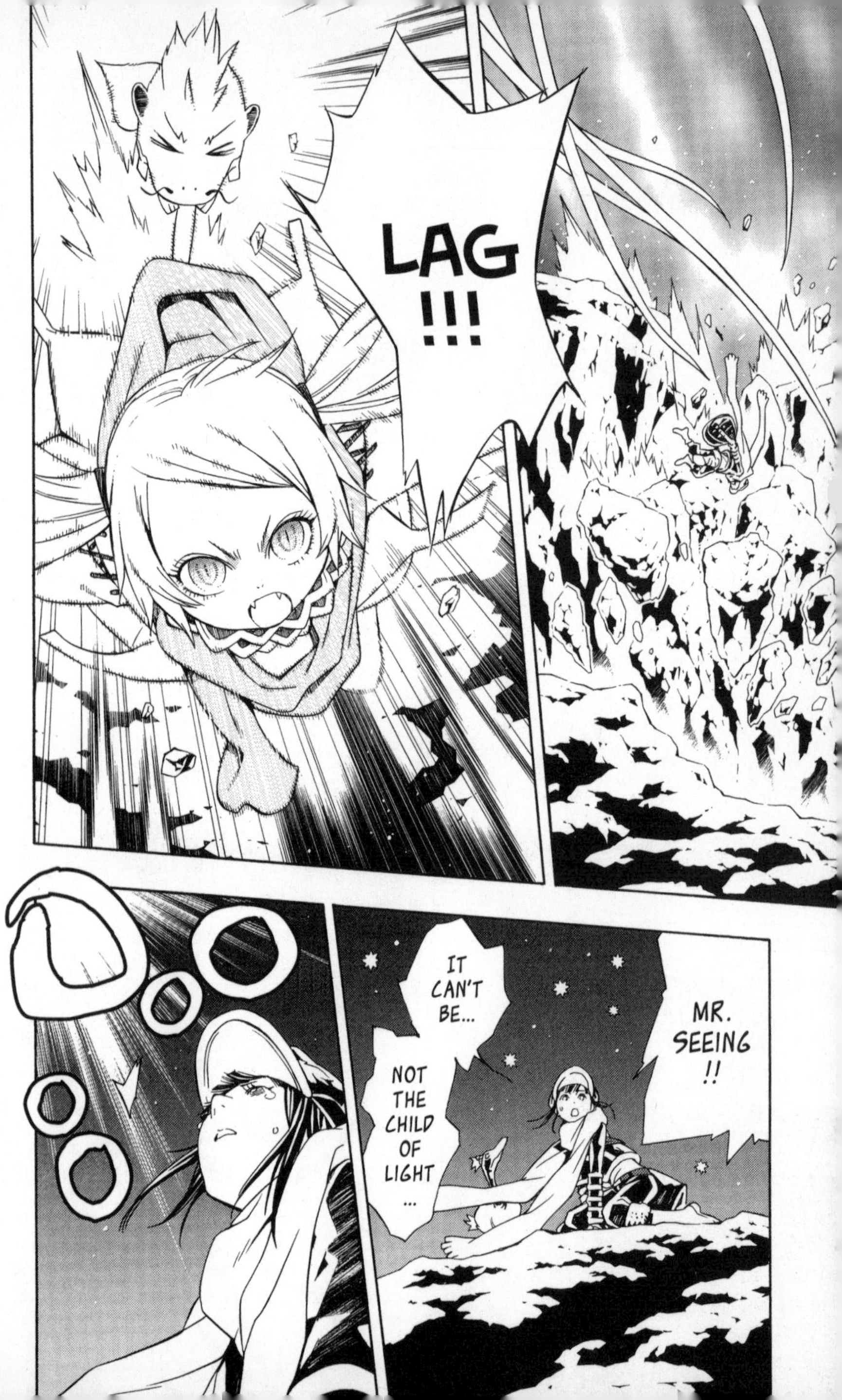
LAG !!!
MR. SEEING !!
IT CAN'T BE...
NOT THE CHILD OF LIGHT ...

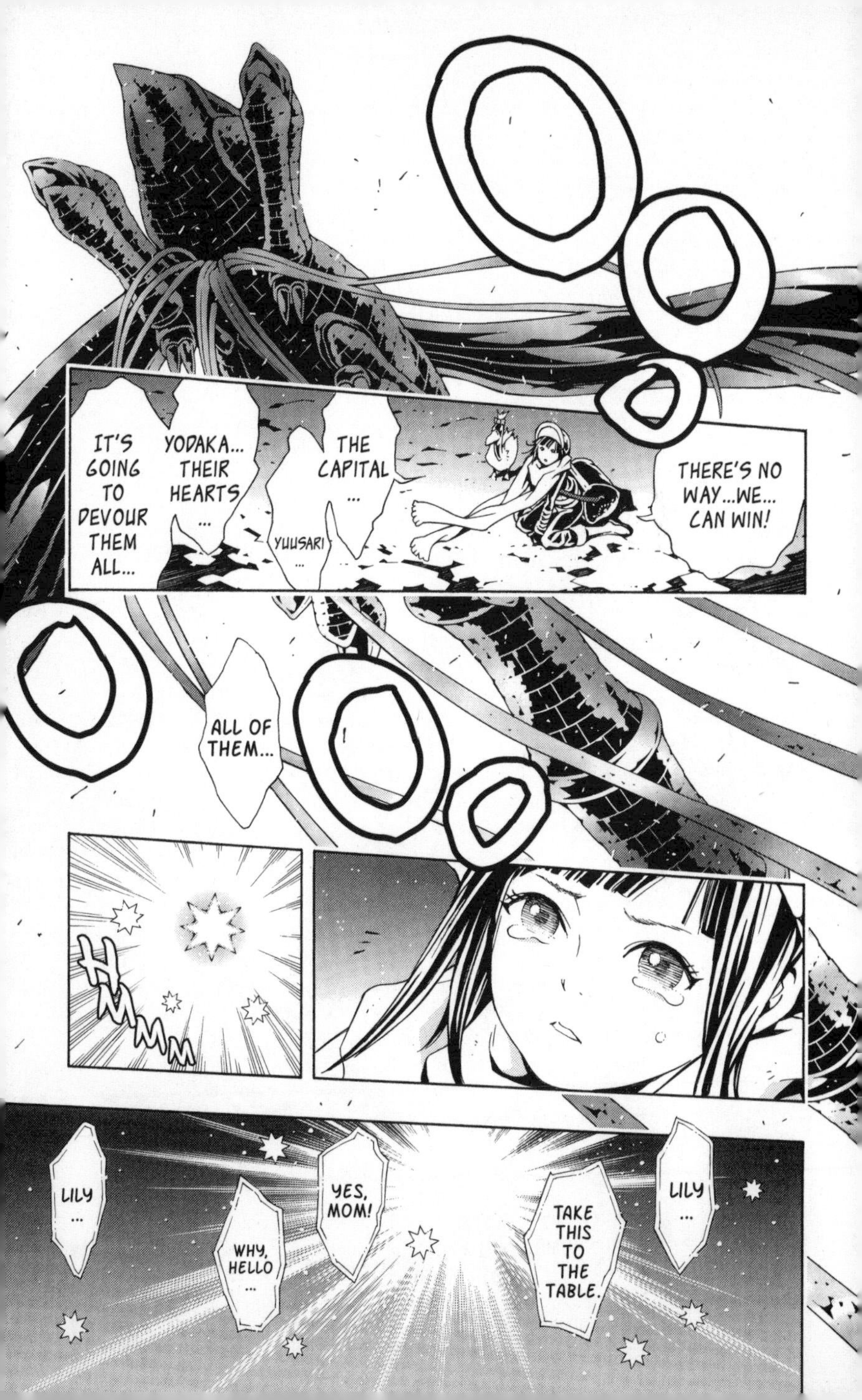
THERE'S NO WAY...WE... CAN WIN!
THE CAPITAL...
YUUSARI...
YODAKA... THEIR HEARTS...
IT'S GOING TO DEVOUR THEM ALL...
!
ALL OF THEM...
HMMMM
LILY...
TAKE THIS TO THE TABLE.
YES, MOM!
WHY, HELLO...
LILY...

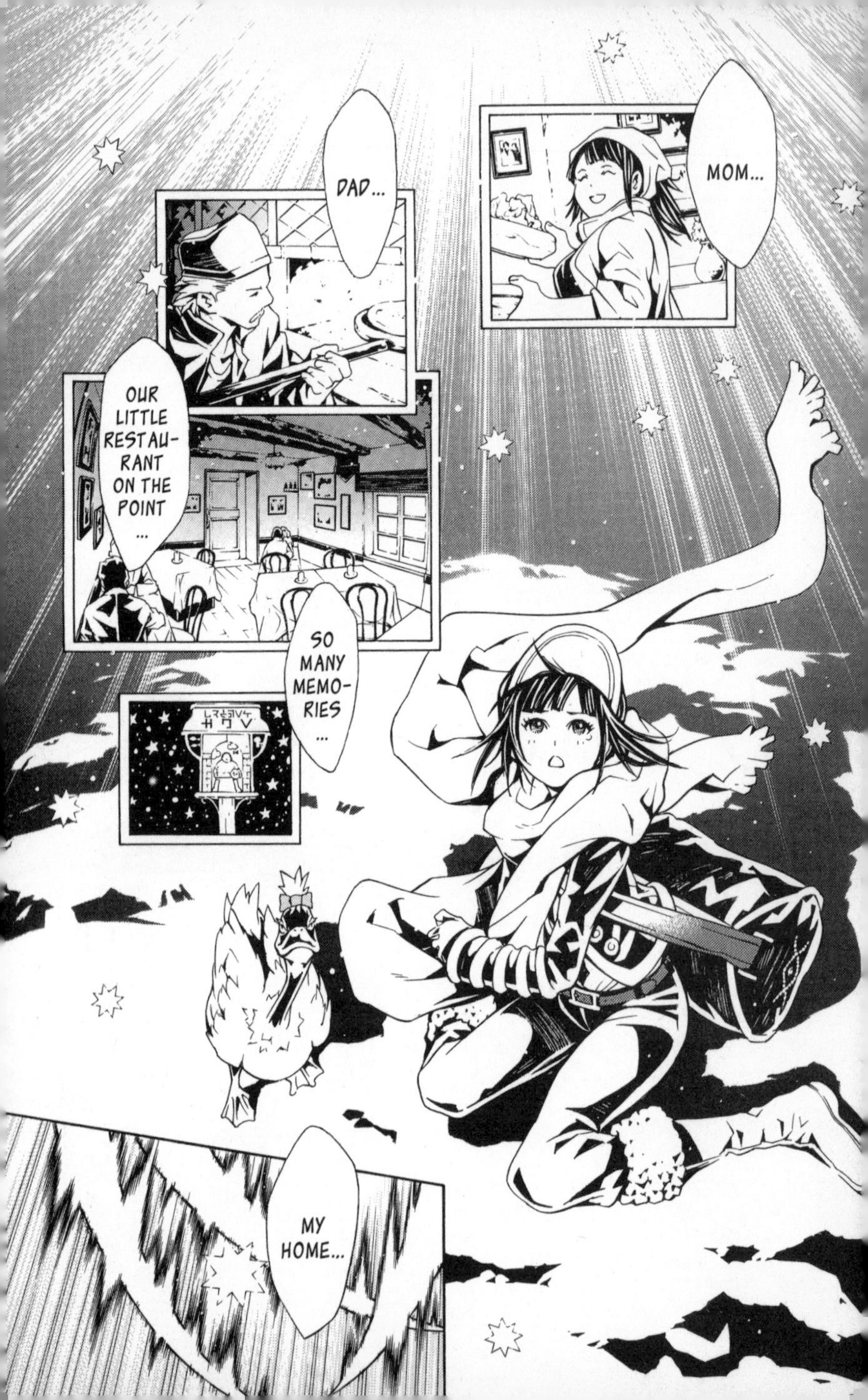
MOM...
DAD...
OUR LITTLE RESTAURANT ON THE POINT...
SO MANY MEMORIES...
MY HOME...

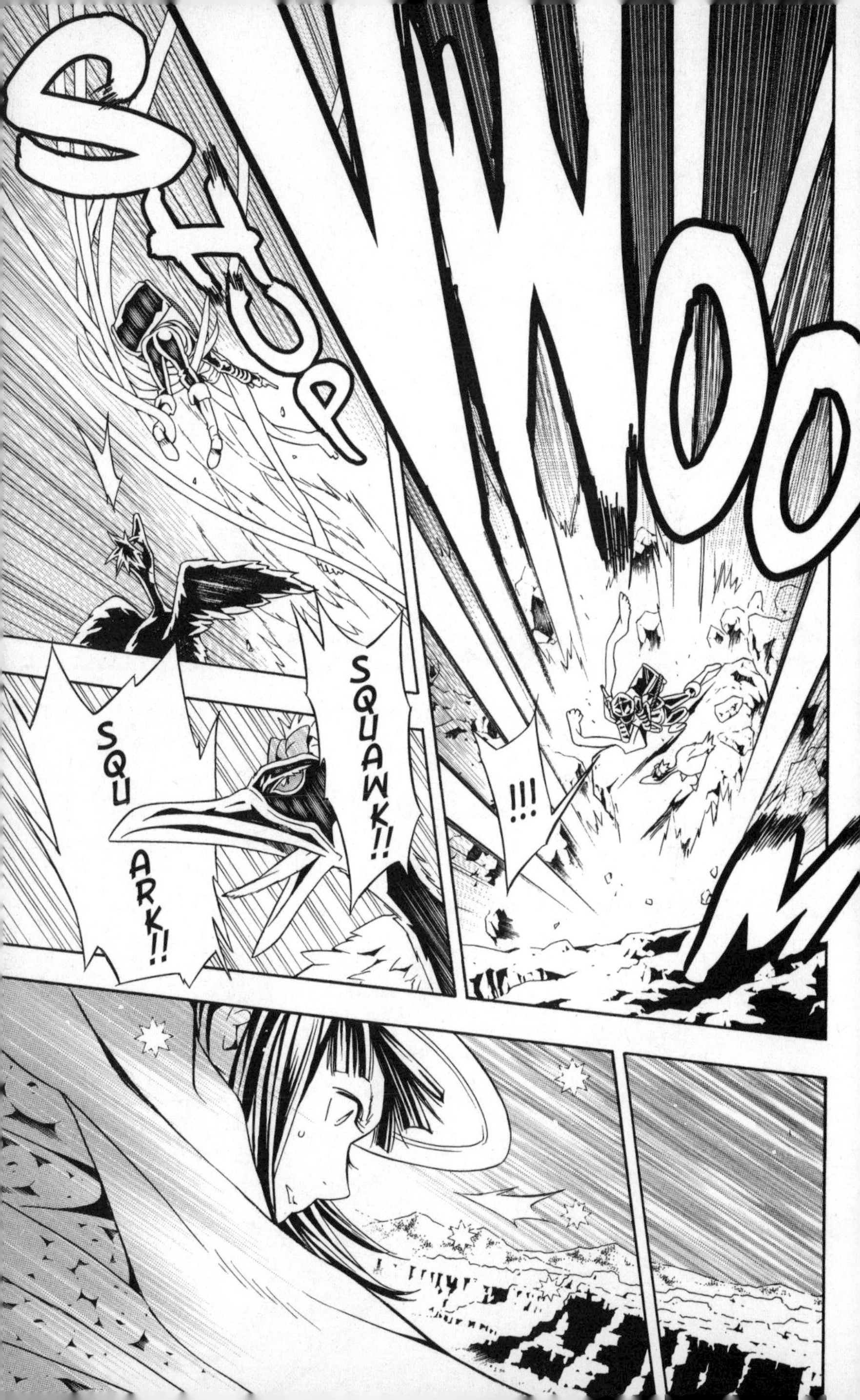
WHOOM
SHUP
!!!
SQUAWK!!
SQU
ARK!!

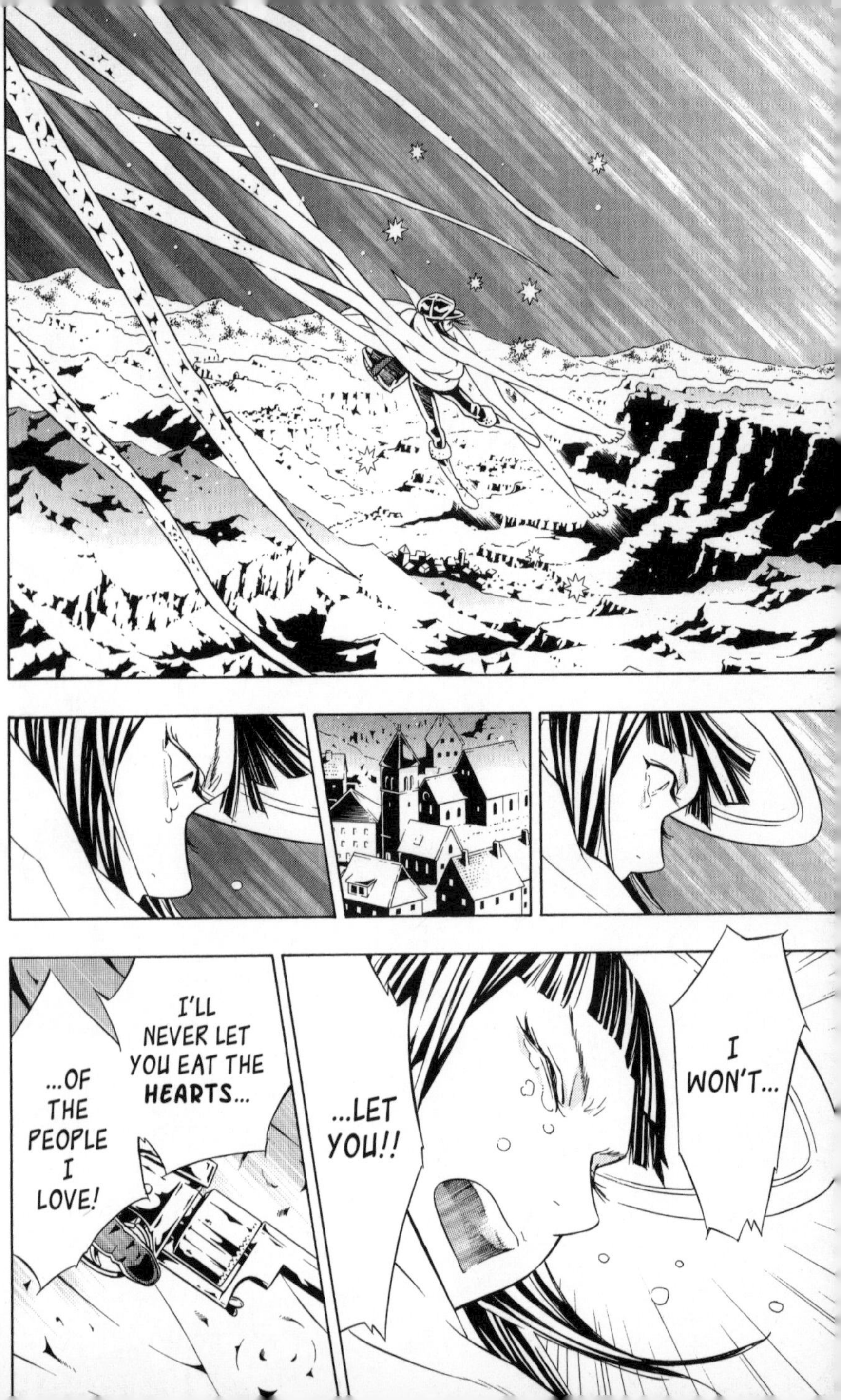
I WON'T...
...LET YOU!!
I'LL NEVER LET YOU EAT THE **HEARTS**...
...OF THE PEOPLE I LOVE!

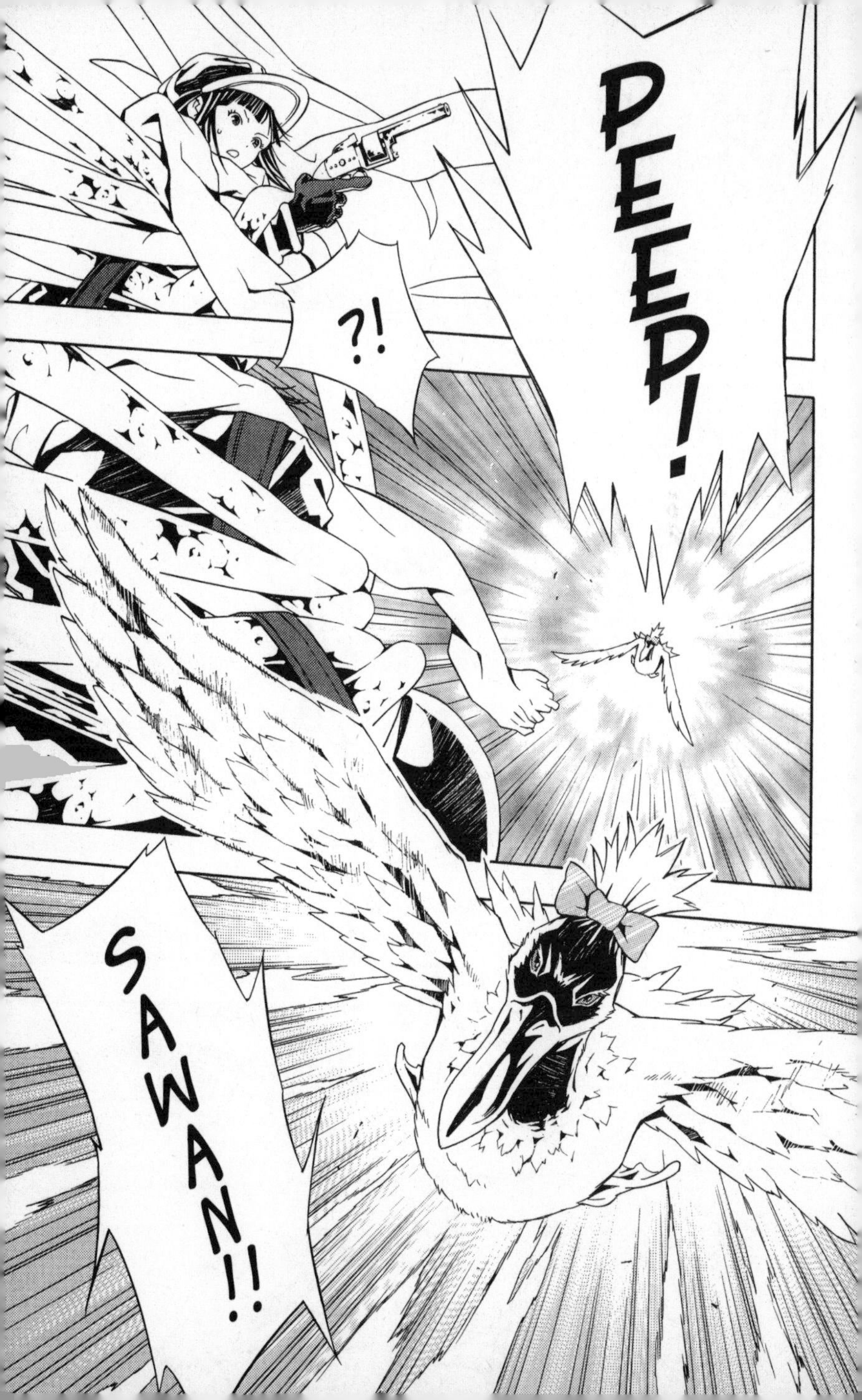

PEEEP!
?!
SAWAN!!

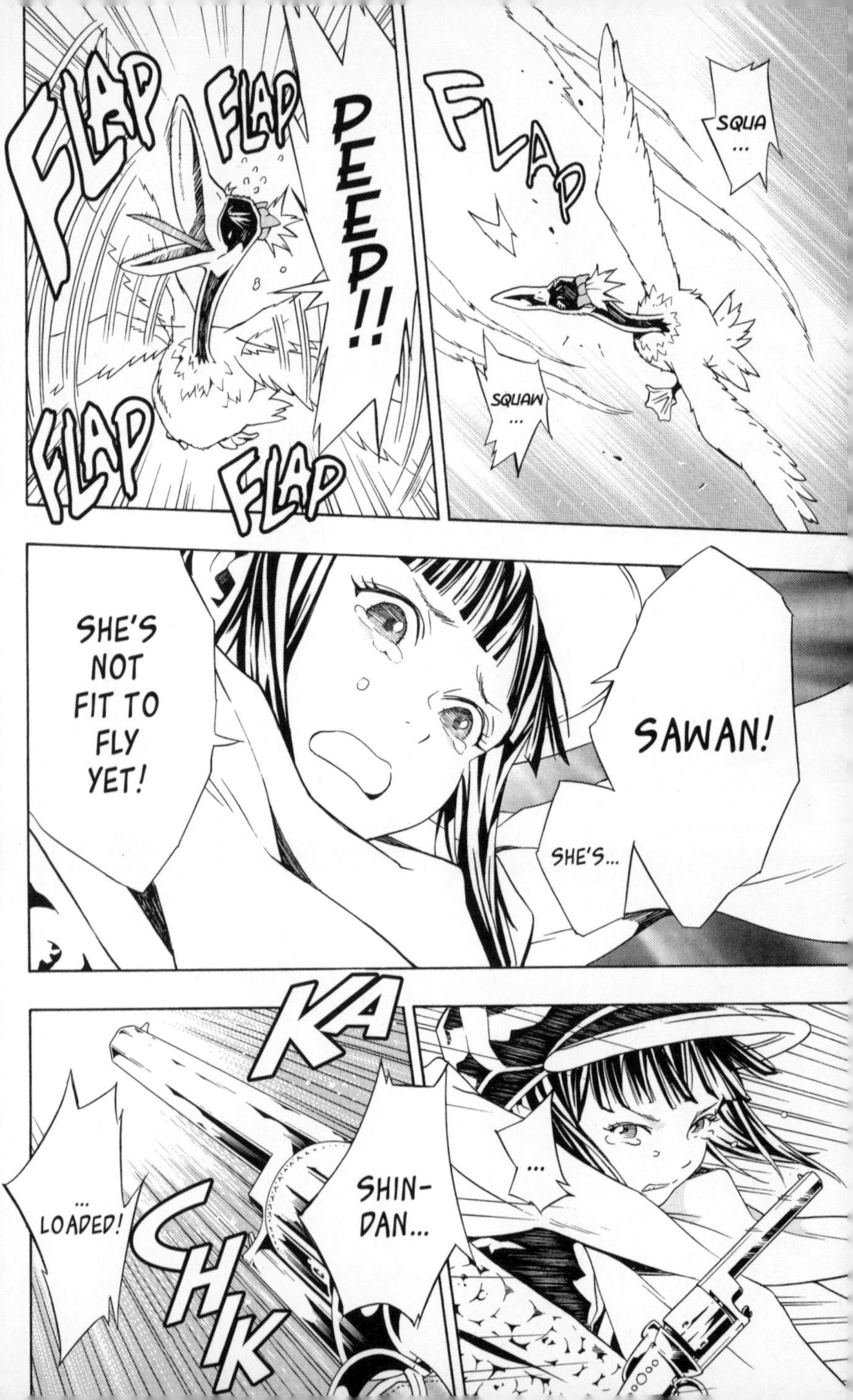
SQUA...
FLAP
SQUAW...
PEEEP!!
FLAP
FLAP
FLAP
FLAP
SAWAN!
SHE'S...
SHE'S NOT FIT TO FLY YET!
KA
...
SHIN-DAN...
CHIK
... LOADED!

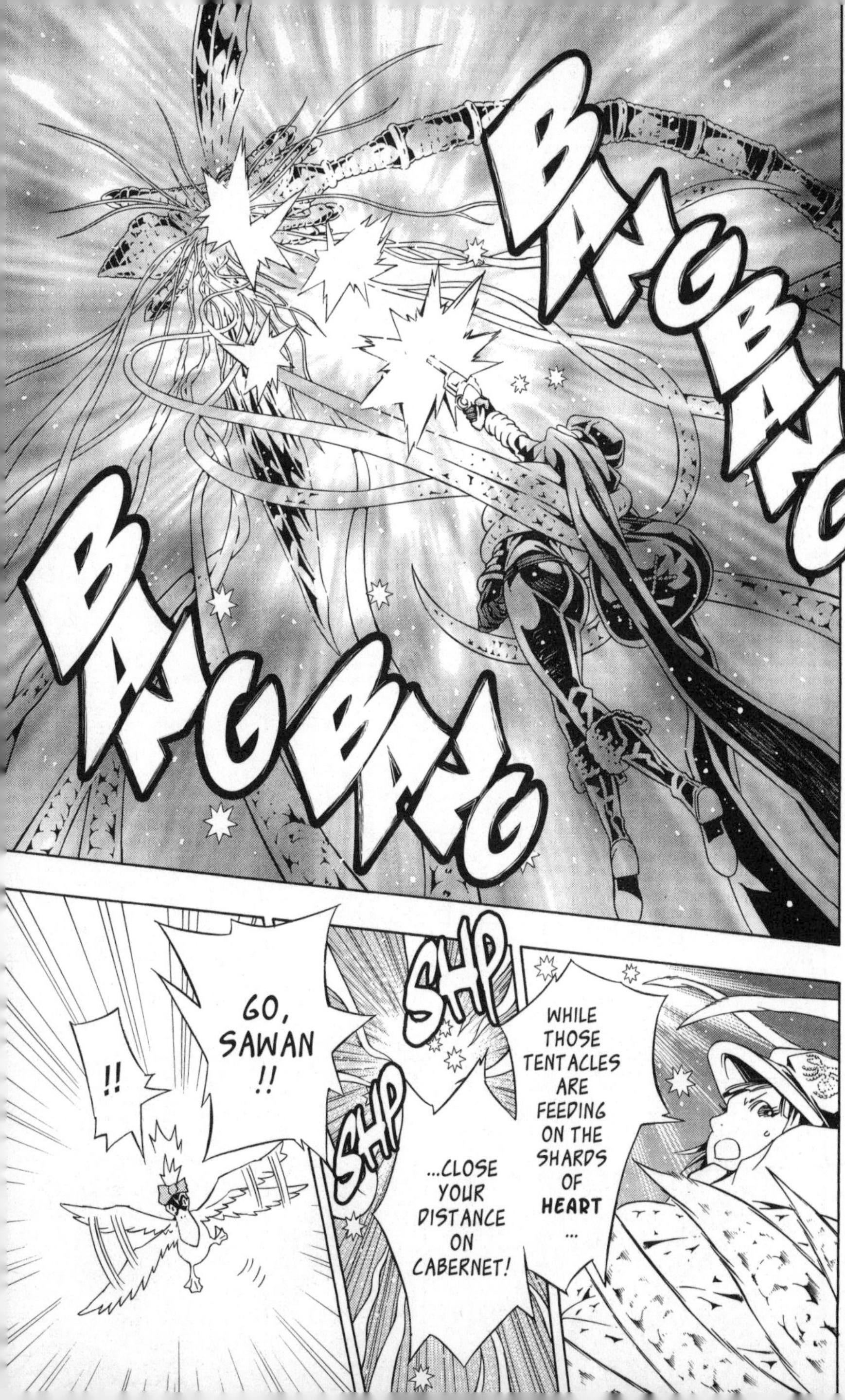
BANGBANG
BANGBANG
SHP
SHP
SHP
WHILE THOSE TENTACLES ARE FEEDING ON THE SHARDS OF **HEART**...
...CLOSE YOUR DISTANCE ON CABERNET!
GO, SAWAN!!
!!

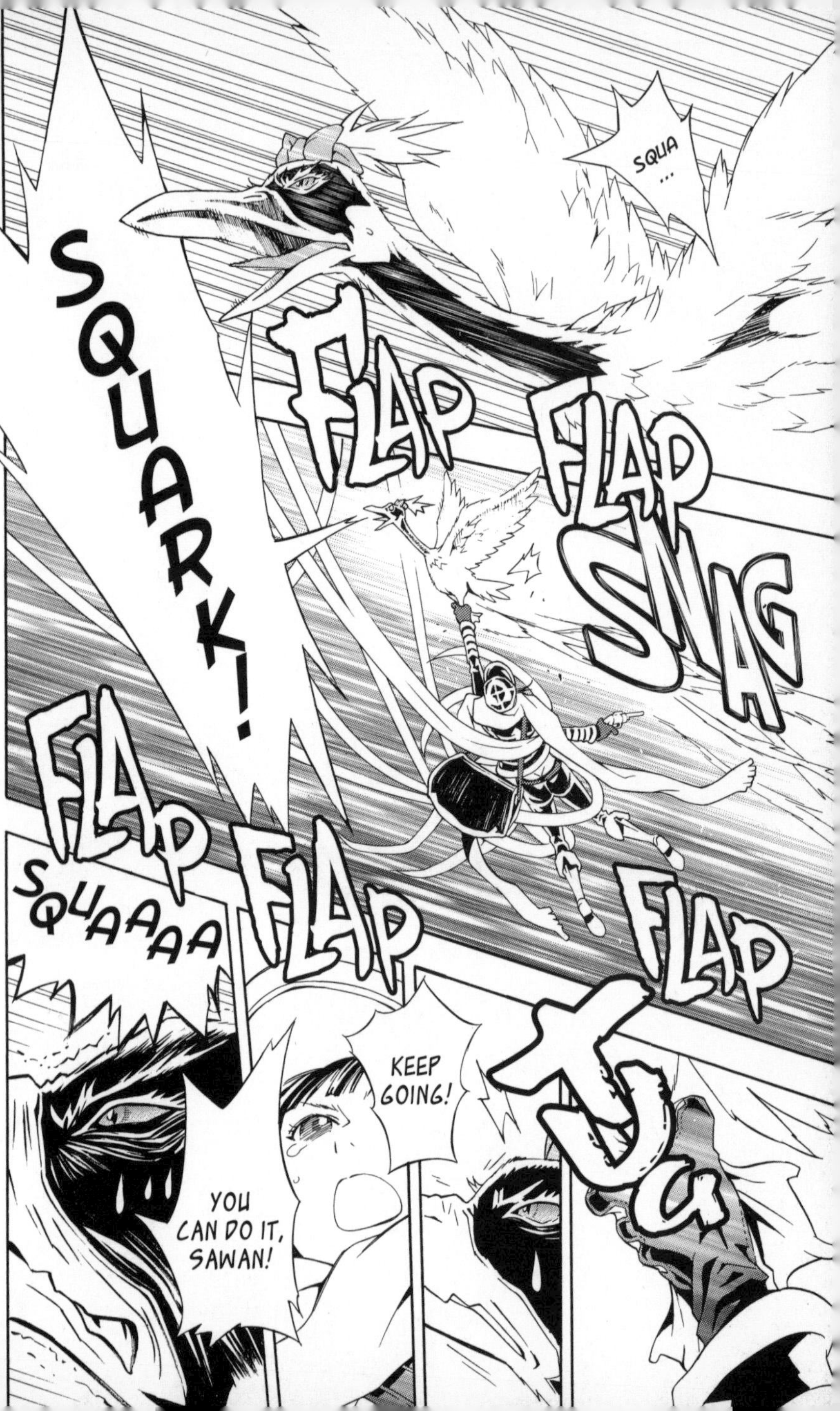
SQUA ...
FLAP
FLAP
SNAG
SQUARK!
FLAP
FLAP
FLAP
TUG
KEEP GOING!
YOU CAN DO IT, SAWAN!
SQUAAAA

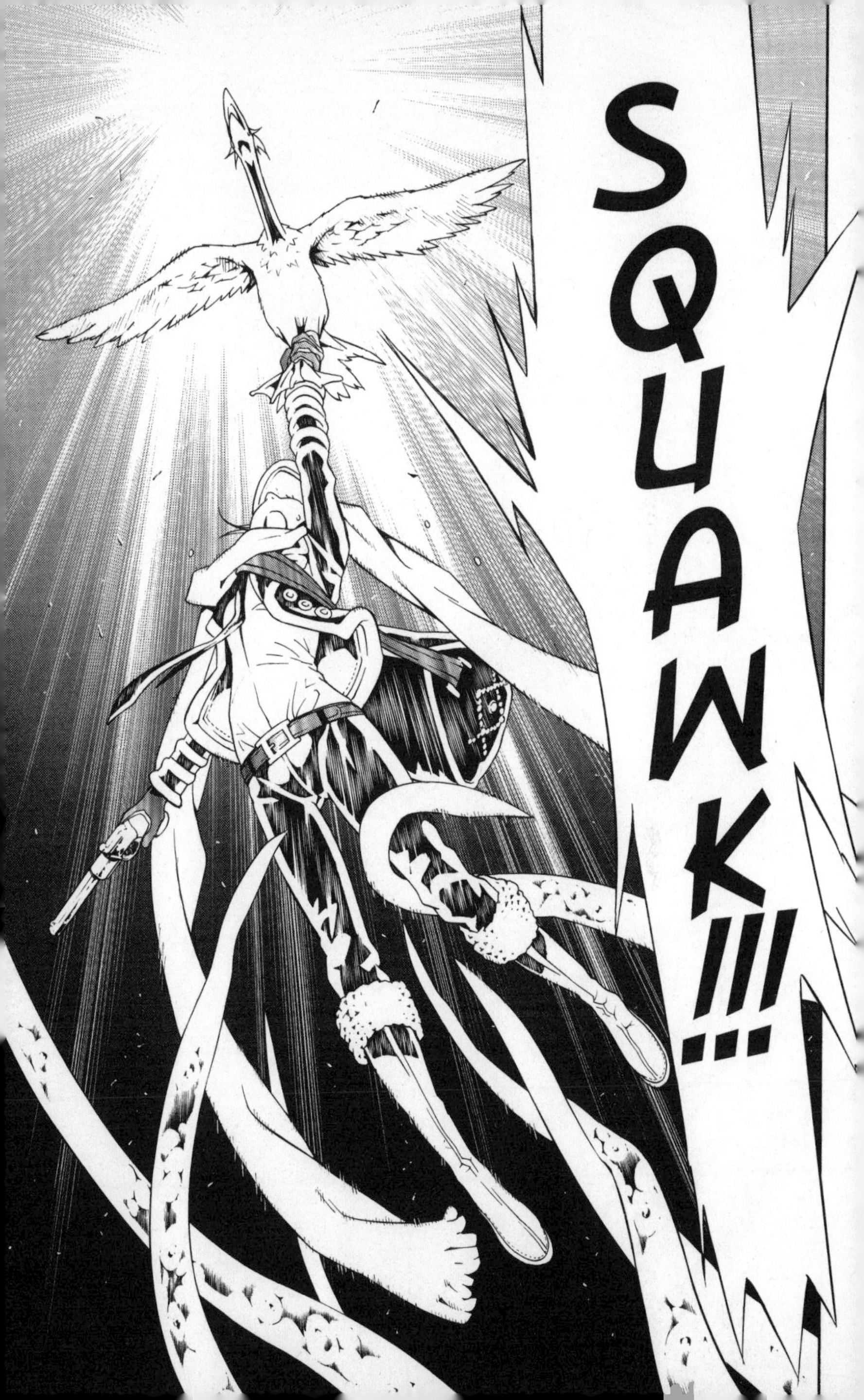
SQUAWK!!!

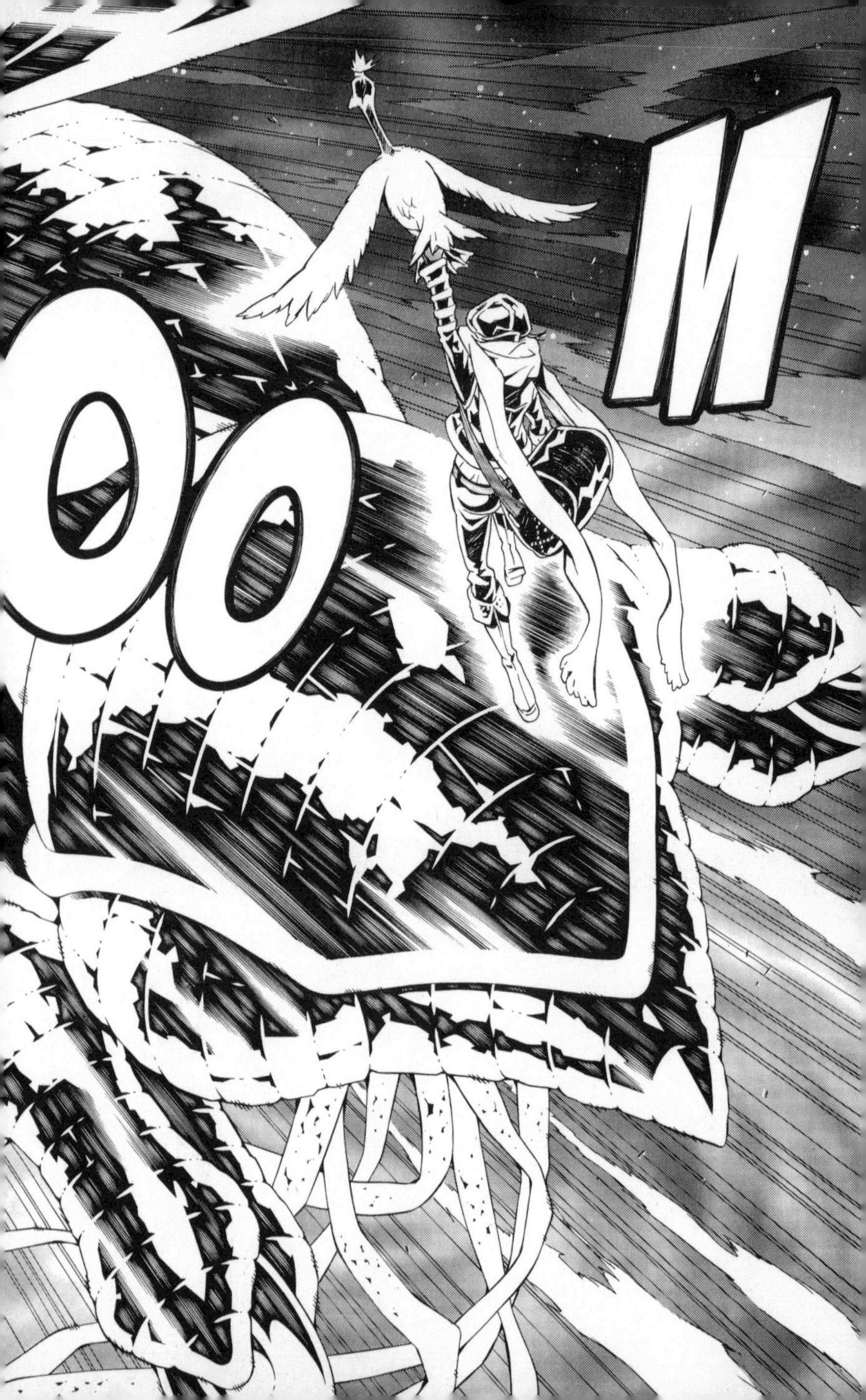
OOM

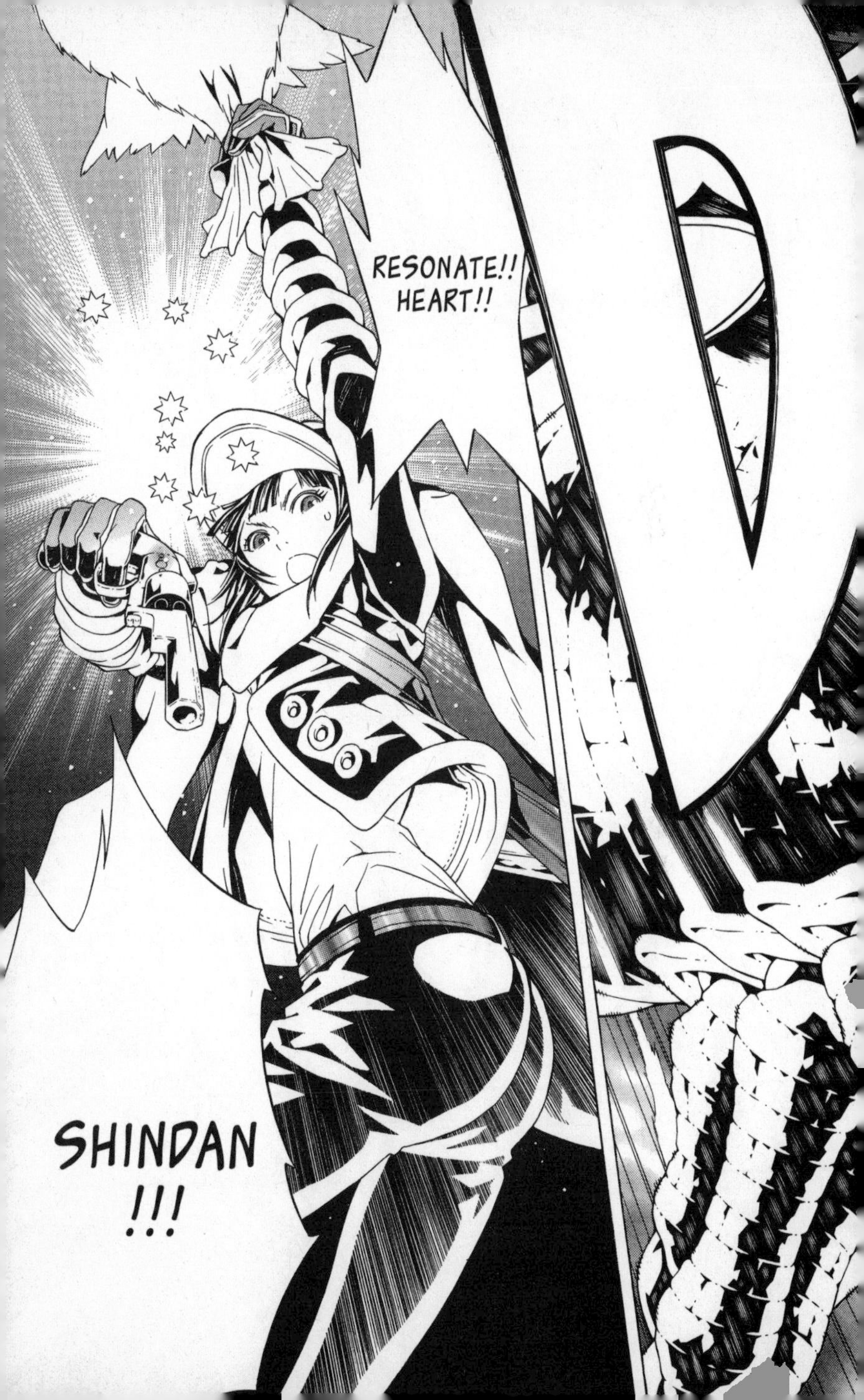
RESONATE!! HEART!!
SHINDAN !!!

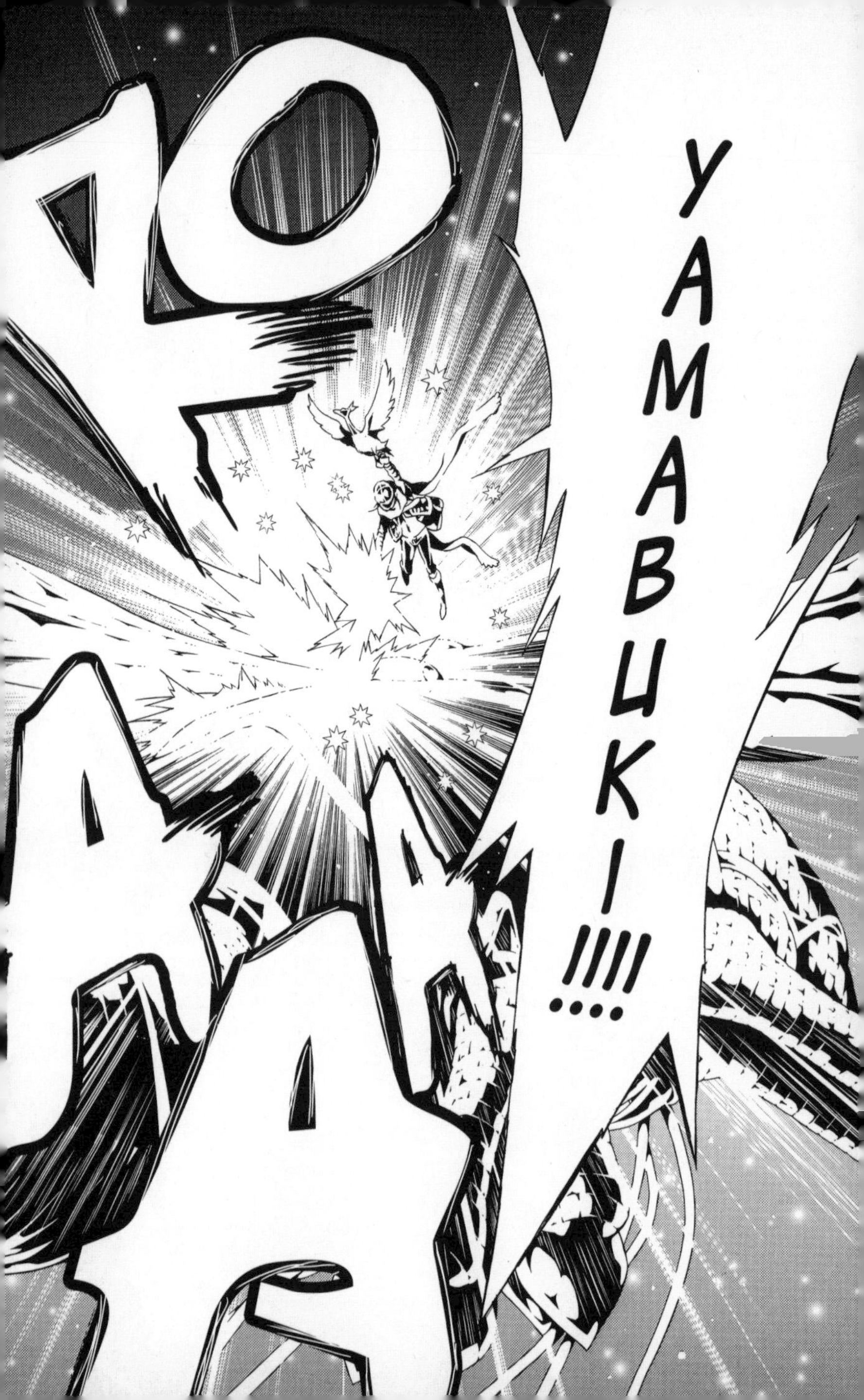
YAMABUKI!!!!

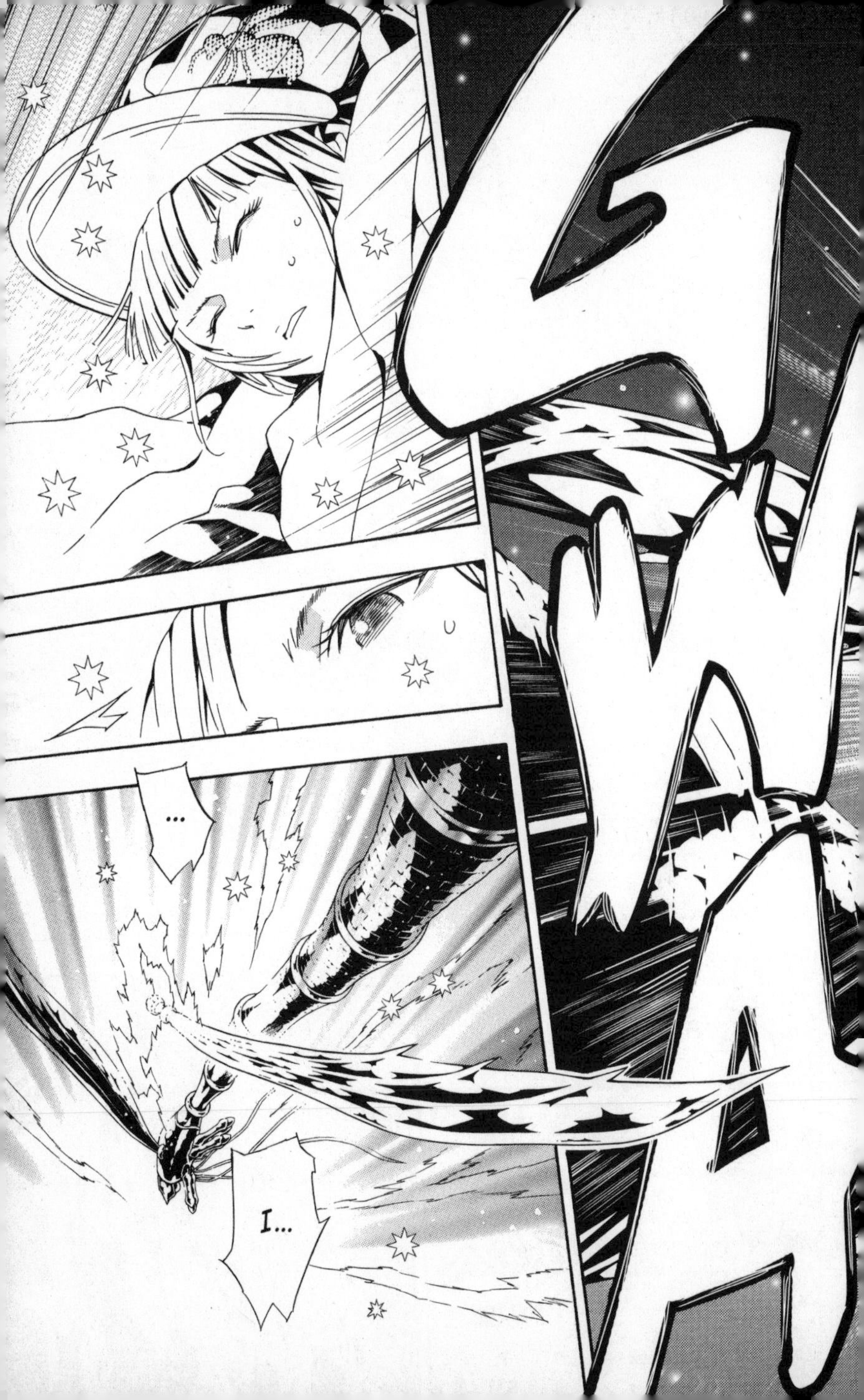
...
I...

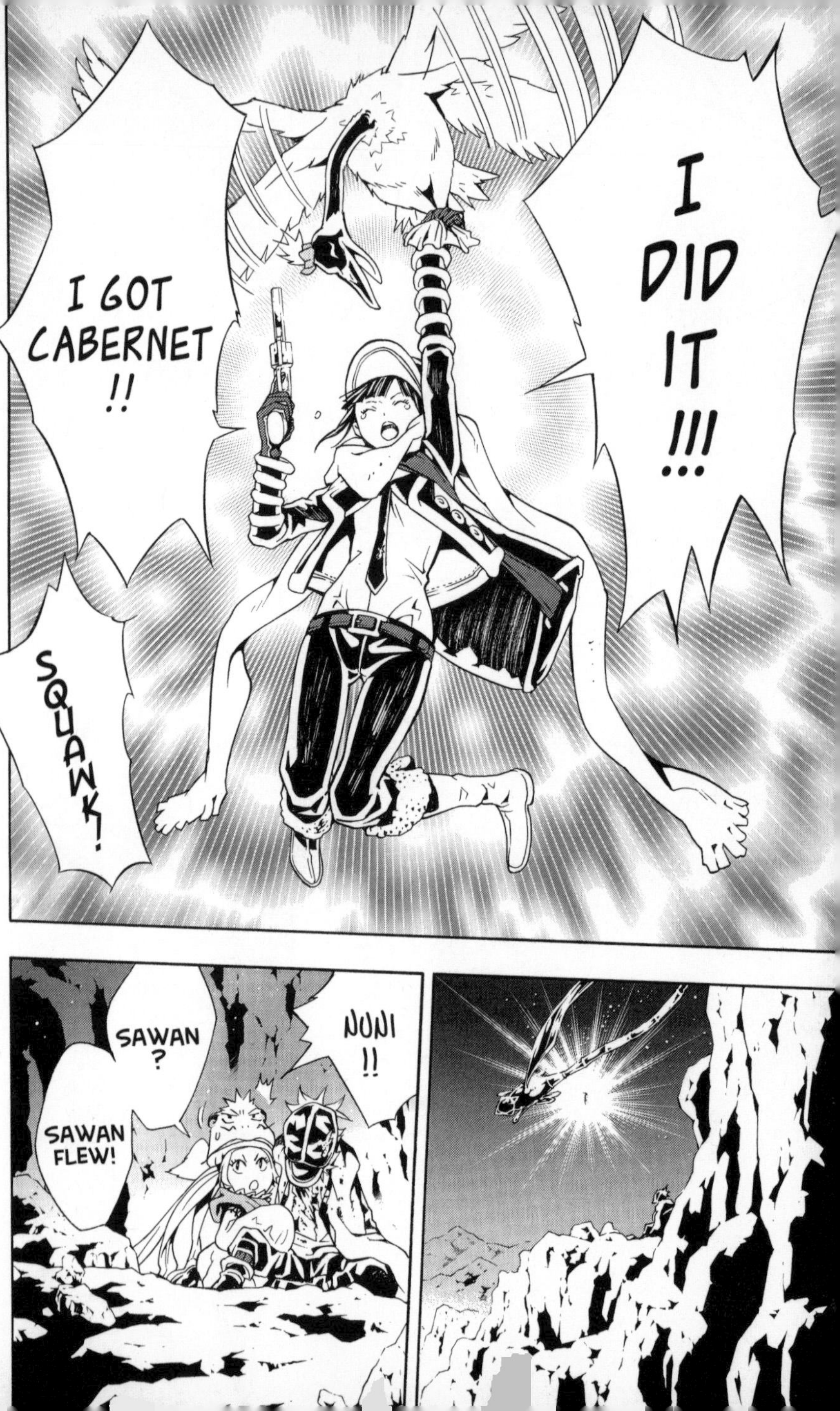
I DID IT !!!
I GOT CABERNET !!
SQUAWK!
NUNI !!
SAWAN ?
SAWAN FLEW!

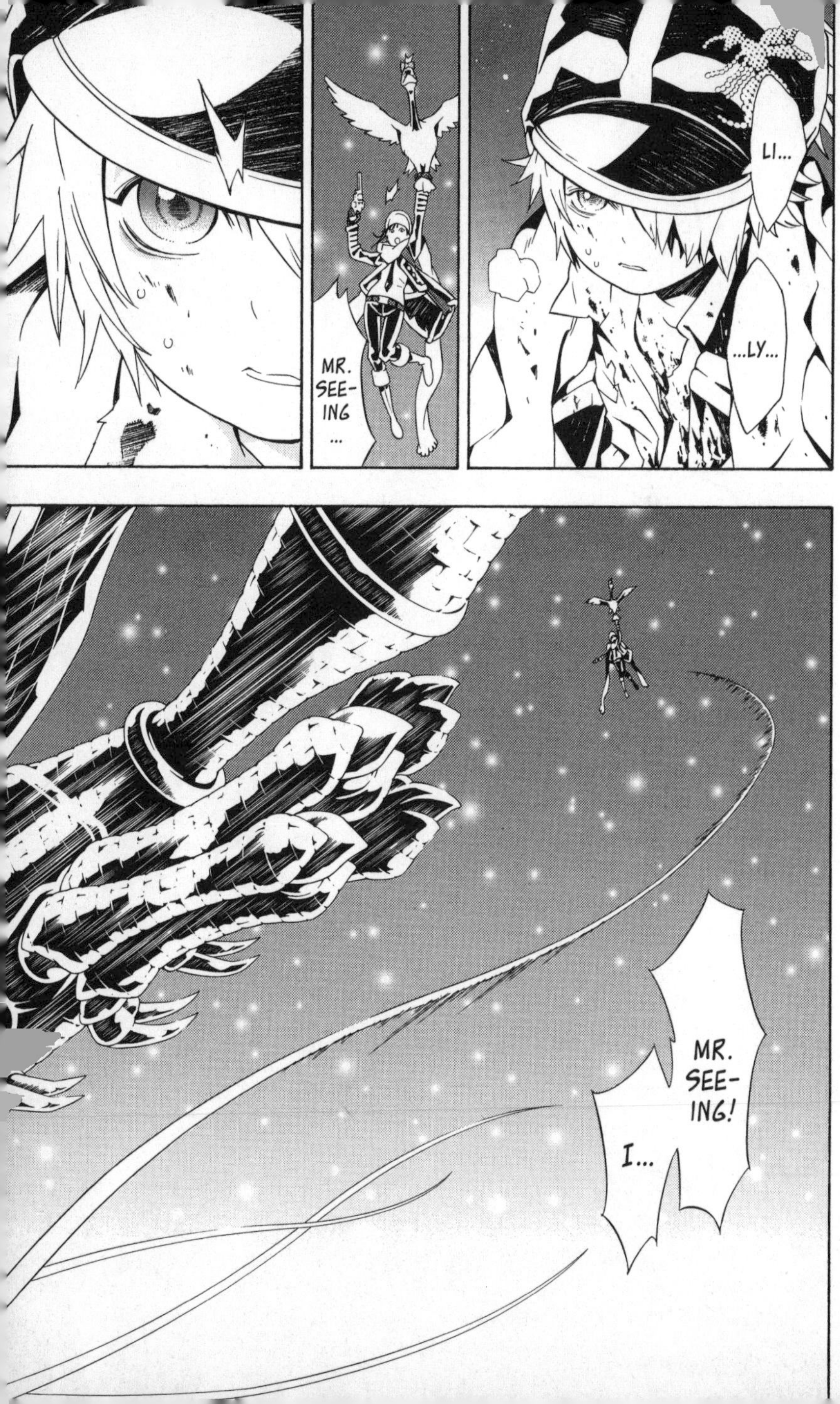
LI...
...LY...
MR. SEE-ING...
MR. SEE-ING!
I...

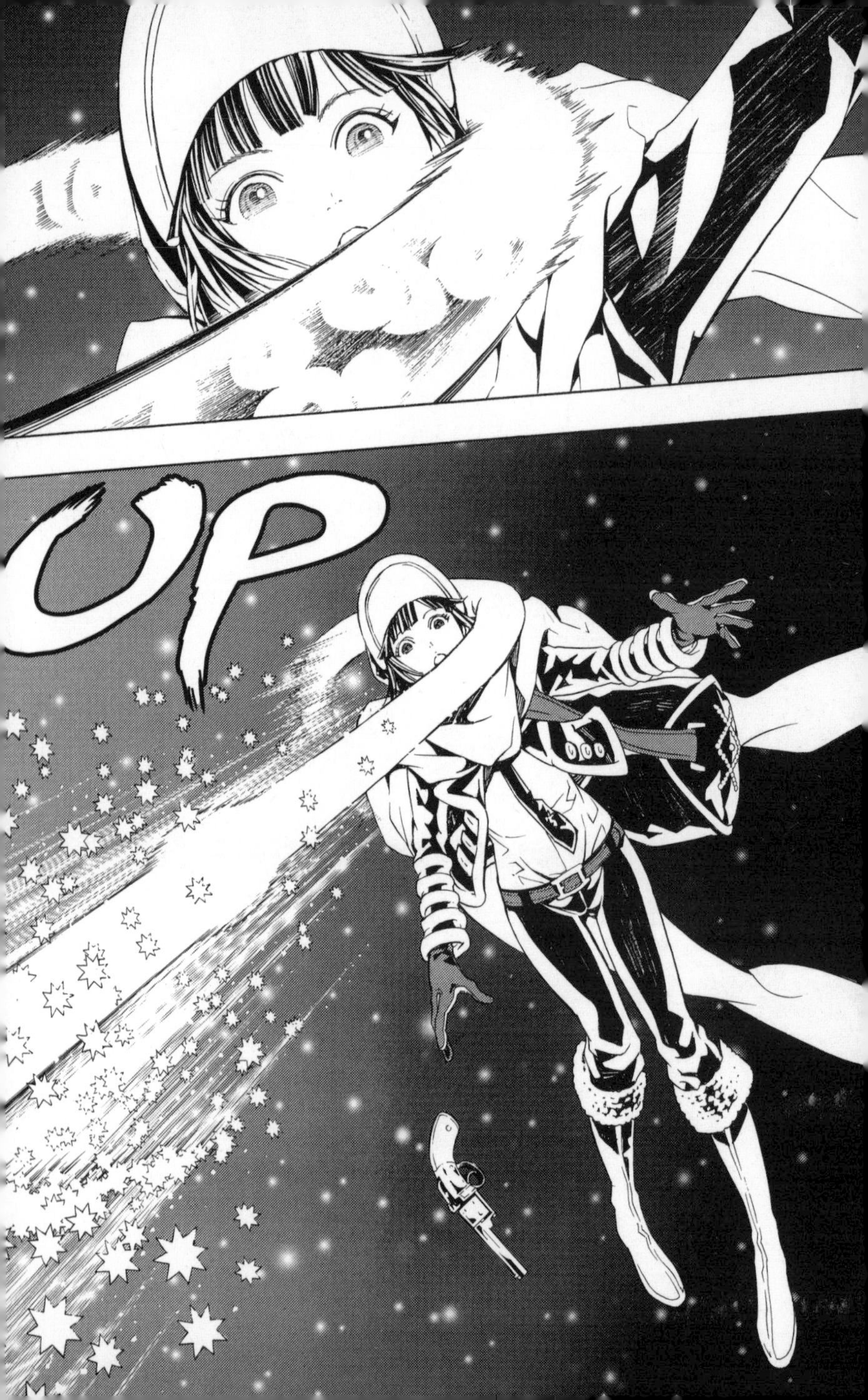
UP

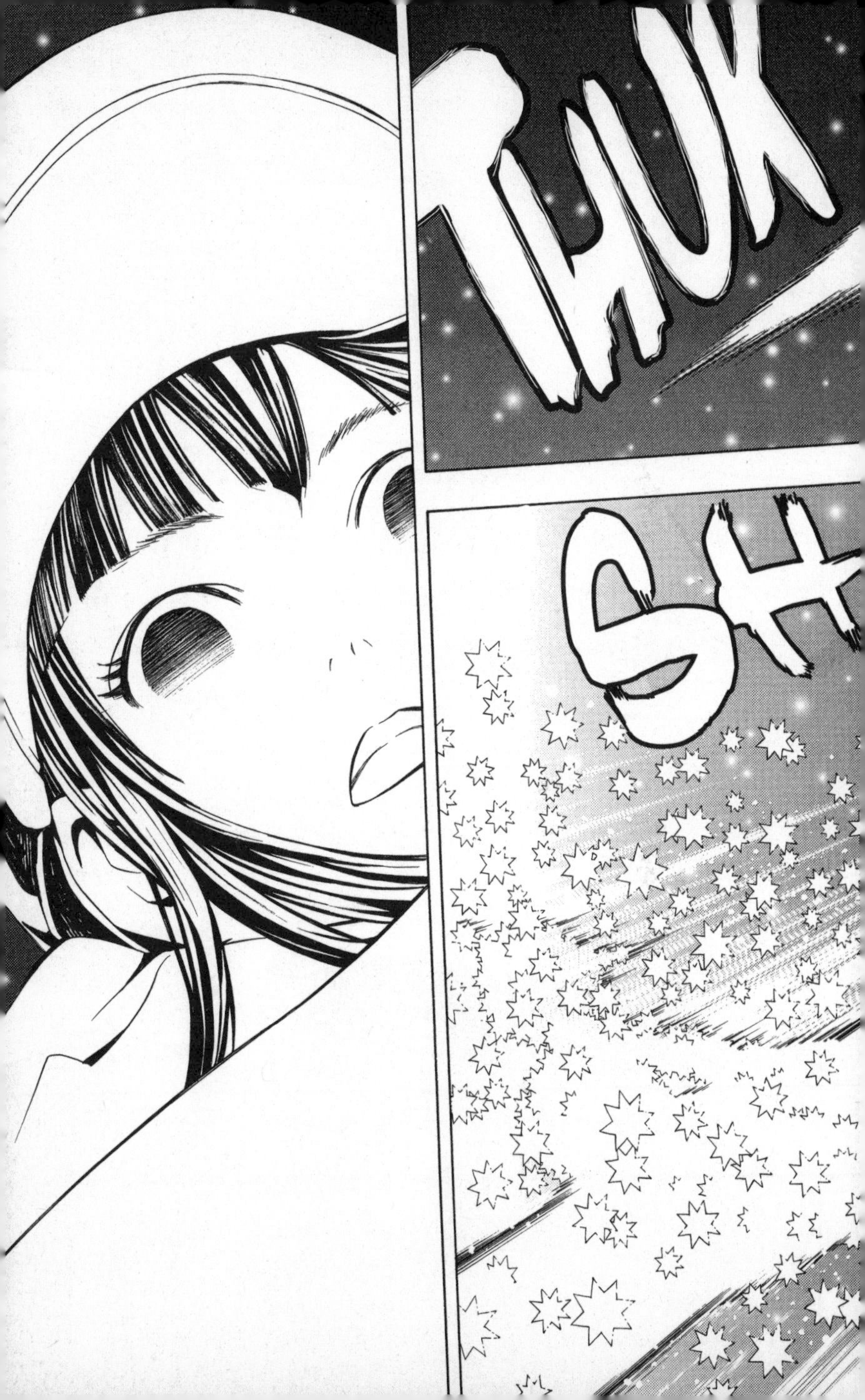
THUCK
SH

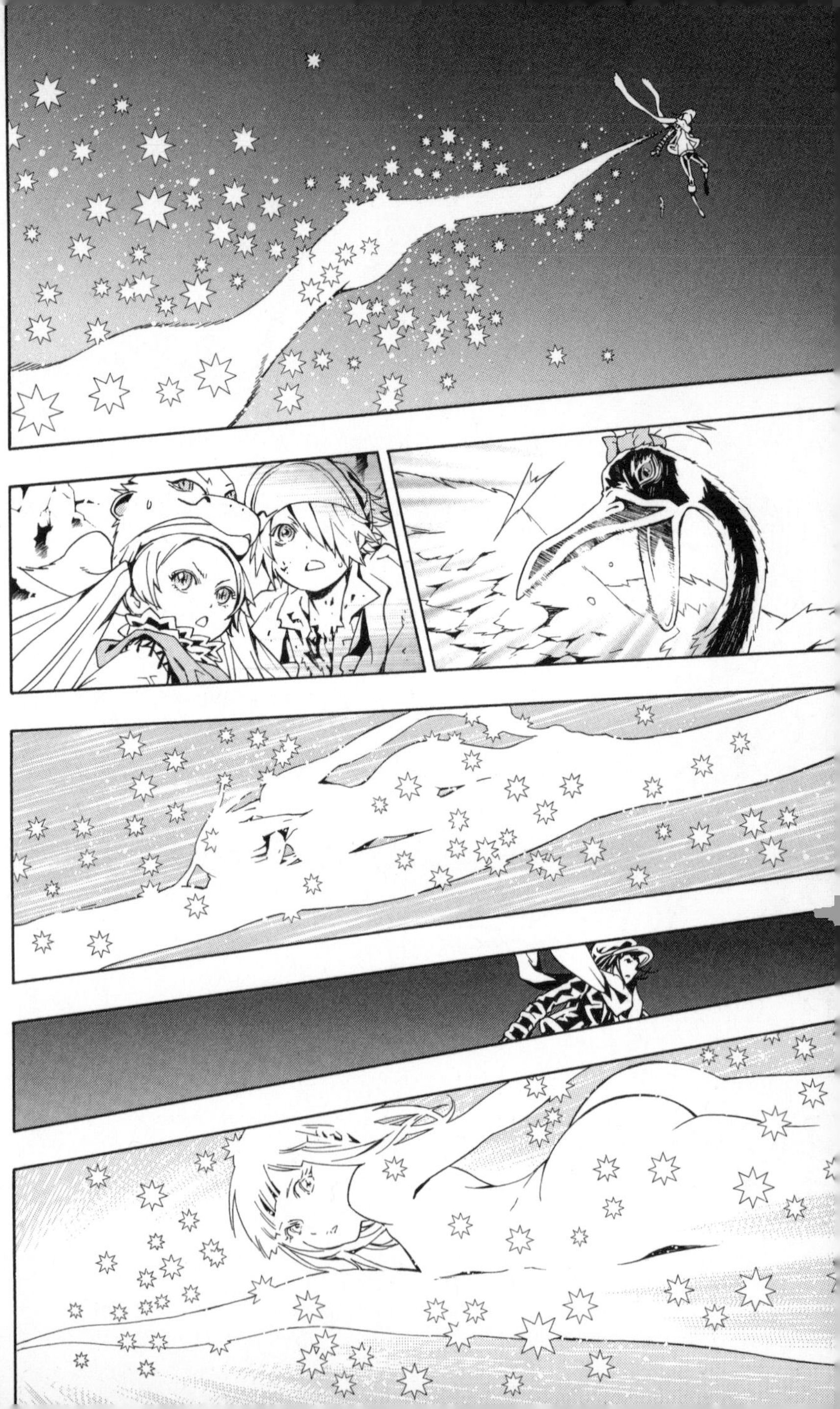

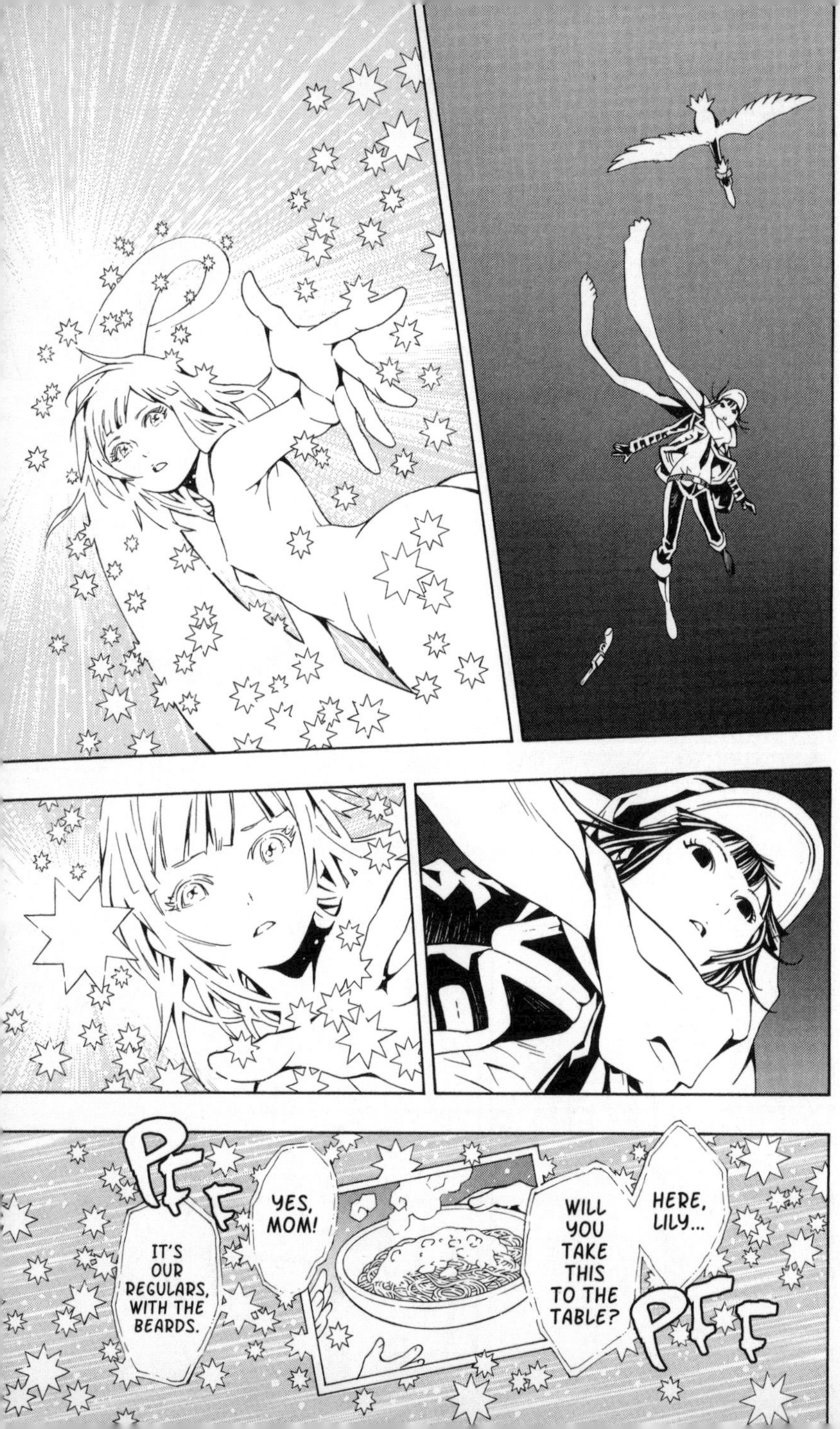

PFF
HERE, LILY...
WILL YOU TAKE THIS TO THE TABLE?
YES, MOM!
IT'S OUR REGULARS, WITH THE BEARDS.
PFF

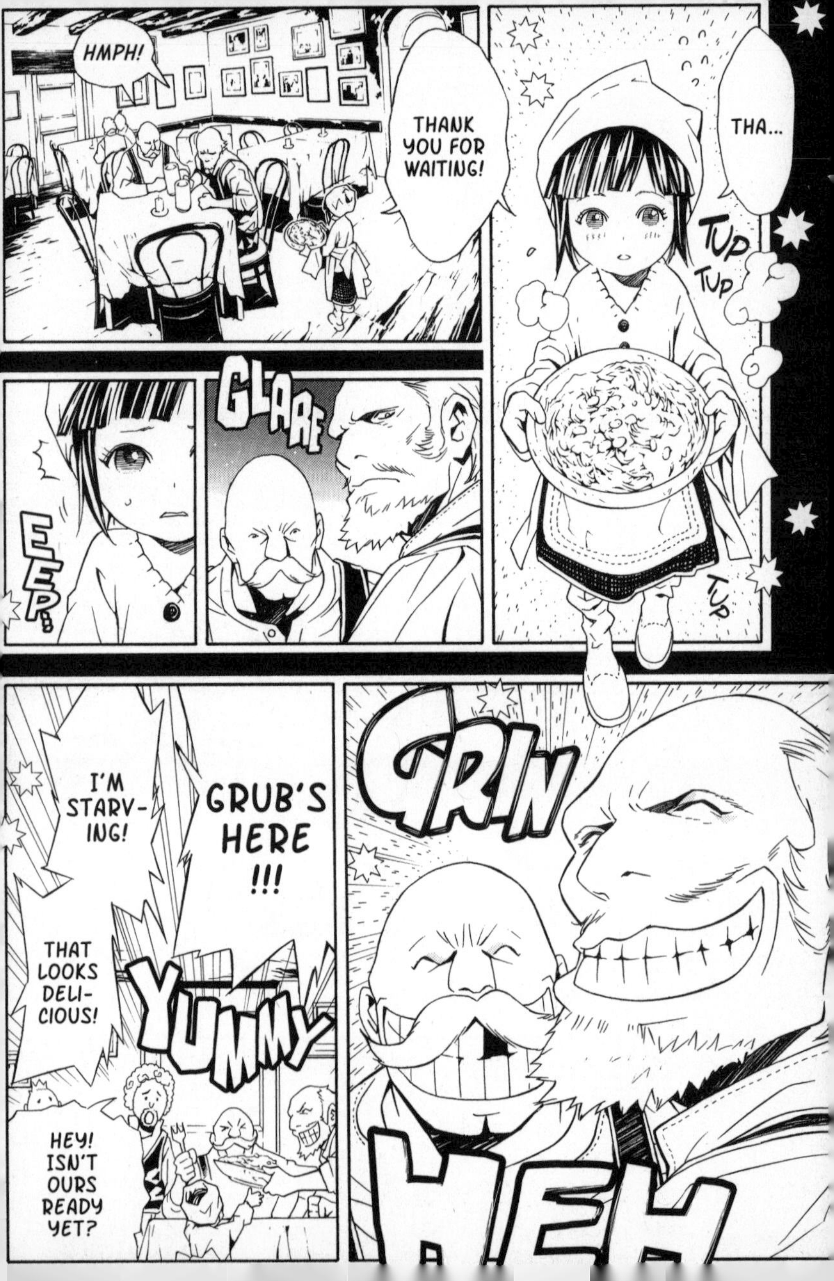

THA...
TUP TUP
TUP
THANK YOU FOR WAITING!
HMPH!
GLARE
EEP...
GRIN
HEH
GRUB'S HERE!!!
I'M STARVING!
YUMMY
THAT LOOKS DELICIOUS!
HEY! ISN'T OURS READY YET?

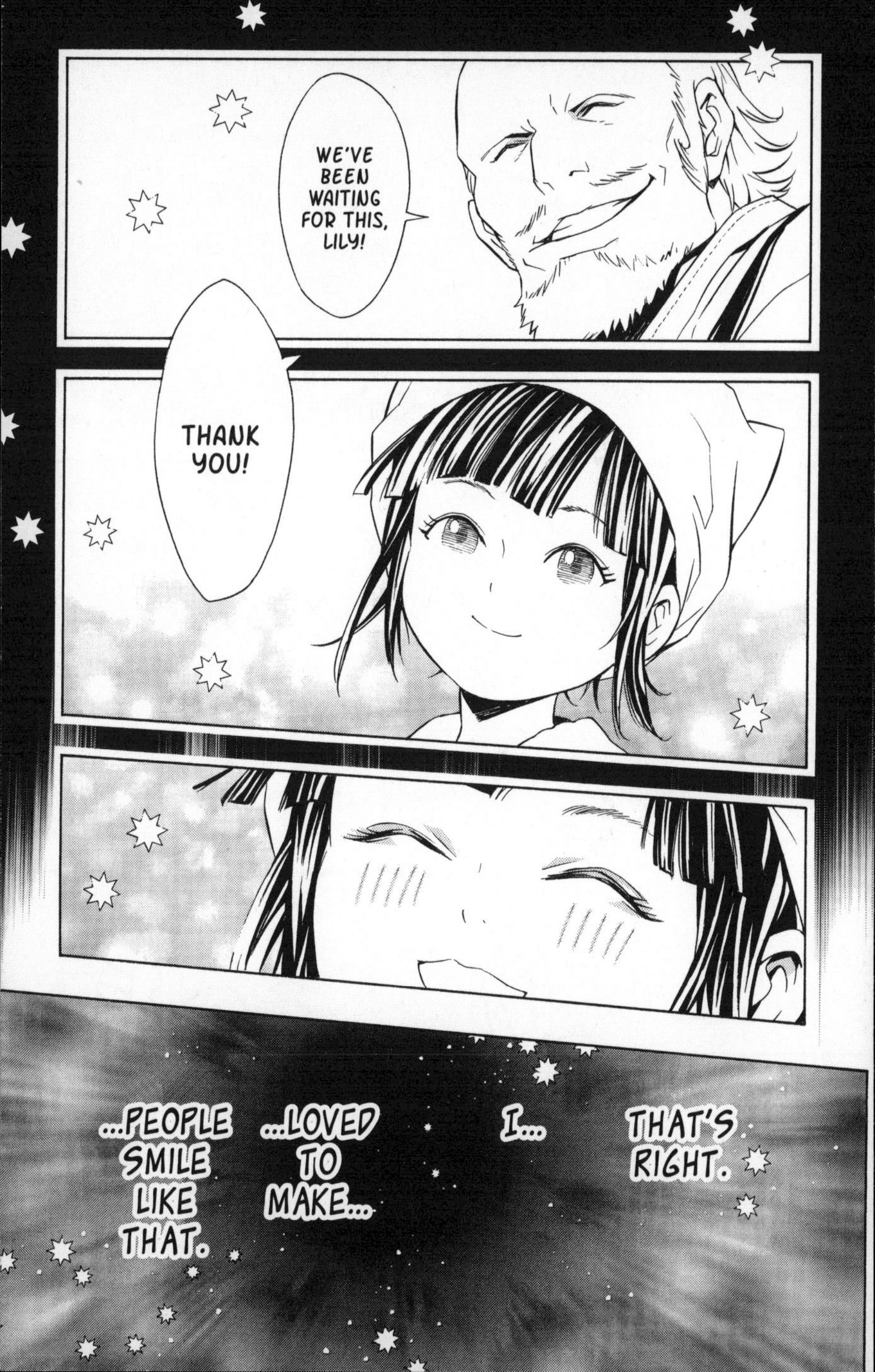
WE'VE BEEN WAITING FOR THIS, LILY!
THANK YOU!
THAT'S RIGHT.
I...
...LOVED TO MAKE...
...PEOPLE SMILE LIKE THAT.

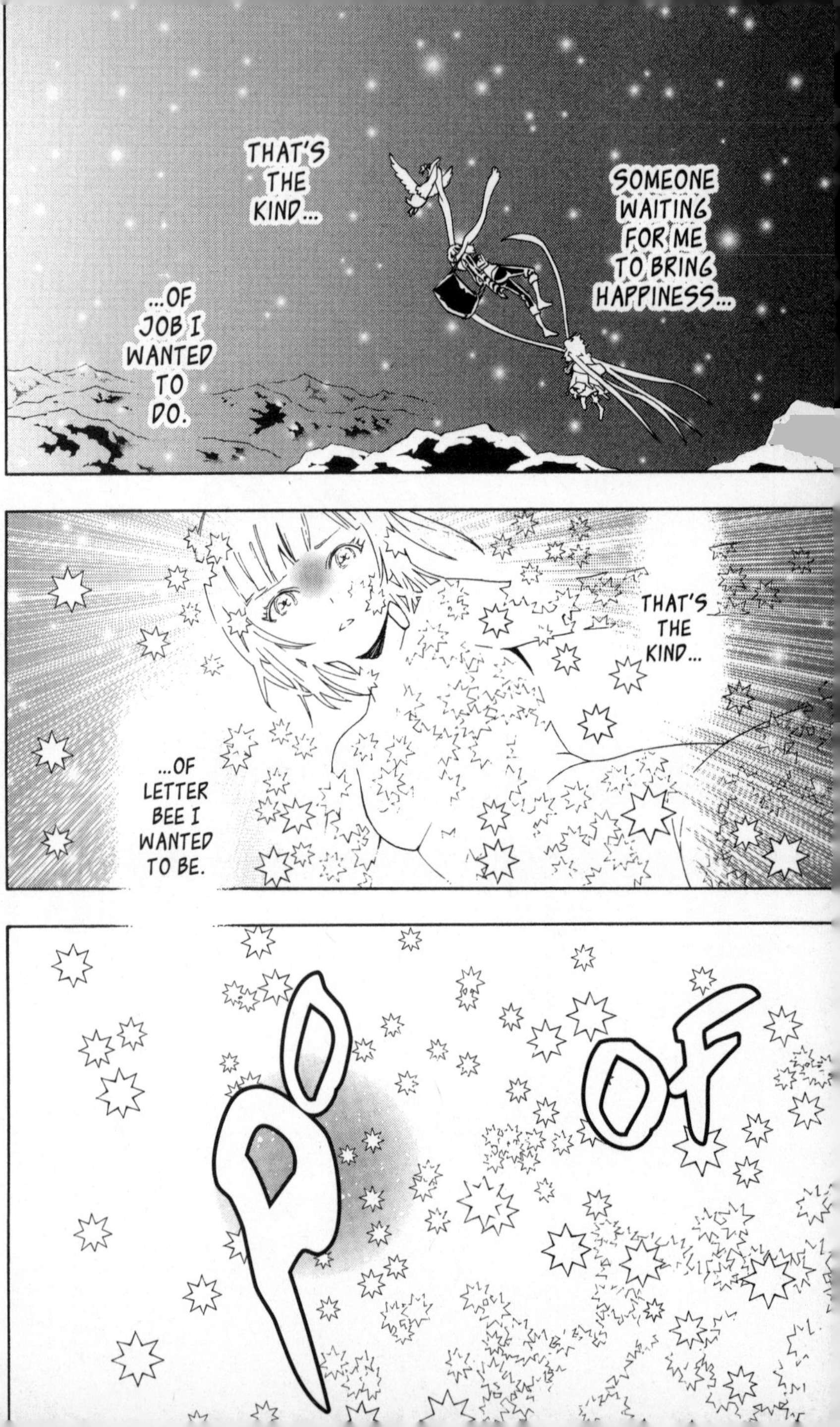
SOMEONE WAITING FOR ME TO BRING HAPPINESS...
THAT'S THE KIND...
...OF JOB I WANTED TO DO.
THAT'S THE KIND...
...OF LETTER BEE I WANTED TO BE.
POOF

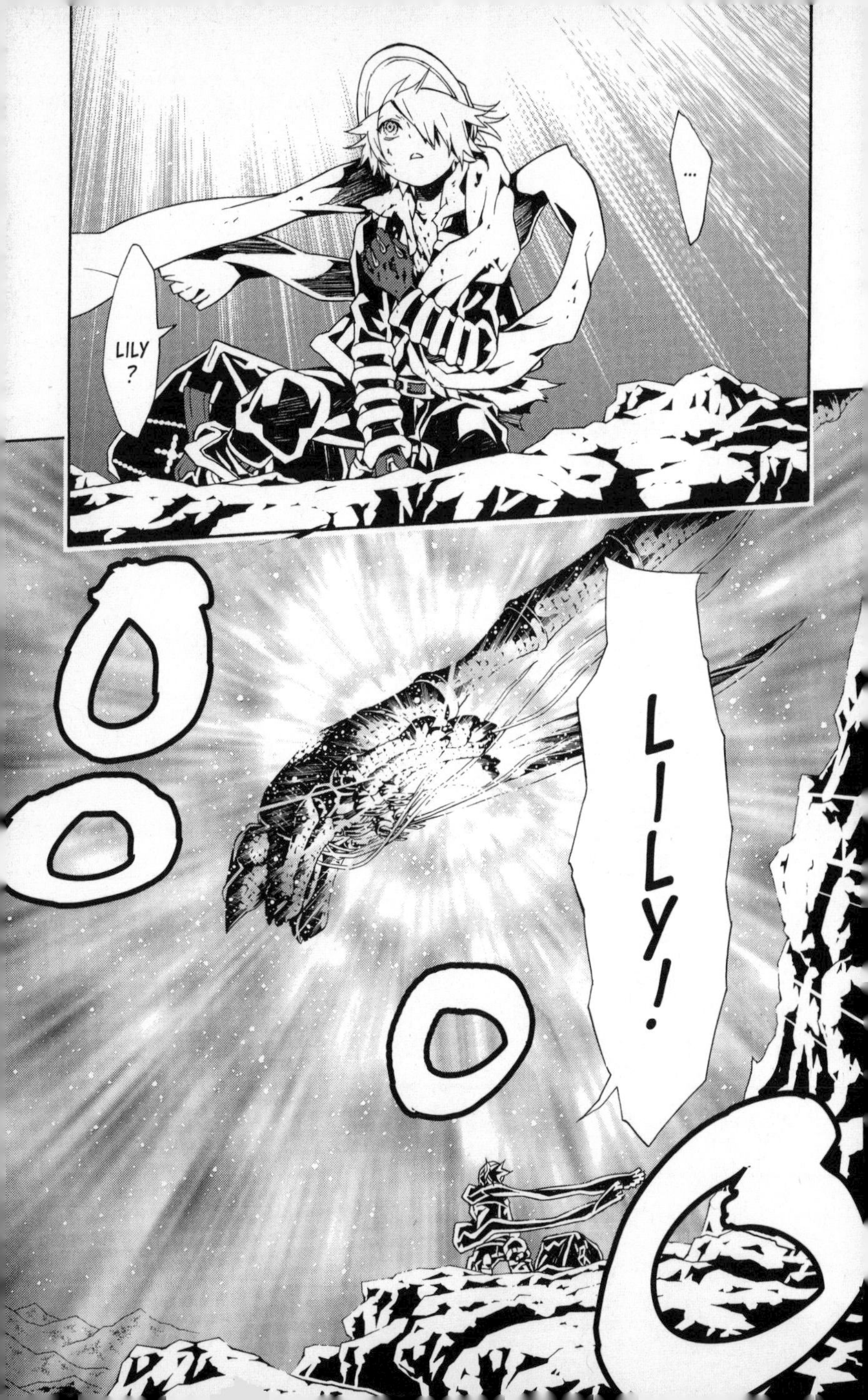
...
LILY?
LILY!
OOOO

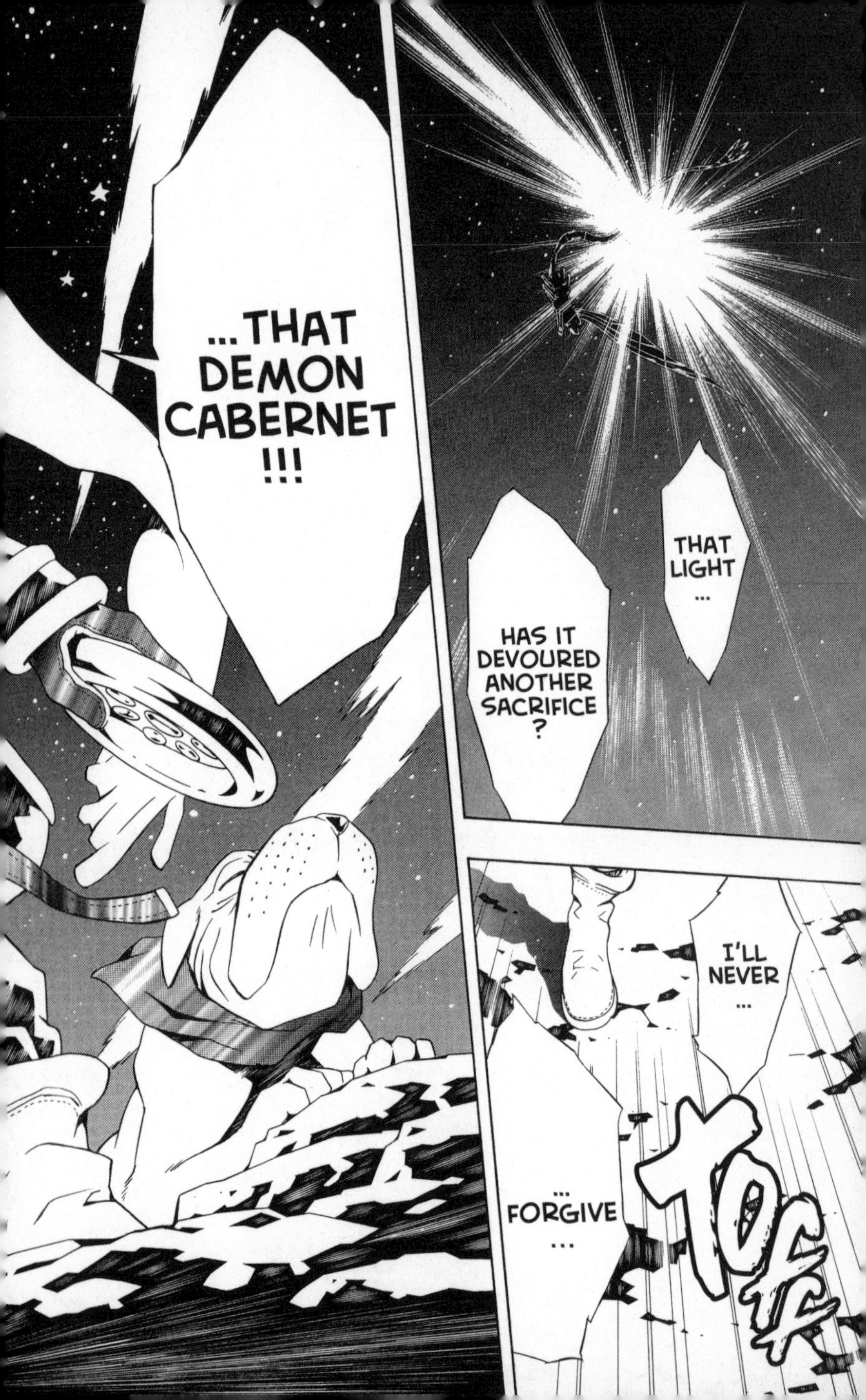
THAT LIGHT ...
HAS IT DEVOURED ANOTHER SACRIFICE ?
I'LL NEVER ...
... FORGIVE ...
TOF
... THAT DEMON CABERNET !!!

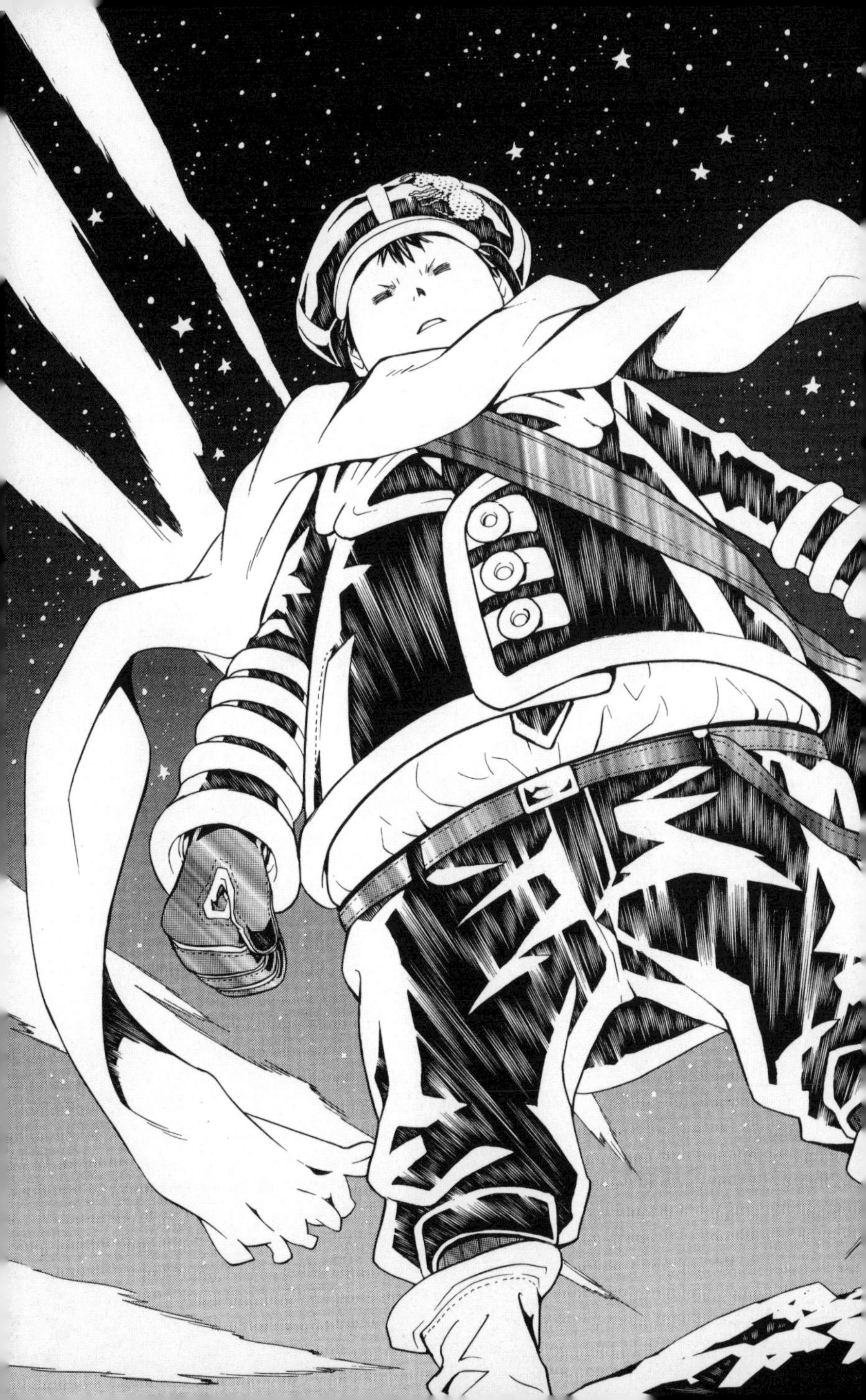

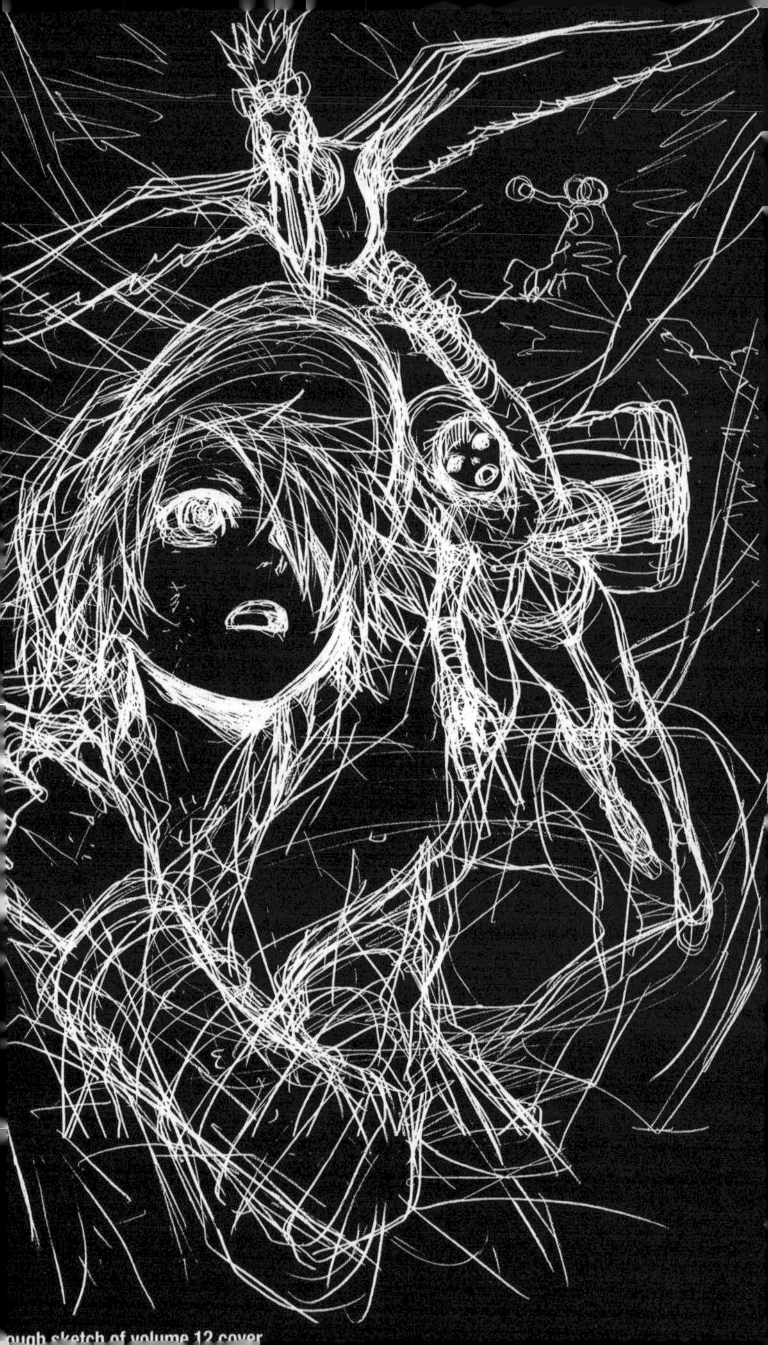

Rough sketch of volume 12 cover

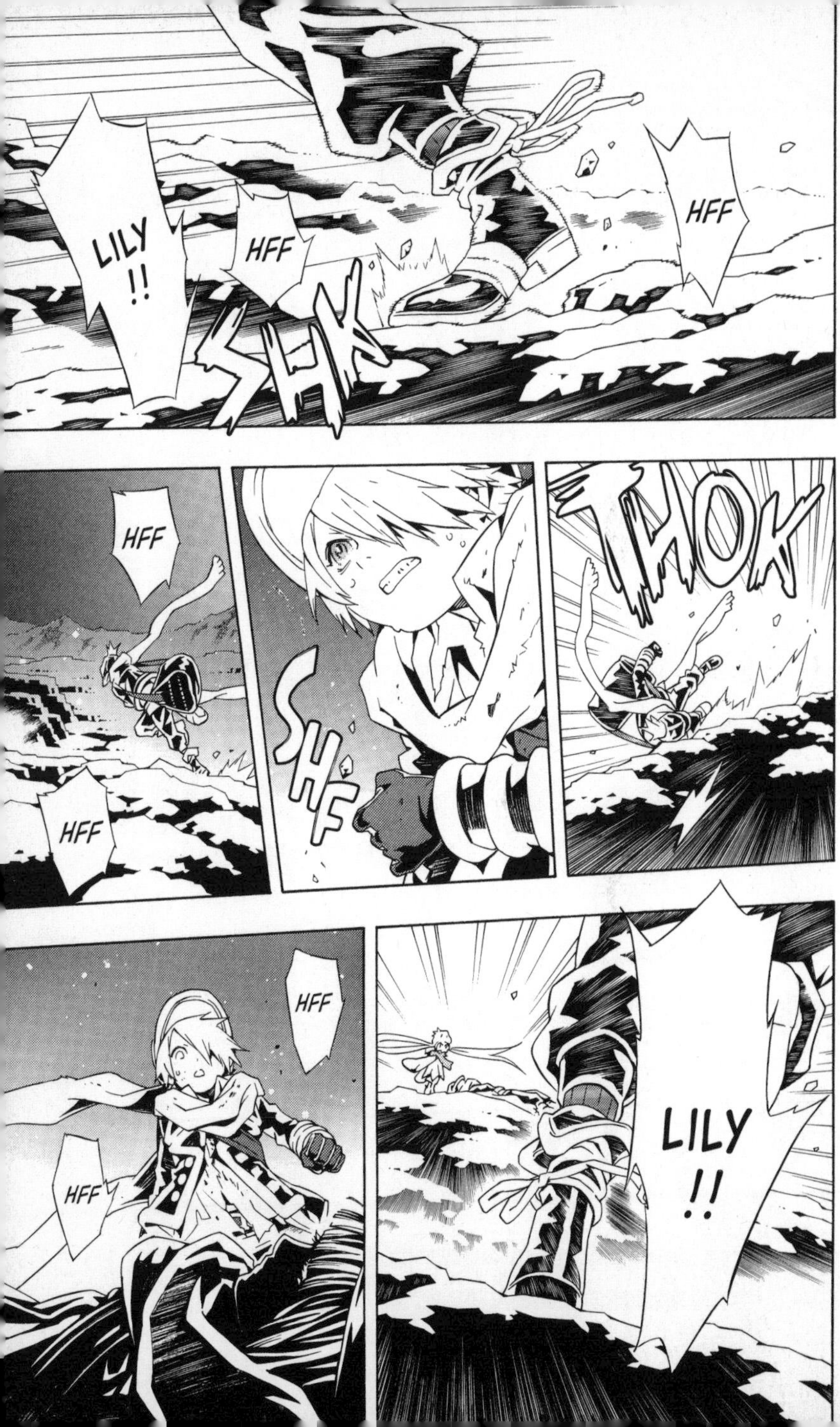
HFF
HFF
LILY !!
SHK
THOK
SHF
HFF
HFF
LILY !!
HFF
HFF

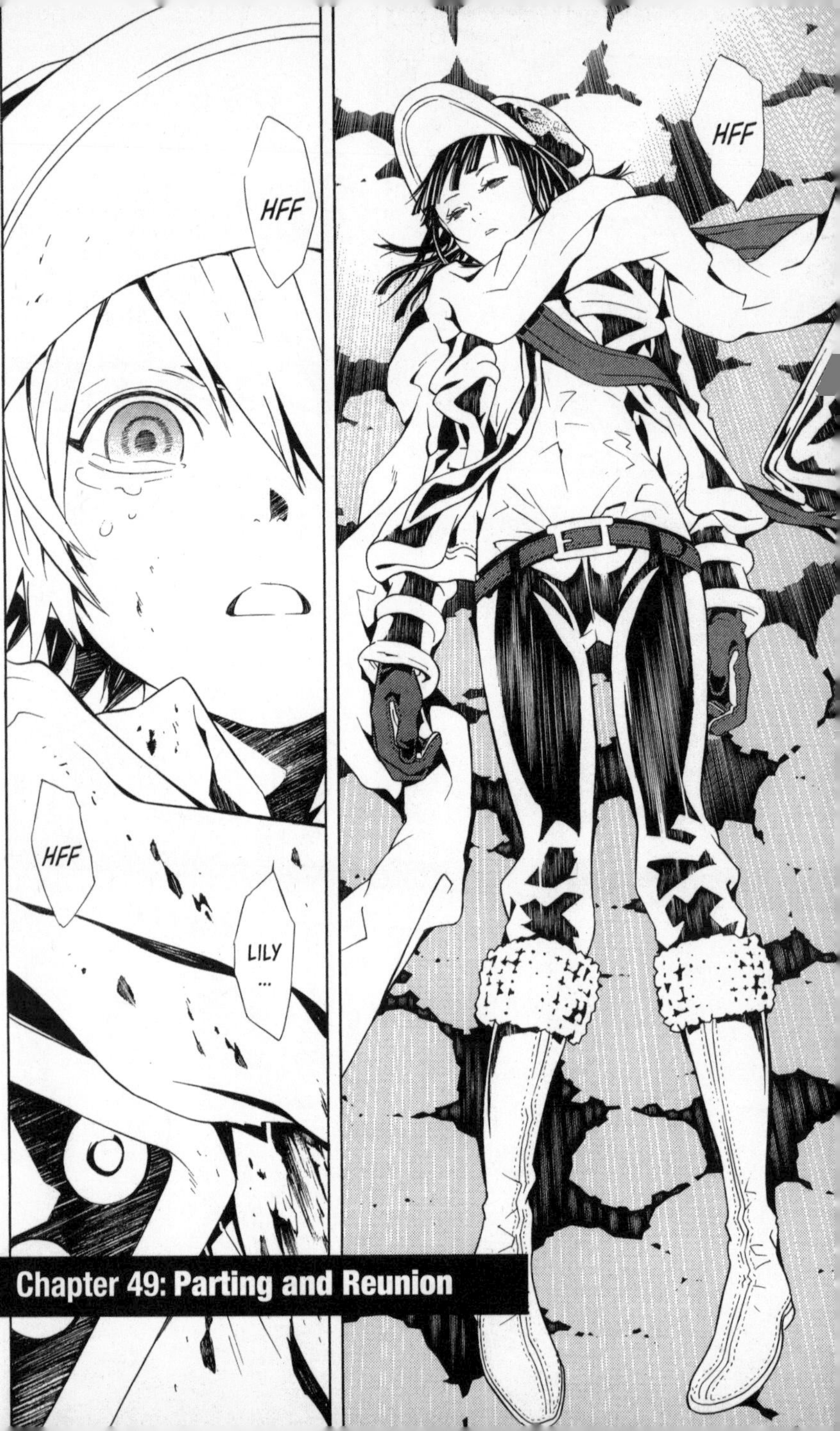
HFF
HFF
HFF
LILY
...

Chapter 49: Parting and Reunion

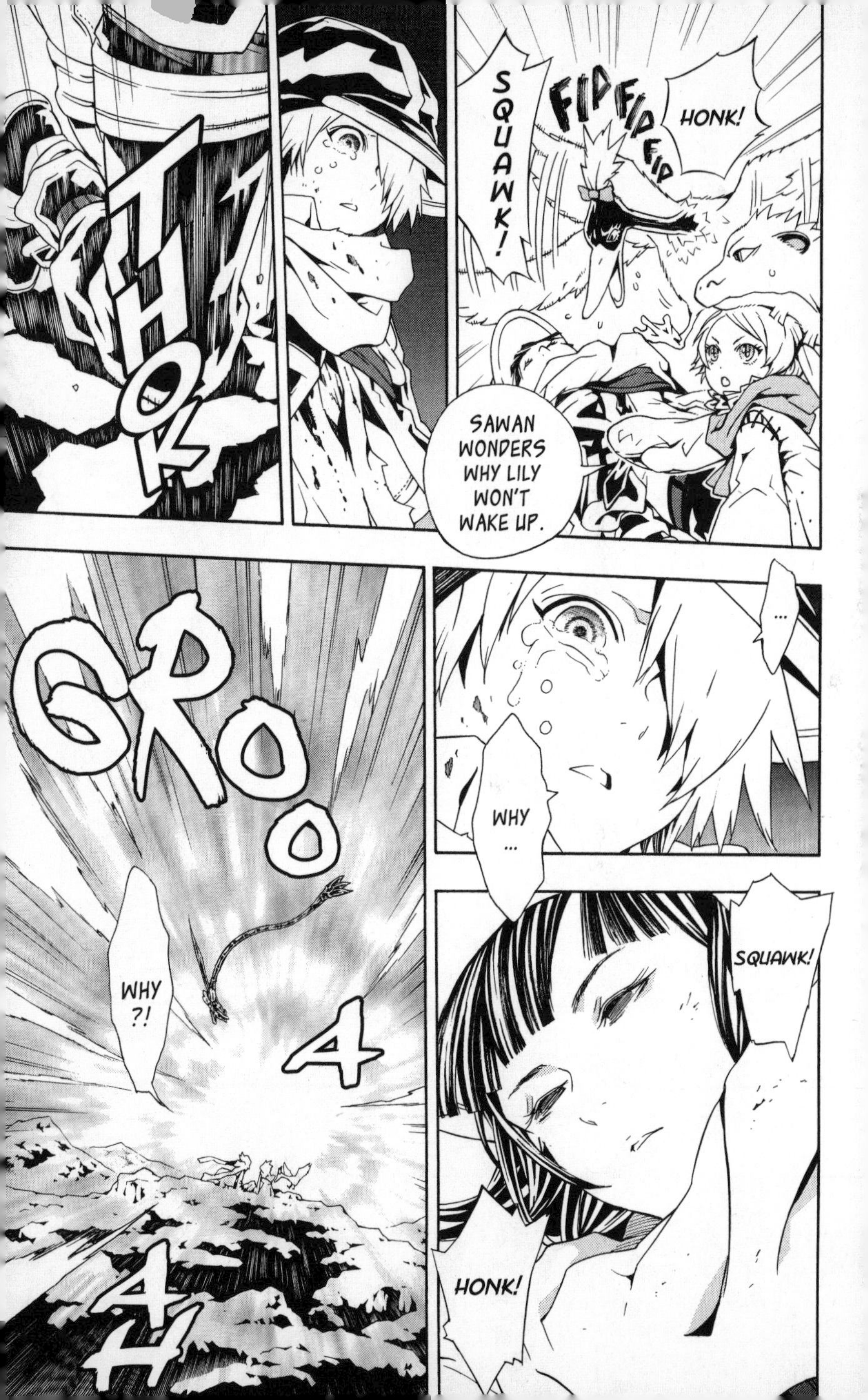
HONK!
FIPFIPFIP
SQUAWK!
SAWAN WONDERS WHY LILY WON'T WAKE UP.
THOK
...
WHY ...
SQUAWK!
HONK!
GROOO
WHY ?!

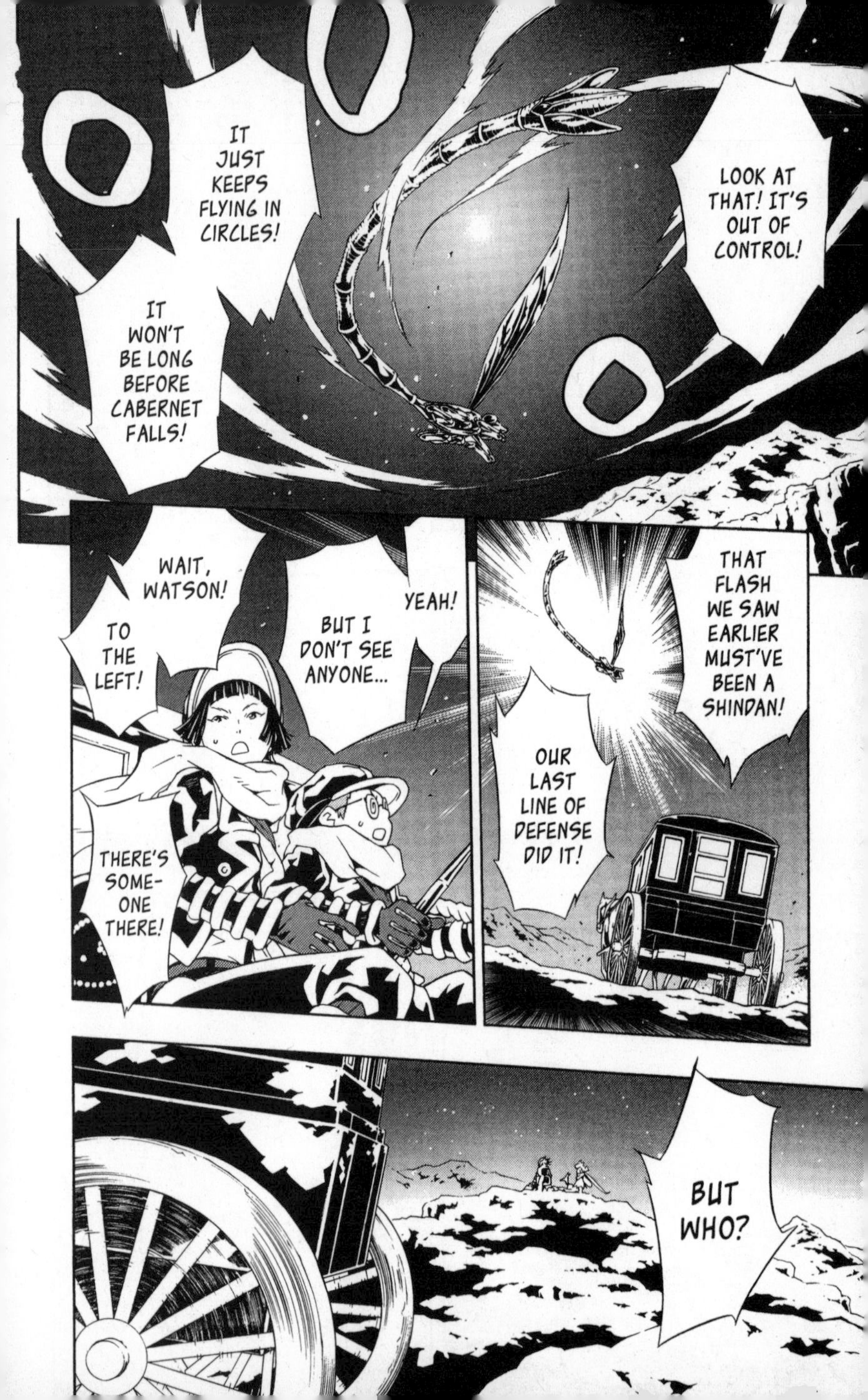
LOOK AT THAT! IT'S OUT OF CONTROL!
IT JUST KEEPS FLYING IN CIRCLES!
IT WON'T BE LONG BEFORE CABERNET FALLS!
THAT FLASH WE SAW EARLIER MUST'VE BEEN A SHINDAN!
OUR LAST LINE OF DEFENSE DID IT!
YEAH!
BUT I DON'T SEE ANYONE...
WAIT, WATSON!
TO THE LEFT!
THERE'S SOME-ONE THERE!
BUT WHO?

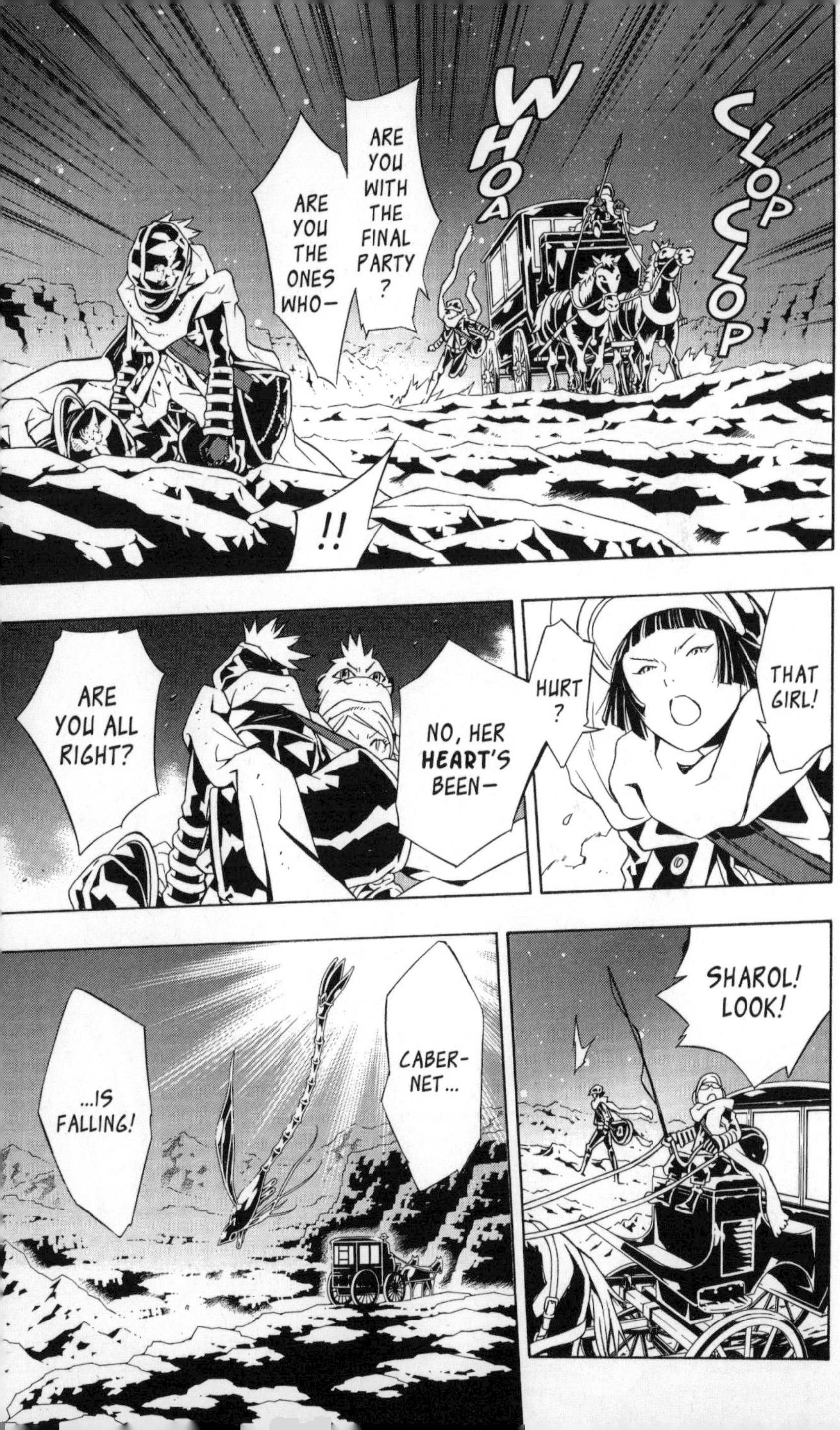
CLOP CLOP CLOP
WHOA
ARE YOU WITH THE FINAL PARTY?
ARE YOU THE ONES WHO—
!!
THAT GIRL!
HURT?
NO, HER HEART'S BEEN—
ARE YOU ALL RIGHT?
SHAROL! LOOK!
CABER-NET...
...IS FALLING!

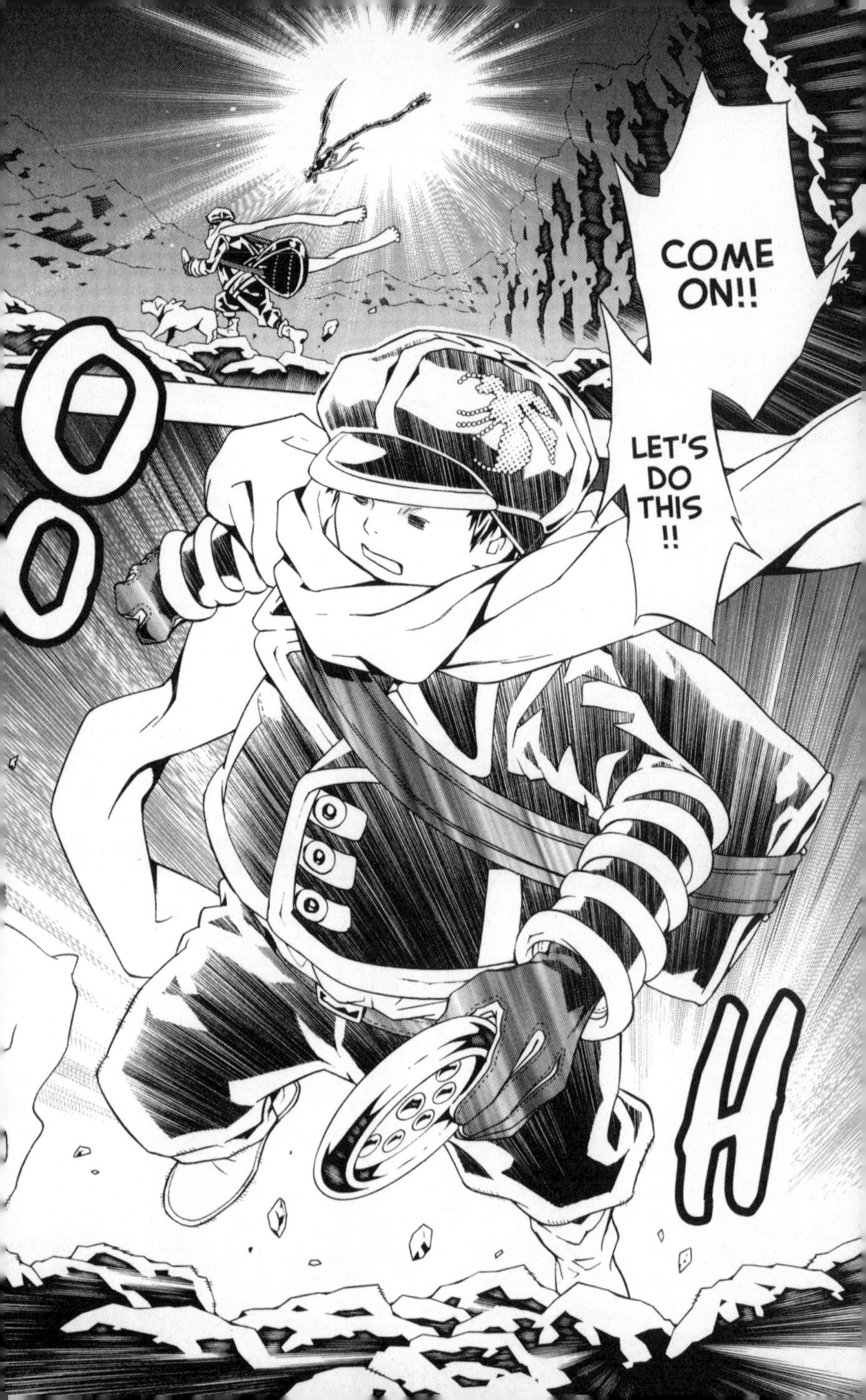
COME ON!!
LET'S DO THIS!!
OOH

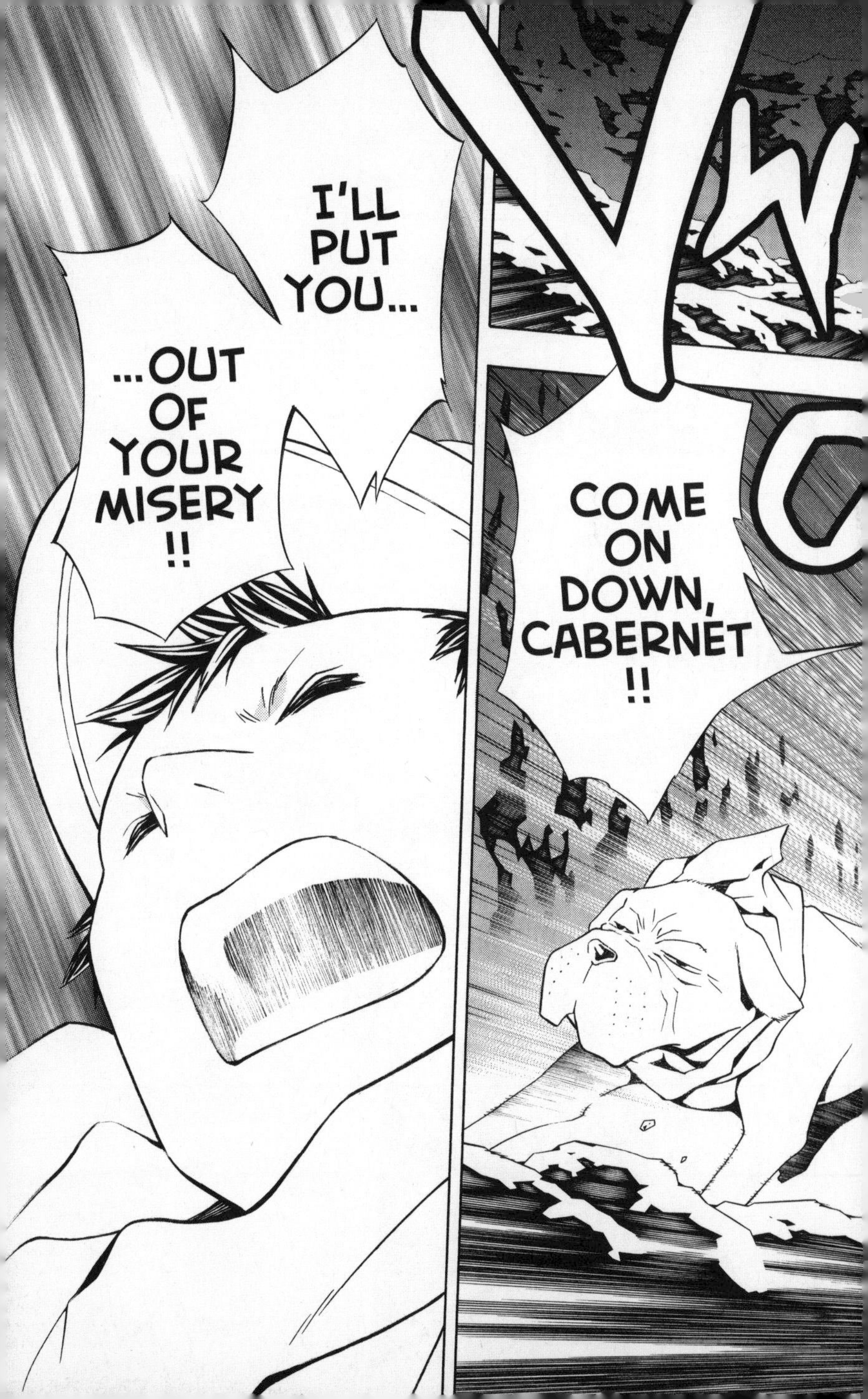
COME ON DOWN, CABERNET!!
I'LL PUT YOU...
...OUT OF YOUR MISERY!!

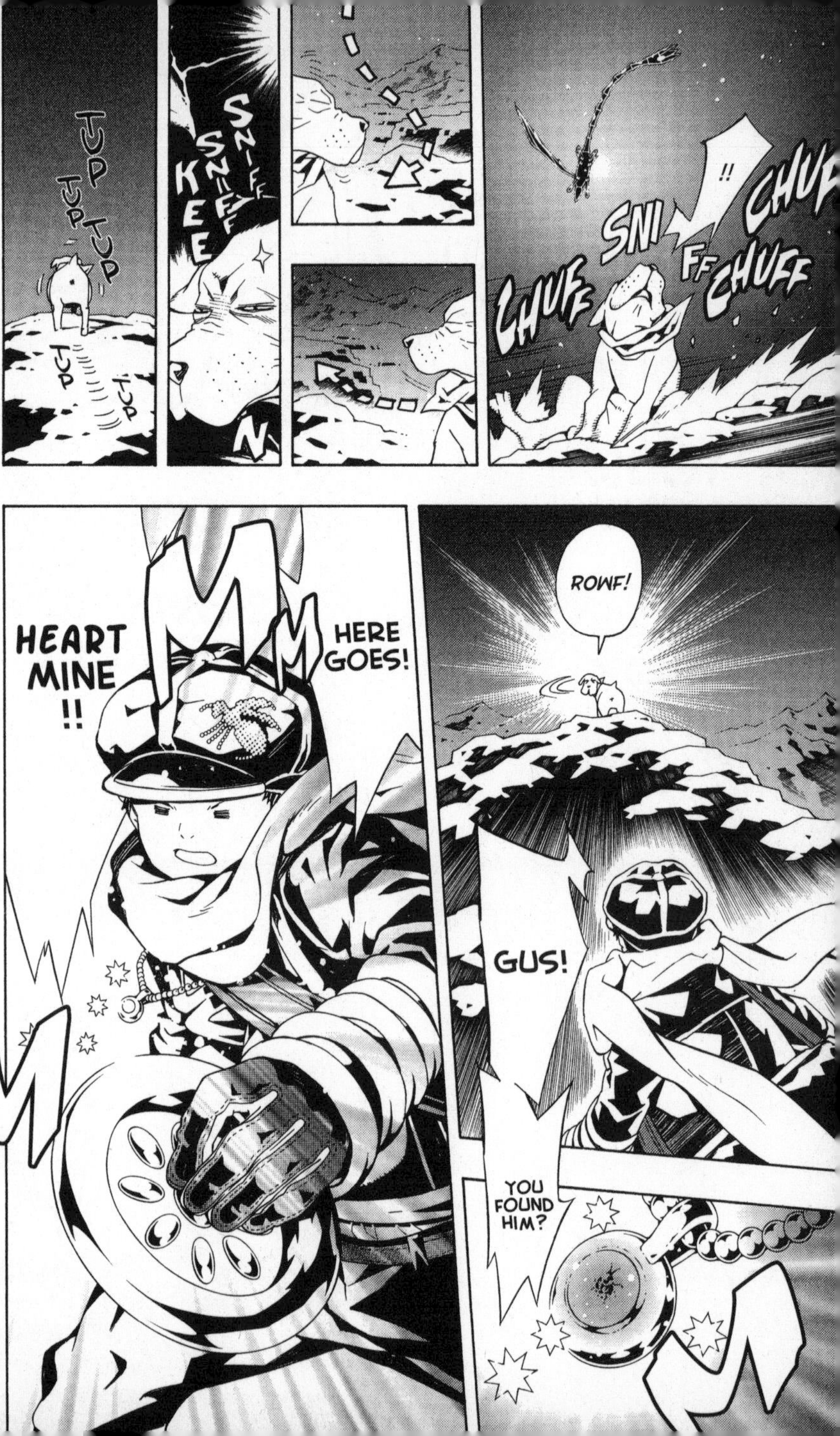

!!
CHUFF
SNIFF
CHUFF
CHUFF
SKEE
SNIFF
SNIFF
SNIFF
TUP
TUP
TUP
TUP
TUP
TUP
ROWF!
GUS!
YOU FOUND HIM?
HERE GOES!
HEART MINE!!

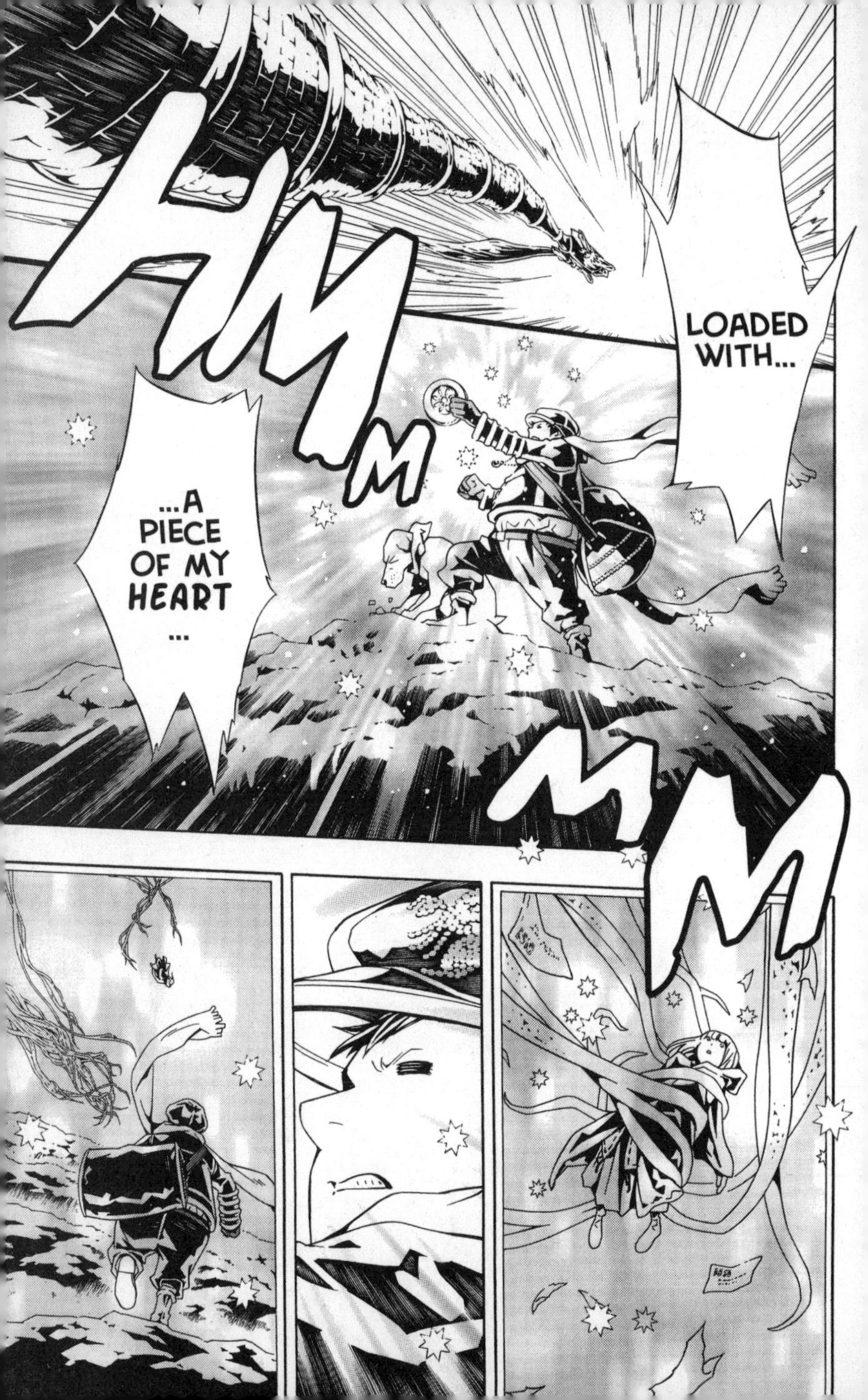
LOADED WITH...
HMMMMM
...A PIECE OF MY HEART ...

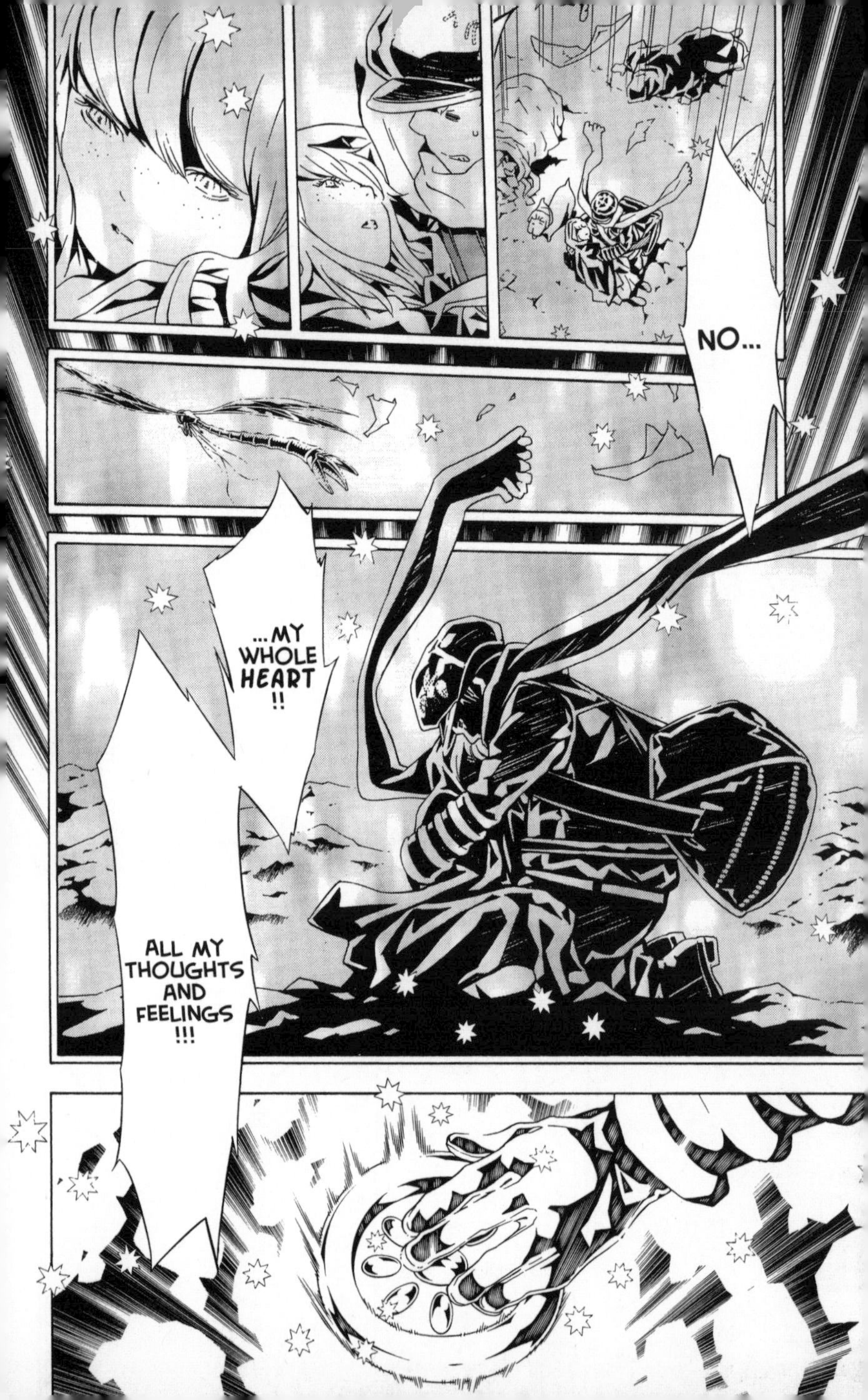
NO...
...MY WHOLE HEART !!
ALL MY THOUGHTS AND FEELINGS !!!

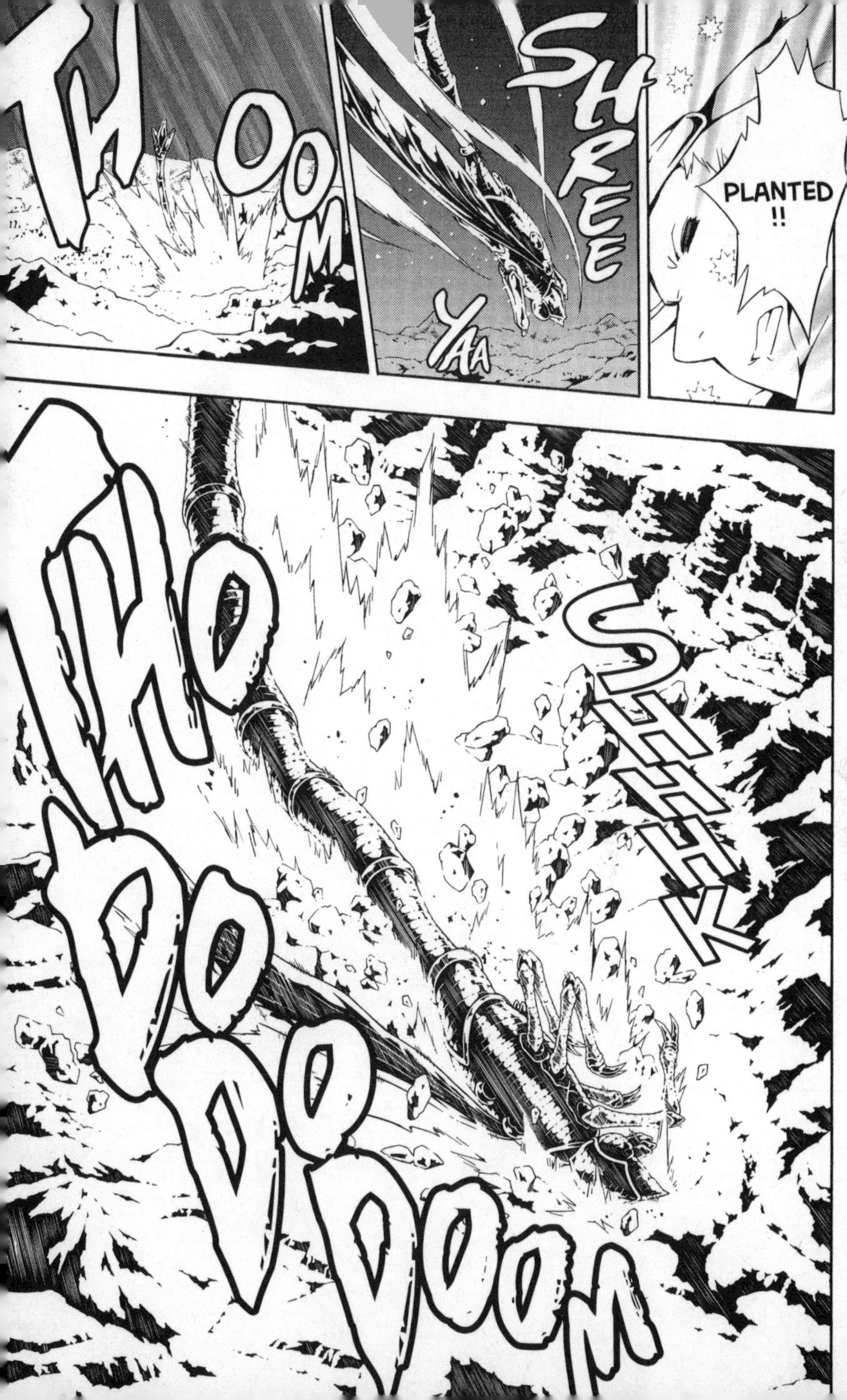
PLANTED !!
SHREEE
YAA
THOOOM
SHEEEK

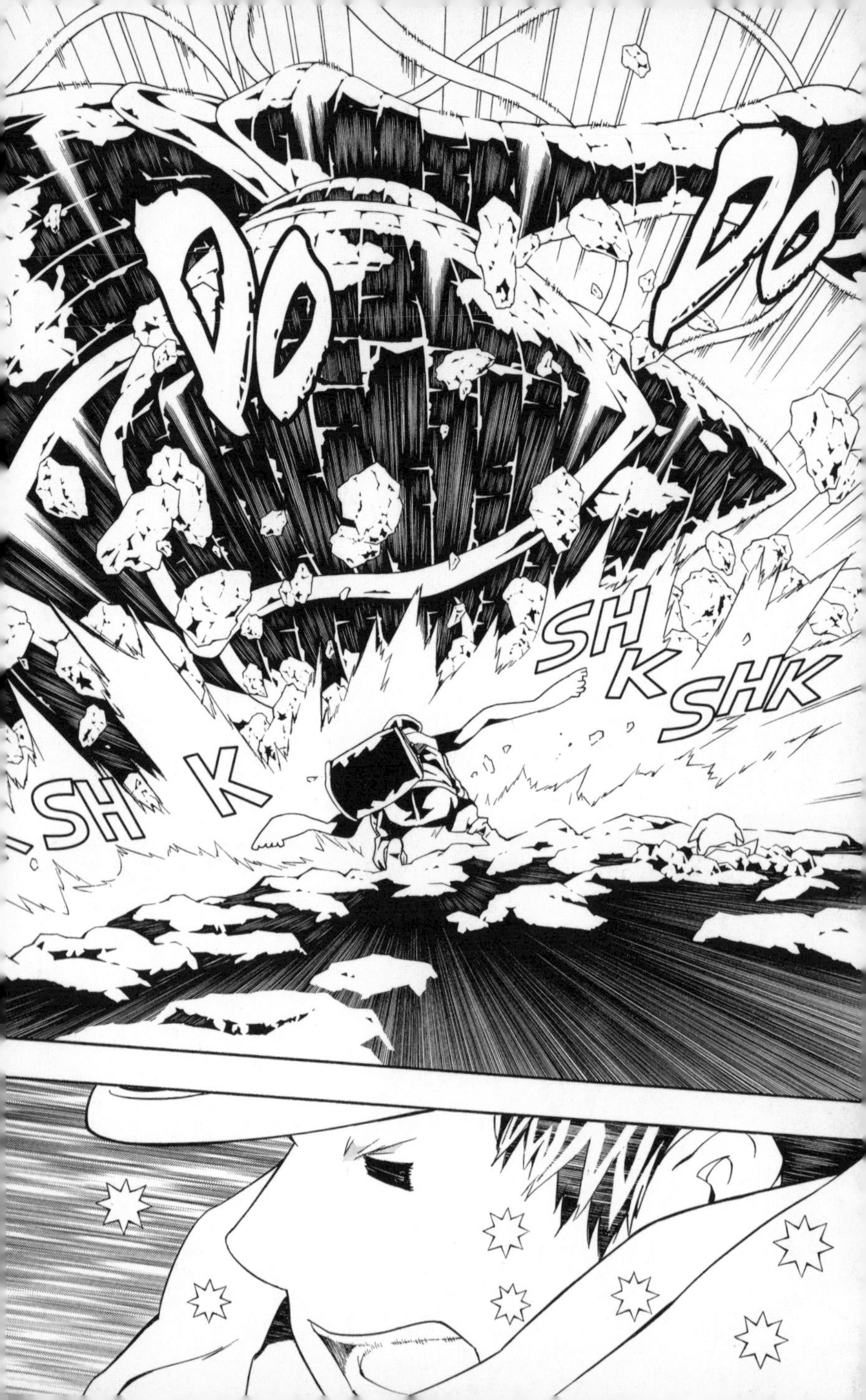
DO
DO
SH K SHK
-SH K

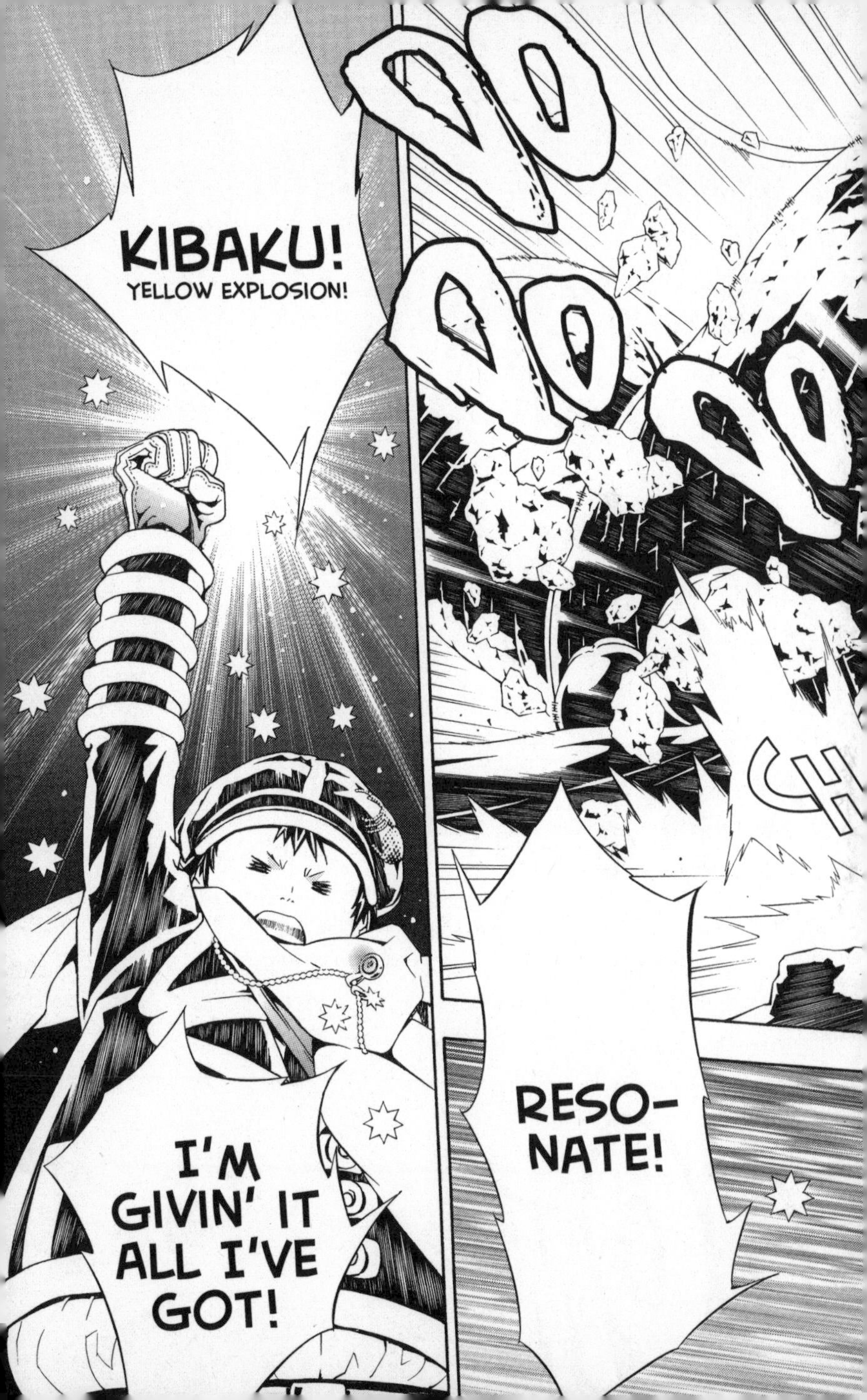
DO DO DO
RESO-
NATE!
KIBAKU!
YELLOW EXPLOSION!
I'M
GIVIN' IT
ALL I'VE
GOT!

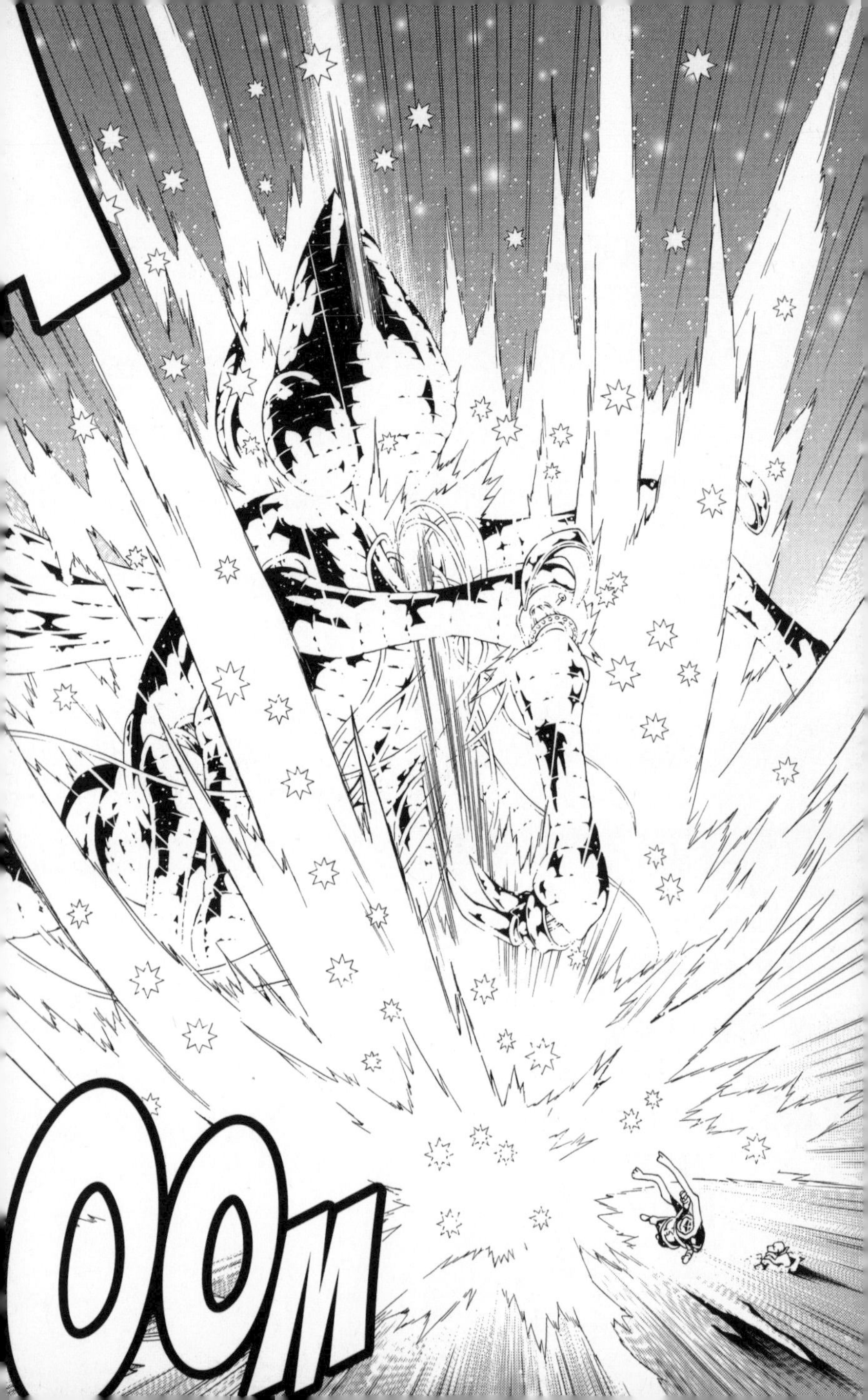
OOM

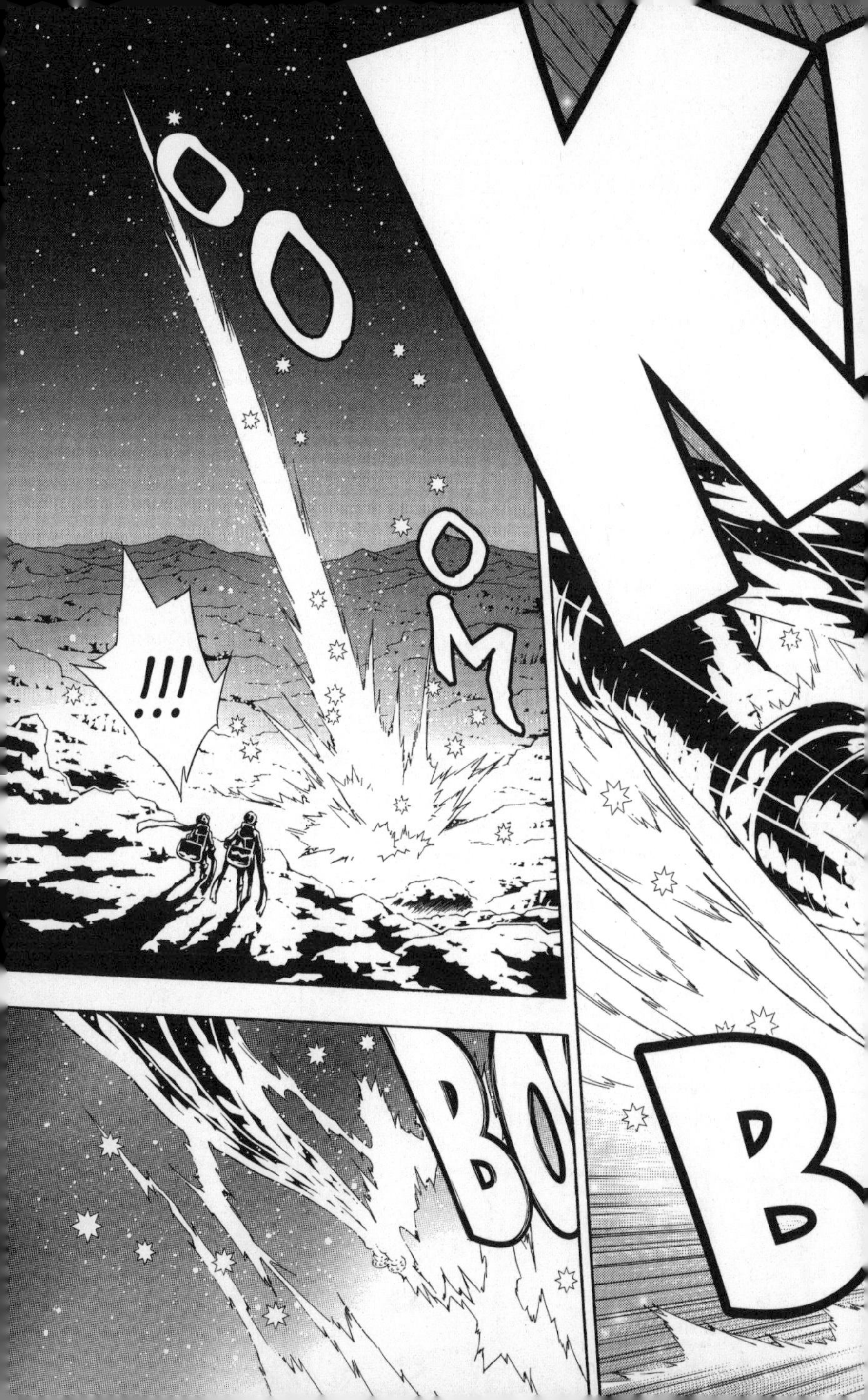
K
B
OOOM
!!!
BO

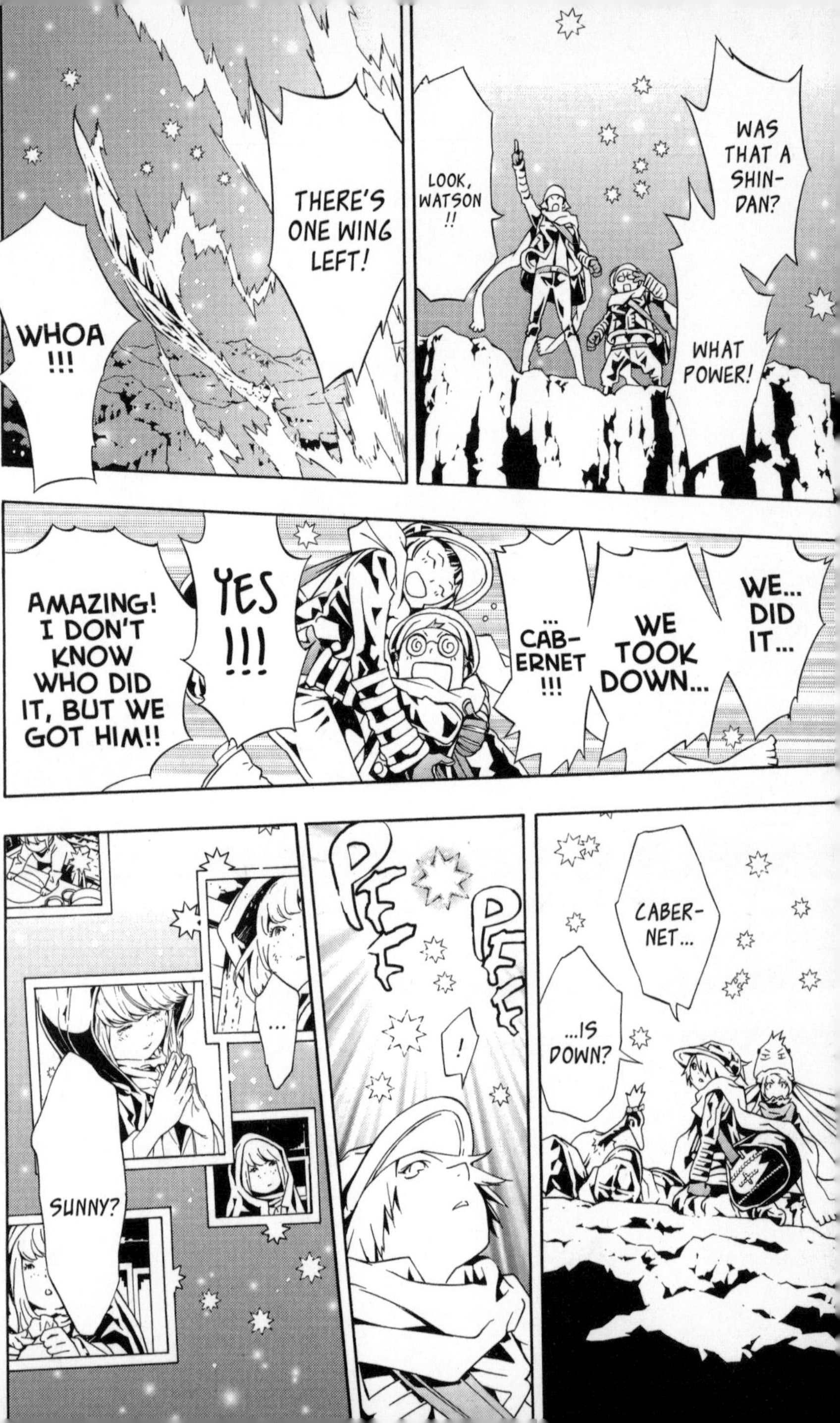
WAS THAT A SHIN-DAN?
LOOK, WATSON !!
WHAT POWER!
THERE'S ONE WING LEFT!
WHOA !!!
WE... DID IT...
WE TOOK DOWN...
...CABERNET !!!
YES !!!
AMAZING! I DON'T KNOW WHO DID IT, BUT WE GOT HIM!!
CABERNET...
...IS DOWN?
PEF
PEF
!
...
SUNNY?

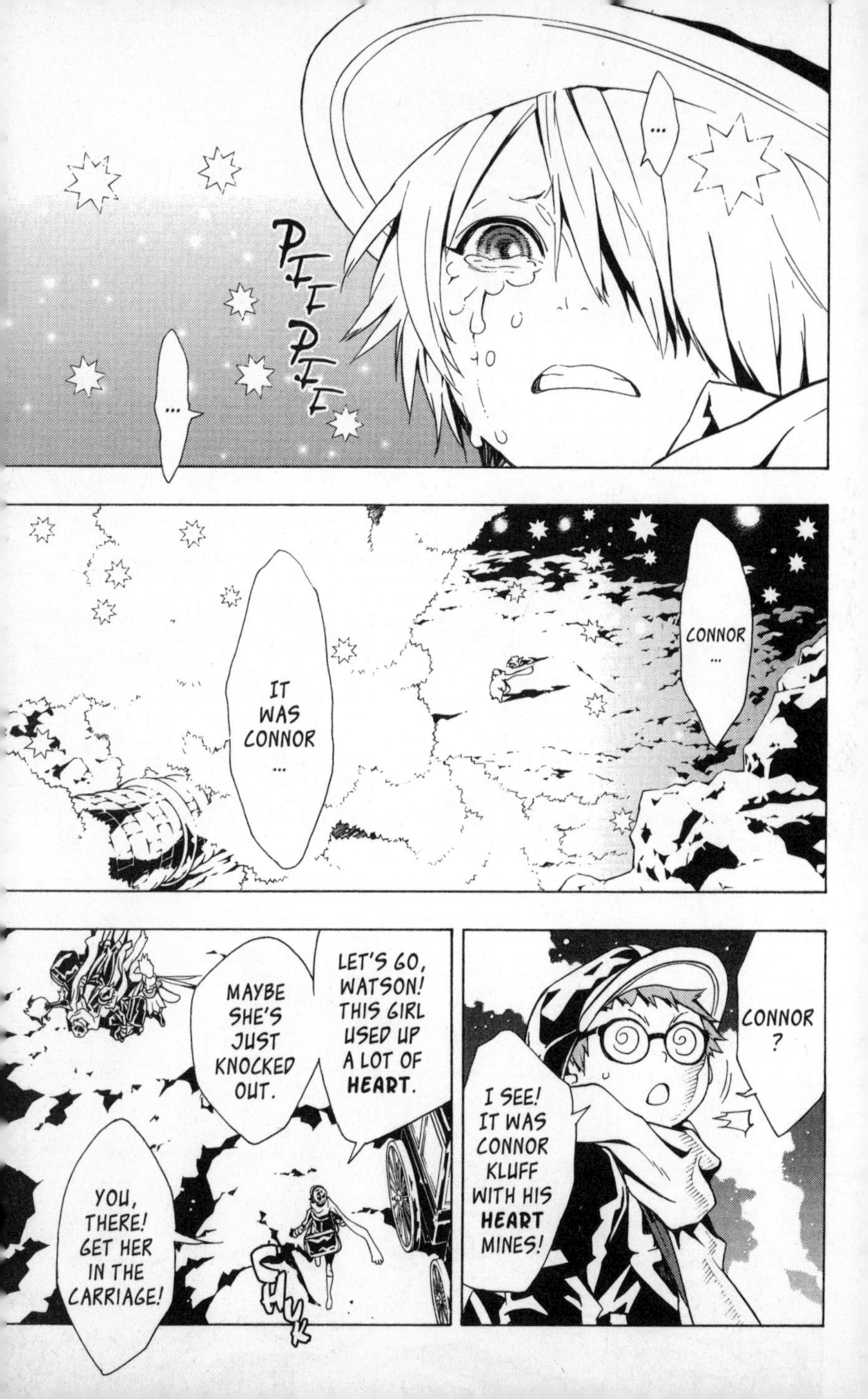
...
PFF PFF
...
CONNOR...
IT WAS CONNOR...
CONNOR?
I SEE! IT WAS CONNOR KLUFF WITH HIS HEART MINES!
LET'S GO, WATSON! THIS GIRL USED UP A LOT OF HEART.
MAYBE SHE'S JUST KNOCKED OUT.
YOU, THERE! GET HER IN THE CARRIAGE!
SHUK

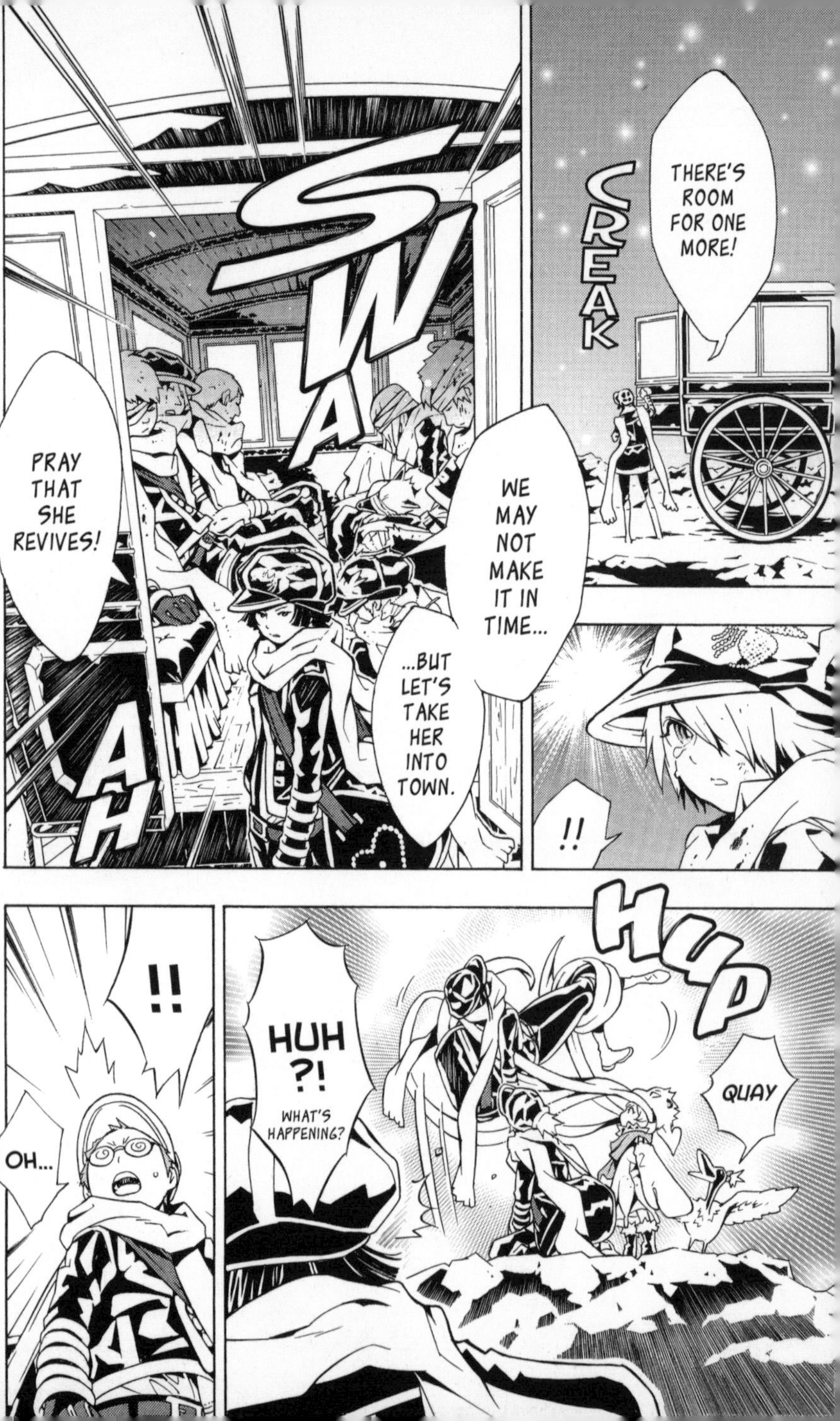
CREAK
THERE'S ROOM FOR ONE MORE!
!!
SWA
WE MAY NOT MAKE IT IN TIME...
PRAY THAT SHE REVIVES!
...BUT LET'S TAKE HER INTO TOWN.
AH
HUP
QUAY
HUH ?!
WHAT'S HAPPENING?
!!
OH...

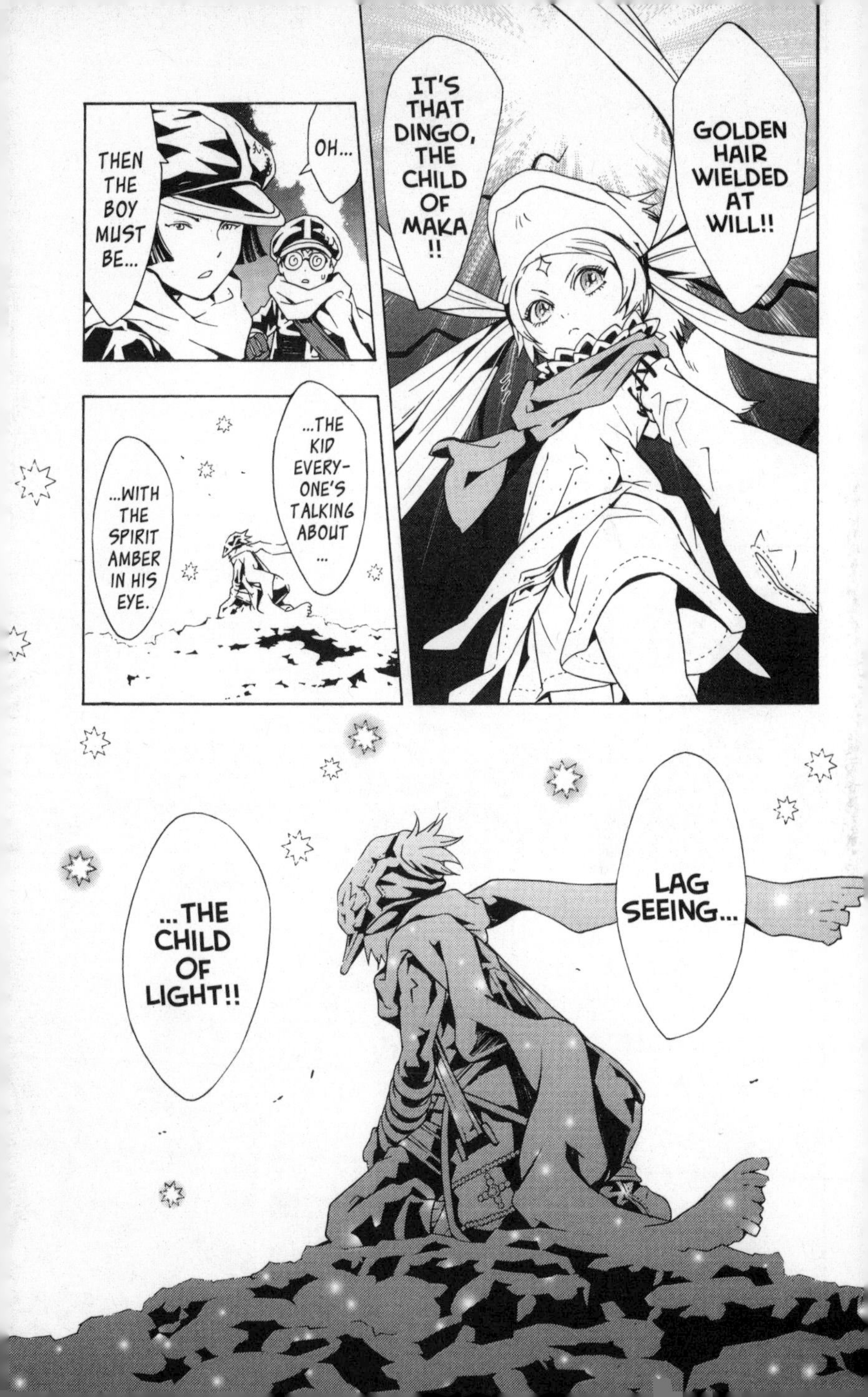
GOLDEN HAIR WIELDED AT WILL!!
IT'S THAT DINGO, THE CHILD OF MAKA!!
OH...
THEN THE BOY MUST BE...
...THE KID EVERY-ONE'S TALKING ABOUT...
...WITH THE SPIRIT AMBER IN HIS EYE.
LAG SEEING...
...THE CHILD OF LIGHT!!

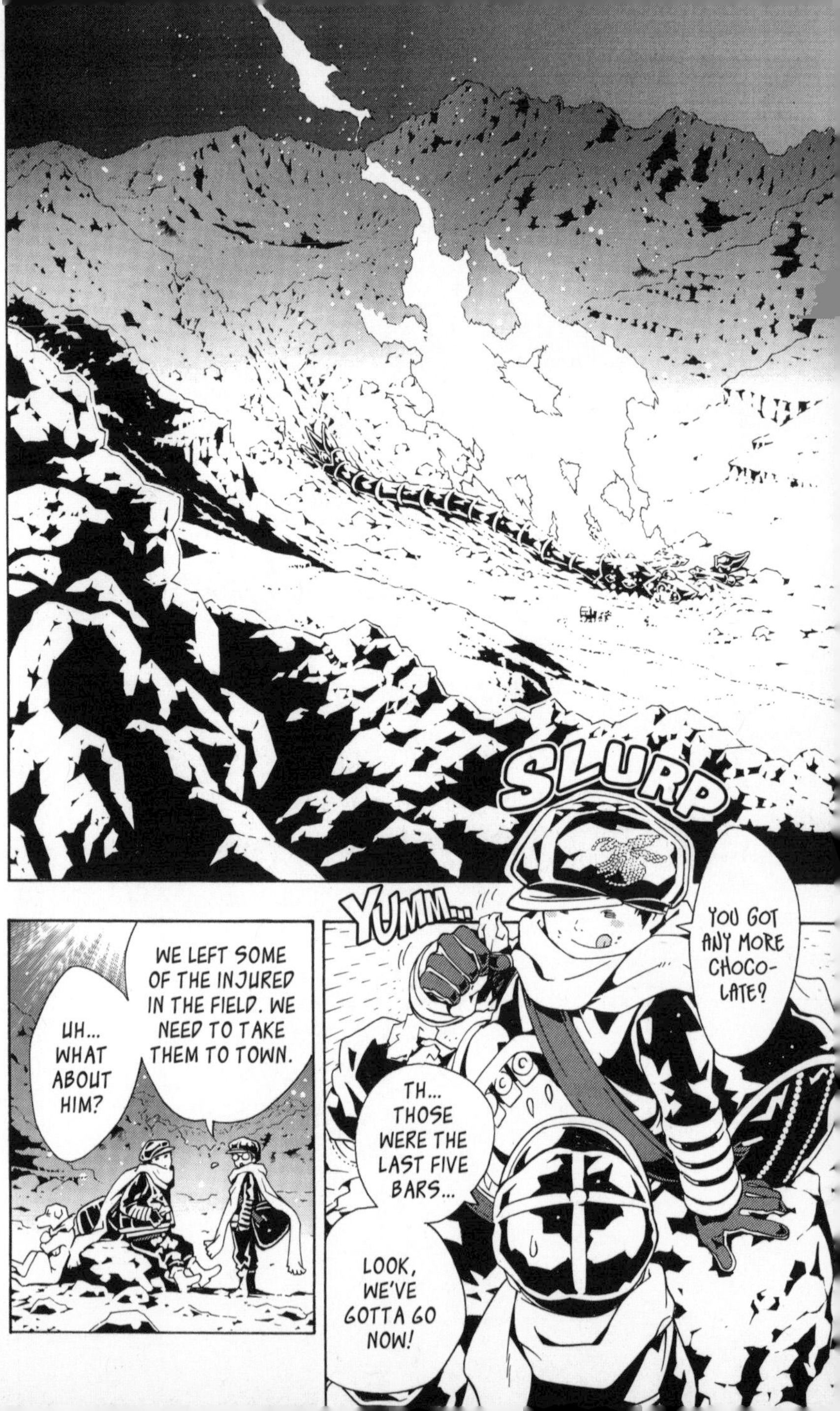
SLURP
YUMM...
YOU GOT ANY MORE CHOCO-LATE?
TH... THOSE WERE THE LAST FIVE BARS...
LOOK, WE'VE GOTTA GO NOW!
WE LEFT SOME OF THE INJURED IN THE FIELD. WE NEED TO TAKE THEM TO TOWN.
UH... WHAT ABOUT HIM?

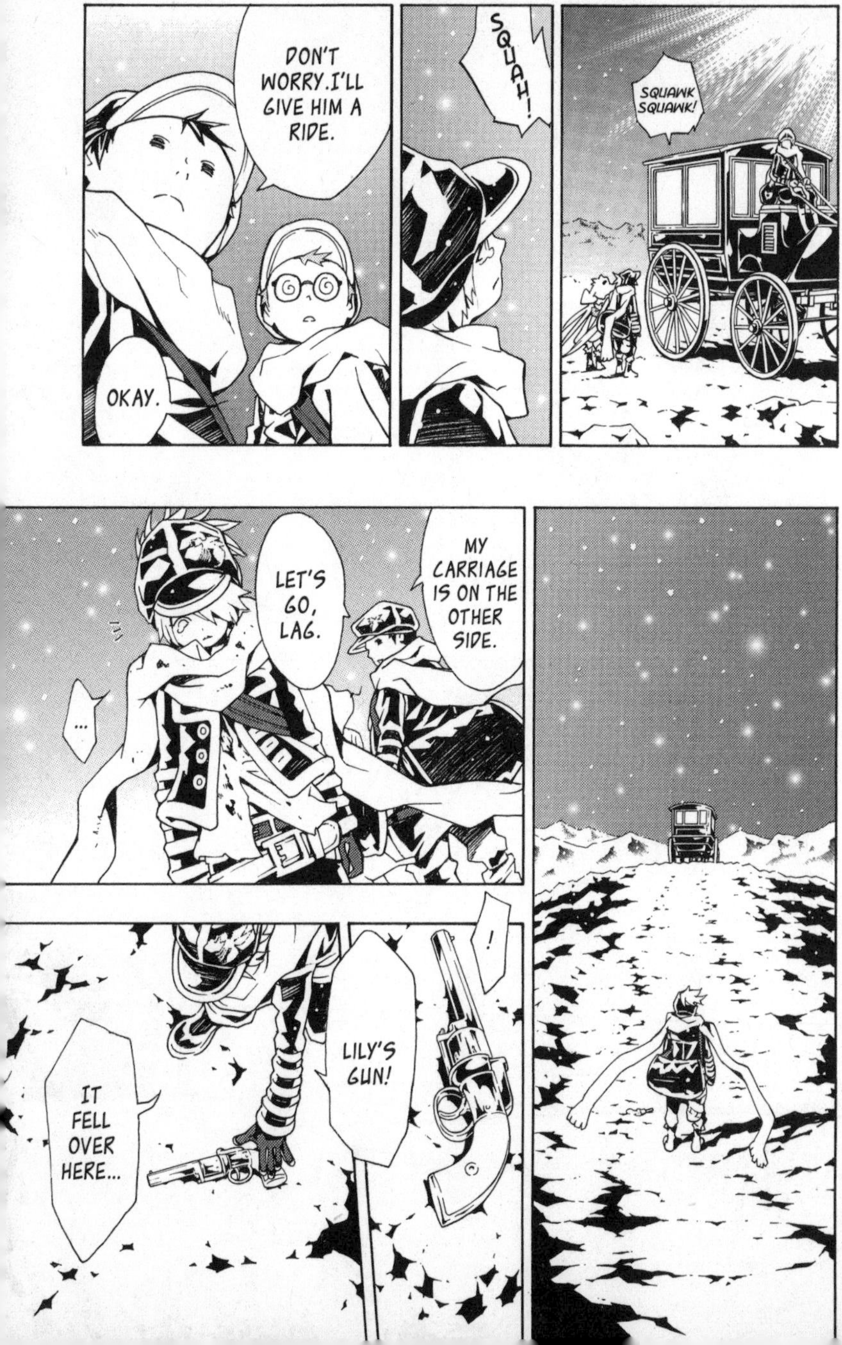
SQUAWK SQUAWK!
SQUAH!
DON'T WORRY. I'LL GIVE HIM A RIDE.
OKAY.
MY CARRIAGE IS ON THE OTHER SIDE.
LET'S GO, LAG.
...
!
LILY'S GUN!
IT FELL OVER HERE...

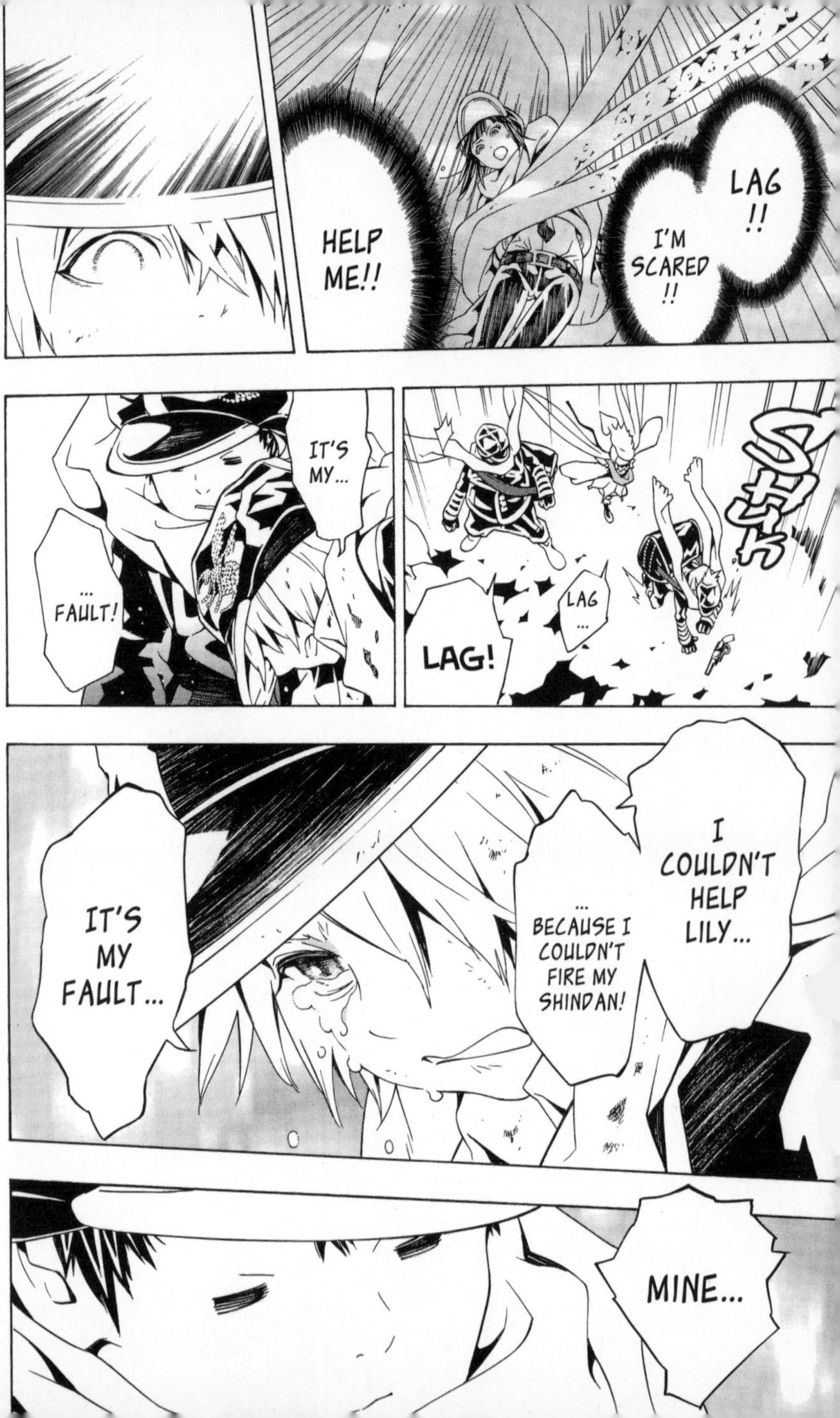
LAG !!
I'M SCARED !!
HELP ME!!
SHUH
LAG ...
LAG!
IT'S MY...
... FAULT!
I COULDN'T HELP LILY...
... BECAUSE I COULDN'T FIRE MY SHINDAN!
IT'S MY FAULT...
MINE...

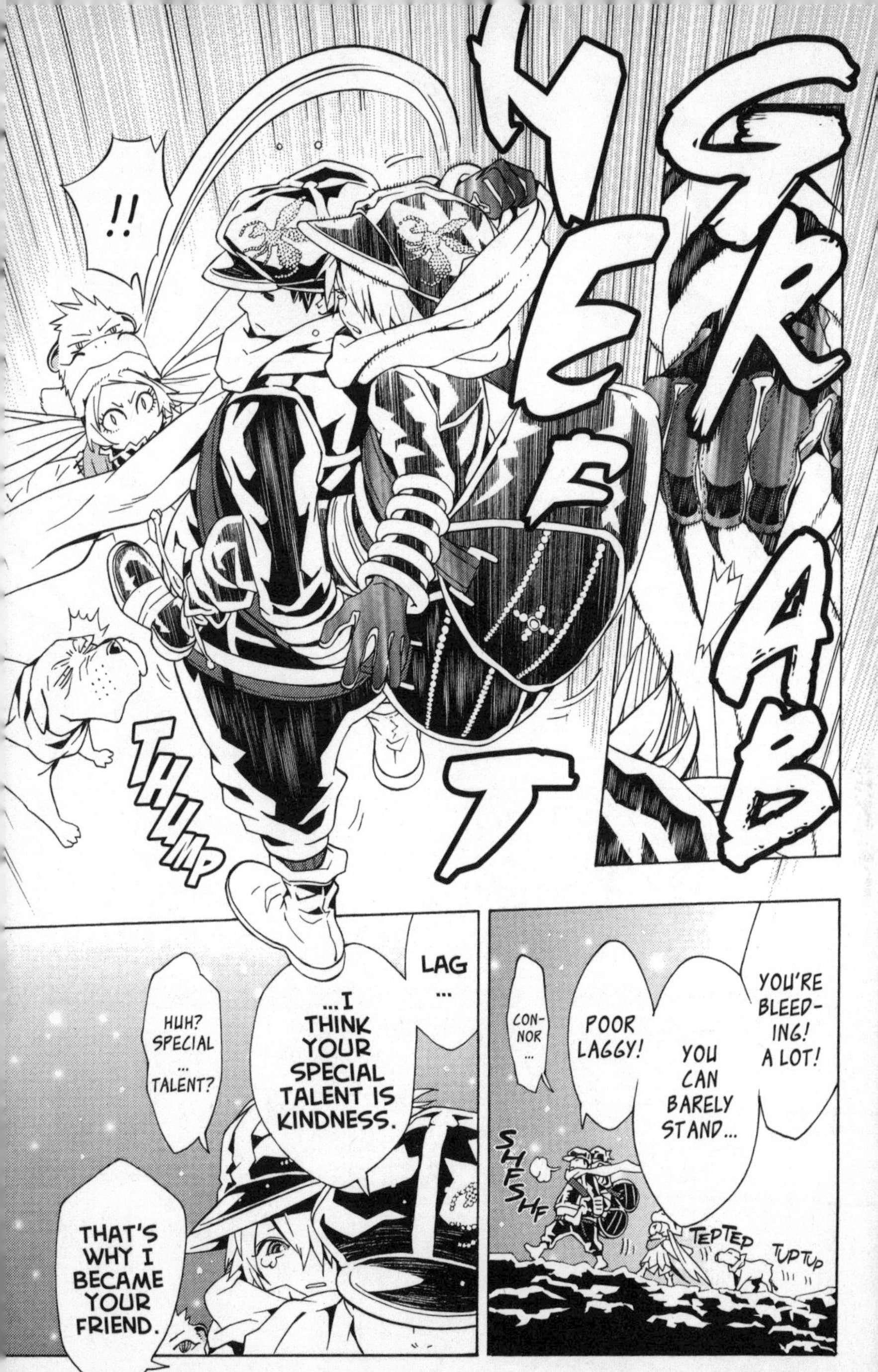
GRAB
HEFT
!!
THUMP
YOU'RE BLEED-ING! A LOT!
YOU CAN BARELY STAND...
POOR LAGGY!
CON-NOR ...
SHFSHF
TEPTEP
TUPTUP
LAG ...
...I THINK YOUR SPECIAL TALENT IS KINDNESS.
HUH? SPECIAL ... TALENT?
THAT'S WHY I BECAME YOUR FRIEND.

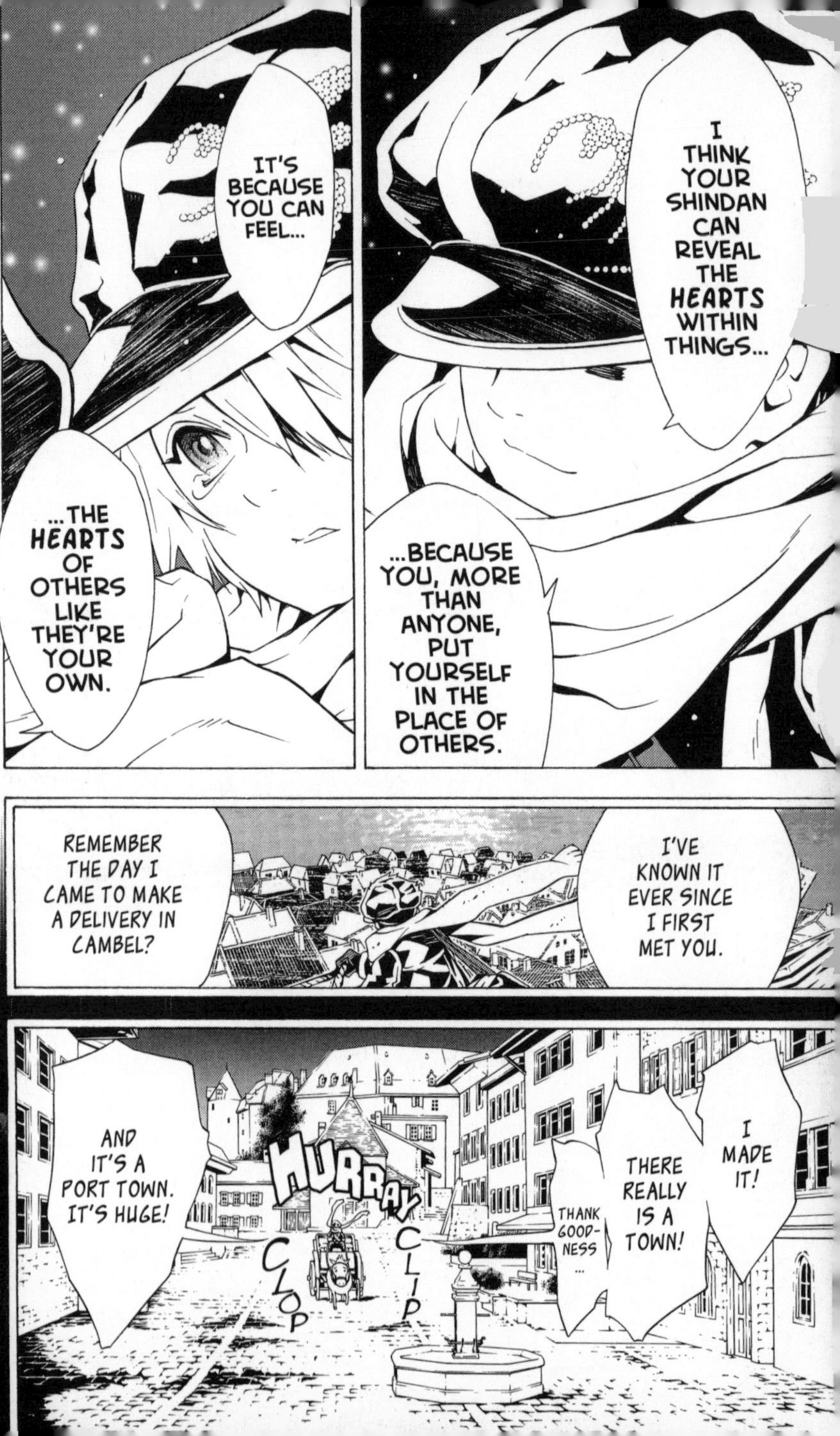
I THINK YOUR SHINDAN CAN REVEAL THE HEARTS WITHIN THINGS...
...BECAUSE YOU, MORE THAN ANYONE, PUT YOURSELF IN THE PLACE OF OTHERS.
IT'S BECAUSE YOU CAN FEEL...
...THE HEARTS OF OTHERS LIKE THEY'RE YOUR OWN.
I'VE KNOWN IT EVER SINCE I FIRST MET YOU.
REMEMBER THE DAY I CAME TO MAKE A DELIVERY IN CAMBEL?
I MADE IT!
THERE REALLY IS A TOWN!
THANK GOODNESS...
CLIP
HURRAY
CLOP
AND IT'S A PORT TOWN. IT'S HUGE!

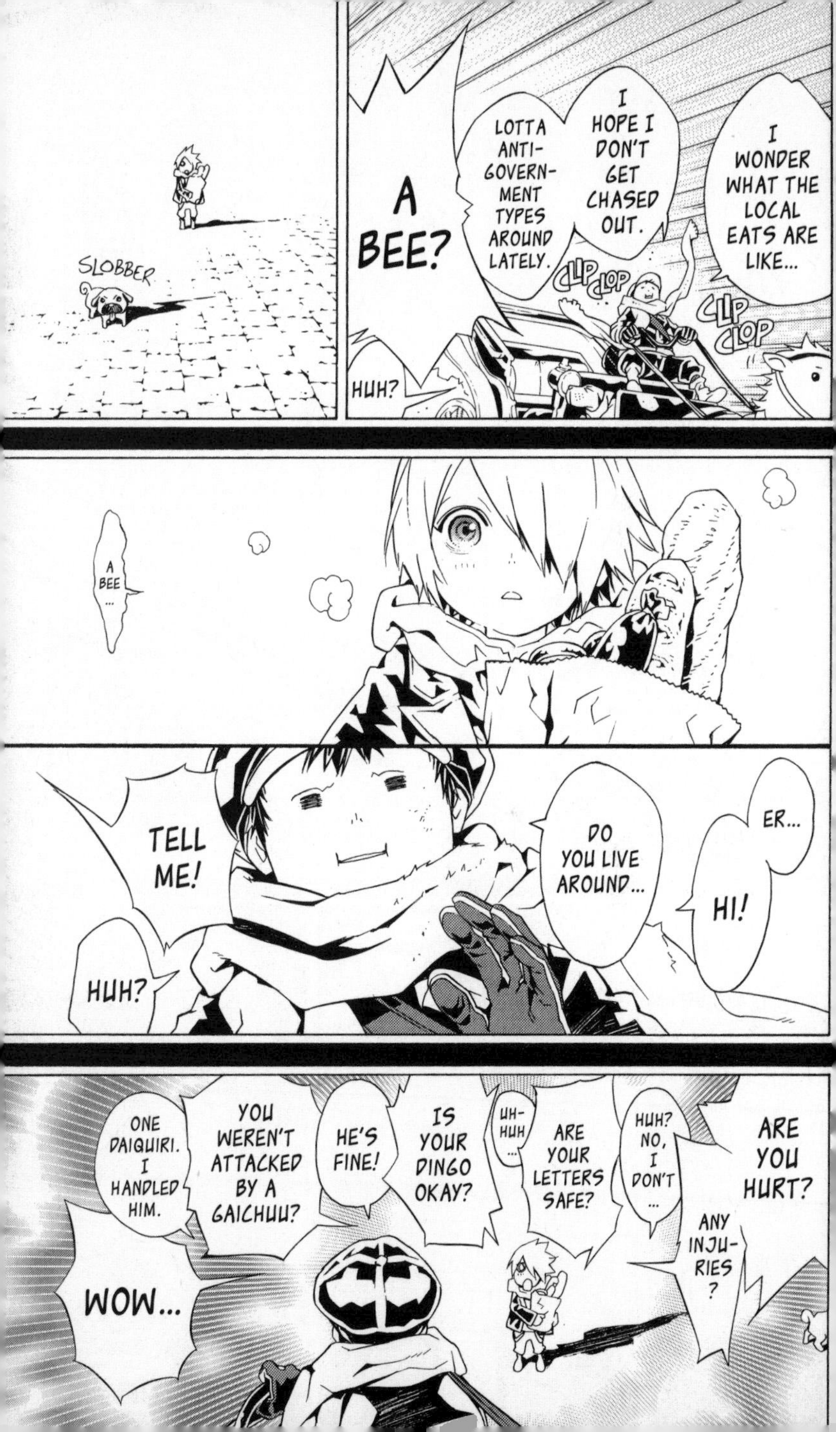
I WONDER WHAT THE LOCAL EATS ARE LIKE...
I HOPE I DON'T GET CHASED OUT.
LOTTA ANTI-GOVERNMENT TYPES AROUND LATELY.
A BEE?
CLIP CLOP
CLIP CLOP
HUH?
SLOBBER
A BEE...
ER...
HI!
DO YOU LIVE AROUND...
TELL ME!
HUH?
ARE YOU HURT?
ANY INJURIES?
HUH? NO, I DON'T...
ARE YOUR LETTERS SAFE?
UH-HUH...
IS YOUR DINGO OKAY?
HE'S FINE!
YOU WEREN'T ATTACKED BY A GAICHUU?
ONE DAIQUIRI. I HANDLED HIM.
WOW...

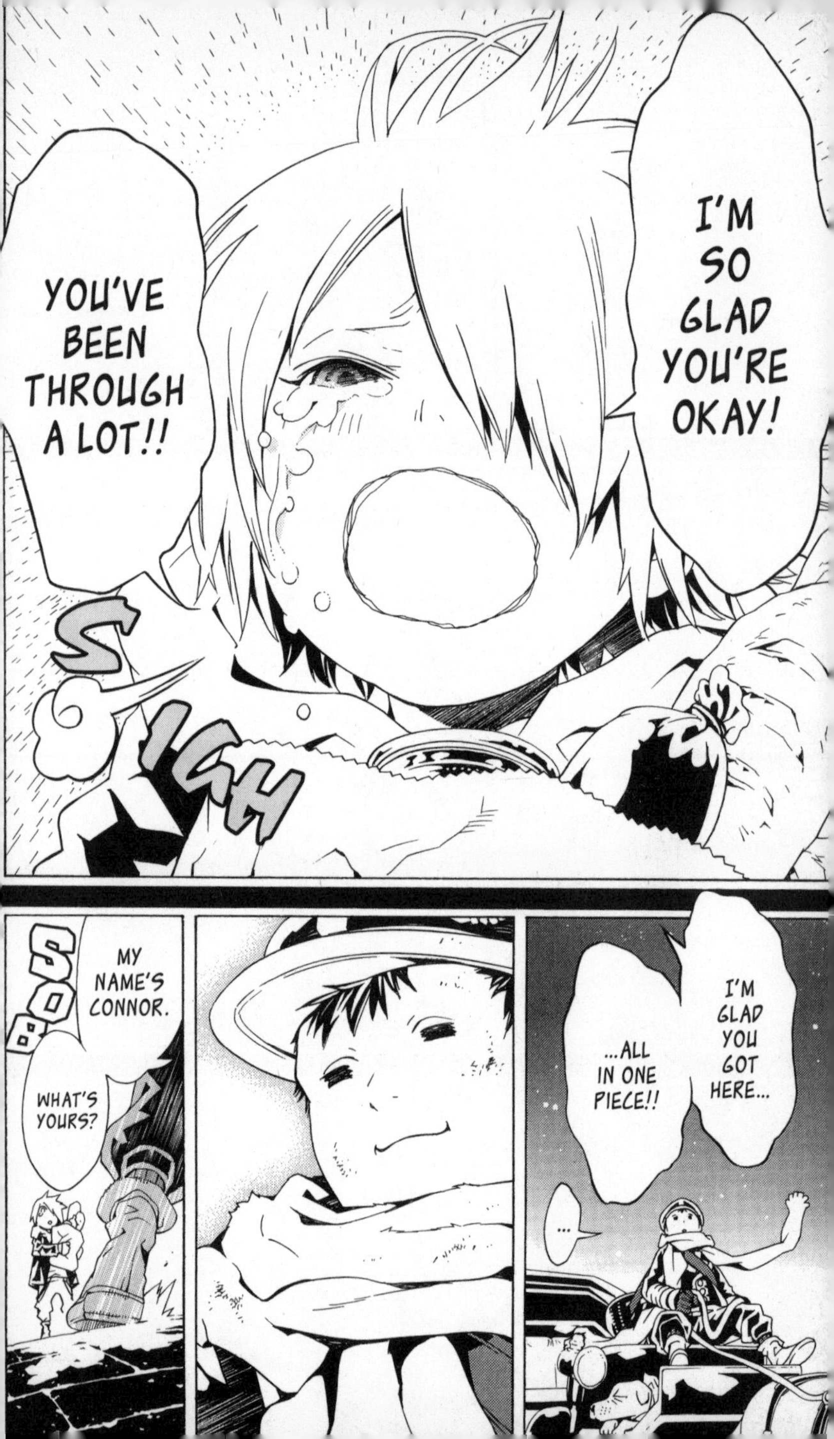
I'M SO GLAD YOU'RE OKAY!
YOU'VE BEEN THROUGH A LOT!!
SIGH
I'M GLAD YOU GOT HERE...
...ALL IN ONE PIECE!!
...
SOB
MY NAME'S CONNOR.
WHAT'S YOURS?

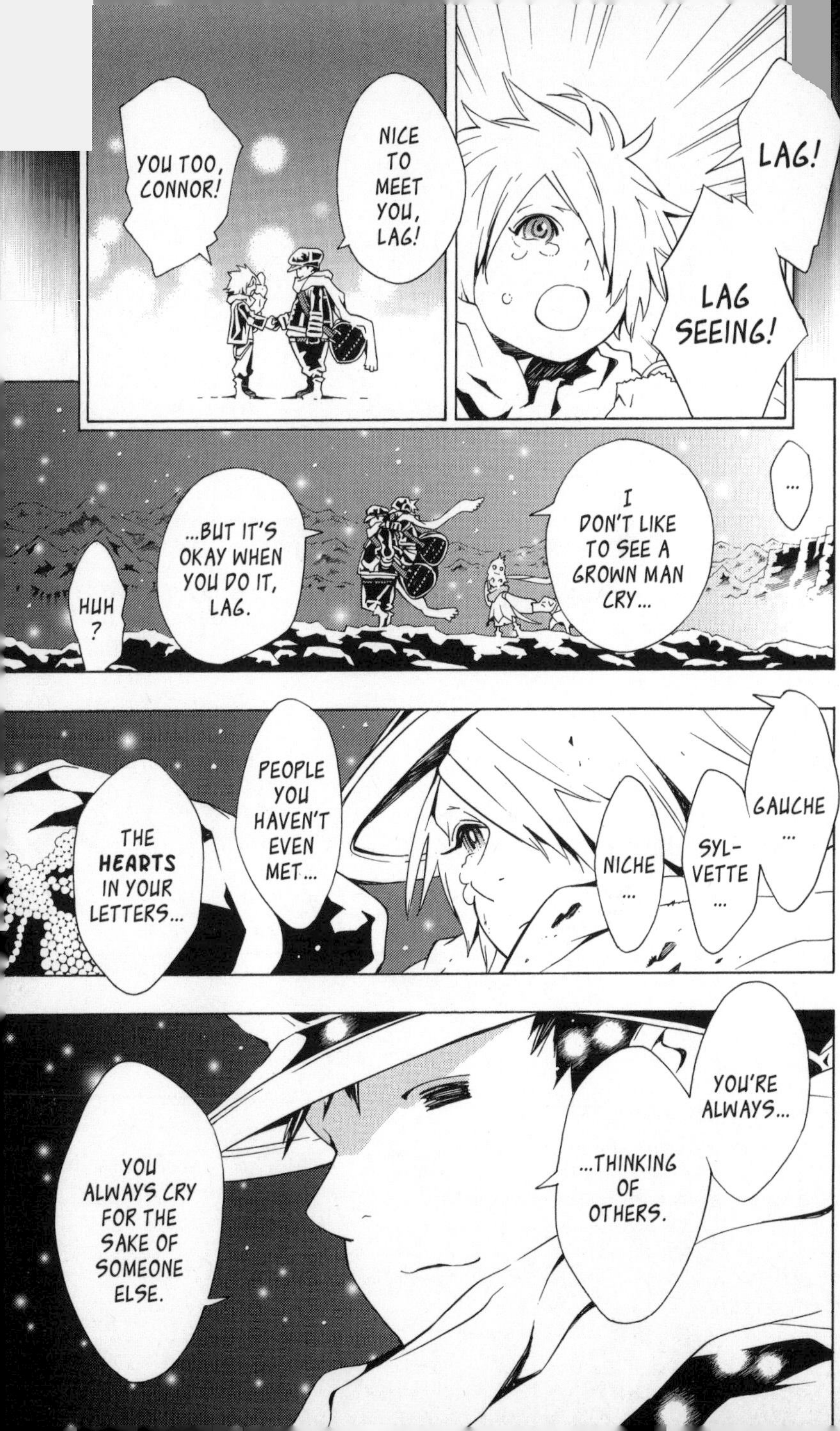
LAG!
LAG SEEING!
NICE TO MEET YOU, LAG!
YOU TOO, CONNOR!
...
I DON'T LIKE TO SEE A GROWN MAN CRY...
...BUT IT'S OKAY WHEN YOU DO IT, LAG.
HUH?
GAUCHE...
SYLVETTE...
NICHE...
PEOPLE YOU HAVEN'T EVEN MET...
THE **HEARTS** IN YOUR LETTERS...
YOU'RE ALWAYS...
...THINKING OF OTHERS.
YOU ALWAYS CRY FOR THE SAKE OF SOMEONE ELSE.

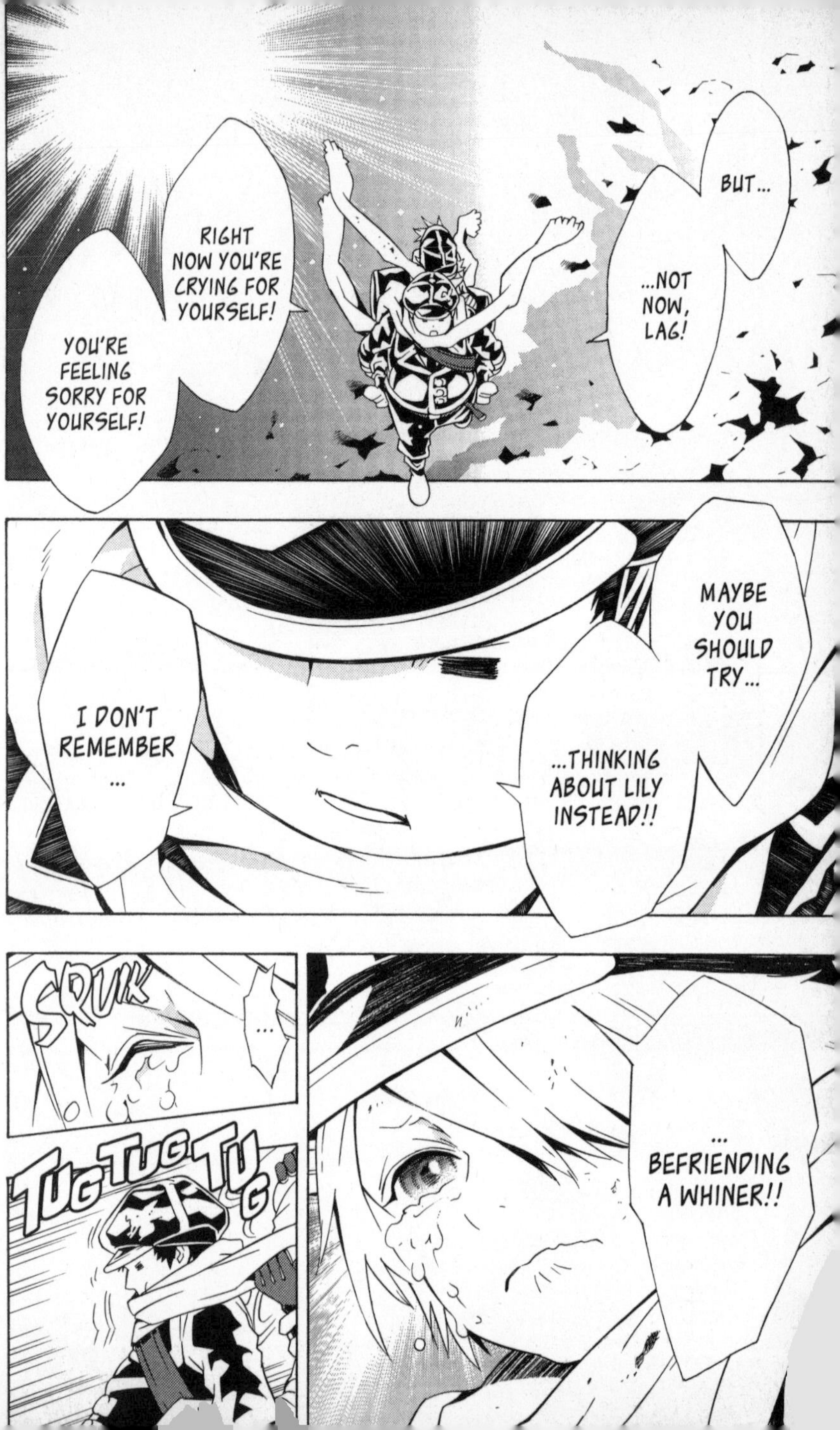
BUT...
...NOT NOW, LAG!
RIGHT NOW YOU'RE CRYING FOR YOURSELF!
YOU'RE FEELING SORRY FOR YOURSELF!
MAYBE YOU SHOULD TRY...
...THINKING ABOUT LILY INSTEAD!!
I DON'T REMEMBER ...
... BEFRIENDING A WHINER!!
SQUIK
...
TUG TUG TUG

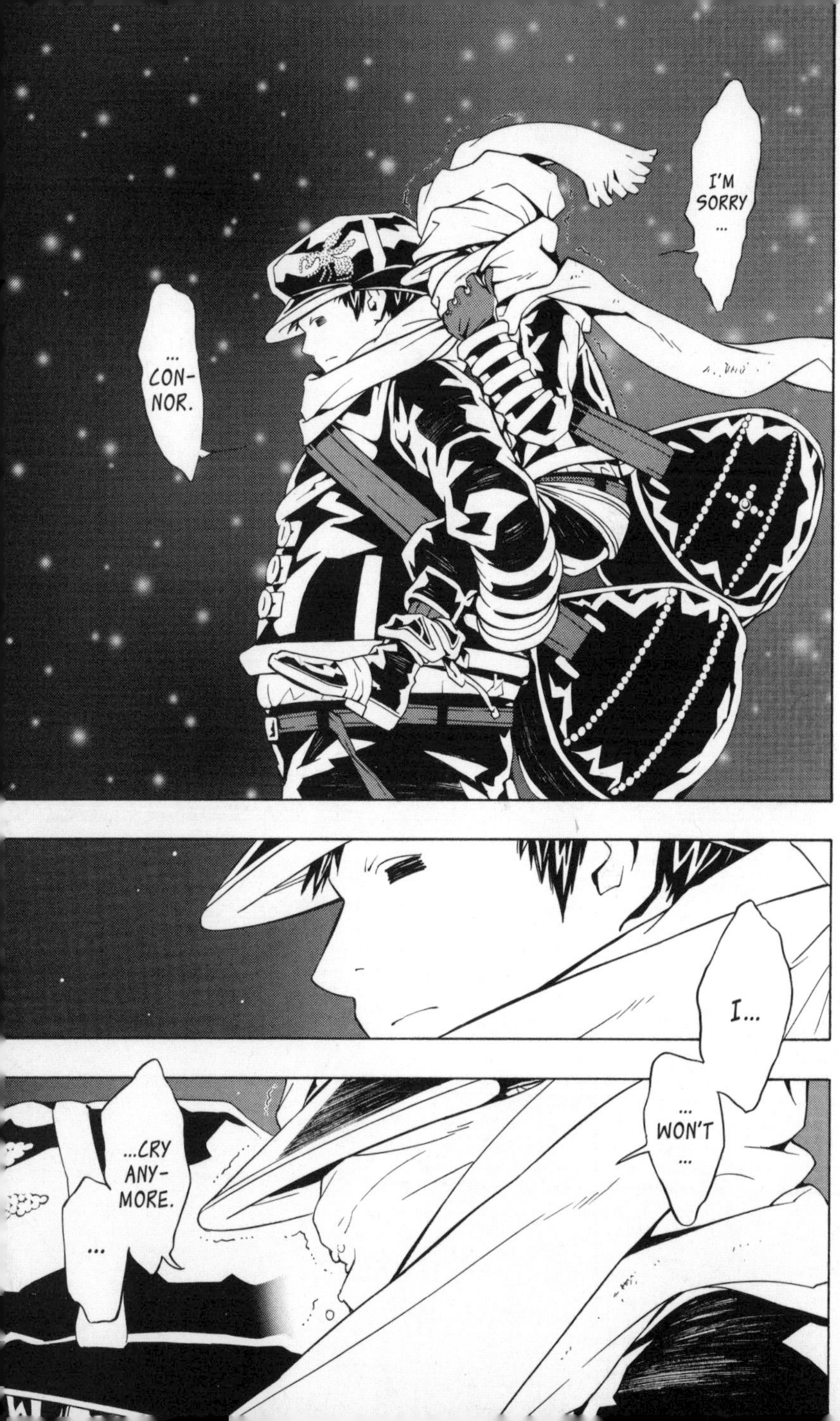
I'M SORRY ...
... CON-NOR.
I...
... WON'T ...
...CRY ANY-MORE.
...

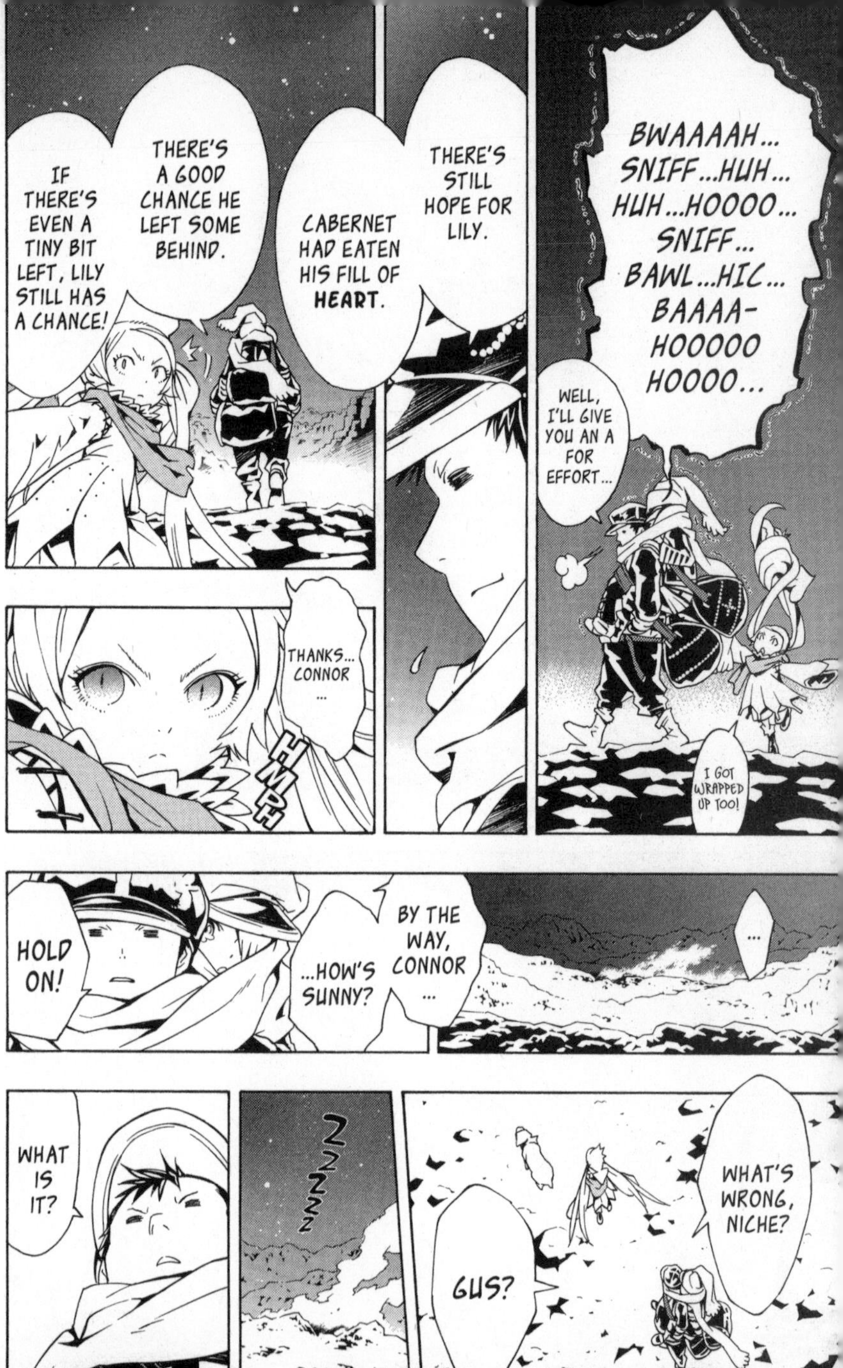
BWAAAAH... SNIFF...HUH... HUH...HOOOO... SNIFF... BAWL...HIC... BAAAA-HOOOOO HOOOO...
WELL, I'LL GIVE YOU AN A FOR EFFORT...
I GOT WRAPPED UP TOO!
THERE'S STILL HOPE FOR LILY.
CABERNET HAD EATEN HIS FILL OF HEART.
THERE'S A GOOD CHANCE HE LEFT SOME BEHIND.
IF THERE'S EVEN A TINY BIT LEFT, LILY STILL HAS A CHANCE!
THANKS... CONNOR ...
HMPH
...
BY THE WAY, CONNOR ...
...HOW'S SUNNY?
HOLD ON!
WHAT'S WRONG, NICHE?
GUS?
ZZZZZ
WHAT IS IT?

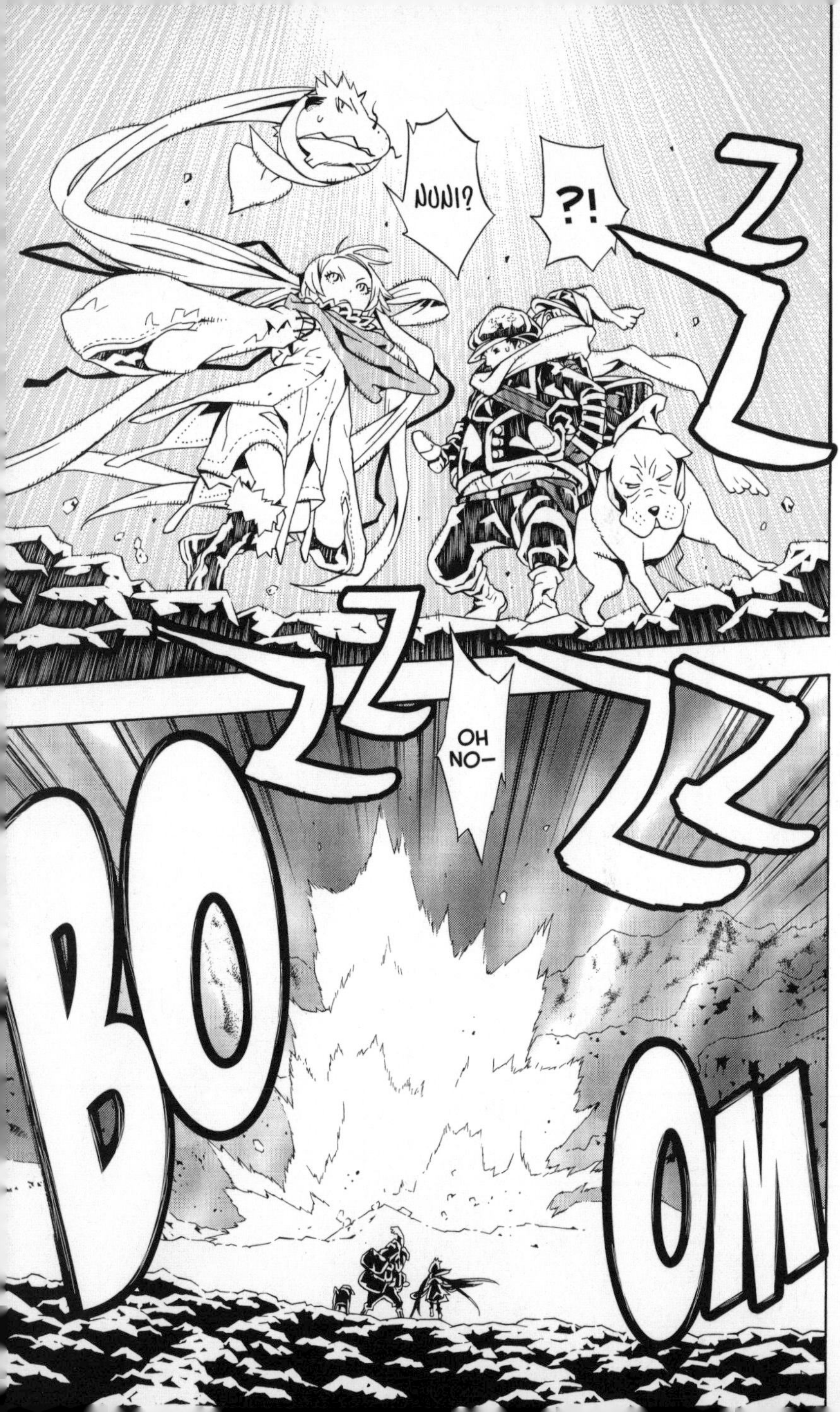

?!
NUNI?
ZZ
ZZ
OH NO–
ZZ
BOOM

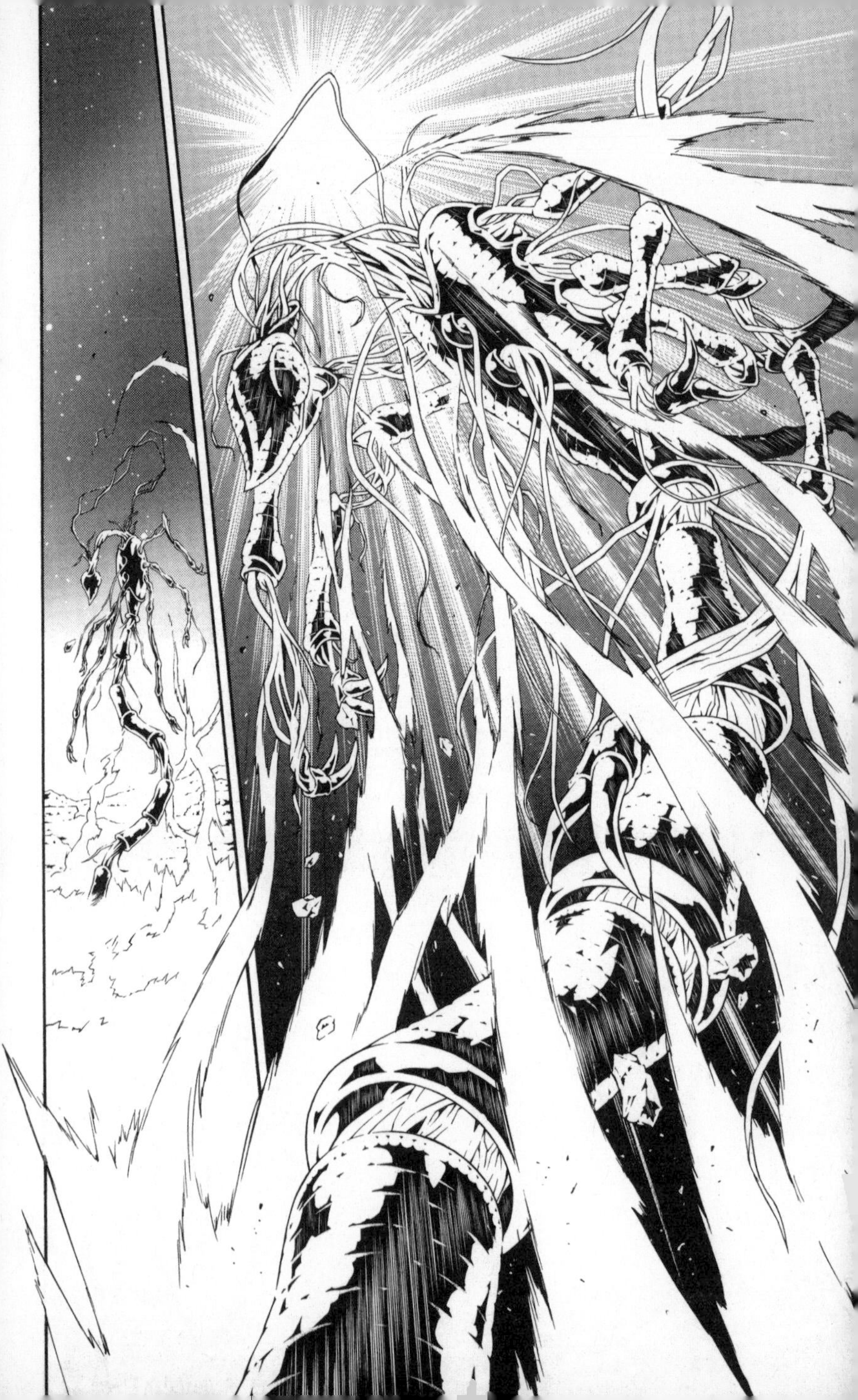

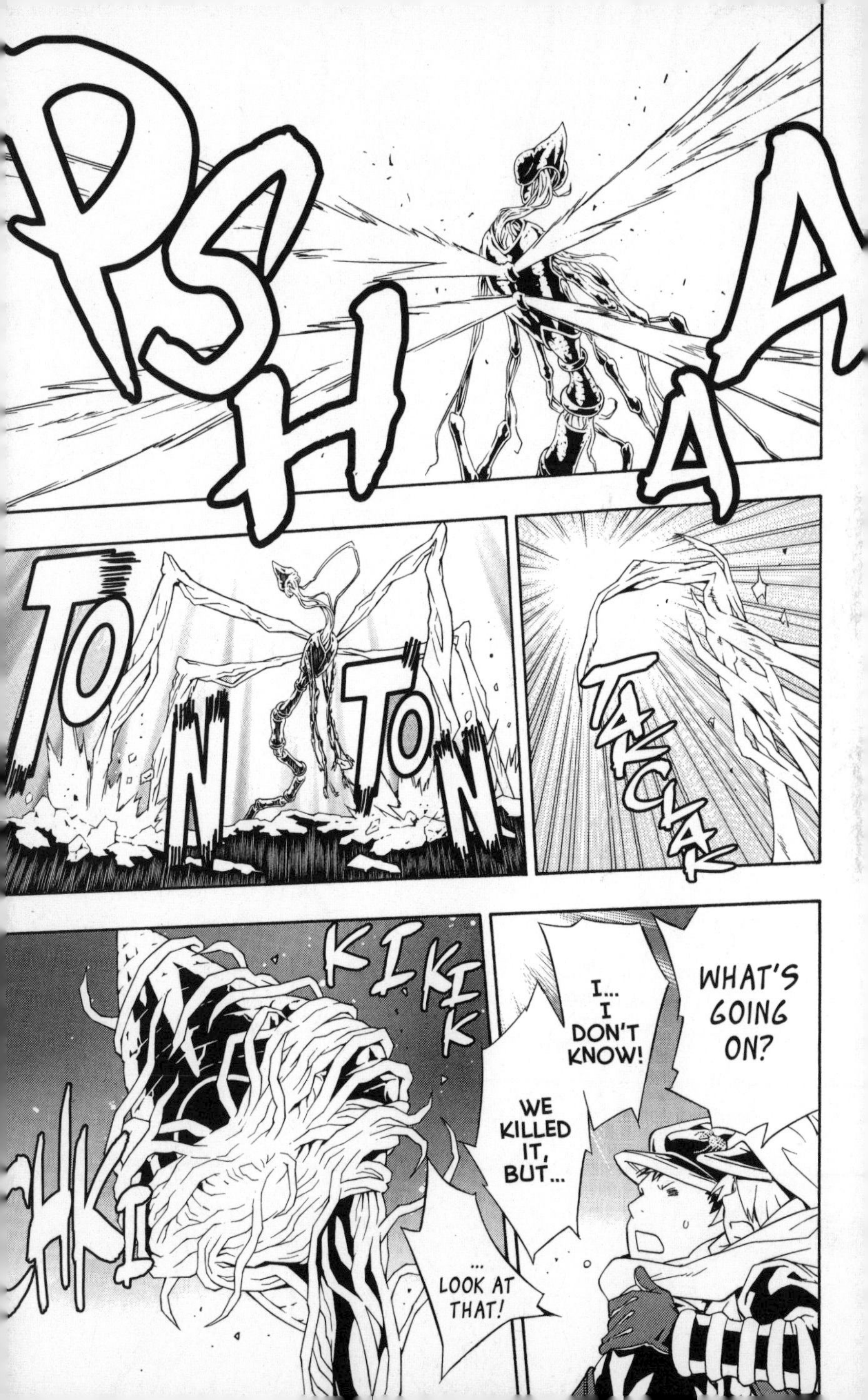
PSHAA
TAKCHAK
TON TON
WHAT'S GOING ON?
I... I DON'T KNOW!
WE KILLED IT, BUT...
... LOOK AT THAT!
KIKIKK
HKI

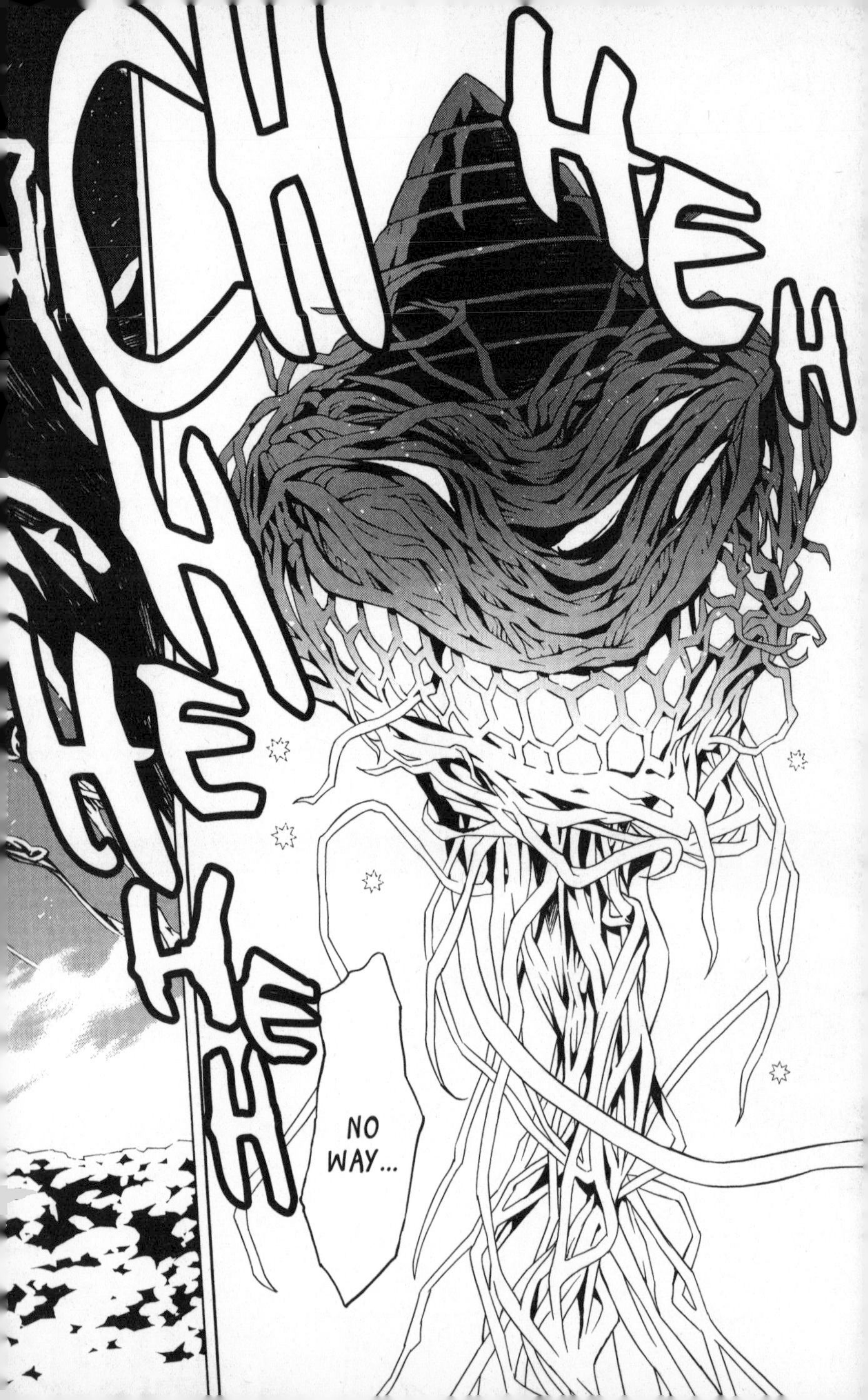
NO WAY...

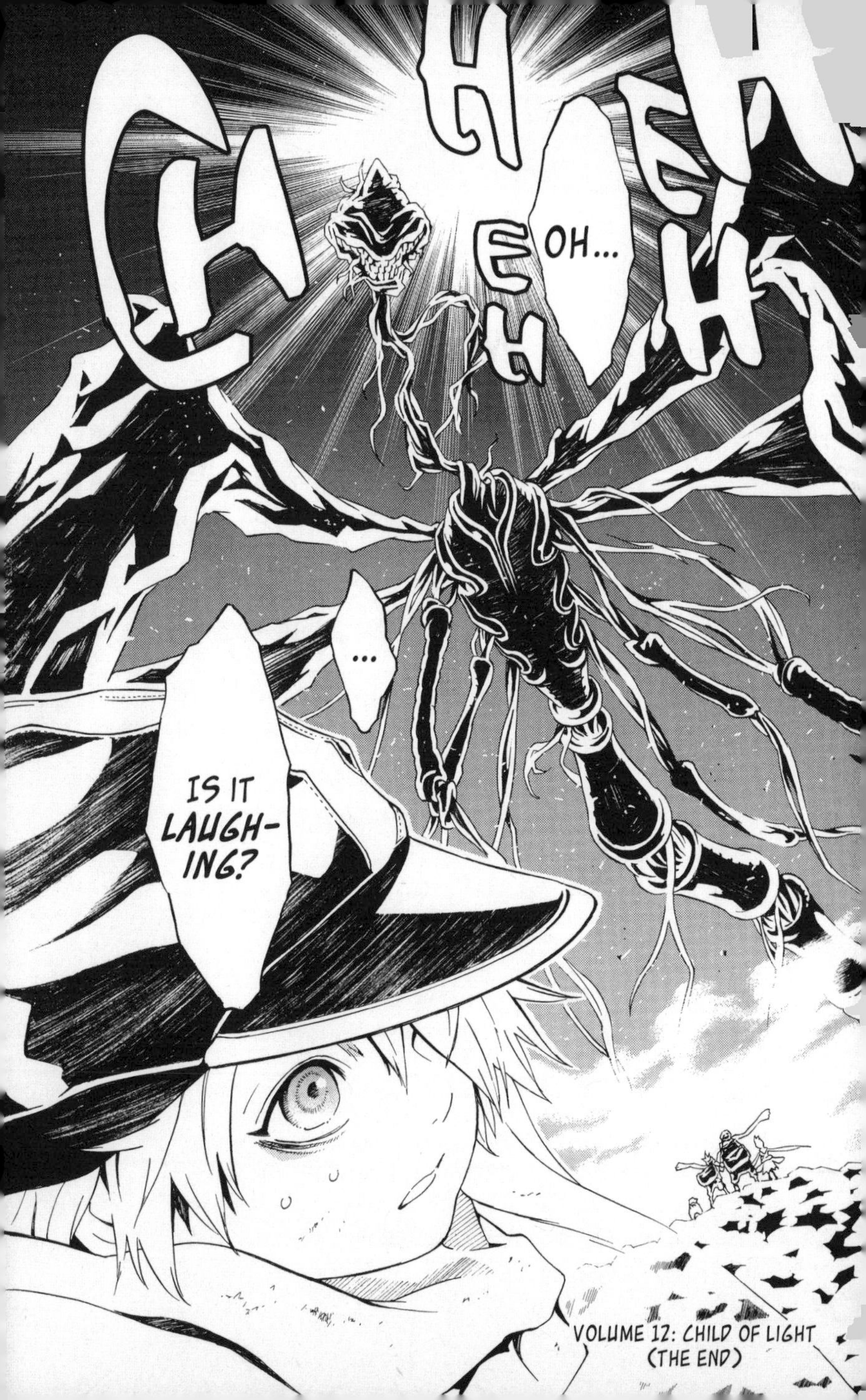
OH...
CHEHEH
...
IS IT LAUGHING?

VOLUME 12: CHILD OF LIGHT
(THE END)

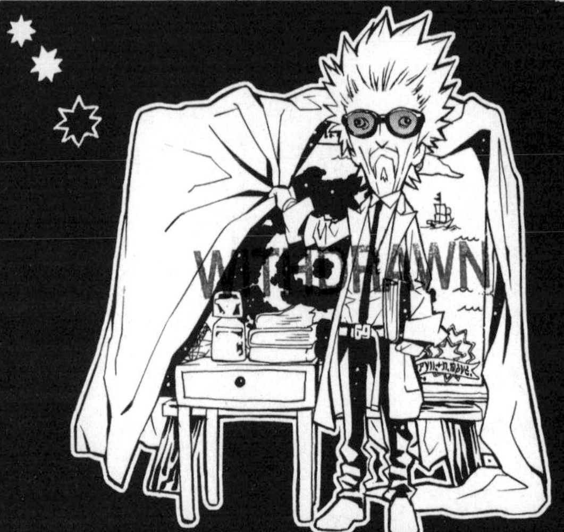

Dr. Thunderland's Reference Desk

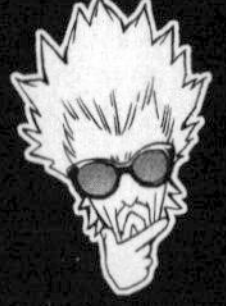

I am Dr. Thunderland.

Wait wait wait!! What's that in chapter 46? An emergency summons? The entire staff of the Beehive is present, right? Well, where am I? Where? Get a magnifying glass! Search carefully! Find me! Not Waldo! Me! Look carefully for meeee!!

I work at the Yuusari Beehive, spending my days researching this and that, but there's my son, front and center, lecturing about Cabernet. I'm supposed to review the features of Amberground mentioned in this volume, but I don't get to appear in it at all! I'm gnashing my teeth with rage! Gnash, gnash, gnash! No, not *Nash Bridges*! Pay attention!

■ NOIR

I AM THE REVERSE MARAUDER...
...NOIR.

I see...So Gauche didn't really recover his *heart*. But I get the feeling Noir was sincere when he said he wished he were Gauche. I'd like to think that Lag's Letter Bullet touched Noir's *heart*. I feel sorry for Lag, forced to lie to Sylvette like that. Almost as sorry as I feel for myself for having no part in this story.

But what about Roda? Could she be regaining some of her memory? I wish someone would resurrect me too...

THANK YOU FOR YOUR LETTER...

nb: Albert Camus (1913-1960) / French novelist and playwright. His writings include *The Stranger*, *The Plague* and *Caligula*. He was awarded the Nobel Prize for Literature in 1957.

■ AKATSUKI AND THE ARTIFICIAL SUN

It seems that even without Gauche's memories, Noir feels fear and loathing for the artificial sun. It also seems like Lag is starting to have his own doubts about the government. Okay, then I'll be the one to uncover all the secrets for him! What do you want to bet?

■ DIVIDING RIVERS

PLASH

Yodaka and Yuusari are divided by the Teardrop River. This rather sentimental name was given to the river because those who manage to cross it into Yuusari need not cry anymore...or the river will cry those tears for them. But the truth is that most people, no matter how much they suffer and weep, will never be able to cross the river.

THE COBALT GLASS RIVER...
OH YEAH.

The river separating Yuusari and Akatsuki is called the Cobalt Glass River because it looks like blue glass when the artificial sun reflects on the water. Does something sinister lurk beneath that beautiful surface?

■ ANCIENT TEXT

What's up with that Largo Lloyd? He's a hard man to read, a little aloof, and then suddenly he starts spouting off about revolution? Wow!

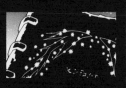

For the first time, there's a serious light in his eyes! And what's this about another area between Yuusari and Akatsuki? How does he know that? Why don't I know it?

Pardon me, but I have a question. If the revolution succeeds, will there be a part in the story for me? If so, I will join the resistance! Revolt at once! Junior, who stole my rightful scene, will get his due! By the way, my son's full name is Aaron Thunderland, Jr. Ha! Revealed here for the first time! What a waste of important information! It's a waste of **me** too!

■ CABERNET VS. BEES

The Bees are usually dispersed throughout the country. They're all sure shots with a shindan, so I can't believe they were defeated so quickly. That Cabernet certainly has developed into a monster! Does he need to eat more *hearts* to regrow the wings he lost, or has he eaten too much already? I bet we'll find out in the next volume.

Perhaps because he'd used too much *heart*, Lag was unable to fire his shindan and was injured, while Lily lost all of her *heart*. Thank goodness Connor is back! Having seen Sunny lose her *heart*, Connor may be the only one who can help Lag now. I wonder whatever happened to Sunny…

Can't anyone throw me a bone in this story? If not, I'll bring the revolution down on all your heads! I'll kowtow and negotiate a pact with *Blue Exorcist*! I just need to figure out how to spell "exorcist"…

nb: *Sawan on the Roof* / One of the key works of author Masuji Ibuse (1898-1993), published in 1929.

■ THE LAUGHING GAICHUU

Wait for volume 13! I shall explain all! Be there!

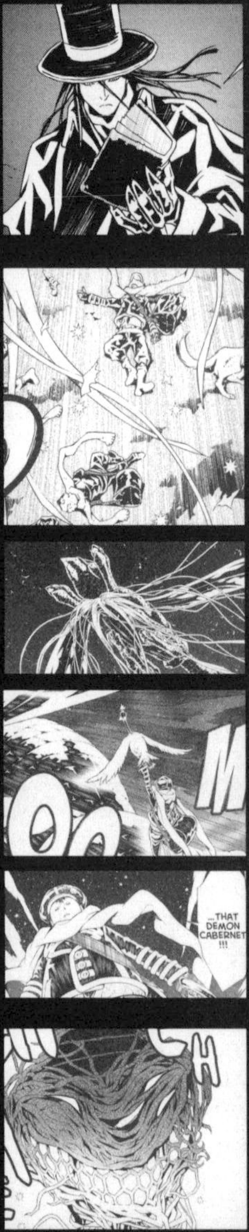
...THAT DEMON CABERNET!!!

Route Map

Finally, I am including a map, indicating Lag's route and Cabernet's flight path, created at Lonely Goatherd Map Station of Central Yuusari.

A: Akatsuki B: Yuusari C: Yodaka

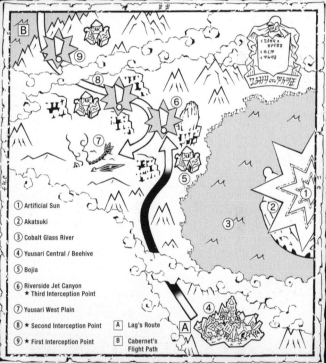

① Artificial Sun

② Akatsuki

③ Cobalt Glass River

④ Yuusari Central / Beehive

⑤ Bojia

⑥ Riverside Jet Canyon ★ Third Interception Point

⑦ Yuusari West Plain

⑧ ★ Second Interception Point

⑨ ★ First Interception Point

| A | Lag's Route |
| B | Cabernet's Flight Path |

Now why aren't I on that map? (I checked chapter 46...for the 6,741st time.) *Sigh.*..Don't tell me!!!!! Maybe I'd gone to the bathroom!!!!!!!!!

...EVEN I...

In the next volume...

A District Called Kagerou

As the battle against Cabernet grows desperate, the secrets of Amberground come to light. Largo Lloyd shares his past with the rebels of Reverse, while Garrard finally reveals what he saw, long ago, on his journey to the capital...in a district called Kagerou.

Available May 2013!